THE MEAT TRADE
IN BRITAIN 1840-1914

STUDIES IN ECONOMIC HISTORY

Editor:
Professor F. M. L. Thompson
Bedford College
University of London

Already published:

Eric J. Evans *The Contentious Tithe*
David W. Howells *Land and People in Nineteenth-Century Wales*

In preparation:

Anne Digby *Pauper Palaces*

THE MEAT TRADE
IN BRITAIN 1840-1914

RICHARD PERREN

Department of Economic History
University of Aberdeen

ROUTLEDGE & KEGAN PAUL
London, Henley and Boston

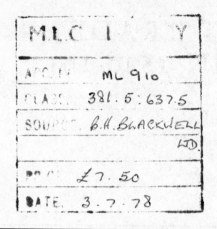
First published in 1978
by Routledge & Kegan Paul Ltd
39 Store Street,
London WC1E 7DD,
Broadway House,
Newtown Road,
Henley-on-Thames,
Oxon RG9 1EN and
9 Park Street,
Boston, Mass. 02108, USA
Printed in Great Britain by
Redwood Burn Ltd
Trowbridge and Esher

British Library Cataloguing in Publication Data

Perren, Richard

    The meat trade in Britain, 1840–1914.
    1. Meat industry and trade – Great Britain –
    History
    I. Title
    381'.45'664900941   HD9421.5   78–40018

    ISBN 0 7100 8841 8

CONTENTS

Contents

Contents

PREFACE

The theme of this book is the changing nature of the meat trade
in Britain over the seventy-four years prior to the First World
War. In certain cases, however, events earlier than 1840 have
been looked at simply because without consideration of these it
is impossible to understand developments after that date. My main
concern has been with supply factors as they affected the availability of this important foodstuff in nineteenth- and early
twentieth-century Britain. In this case, the exploitation of
overseas sources of supply to supplement home production was of
prime importance. But also the trade itself was subject to an
increasing amount of government intervention and control, partly
aimed at preserving public health and partly to protect the
farmer against losses from livestock disease.

As this book has been written over a number of years, I have
incurred a number of debts to individuals and to institutions for
helpful comments, suggested improvements and the correction of
errors. Mr Sherwin A. Hall of the Veterinary Investigation Centre,
Cambridge, provided much useful information on sources of
veterinary history for the nineteenth century. Professor G.R.
Hawke, Dr M. Walsh and Dr E.J.T. Collins have at various times
made helpful comments and corrected some of the mistakes in
different sections of this book. In Aberdeen there are a number
of persons to whom I am grateful. Professor G.R. Allen and Mr A.
Beavan, both formerly members of the Department of Agricultural
Economics at the North East Scotland College of Agriculture, gave
valuable advice and information. Also the librarians of that
institution and those at King's College Library in the university
have assisted greatly in tracking down some of the obscure
publications I have needed to consult. My colleagues in the
Economic History Department, in particular Mr C.H. Lee, Dr A.J.
Durie and Dr R.J. Irving (now with the British Steel Corporation),
made many useful suggestions and Professor P.L. Payne has given
me much helpful encouragement during the preparation of this
volume. I am grateful to the Carnegie Fund who have provided
grants for travel in connection with the book. Various drafts
have been typed with skill and patience by Mrs E.A. Hutton, Miss
L.M. Cockburn and Mrs P.A. Smith. Some of the material appeared

in the 'Economic History Review' and I am grateful to its editors
and to the Economic History Society for their kind permission to
reproduce those sections here. Chapter 3 is an extended version
of my article, The Meat and Livestock Trade in Britain, 1850-70,
'Economic History Review', 2nd series, vol. XXVIII, no. 3, 1975,
pp.385-99, and parts of chapters 7 and 9 contain sections from
my article, The North American Beef and Cattle Trade with Great
Britain, 1870-1914, 'Economic History Review', 2nd series, vol.
XXIV, no. 3, 1971, pp.430-44. Finally I must thank my wife,
Helen, for her cheerful forbearance. Confusions and errors
remaining are entirely my own.

University of Aberdeen
Department of Economic History   R.P.

CHAPTER 1

IMPORTANCE OF THE MEAT TRADE, 1840-1914

1 AMOUNT CONSUMED

It is true to say, as a generalization applied to the nineteenth
and early twentieth centuries, that next to bread, meat was the
most important food of the British people. If one goes beyond
generalities and tries to define this importance with greater
precision, such as finding out what was the average consumption
of meat by individuals, or the expenditure on meat in relation to
that on other foodstuffs, the investigator soon discovers that
here the ground is most uncertain. An answer to these questions
requires specific pieces of information which were in some cases
never collected and in others were only guessed at. For instance
to find out the total amount of meat consumed in any year we need
to know the following: (a) the numbers of each type of livestock
in the country at that time; (b) the percentages annually
slaughtered for food; and (c) the average amount of meat obtained
from each type of animal. In the case of the United Kingdom we
also need to know the amount of meat, if any, that was imported.
Prior to the regular collection of agricultural statistics in
Ireland from 1847 and Great Britain from 1867 (1) there are no
accurate livestock statistics. However there do exist certain
estimates made by contemporaries at very irregular intervals.
These earlier figures were synthesized and extensively used by
the economist, J.R. McCulloch, in his 'A Statistical Account of
the British Empire' which was published in four editions between
1837 and 1854. (2) McCulloch's estimates were also conveniently
summarized and placed beside those derived from official surveys
for the later years by W.G. Mulhall. (3) The percentages of livestock annually slaughtered for food are usually estimates made by
authors interested in current economic trends. The information
available to them is less comprehensive the farther back one goes
in time. The same applies to any assessment of the weight of meat
obtained from these animals.

   No official attempts were made to measure the output of meat
in the United Kingdom prior to the first census of production in
1907. (4) However, some of the unofficial estimates for earlier
years were very comprehensive and the agricultural and other

1

writers who made them were well informed as well as being
competent statisticians. This applies particularly to the works
of Craigie, (5) Crawford, (6) Rew (7) and Hooker. (8) In addition
to the articles that present finished estimates of the domestic
production of meat, there are a further number of articles which
give some of the components that must be considered when arriving
at these estimates. These were listed and the information
contained in them was summarized by Rew. (9) All the estimates
of these writers are based on the number of livestock in the
official agricultural returns and the earliest, Craigie's, does
not go back earlier than 1868.

For the period before 1867, McCulloch also provided his own
uncertain estimates of meat production for individual years and
Mulhall, building on McCulloch's work, gives estimates for some
decades. In addition, Robert Herbert who wrote about the sale
of livestock in London in the 1850s and 1860s gave figures for
the weights of beef and mutton obtained from the different breeds
of animals sold there (10) as well as a rather brief estimate of
the numbers of cattle and sheep in the United Kingdom in the
1840s and 1850s. (11)

On the question of imported supplies of meat, there is more
certainty. Imports of meat and livestock did not begin until
1842. Quantities of meat, though not always the types, were
pretty faithfully recorded and are published in the 'Annual
Statement of Trade'. So, too, are imports of livestock. However, when converting these cattle, sheep and pigs into quantities
of meat the investigator has to remember that imported animals
did not necessarily weigh the same as home-produced ones. Also
some imported livestock were not killed immediately but were
purchased as stores by farmers for further fattening before passing into consumption. However, this is not a serious source of
inaccuracy as only a relatively small proportion of total imports,
and of these mostly cattle, were store animals. Authors who
computed the total meat supplies of the United Kingdom had to
make an allowance for imports and so some of the works already
referred to make estimates for this item. Also the growth in the
importance of imported supplies after the 1860s encouraged some
writers to consider them separately. (12) In addition there were
various investigations conducted by Royal Commissions and
Parliamentary Select Committees, etc., into or including aspects
of the international food trade. Most of those appointed after
1880 were associated with some aspect of the decline in British
agricultural prices from 1873. These often give summaries of
meat (and other food) imports in appendices. (13)

The results of some of these investigations are presented in
Table 1.1 which gives estimates of the amounts of meat consumed in
the United Kingdom from 1831 to 1914. The earlier decennial
estimates have been taken from Mulhall and it must be admitted
that these belong more to the realm of conjecture, in the absence
of any reliable count of livestock in Great Britain. The quin-
quennial figures from 1870 onwards are more reliable because the
official agricultural statistics for the whole United Kingdom
after 1867 can be used to estimate the output of home-produced
meat. The most important features of the United Kingdom meat

TABLE 1.1 Average consumption of meat, per annum, in the United Kingdom, 1831-1914

Years	Domestic		Imported		Total	Consumption per head
	tons	%	tons	%	tons	lb
1831-40	980,000	100	-	-	980,000	86.8
1841-50	1,014,000	100	-	-	1,014,000	82.5
1851-60	1,047,000	96	44,000	4	1,091,000	87.3
1861-70	1,078,000	89	131,000	11	1,209,000	90.0
1870-4	1,330,200	86	210,100	14	1,540,300	108.3
1875-9	1,322,600	79	341,900	21	1,664,500	111.0
1880-4	1,277,600	74	447,900	26	1,725,500	109.8
1885-9	1,334,400	73	490,000	27	1,824,400	111.7
1890-4	1,410,200	68	673,500	32	2,083,700	122.4
1895-9	1,401,000	60	933,000	40	2,334,000	130.7
1900-4	1,455,200	59	1,015,400	41	2,470,600	132.1
1905-9	1,457,400	58	1,051,000	42	2,508,400	128.5
1910-14	1,484,400	58	1,091,000	42	2,575,400	126.9

Sources: Domestic, 1831-70, M.G. Mulhall, 'Dictionary of Statistics', London, 1892, p.287. Imported, 1831-70, ibid., p.15; Domestic and imported, 1870-9, P.G. Craigie, On the Production and Consumption of Meat in the United Kingdom, 'British Association for the Advancement of Science, Report', 1884, p.844; Domestic, 1880-99, calculated from the numbers of livestock in the United Kingdom from the 'Agricultural Returns', using the percentages killed for food (cattle 25%, sheep 40%, pigs 116%) and the average weight of meat obtained from each animal (cattle 600 lb, sheep 70 lb, pigs 134 lb) suggested by Craigie, ibid., p.842; Imported, 1880-99, 'Departmental Committee on Combinations in the Meat Trade', P.P., 1909, XV, Appendix II, Table IX, p.273; Domestic and imported, 1900-14, 'First Report of the Royal Commission on Food Prices', P.P., 1924-5, XIII, Annex IV, p.162.

supply situation are, first, the rise in per capita consumption after 1850 and, second, the growth in the importance of overseas supplies. One of the most obvious indicators of an improvement in the living standards of any nation is to be found in an increased consumption of the more expensive protein foods, like meat, butter, cheese and eggs. In the United Kingdom this was only made possible by the mechanism of international trade and the ability to purchase greater amounts of these things from abroad. Although there was some improvement in the productive capacity of the United Kingdom's agriculture during this time, it in no way matched the growth of population. In 1831 the population was 24.1 million and in 1914 it was 46 million. The production of meat from British farms increased at about half the

rate of population growth. In addition, part of the rise in meat
output was achieved by some redistribution of agricultural
resources, especially land, away from grain production and into
livestock farming following the large fall in cereal prices of
the 1870s. (14)

2   IMPORTANCE OF MEAT PRODUCTION IN UNITED KINGDOM AGRICULTURE

The value of meat production in relation to the total agricultural output of the United Kingdom can only be guessed at before
1867. McCulloch gave estimates that applied to the whole of the
British Isles for 1846. In that year he made the distinction
between 'agricultural' and 'pastoral' production. The former
category presumably includes all grain, vegetables, timber, etc.,
and the latter are all animal products. The small weighting of
the pastoral sector in Irish agriculture seems surprising, but
this will take account of the enormous destruction of livestock
during the famine, a fact that was commented upon by contemporaries. The total of £142 million for the value of English
agricultural output in 1846 can be analysed more closely. From
Table 1.3 it can be seen that meat accounted for 18.5 per cent of

TABLE 1.2 Value of all farm products, 1846, £ millions

	Agricultural	%	Pastoral	%	Total	%
England	80	56	62	44	142	100
Scotland	19	68	9	32	28	100
Ireland	28	58	20	42	48	100
United Kingdom	127	58	91	42	218	100

Source: M.G. Mulhall, 'Dictionary of Statistics', London, 1892,
p.16.

TABLE 1.3 Value of all farm products, England and Wales, 1846

Products	£m.	%
Grain	51.5	36.3
Green crops	28.5	20.1
Hay and straw	13.0	9.2
Timber	1.8	1.3
Meat	26.2	18.5
Dairy	12.0	8.5
Eggs and poultry	1.4	1.0
Hides and wool	4.3	3.0
Foals	3.0	2.1
Total	141.7	100.0

Source: M.G. Mulhall, 'Dictionary of Statistics', London, 1892,
p.16.

agricultural output in 1846. If the whole animal sector is taken
into account, i.e. meat, dairy products, hides and wool, then
these account for 30 per cent of the total.

For the years after 1867 there is a standard source for all
estimates of agricultural output in the United Kingdom. (15) This
has been used for the comparisons over the period from 1867 to
1913. Ojala presents two main tables of gross agricultural
output showing the breakdown of the total into the various farm
products. The first gives their value at current prices and the
second table values these at constant (1911-13) prices. (16) As
cereal prices fell by approximately 25 per cent between 1870 and
1913 and meat prices rose slightly, the series valuing output at
constant prices gives meat a greater weighting within the total
agricultural output than the current prices series. Ojala's
tables, covering the period 1867-1913, are presented here in
Tables 1.4 and 1.5. Within the agricultural sector the annual
output of meat, at current prices, rose from 34.5 per cent of
total output in 1867-9 to 41.9 per cent of total output in 1911-
13. Valued at constant prices the contribution of meat in the
earlier years is more impressive, in 1867-9 it accounted for
41.5 per cent of total output (see Table 1.5). But the importance of meat within the gross agricultural output is relatively
stable over time when valued at 1911-13 prices. This again is
consistent with the fact that there was very little increase in
the amount of meat produced after 1870: in the quinquennium 1870-
4 this averaged 1,330,200 tons per annum, and by 1910-14 average
annual output had only risen by a further 11.5 per cent, or
154,200 tons (see Table 1.1).

Certain adjustments were made to some of Ojala's figures by the
late T.W. Fletcher. This mainly involved the substitution of a
more appropriate price series for hay, straw, fruit and vegetables
(all minor parts of the 'crops' component) and for beef, mutton,
pigmeat, milk, poultry and eggs. In addition he revised the
estimates of output for oats, hay and straw and the Irish potato
crop. The end result of his labours is to reduce the fall in the
value of output over the great depression period of 1873-96. He
only carried his estimates as far as 1894-1903, but in those years
total livestock products accounted for £146.18 million or 70.2 per
cent of his new estimate of total agricultural output for the
United Kingdom (£208.13 million). (17) Ojala's estimates for the
same period are £133.01 million, 72.8 per cent and £182.78
million, respectively (see Table 1.4). In addition Fletcher also
presented a separate output series applying to England alone for
two groups of years, 1867-71 and 1894-8. Although they cannot be
compared directly with the United Kingdom estimates, they do
reveal the relatively smaller importance of the livestock sector,
and consequently meat, within the total output for England, as
shown in Table 1.6. It is what would be expected, given the
greater importance of livestock farming in the pastoral west and
north of the British Isles.

Taken alone the production of meat constituted just over 40 per

TABLE 1.4 United Kingdom gross agricultural output at current prices, estimated annual averages of groups of years, 1867-1913

	1867-9		1870-6		1877-85		1886-93		1894-1903		1904-10		1911-13	
	£m.	%	£m.	%	£m.	%	£m.	%	£m.	%	£m.	%	£m.	%
Crops	104.17	45.3	94.99	38.4	75.99	34.7	56.75	30.2	49.77	27.2	50.68	25.2	56.23	25.3
Beef & veal	34.90	15.2	44.53	18.0	43.14	19.7	37.95	20.2	39.88	21.8	43.39	21.6	47.43	21.3
Mutton & lamb	25.92	11.3	29.77	12.0	27.34	12.5	23.94	12.8	23.16	12.7	23.87	11.9	25.01	11.3
Pigmeat	18.60	8.0	22.55	9.1	19.90	9.0	18.05	9.6	18.31	10.0	19.19	9.6	20.63	9.3
Horses	0.40	0.2	1.60	0.7	3.00	1.4	3.20	1.7	2.55	1.4	2.40	1.2	2.31	1.0
Milk	33.78	14.7	38.51	15.6	37.99	17.3	36.36	19.4	36.89	20.2	46.06	22.9	52.83	23.8
Wool	7.49	3.3	8.27	3.4	4.48	2.0	3.80	2.0	3.24	1.8	3.51	1.8	3.71	1.7
Eggs & poultry	4.57	2.0	6.96	2.8	7.36	3.4	7.75	4.1	8.98	4.9	11.65	5.8	13.97	6.3
Total livestock	125.66	54.7	152.19	61.6	143.21	65.3	131.05	69.8	133.01	72.8	150.07	74.8	165.89	74.7
Grand total	229.83	100.0	247.18	100.0	219.20	100.0	187.80	100.0	182.78	100.0	200.75	100.0	222.12	100.0

Source: E.M. Ojala, 'Agricultural and Economic Progress', p.208.

TABLE 1.5 United Kingdom gross agricultural output at 1911-13 prices, estimated annual averages of groups of years, 1867-1913

	1867-9		1870-6		1877-85		1886-93		1894-1903		1904-10		1911-13	
	£m.	%	£m.	%	£m.	%	£m.	%	£m.	%	£m.	%	£m.	%
Crops	70.37	35.4	69.86	33.9	63.73	31.8	60.14	28.9	57.21	27.1	57.54	26.3	56.23	25.3
Index, 1911-13 = 100	125		124		113		107		102		102		100	
Beef & veal	35.59	17.9	39.07	19.0	39.90	19.9	43.14	20.7	44.34	20.9	46.42	21.2	47.43	21.3
Mutton & lamb	27.58	13.9	26.33	12.8	23.98	12.0	24.68	11.9	24.39	11.5	24.11	11.0	25.01	11.3
Pigmeat	19.19	9.7	20.72	10.0	19.90	9.9	20.76	10.0	21.25	10.0	20.88	9.5	20.63	9.3
Horses	0.35	0.2	1.40	0.7	2.10	1.0	2.80	1.3	2.98	1.4	2.80	1.3	2.31	1.0
Milk	34.46	17.4	36.68	17.8	38.37	19.1	42.77	20.5	45.54	21.5	50.62	23.0	52.83	23.8
Wool	4.51	2.3	4.33	2.1	3.93	1.9	4.04	1.9	4.00	1.9	3.86	1.8	3.71	1.7
Eggs & poultry	6.44	3.2	7.58	3.7	8.77	4.4	9.93	4.8	12.14	5.7	12.94	5.9	13.97	6.3
Total livestock	128.12	64.6	136.11	66.1	136.95	68.2	148.12	71.1	154.64	72.9	161.63	73.7	165.89	74.7
Index, 1911-13 = 100	77		82		83		89		93		97		100	
Grand total	198.49	100.0	205.97	100.0	200.68	100.0	208.26	100.0	211.85	100.0	219.17	100.0	222.12	100.0
Index, 1911-13 = 100	89		93		90		94		95		99		100	

Source: Ojala, op.cit., p.209.

TABLE 1.6 Gross output of agriculture in England, 1867-71 and
1894-8

	1867-71		1894-8	
	£m.	%	£m.	%
Crops	65.43	50.4	41.47	37.0
Beef	14.59	11.2	16.02	14.3
Mutton	14.60	11.3	12.59	11.2
Pigmeat	9.59	7.4	10.52	9.4
Horses	1.00	0.8	2.00	1.8
Milk	15.40	11.9	20.29	18.0
Wool	5.62	4.3	2.36	2.1
Poultry & eggs	3.50	2.7	7.00	6.2
Total livestock	64.30	49.6	70.78	63.0
Grand total	129.73	100.0	112.25	100.0

Source: T.W. Fletcher, The Great Depression of English
Agriculture, 1873-1896, 'Economic History Review', 2nd
series, vol. XIII, 1961.

cent of United Kingdom gross agricultural output before 1914. In
England meat output rose from 29.9 per cent of the total in 1867-
71 to 34.9 per cent by 1894-8. This made it the largest single
category within British agriculture. In 1867-9 the output of
small grains (wheat, barley and oats) was at its highest, but in
those years they only accounted for £62.7 million or 27.3 per
cent of the United Kingdom total agricultural output. (18) It
also has to be remembered that the production of meat is linked
to other agricultural outputs. The most important of these was
milk which rose from around 15 to 24 per cent of output between
1867 and 1913. The production of wool was much less important
and only accounted for around 2 per cent of output between these
dates. The importance of wool declined in the last quarter of
the nineteenth and early part of the twentieth centuries. This
was the result of a long-term fall in wool prices over this period.
In addition the sheep numbers in the United Kingdom suffered a
long-term decline after 1870. Part of this was the effect of a
period of serious disease between 1879 and 1882. In 1874 there
were in Great Britain 29,427,635 head of sheep and by 1913 this
had fallen to 23,931,412. (19) a more fundamental reason for
this decline was probably the fact that the fall in mutton and
lamb prices after 1880 was greater than that for beef. Therefore,
where it was possible, there may have been some limited transfer
of resources out of sheep and into cattle. In 1870 the number of
cattle in the United Kingdom was 9,199,967 but by 1913 this had
increased to 11,896,470. (20) In 1867-9 beef and veal accounted
for 15.2 per cent of the agricultural output of the United Kingdom
at current prices and by 1911-13 this was 21.3 per cent. However,

the major part of this increase was accommodated on land taken out
of arable production, following the serious decline of grain
prices after 1873, rather than on land which had formerly been
sheep pasture. On the question of cattle by-products, by far the
most important one being hides, Ojala has nothing to say. As
this is not a very important item in comparison with the value of
meat, its omission is not a serious matter.

3   EMPLOYMENT

No attempt can be made to estimate the number of persons among the
agricultural labour force who were engaged in meat production.
The census returns give the numbers employed in agriculture, but
any attempt to sub-divide this group and apportion it between the
various constituents of total agricultural output would be
meaningless. On many farms the job-specification for workers was
an unspecialized one. This applied particularly to small farms
that relied mainly on family labour to perform all the tasks
associated with the management and running of the holding. Larger
farms did employ specialized herdsmen to look after the cattle,
and on sheep farms the occupation of the shepherd was clearly
defined. But on those holdings that were partly pastoral and
partly arable the general labourer would perform tasks for both
departments. Sometimes it was difficult to define precisely
where the division between arable and pastoral lay. For instance,
ploughing followed by the sowing, weeding and harvesting of root
crops was an arable occupation. But turnips and mangolds, etc.,
were used for animal fodder and as such became inputs for the livestock side of a farm's operations. Therefore any labour costs
incurred in their production would have to be set against and paid
for by revenue from livestock. In other cases this sort of
argument applied in the reverse direction. The storage and cart-
ing of cattle dung was a cost involved with the upkeep of the
herds. But when this material was applied to the fields the
arable crops benefited from the increased fertility and higher
yields were obtained. When these crops were sold off the farm,
as in the case of grain, then some of the revenue obtained should,
in theory, be set against the livestock costs.
     Also livestock husbandry did not have meat production as its
sole output. A lot of beef was itself the by-product of dairying. When milch cows reached a certain age, or their yield
declined, they were then dried off and fattened for the butcher.
Very often this final stage was carried out by the dairy farmer
on his own premises and so some of the labour spent in milk
production also contributed to the output of meat. Then there
were those farmers who did not sell their animals to butchers,
but sold them as stores to other farmers to fatten. In Britain
this livestock traffic was broadly from the west (21) and north
to the east and south. Pasture farms in the more mountainous
regions of the west and north were breeding and rearing centres,
but these did not have the arable land to grow enough fodder to
fatten their animals. Instead they were sold to farmers on the
more fertile eastern side of Britain who grew sufficient fodder

crops to specialize in meat production.

From this it can be seen that any attempt to estimate the proportion of the agricultural labour force employed in the production of meat would produce meaningless results.

The census returns are more helpful when an attempt is made to quantify the numbers employed in distribution of meat. The occupational category of 'butchers and meat salesmen' is a more or less clearly defined one that appeared in all the censuses after 1841. For purposes of comparison the numbers engaged in other food trades in the United Kingdom are given also (see Table 1.7). In some of these occupations the groups included both makers and dealers. Thus the term 'baker' encompasses both bakehouse workers (who manufactured bread) and workers in bakers' shops (who sold bread) and in 1881 and 1891 they were included with confectioners. Only in 1901 and 1911 did the census make a clear and satisfactory distinction between these three occupations. In the table presented here the occupational definitions have, in some cases, been simplified to include more than one specific job group, as with bakers. By doing this it is possible to compress those working in food into some ten main occupational categories, whereas in some of the censuses these cover eighteen separate occupations.

The number of butchers and meat salesmen increased over this whole period but not as fast as the total employed in food. In 1841 they accounted for 21.2 per cent of the total in Table 1.7 but by 1911 they had fallen to 14.9 per cent. In addition they were in 1841 the second largest single group in these trades, being second only to bakers. By 1911 they occupied the third place after bakers and grocers respectively. In terms of handling a homogeneous product, however, the butchers were probably the largest single group; grocers sold a whole variety of goods including some meat in the form of bacon and tinned products, also their stocks were not exclusively foodstuffs, although these constituted a majority. As about half the bakers were bakehouse workers and the other half were sales personnel they were not a homogeneous group with regard to the tasks performed, even though the product sold was more homogeneous than a grocer's wares. (22) It may be asked to what extent was meat sold by itinerant traders who did not confine themselves exclusively to one product. In this context the relevant group of individuals were the London costermongers and the street traders who sold their wares from barrows in the large towns. Over the nineteenth century this class declined numerically as retail trading became more institutionalized and concentrated in fixed premises. However, this change did not have much impact on the meat trade as the barrow boys concentrated mostly on fruit and vegetables. Their practice was to hang around the wholesale markets and buy cheap any surplus remaining at the end of the day's trading that was not required by the regular shopkeepers. But this was not common within the wholesale meat markets, possibly because the flow of supplies was more predictable and easier to control. (23)

All the trades engaged in food sales also employed additional workers who, because of their job description, did not appear in the occupational tables of the census under food. Thus, many

TABLE 1.7 Main occupational categories of workers and dealers in food in the United Kingdom, 1841–1911

	1841	1851	1861	1871	1881	1891	1901	1911
Milk	13,112	20,393	22,558	26,628	33,846	47,103	50,408	66,265
Provisions	10,997	20,061	22,195	25,382	28,058	28,522	32,111	37,577
Fish & poultry	8,646	17,141	19,156	23,435	27,873	39,985	46,546	64,433
Butcher, meat salesmen	54,029	69,643	78,845	88,905	95,563	115,613	127,925	155,732
Corn & flour	33,793	56,502	58,231	53,610	48,875	43,543	47,912	53,360
Bakers	59,462	85,948	92,322	101,628	126,727	166,572	216,442	275,446
Grocers	53,789	95,122	124,528	142,017	169,577	225,615	251,715	285,282
Greengrocers	18,013	18,688	26,472	30,061	44,332	47,151	59,810	80,024
Sugar refiners	1,082	2,820	3,756	3,085	4,484	4,984	3,231	4,603
Soft drinks	675	1,189	1,599	3,090	5,250	8,127	13,638	13,655
Others	182	577	631	975	1,593	2,752	4,570	7,764
Total	253,780	388,084	450,293	498,816	586,178	729,967	854,308	1,044,141

Notes on occupational categories. Milk – milkseller, dairyman. Provisions – cheesemonger, provision dealer, provision curer. Fish and poultry – poulterer and game dealer, fishmonger, fish curer. Corn and flour – corn, flour, and seed merchants and dealers, millers, cereal goods manufacturers. Bakers – bakers, i.e. makers and dealers, confectioners. Grocers – grocers, tea, coffee and chocolate dealers, chocolate and cocoa makers. Greengrocers – greengrocers, fruiterers, vegetable dealers. Soft drinks – ginger beer, soda water, mineral water manufacturers. Others – mustard, vinegar, spice, pickle, etc., makers. Broadly, these are the occupational categories used in the 1881 and 1891 census and are much less detailed than those used from 1841 to 1871 and for 1901 and 1911.

grocers' shops employed messengers, porters, watchmen, clerks and carmen, etc., who appeared in the census under those occupations. The general Report of the 1911 census published details of these persons for England and Wales, and they provided some indication of how far the food trade in general, and the meat trade in particular, made use of such workers (see Table 1.8). If these figures are applied to the whole United Kingdom then the numbers employed in butchers' shops and by meat wholesalers would be

TABLE 1.8 Workers and additional workers in food trades, 1911: England and Wales

Occupations	Number in occupation tables	Additional workers	Total	(2) as a percentage of (3)
	(1)	(2)	(3)	(4)
Milksellers, dairymen	56,971	9,056	66,027	13.7
Butchers, meat salesmen	135,133	16,651	151,784	11.0
Grocers	219,619	56,562	276,181	20.5
Greengrocers	72,289	10,973	83,262	13.2
Bakers (makers and dealers)	198,550	17,100	215,650	7.9
Cheesemongers, butter-men, provision dealers	24,567	12,334	36,901	33.4
Corn merchants	20,168	14,515	34,683	41.9
Fishmongers	44,684	5,909	50,593	11.7

Source: 1911 Census, 'General Report', p.140.

increased by approximately 11 per cent (or 17,000) to 172,800. It must be noted that butchers' use of additional labour was less than some trades (notably grocers, provision dealers, etc., and corn merchants) but it is broadly comparable with those trades where the majority of the members were in retailing and handled a largely homogeneous type of product (i.e. milksellers, green-grocers and fishmongers).

Besides the fetchers and carriers, etc., who were directly employed by butchers' establishments, the railway companies also performed a lot of the long distance carriage for meat, although this item only constituted a fraction of the merchandise that they handled. Also the cold stores erected in Britain in the 1890s were built mainly to hold meat, even if they took other products as well once they became operational. The cattle and pig dealers who were also recorded in the censuses were not exclusively con-fined to the meat trade. For instance some of these were farmers as well, and again others did not deal directly in fatstock but concentrated on the store trade. Finally there is the question of

the number of slaughtermen. The early censuses do not enumerate
this occupation separately, probably because there was little need
for specialist slaughterers outside London. In most cases the
butcher who was a small 'scale retailer performed this job himself.
Later on, as a greater degree of specialization was introduced
and the municipal abattoir movement gathered strength, they are
listed separately. However, their number was small in comparison
with the number of butchers: in 1911 there were in England and
Wales only 2,634 slaughtermen or less than one to every fifty
butchers.

4   EXPENDITURE ON MEAT

The amount spent on meat, as with all food expenditure, is the
total of three separate items. In the first place there is the
initial production cost. Second, there has to be added to this
the cost of any processing that is required. Finally, an
appropriate allowance has to be included to cover the costs of
distribution, both wholesale and retail. In practice these last
two items are sometimes treated as one. This approach is
particularly useful for bread where the flour is valued at current
wholesale prices and an appropriate percentage is added to cover
the baking and distribution which were often carried out by the
same firm.

The first really comprehensive attempt to estimate, on a
national scale, the current expenditure on food was made by the
committee of the British Association for the Advancement of
Science which was set up in 1880 to report on the appropriation of
wages. This committee allowed margins of between 20 and 30 per
cent to cover distribution and some processing costs for foodstuffs. (24) This procedure involved the use of certain heroic
assumptions. For instance, with meat the total consumption of the
country was based on figures for per capita consumption in London
which was then applied to the whole United Kingdom population and
valued at $6\frac{1}{4}$d. per lb wholesale and $7\frac{1}{2}$d. per lb retail. (25)
Knowledge of retail prices for the nineteenth century is very
sketchy. In the case of meat there are special problems because
a carcase is cut into joints which represent different qualities
and are priced accordingly. In addition there is strong evidence
of marked regional variations in the price of similar joints. (26)

Rather than make hazardous guesses to allow for these
differences Table 1.9 gives two estimates of the value of total
food consumption at wholesale prices only. The average annual
values of imported foods are taken from the 'Annual Statement of
Trade' for quinquennia centred around 1880 and 1900. The
estimates for home-produced food are based on the 'Agricultural
Returns' where available. In some cases the sources do not provide
full information. This applies mainly to the less important items
of food like home-grown fruit and fish caught by British vessels.
However, there is sufficient information to indicate the relative
importance of expenditure on different items of foodstuffs in
1880 and 1900.

The proportion accounted for by meat is remarkably constant at

TABLE 1.9 Estimated value of United Kingdom food consumption at current wholesale prices, 1880(a) and 1900(b)

			1880			1900		
		£m.	£m.	%		£m.	£m.	%
Wheat: Imports		39.3)	62.7	20.5	33.6)		42.4	13.6
Home-Produced		23.4)			8.8)			
Potatoes: I		2.0)	26.8	8.8	1.8)		19.4	6.2
H-P		24.8)			17.6)			
Vegetables: I		.9)			2.3)		8.3	2.7
H-P		14.0(c))	18.5	6.1	6.0)			
Fruit: I		3.6)			7.2)		16.7	5.3
H-P		)			9.5)			
Fish: I		1.0)	6.5	2.1	2.9)		9.5	3.0
H-P		5.5)			6.6)			
Meat: I		22.8)	101.1	33.1	43.9)		104.3	33.3
H-P		78.3)			60.4)			
Milk: H-P		14.4	14.4	4.7	27.6		27.6	8.8
Eggs: I		2.4)	9.4	3.1	5.3)		13.5	4.3
H-P		7.0)			8.2)			
Butter) I		15.7)	29.2	9.6	23.7)		41.1	13.1
& cheese) H-P		13.5)			17.4)			
Other imports(d)		36.6	36.6	12.0	30.2		30.2	9.7
	Total		£305.2	100.0	Total		£313.0	100.0

(a) James Caird, 'The Landed Interest and the Supply of Food', London, 1878, p.14. Report of the Committee ... on the present Appropriation of Wages ... 'British Association', 1881 and 1882. 'Agricultural Returns of Great Britain', 1883. 'Statistical Abstract for the UK ... from 1869 to 1883'. 'Annual Statement of the Trade of the UK'. 'Statistical tables and memorandum relating to the Sea Fisheries of the United Kingdom ...', B.P.P., 1887, LXXV. R.E. Turnbull, Farm Capital and Revenue, 'Transactions of the Highland and Agricultural Society', 5th series, vol. X, 1898.
(b) 'Annual Statement of the Trade of the UK. R.C. on the Supply of Food in Time of War', 1905. R.H. Rew, The Food Production of British Farms, 'Journal of the Royal Agricultural Society of England', no. 64, 1903. Production and Consumption of Meat and Milk ..., 'Journal of the Royal Statistical Society', no. 67, 1904. R.E. Turnbull, The Household Food Supply; With Special Relation to Dairy Produce, 'Journal of the British Dairy Farmers' Association', no. 17, 1903. 'Economist: Statistical Abstract for the UK ... from 1889 to 1903'.
(c) Fruit and vegetables.
(d) Sugar, tea, coffee, rice, dry fruit, spices, confectionery.

a little over 33 per cent. The total value of all foodstuffs is
roughly the same between the two dates at £305.2 million in 1880
and £313 million in 1900. With the sharp fall in the price of
wheat and potatoes between these dates most of the released
purchasing power was redistributed in favour of fruit and dairy
products rather than meat. But as the prices of all foodstuffs,
fell, though not to the same extent, the combined quantities of
wheat, potatoes, fish, meat, milk, butter and cheese, sugar, tea
and coffee that were consumed rose by almost 20 per cent between
1880 and 1900.

CHAPTER 2

CHANGES IN THE DOMESTIC LIVESTOCK TRADE, 1840-64

1 STEAM NAVIGATION

In the middle of the nineteenth century livestock markets were of
two main kinds. First, in all large towns, such as London,
Liverpool, Manchester, Newcastle, Edinburgh, Glasgow and Dublin
and some others, weekly or twice-weekly markets were held for all
kinds of fatstock to supply the inhabitants of those places with
butcher-meat. Second, there were other localities away from large
towns, in different parts of the United Kingdom, where very large
and important sales were held on stated dates for lean cattle and
sheep to supply farmers with fattening stock. Markets of this
description, such as the Falkirk Tryst, the Inverness Sheep and
Wool Market, the Brechin Muir, the Doune market in Scotland and
other similar gatherings south of the Border and also in Ireland,
were not a direct part of the meat marketing network and so are
not included in the following account. (1) Fatstock markets were
also held locally on a smaller scale than those already mentioned.
Nearly every town of any note had a monthly cattle market, at which
resident butchers supplied themselves with what was needed for
local consumption and the surplus was bought by dealers who sent it
by rail or sea to the larger towns.
  The traditional method of transporting cattle had been on the
hoof, that is by sending them in droves along the public highways.
In the nineteenth century this method of sending cattle faced
pressure from two directions. In the first place the adoption of
improved farming techniques, with the accompanying enclosures,
reduced the amount of common grazing land available by the road-
sides. The drovers had always relied on freely available grazing
to sustain their herds on their journeys. In Scotland, when the
droving of cattle became substantial, proprietors began to charge
the drovers for wayside grazing. Later in the nineteenth century
the drove roads themselves came under pressure and attempts were
made to close them in places where local proprietors found the
transit of large herds of cattle inconvenient and unwelcome. (2)
The Scottish droving business appears to have reached its height
around 1835; thereafter decline was relatively sudden. In England,
with the earlier progress of agricultural improvement, pressure

upon grazing land was bound to have come sooner than in Scotland.
Again, in England the turnpikes imposed another cost on the cattle
drovers. Also the heavier breeds of cattle brought about by
improvement were less fit to travel by road than the smaller
cattle of the eighteenth century. Writing in 1868, one authority
gave 50 miles as the upper limit that cattle were ever sent by
road. (3)

Already by 1850 important changes had been made in the meat and
cattle trade through the agency of the steam engine. The first
development was the use of steamboats as cattle ships to provide a
more satisfactory method of transporting animals over long
distances than driving them by road. By 1830 it was possible to
send fat cattle from the ports on the east and west coasts of
Scotland for sale in London. Probably the greatest change by 1850
was in the position of Ireland as a supplier of foodstuffs. Steam
navigation opened up the ports of England and Scotland from London
round to Bristol and Glasgow to increased supplies of Irish agricultural produce. By 1835 it was common for dealers to buy fat
cattle at the Dublin Smithfield which was held on a Thursday, to
ship them to Liverpool by the Saturday and sell them there on the
Monday, or else send them to be sold in Manchester on Wednesday,
and to return themselves to Dublin in time for the market again
on Thursday. In this way dealers in livestock brought consignments as large as eighty to a hundred cattle, or as small as a
score or so pigs, to Liverpool as a regular weekly traffic. In
addition to livestock, both large and small dealers in eggs,
poultry, butter, fruit, etc., made regular voyages to the west
coast ports to dispose of their goods in the English markets.
The quality of product required for this trade stimulated some
limited improvement to Irish agriculture. The condition of Irish
cattle was strengthened by crosses with shorthorn and Devon bulls
bought from England for the purpose, and flocks of Leicester sheep
were imported to feed on Irish pastures and ultimately find a sale
for both meat and wool in Liverpool. Formerly the Irish beef trade
had been confined to curing beef for the army and navy and no
doubt the spartan requirements of these customers provided little
encouragement for the improvement of the quality and condition of
Irish cattle. The steam ship effectively opened to the Irish
farmer and livestock dealer the entire civilian market for food of
the west coast of England and Scotland. As the requirements of
this market, and the prices paid, were superior to those of the
government contractor, it was necessary for the Irish agricultural
community to improve the quality of their product to capture a
share. Although the improvements effected were not startling,
they were partially successful in this endeavour, at least in the
1850s when between 9,000 and 17,000 Irish beasts were sent annually
to the London cattle market. (4)

Steam navigation conferred benefits of a rather different
nature on Scotland. Scottish livestock farming had been in contact
with the English market for centuries, though the rigours of
driving animals south by road had imposed severe limitations on
the nature of this traffic. Scotland was chiefly a source of lean
cattle that were fattened on English pastures nearer the great
market of London. The loss of weight involved in walking animals

several hundred miles made the provision of Scots fatstock for the
English markets an economic impossibility. However, despite the
losses incurred, fat cattle were being driven into England from
southern Scotland in the early nineteenth century. Mixed farming
with the cultivation of root crops was first adopted in the
southern counties of Scotland after 1780 (5) and the winter
feeding of stock which this permitted expanded the previously
meagre supply of fat cattle produced in Scotland. For many years
the fairly large markets of Edinburgh, Glasgow and Morpeth (6)
were able to absorb the extra supply of animals quite adequately.
Also the distances involved did not mean there was a tremendous
loss of flesh on the journey to these places. But as the improved
methods of cultivation spread to the lowland areas of northern
Scotland from around the 1790s and onwards, the quantity of fat
cattle produced began to exceed the demand of these markets and
the country as a whole. Therefore these animals had to be driven
to markets in England further south, and the market in question was
usually London. The losses involved on this journey in terms of
weight and a general deterioration of condition made the trade an
unsatisfactory one. The improved cattle produced by winter feeding were less able to withstand the rigours of the long journey
into England than those at the very start of the century which
were able to live hard on the meagre supplies of food then available. (7) It was only the fact that prices in London were usually
above those of Scotland and the borders that made the trade worth
following at all. For instance, to drive a fat ox of 50 stones to
Barnet or Norwich involved a loss of 6 stones and at 6s. per stone
this was 36s. In addition the expenses of driving an animal 400
or 500 miles averaged 35s., making the total cost of the journey
£3 11s. Therefore to cover these expenses the London price had to
be in excess of 16 per cent above prices in Scotland, which were
themselves unprofitable for feeders. Usually after such a journey,
to be in any condition at all for sale a beast needed four weeks'
feeding on good pasture, which would cost 5s. a week in the neighbourhood of the metropolis and would add a further £1 to the cost
of bringing cattle south for sale in London. (8)

The use of the steamer from Scotland (9) reduced the loss in
weight on the journey from 6 to 2 stones per beast. In addition
the charges for attendance, freight, and wharfage in London
amounted to £2 15s. per beast, so the final cost of the sea journey
was £3 7s. an animal. This was not much less than the road journey,
but there was no need to feed the animals again before sale and the
prices they fetched were commensurate with the altogether better
condition in which they arrived. The sea-borne trade started first
from Leith and then extended itself to Dundee, Berwick, Montrose,
Aberdeen and Inverness for London; and from the Solway Firth for
the market at Liverpool. By the 1830s on the east coast the trade
was quite extensive. In 1836-7 the numbers of livestock shown in
Table 2.1 were shipped from Inverness, Aberdeen, Dundee and Leith;
the majority of them to London. In addition a total of 11,621
barrels of meat were shipped from these ports between the same
dates, which at 2½ cwt per barrel came to 1,452½ tons. (10)

It was estimated that by the 1830s eastern Scotland produced
an excess of 20,000 fat cattle over what were necessary to supply

TABLE 2.1

	Cattle	Sheep	Lambs	Pigs
From Inverness (29 Sept. 1836 to 31 May 1837)	111	80	-	-
From Aberdeen (31 May 1836 to 31 May 1837)	7,443	945	-	2,162
From Dundee (31 May 1836 to 31 May 1837)	1,800	2,392	3,510	-
From Leith (31 May 1836 to 31 May 1837)	252	3,196	4,059	-
	9,606	6,613	7,569	2,162

the local population with meat. Therefore these exports did not immediately relieve these regions of their meat surplus. One difficulty in the way of the sea-borne trade with London from the northern ports of Invergordon, Inverness, Findhorn and Burghead was the lack of coal, which had to be brought from the Firth of Forth.

Western Scotland was also affected by these changes, though here the most convenient market in England was not London but Liverpool. The counties in the south west of the country - in particular Dumfries and Galloway - were already in a position to supply Glasgow with fat cattle and sheep. Freights from the west coast to Liverpool were much cheaper than to London. The west coast shippers were also prepared to encourage the traffic in lean stock by charging lower rates than for fat animals, a practice not followed on the east coast. The rate for large cattle was only 12s. per head from Port Carlisle, Annan, Waterfoot, Wigton, Kirkcudbright, Garlieston and Dumfries to Liverpool but stores were only charged 8s., fat sheep cost 1s. 6d., and lean sheep and lambs 1s. a head. The advantage of this policy to the shipping companies was that the store traffic involved a more continuous employment of carrying capacity. The fat trade was chiefly carried on in winter and spring with a little grass-fed stock taken south in summer and the trade in lean stock provided cargoes for summer and autumn.

The coastal steamer was also employed to carry dead meat from Scotland to England. According to Andrew Wynter, writing about the London meat supply in 1854, and with the railways in mind, 'Twenty years ago, 80 miles was the farthest distance from which carcases ever came'. (11) The railways were preceded by steamships as carriers of carcase meat and the possibility of a substantial traffic in sea-borne Scottish meat was discussed in 1837 and the descriptions given already indicate that the trade was established by then. However, the extreme ignorance shown by traders as to the precise requirements of their new market was a sign of its comparative novelty. This fault also applied to the exporters of livestock and can be traced to the curious variety of businessmen who pioneered the trade with London. It was said that men from a mixture of trades and professions, besides butchers, sent animals to England by steamship. Entry into the trade was comparatively

easy. The droving trade, where hundreds of animals were involved,
required large amounts of capital, (12) but anyone with £20 or £25
could buy an ox, ten sheep or a score of pigs to send by sea. The
trade also needed comparatively little personal supervision; the
purchase of stock could be left to the shipper and their disposal
to the market salesmen in London. The people who entered this
business purely as a speculation, like merchants, bakers or grocers,
etc., were unfitted either by experience or training as competent
judges of livestock and were sold animals that were in less than
prime condition. The same also applied to the condition of the
meat that they consigned to salesmen in London. Complaints that
beef and lamb was from half-fed animals, slaughtered in a filthy
manner, cut up in ignorance of the wants of the London market, and
packed for the journey in such a way as would injure even the
finest quality meat, were commonplace remarks that persisted well
after the trade had passed its infancy. The long distance meat
trade with Scotland and England revealed for the first time the very
different requirements of customers in various regions. The London
market, for instance, had a very heavy demand for the best cuts of
meat for roasting - much more so than Scotland. The greatest
profits were made in sending this quality of produce rather than
the poorer stewing joints. But some Scottish dealers ignorant of
the market requirements sent whole salted carcases to London -
salted to prevent the meat spoiling in hot weather. As Londoners
only used fresh meat for roasting, the prime parts of the carcase
sold for no more than the coarsest boiling pieces.
    A steady stream of meat and livestock was not sent to London
throughout the year. As Aberdeen was a winter feeding area the
supplies coming to the market in the city dried up from July to
November. Indeed, the whole of the trade in dead meat from all
areas was heaviest in the cooler months of the year when it was
less of a problem to ensure freshness. The growth of the dead meat
trade appears also to have been accompanied by a change in the
personnel involved. Prior to 1850 most of the cattle sent south
by sea appear to have been dispatched by the graziers, and they
took responsibility for them before they reached the London buyers.
With the growth of the dead meat trade the farmers relinquished
control of the animals when they sold them in the town markets in
Scotland. In the case of Aberdeen, after the amateurish efforts
of some of the pioneers in the dead meat trade in the 1830s, by
1850 wholesale butchers had come to dominate meat exports from the
city. In this way it was easier to get the animals butchered in
accordance with the requirements of the London market.

2 THE RAILWAYS

Even before the railways cattle and other livestock found their way
to the London meat market from most parts of Britain. But as they
were mostly driven by road the journey was sometimes, for those
originating in Scotland, an indirect one of the kind already
referred to above. (13) However there were seasonal variations in
all aspects of this trade and each district sent its greatest
numbers at particular times of the year. These seasonal variations

were determined by the regional variations in the nature of the
livestock industry and the availability of feeding stuffs. According to Youatt, writing in the 1830s, (14) it was in December
that fat cattle to furnish the prime beef for the London Christmas
tables were sent there from the stall yards around the metropolis
as well as from Norfolk, Northants, Leicestershire, Lincolnshire,
Sussex and the east and west Midlands. In the spring the stall-
fed animals from the eastern counties of England furnished the
heaviest supplies with smaller numbers sent by sea from Galloway
and eastern Scotland. (15) These tended to dominate the London
market through the early summer months and only became exhausted
by late July. In July, August and September the grass-fed animals
from Essex, Northants, Leicestershire and Lincolnshire poured in,
and these occupied the main place in the market through to the
early part of December. Thereafter the stall-fed animals took over
once again.

By 1850 the railways and steamships had added another dimension
to this traffic. Youatt's description dealt only with the cattle
driven by road to the metropolis, and the most distant of these
only came from Lincolnshire. The trade from Scotland, which was
still comparatively minor in terms of the numbers received from
England, was ignored by him. But less than a generation later the
combined rail and sea routes had opened the London markets to
considerably more cattle and livestock from Ireland and Scotland
as well as the more distant parts of England. This encouraged a
general increase in supplies from all districts of the British
Isles and in addition, after the free trade budget of 1842, the
London market was open to livestock from Europe. The last group
was a comparatively small proportion of the total but the yearly
and seasonal variation in arrivals from the United Kingdom from
1855 to 1860 can be seen in Table 2.2.

The distinction between the northern summer pasture counties
and the eastern arable districts, where the changing emphasis of
mixed farming encouraged a greater concentration on livestock
fattening by 1850, (16) is readily apparent. The contrast between
Scotland and Ireland was also marked. Arrivals from eastern
Scotland, where the agriculture of the Lothians bore most resembl-
ance to that of Norfolk, were predominantly stall-fed winter
beasts; but in Ireland summer fattening on grass supplied the
majority of animals that were sent to the metropolis.

Arrivals of mutton were also on a year-round basis. Thus both
meats were always available, as was pork. Yet all meats varied
in abundance and were better at certain seasons. Lamb and veal,
however, were more strictly seasonal trades; lamb was most plentiful between April and June and veal was at its best between
February and July. (17) Prices also varied seasonally in a normal
year. Generally at the start of a normal year beef and mutton
were found to be in short supply and so the price of both these
meats was relatively high. In February and March, as more stall-
fed animals became available so the price of beef dropped. Mutton,
however, was in short supply in those months which are close to
lambing time and so the price of this meat rose. In the spring
and summer, as grass-fed animals became available in greater
numbers, the movement of prices for both meats was generally down-

TABLE 2.2   Metropolitan cattle market, district bullock supplies,
1855-60

		1855	1856	1857	1858	1859	1860
Northern Districts	(a)	600,	900	-	4,000	4,000	4,000
	(b)	52,800	60,760	81,600	66,260	64,470	66,140
Eastern Districts	(a)	54,989	51,700	60,500	66,890	67,460	68,520
	(b)	9,800	-	7,000	6,970	3,600	9,500
Other parts of England	(a)	12,530	13,850	14,490	14,560	19,090	21,420
	(b)	11,050	20,700	15,370	13,830	23,220	20,500
Scotland	(a)	9,827	10,008	8,860	8,456	10,030	5,033
	(b)	2,993	2,734	1,836	2,674	4,640	1,151
Ireland	(a)	4,000	3,400	2,700	4,820	2,217	1,477
	(b)	9,800	11,000	12,000	13,760	10,544	7,852

Source: Robert Herbert, Statistics of Live Stock and Dead Meat for
Consumption in the Metropolis, 'Journal of the Royal Agricultural
Society of England', vol. XXI, 1860, pp.177 and 383.

(a) January to June, (b) July to December.

'Northern Districts' were understood to include the counties of
Lincolnshire, Leicestershire, Northamptonshire and Warwickshire.
These were chiefly grass-feeding counties. The 'Eastern Districts'
- mainly devoted to stall-feeding - comprised the corn-growing
counties of Norfolk, Suffolk, Cambridgeshire and Essex. ('Journal
of the Royal Agricultural Society of England', vol. XIX, 1858,
p.500.)

wards, the lowest point being reached in June. In the hot summer
months there was less demand for meat and this also contributed to
lower prices. By September beef prices began to rise again as the
grass-fed beasts tailed off and before the stall-fed animals
became fully available. For mutton the movement of prices was more
uncertain, but from September through the winter the supply consisted of fattened ewes and wethers. For both meats October and
November were months of abundance and also of relatively high
demand as the weather became cooler.

In the 1850s London drew its own meat supplies from a number of
separate regions of Britain and also from abroad. If we exclude
the 'town made' pork we find that there are four more or less
distinct sources of supply.
1 Live animals from Ireland, England, Wales and Scotland.
2 Dead meat from England and Scotland.
3 Live animals from the Continent.
4 Cattle from the London dairies.

Domestic sources of supply provided the major part of the meat
eaten in London between 1850 and 1864. The railways played a vital
part in extending the distance, and hence the number of regions
from which London drew its meat supplies. In the early part of the

nineteenth century cattle were walked into London. This was a
wasteful practice because the animals lost a certain amount of
weight on their journey. It must also have placed certain limits
on the size to which the farmers could afford to fatten the
cattle. A very fat, overweight beast is much less fit to undertake a long road journey than a somewhat leaner animal. The
transformation of meat distribution brought about by the railways
took place in stages. The first step was the transport of live
animals by rail instead of walking them in by road. This development caused important economic changes for those places on the
road to London that had previously catered for the drovers' flocks
and herds. The village of Southall on the Uxbridge Road straddled
the main route into London from Oxford. Southall had a cattle
market which was attended by local farmers and dealers as well as
men from London buying animals. The farmers of the village were
in a fortunate position to buy stock to fatten on their land, or
to rent out their fields to salesmen who had brought cattle a long
distance and required the use of land to provide sustenance for
the beasts prior to sale. The local farmers were in a monopoly
position as they could buy cheaply if there was no ready sale for
animals and wait till prices improved before selling, or they could
charge heavily for the use of their land by dealers with animals
on their hands until the next market. The introduction of the
Great Western Railway with a station at Southall gave dealers the
ability to transfer rapidly large numbers of stock from one county
to another. If the Southall market was over-stocked the dealers
would send their animals to another the same day by rail. This
deprived the Southall farmers of their monopoly position. They
found their grazing land and animal feed was in less demand and
prices of these accordingly moved downwards. The railway was also
able to put far bigger numbers of stock into Southall market on a
single day than the drovers had ever done. At times 500 head of
sheep and 100 head of cattle from the west of England appeared and
forced down prices accordingly, compelling the Middlesex farmers to
sell their stock at a loss or withdraw them from competition. (18)
As the complaints of the farmers were voiced in 1843 this was a
development which had started well before 1850. In later years the
extension of the railway network brought Irish and Scottish cattle
besides those of Devon and Hereford. (19)

These economic changes were a two-way process affecting districts
further afield than former suburban fattening areas like Southall.
Regions that had been too far from main centres of consumption to
fatten animals profitably, because of the weight losses involved in
walking the animals to town, were able to undertake this branch of
agriculture with profit. As the map of the railway network spread
in the 1840s and 1850s districts increasingly remote were able to
develop fattening industries.

In the case of the Scottish meat trade to London, this came to
be centred on Aberdeen. However, its growth was not entirely
dependent on railway transport as it was possible to take beasts by
sea to London and the south, even before the first load of cattle
was carried by rail with the opening of the through railway to
London in 1850. (20) The sea route suffered from a number of dis-
advantages and limitations which restricted the size of the trade.

The greatest fear was the loss of animals from storms at sea, occurrences which also delayed the arrival of the cargoes in port and added to costs. Therefore the London market was accessible to a limited number of farmers before 1850 who wished to send fatstock south by sea. At this time a considerable number of cattle sent to England were still stores that were driven south from Aberdeenshire and north east Scotland to be fattened in Norfolk for the metropolitan market. But with the opening of a through rail connection with London the trend towards fattening in the north east of Scotland was accelerated.

Even before the opening of the direct link with London the trade in fatstock was already large and expanding. According to one authority, except for one year, the yearly shipments of cattle from the port of Aberdeen increased from 9,543 to 15,858 between 1842 and 1849. (21) The opening of the through rail route to London did not mean the overnight disappearance of the sea traffic. Instead, for a complex set of reasons, rail and sea persisted alongside each other as alternative and competing methods of distribution for the fatstock owners of the north east of Scotland for at least the next twenty years after 1850. In a recent article C.H. Lee has shown that there was an agreement in 1857 between the Aberdeen Steam Navigation Company and the Scottish North East Railway Company to divide the numbers of cattle going to London by sea and rail on a quota basis according to the percentages travelling by each mode of transport in the year before. If the railways exceeded their percentage quota in the future they could pay a fine for each animal in excess and if the steamship company did the same they paid the railway. The total of cattle carried in the year on which the agreement was based was 15,092 of which 39 per cent (5,863) went by steamship and 61 per cent (9,229) by rail. (22) Again after the introduction of the railways there was no sudden fall in the rates for cattle sent by sea. The evidence here is fragmentary but, according to Lee, between 1839 and the mid-1860s the price for sending cattle by sea from Aberdeen to London ranged between 25s. and £1 a head. (23) However, his figures are for freight only and they do not include the charge for attendance and provisions en route or for wharfage in London, and so they cannot be directly compared with the costs of sea transit already cited on page 18. But the sea traffic in livestock was materially reduced by the opening of the railway link. No figures exist for the first five years but from 1855 to 1870 the railways carried most of the livestock except in 1868. (24) In this period an average of 14,173 cattle per annum were sent south from Aberdeen by sea and rail together. The sea traffic, however, sank to about a third of its former size and only 4,452 of their cattle, or 31 per cent of the total, went this way!

The railways did not present farmers and butchers with a clear choice between sending their animals south by sea or by rail. There was a third possibility open to them which has already been mentioned in general terms. This was to slaughter the animals in Aberdeen and to send the carcases south by rail. The introduction of the railway service made it possible to develop a trade in a product which the sea route had little capacity to handle. Some fresh meat was sent by sea before 1850 but it only amounted to a

very small part of the total meat, alive and dead, carried by sea.
(25) In 1855 the bulk of meat carried from Aberdeen was dead meat
and this was carried by rail. The steamship companies did not so
much lose trade in carrying animals to the railways as the whole
live meat trade declined in the face of the rise in the importance
of the dead meat trade. Commenting on the changes he saw in the
meat supply, George Dodd observed: (26)

> There has been an increasing tendency in recent years to send up
> to London country-killed meat; ... but nothing less than swift-
> ness of conveyance could render such a system practicable. The
> meat must be fresh and appear fresh to command a good position
> in the market; and taint arising from the long-continuance of a
> journey would exercise a most injurious influence on the price
> obtained.

In this respect the railways had the competitive edge over the
steamships.

3   REGIONAL DIFFERENCES IN THE DEMAND FOR MEAT

There was a considerable difference between the methods of retail
butchers in the regions of the United Kingdom. (27) These variations can be explained by reference to the particular social and
economic circumstances of the areas where they existed. The way in
which the retailer cut up a carcase for sale in any place or
district was governed by the local demand for particular portions
and the price which each of the different cuts of meat would
command. In London, the presence of the Court and aristocracy,
Parliament, and also the wealthy City business community meant the
capital contained a large population with the means of indulging
their taste for conspicuous consumption. As a result the luxury
joints of meat for roasting, from the prime parts of all animals,
were in heavy demand. To accommodate this demand London butchers
took pains to divide their carcases in such a way as to obtain the
greatest quantity of the most esteemed joints. Also there was a
very wide difference in London between the price of the most
expensive and the price of cheaper cuts of meat. Mid-nineteenth-
century London was, perhaps to a greater extent than most cities,
a place of social extremes; besides the wealthy top stratum the
capital contained a large number of families in casual irregular
employment whose purchasing power was very limited. To supply this
demand inferior joints were sold at prices far below the best. At
the prices current in 1837-8 the rumps, loins and fore-ribs of a
good ox in London fetched 8d. per lb; the thick flank, buttock, and
middle rib 6d.; the aitch bone, thin flank and brisket 5d.; the
neck 3d.; and the legs and shins 2d. Those inferior parts that were
not purchased directly from the retailer found their way into
working-class consumption via the makers of sausages, pies and
cooked meats. In other towns and places where the disparities in
wealth and income were not so extreme the relative strength of
demand for different parts of the carcases tended to be more equal.
Therefore in the provinces the prices paid for better and inferior
joints of meat were closer together than in London. Accordingly
in these places the butcher did not pay so much attention to getting

the most out of prime parts of an animal when he came to cut up a
carcase. In the rural districts, where the means to indulge the
taste for luxury hardly existed - if at all - butchers paid little
attention to how they divided up a carcase as there was little
price incentive to separate the best from the inferior parts.

A difference also existed between Scottish and English towns.
In Edinburgh, Glasgow and a few other of the large Scottish towns
roasting and steak joints fetched 6d. and 7d. per lb when the
boiling pieces like neck and brisket were priced at 5d. or 5½d.
The best meat was less expensive than in London but the poorest
was dearer. In the smaller towns and the country districts throughout Scotland price disparities between high and low quality joints
almost disappeared. Here the situation was the same as in rural
England; there was no consumer preference for particular joints,
nor was there any difference in the price for different parts of
the carcase. The explanation for this peculiarity was not that
Scotland possessed a more egalitarian society than existed south
of the Border; instead it was a question of dietary habits. In
England, and in particular London, there was a strong preference
for the taste of roasted meat, but in Edinburgh and in the rest of
Scotland people were very much in the habit of living on broth and
boiled meat. As the subtle differences of taste that are apparent
between different joints of meat when they are roasted disappear
when it is stewed, there was no strong consumer preference for
particular joints in Scotland. Therefore, the butcher was not
induced to cut the best joints so large, or to exercise the nice
division of quality which characterized the London manner of cutting
up a carcase of beef.

Other English towns occupied an intermediate position between
both the London and Edinburgh patterns of demand and methods of
cutting up meat. Newcastle, for instance, contained a numerous
class of well paid professional men, wealthy merchants, extensive
manufacturers and wealthy shopkeepers and traders. These all able
to afford, and with a strong liking for, traditional English roast
beef meant that there was a steady demand for the roasting parts of
the carcase at all times in that town. In addition, there was a
strong demand for the cheaper boiling parts of the carcase.
Newcastle did a steady trade provisioning the coasting vessels
based on or calling at that port, and from this source there was a
demand for cheap meat which ships usually purchased by the hundredweight. The town itself employed a large number of workers,
principally in heavy engineering, and there was an even larger
number of coal miners in the surrounding districts who were supplied
with meat from the Newcastle market. With a preference and an ample
demand for choice meat by one class of the inhabitants, and yet
with an equal demand for the coarser joints by the poorer members,
there was less difference in the price of different joints in
Newcastle than in London, but a greater difference in price than
in Edinburgh. Again, this pattern of demand was reflected in
butchering practice. In Newcastle the retailers had a greater
incentive to cut the roasting joints larger than was practised in
Scotland and less reason for cutting them so large as in the London
method of dividing a carcase of beef. (28)

These differences in dietary habits, consumer preferences and

the structure of demand were apparent in relative prices of beef
for London, Newcastle and Edinburgh. In London the demand for good
meat was so strong that at times the very best steaks retailed at
1s. per lb, but the more usual price range was of five distinct
qualities of meat costing between 8d. per lb for the best and 2d.
per lb for the worst. In Newcastle there were four qualities of
beef costing 7d. per lb for the best down to 3d. per lb for the
lowest. In Edinburgh such distinctions were vaguer and there seem
to have been only two divisions as to quality and prices. There
they ranged from around 7d. per lb for best beef and around 5d. or
5½d. for the rest. Somewhat similar distinctions existed between
the London and provincial modes of cutting up carcases of mutton.
In London particular attention was paid to obtaining prime roasting
joints of mutton - either saddles or haunches (29) - to supply the
keepers of eating houses or to provide the meat for large banquets
and entertainments. Also at the wholesale dead meat markets the
hind quarter usually fetched 2d. per lb more than the fore quarter
of the same carcase. In Scotland the loin was cut smaller than in
London, thus reducing the size of the higher priced hind quarter.
In Newcastle the hind quarter was cut the same as in Edinburgh and
the differences in prices for the various joints were less than
those of London. In London the leg sometimes fetched 10d. per lb
while the breast was only worth 4d. or 5d.; in Newcastle the leg
and loin fetched 7d.; shoulder 6d.; breast and scrag 4½d. to 5d.
(30) For mutton and for beef the main difference between London
and elsewhere lay in the strength of demand at the top end of the
market, which forced up the price of the very best - and therefore
most expensive - cuts of meat in the metropolis.

Variations in the manner of cutting up meat and disparities in
prices were not fully equalized when they were averaged over a
whole carcase to compare the level of regional prices. A comparison
of wholesale beef and mutton prices in four various parts of the
United Kingdom between 1828 and 1864 (Figures 2.1 and 2.2) reveals
that for most of that time London prices were ahead of those in
Edinburgh and Newcastle. (31) London prices were higher, absolutely, than most other places, for beef and mutton. The only
exception to this rule appears to have been Glasgow where wholesale
beef prices between 1851-3 and 1857-64 were higher than in London.

4 PROVINCIAL MARKETS

The existence of livestock and meat prices in regular and continuous series is not a common occurrence for the United Kingdom before
a record of prices at selected markets was kept after 1891. (32)
Given the practices of both sellers and purchasers at livestock
markets and auctions in the middle of the nineteenth century, the
absence of such records is not wholly a matter that the economic
historian need regret. In the case of livestock markets the
accurate recording of prices was made difficult by the existence of
fictitious sales and the more or less universal custom of 'luck-
money'. Fictitious sales were prevalent in Scotland, either to
satisfy the vanity of the seller by enabling him to boast of the
high prices he had obtained, or in the more or less vain hope of

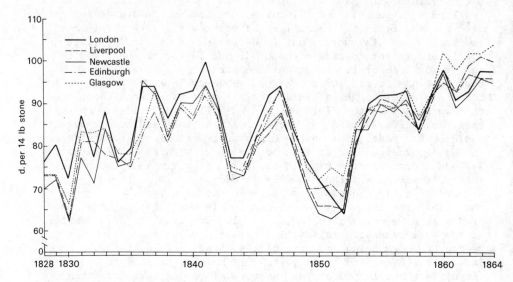

FIGURE 2.1 Wholesale beef prices, 1828-64

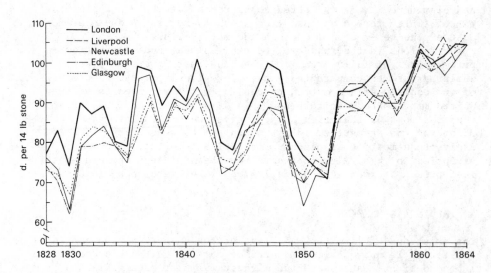

FIGURE 2.2 Wholesale mutton prices, 1828-64

keeping up the future market prices of sheep and cattle. Such sales
were worked in the following manner. The buyer would agree to
purchase a particular lot of animals at a certain sum per head above
the going market price, on the understanding that the seller would
privately hand back to him the excess money after the market had
closed. The fictitious sale was also prevalent in Ireland -
perhaps more so. Of course no regular dealers in the country

markets were fooled by the practice - they were aware of current
values and the methods of doing business and so made their offers
accordingly. However it was often the fictitious price and not
the real one that passed into the public record. For instance, in
Ireland the market returns were based on the maximum prices
entered in the sellers' books which took no account of the fact
that the seller might hand back from 5 to 15 per cent of the cash
paid. These market returns were then paraded through the metropolitan newspapers and extracted from them by the provincial as
well as the English and Scottish newspapers, thus gaining a
general currency. Ireland may have been a more extreme example
but it is likely that the same methods existed in country markets
of England as well as Scotland.

The practice of the luck-money was very similar to the fictitious sale. Indeed the variation was only one of degree. The
luck-money was an amount for each beast which the seller handed
back to the buyer after the transaction had been completed. In
different regions this practice had its own particular name - in
parts of England it was called 'chap-money' or even the 'luck-
penny'. It was also not confined to livestock sales but applied to
practically any sort of farm produce. The origin of the practice
is obscure - it may have been by way of a superstitious offering
that the purchaser (and his purchases) might thrive by its agency.
In the case of a dealer who bought stores for others it may have
been an important consideration as this money went towards defray-
ing his expenses and may have been concealed from the farmers who
paid the price as recorded by the seller plus the commission already
agreed with the dealer. Of course if a very large luck-penny was
exacted - the 'penny' in this case being virtually a synonym for
'money' - there was in fact no difference between this transaction
and a fictitious sale. In some places the value of the luck-money
was more or less fixed by custom and was small enought to be dis-
regarded when consulting livestock market prices in the press. By
the 1860s in most places in England 1s. a head for beasts and 1s. a
score for sheep was the usual amount. In Scotland, however, the
amounts tended to be less institutionalized, and in all places
disputes could arise because the seller refused to return a sum to
the purchaser. In some cases it was said that it took buyers and
sellers longer to settle the luck-money than to make the original
bargain, and at times sales would be called off because the parties
were unable to reach agreements over the amounts. (33)

These methods of marketing were hangovers of the past from a time
when prices and values were harder to determine in the absence of
newspapers and when both buyers and sellers were prepared to devote
considerable time and effort to striking the right bargain. Also,
the practice of luck-money persisted in rural markets beyond the
end of the nineteenth century. (34) In these markets the farmers
themselves took a prominent part in selling, and the conservatism
of this class of men no doubt reinforced the practices of long
usage. Also, these sales were face-to-face bargains struck
between the parties whose financial interests were closely involved
in their outcome. The method of selling by auction was not generally applied in 1850 and so there was no substitution of an

impersonal intermediary with whom the buyers made their bargain.
The unpopularity of this method was on account of the collusion
that usually sprang up sooner or later between the buyers - either
butchers or cattle dealers usually all known to each other being
comparatively few in number - to abstain from bidding long before
the real value of the animals was reached by the auctioneer.
Auction sales were really only popular with the great breeders of
livestock who held annual sales on their farms for their surplus
stock, with luncheon for the buyers, who in any case were more
often farmers and breeders than butchers. (35)

A further complication in the measurement of prices applies to
dead meat. The weight by which carcases were sold varied in
different parts of the United Kingdom. In London the butcher's
stone was 8 lb avoirdupois; in Edinburgh and throughout Scotland
generally they employed the Dutch stone which was 16 lb of 17½
ounces though in some places cattle were sold by the tron stone of
22 lb avoirdupois; in Lancashire and the Midlands carcase meat was
generally sold by the score of 20 lb avoirdupois; and in other parts
of the United Kingdom the imperial stone of 14 lb avoirdupois was
general. In Leeds yet another local variation, that of a stone of
16 lb avoirdupois was employed. (36)

After London the other regional fatstock markets of 1850 were
considerably smaller. The Glasgow and Edinburgh ones were roughly
equal in size. In Edinburgh the weekly market was held on a
Wednesday and the average number of stock on show was about 700
cattle and 2,000 sheep. The Glasgow market had the same amount of
cattle and approximately 1,500 sheep: this market was on a Thursday.
In the 1851 census Edinburgh had a population of 194,000 persons
and Glasgow 345,000. There was no firm rule about the size of
market and the population that it served. The fact that Glasgow
had a larger population than Edinburgh's does not mean that it was
supplied with less meat. The distance by rail between these towns
was short and it was possible for Glasgow butchers to buy stock or
receive meat from Edinburgh. Also Glasgow was well situated to
receive supplies of fatstock from Ireland.

At Newcastle the weekly market for cattle, sheep and pigs was
held on Tuesdays. The market at Newcastle was a comparatively
modern one, dating its first appearance only from 1836. Prior to
that the town was supplied with its fatstock from the weekly market
at Morpeth, some 15 miles to the north. As a market, Newcastle
received an average of 700 beasts a week in the 1850s and some 5,000
sheep and lambs. As with all markets the supplies of fat sheep and
cattle varied at different seasons. From January to the end of July
the numbers of cattle were much greater than from the end of July to
the close of December. During the first part of the year the
average weekly supply of cattle was nearly double that during the
latter period. Also the average weight per head of beasts from
January to July was around 7 cwt, carcase weight, whereas those
coming forward from July onwards were lighter, only averaging 6 cwt
per carcase. Therefore taking account both of numbers and weights
the ratio of beef available in the two parts of the year was about
14 to 6. From the start of January to the end of April the majority
of beasts came from Northumberland, southern Durham and the Border
counties of Roxburghshire and Berwickshire, and were mostly short-

horns.   From the end of April to the end of July these areas were
supplemented by cattle drawn from the east coast of Scotland from
Kincardineshire, Aberdeenshire and Forfarshire.   The Scots animals -
mostly cross-bred shorthorns - made the journey to Newcastle by
steamer and constituted between a third and a quarter of the beasts
exhibited in those months.   Up to the end of July the cattle in the
market were all 'house-fed' - that is on roots or oil-cake in straw
yards or stalls.   But from the beginning of August until the end of
the year the lighter weight grass-fed stock became available from
the surrounding neighbourhood and from Cumberland.   These animals
comprised a great variety of breeds of which Kyloes, polled
Galloways and Irish runts made up a considerable part. (37)

Like the other markets of this size, the Newcastle fatstock
market provided butcher-meat for the surrounding districts besides
the immediate population of the town itself which only totalled
88,000.   An important part of this trade were the meat and animals
supplied to the mining villages of Durham and Northumberland.
From further afield dealers from south east Lancashire and west
Yorkshire also purchased fat cattle to supply the industrial populations in those districts.   However the opening of fortnightly
markets at Alnwick and Berwick after 1850 also attracted these men
and some stock was moved south without ever passing through the
chief market in the county.

CHAPTER 3
CHANGES IN TOWN MARKETS, 1840-64

Because of its size and importance, the London market for meat and
livestock deserves separate examination. London provides a
special case study of all the changes and problems associated with
meat distribution in the mid-nineteenth century. Developments in
transport altered the nature of London's meat supplies and changed
the sources from which those supplies were drawn. The demographic
growth of London also placed severe strains upon the distribution
and marketing system within the capital. As urban growth was not
confined to the metropolis, the way in which these problems were
solved for London also has some relevance to the problems faced
and the solutions adopted in provincial cities.

1 LONDON: THE PROBLEM OF SMITHFIELD AND THE MEAT MARKETS

The livestock market for London was at Smithfield, and had been
located on the same site since A.D. 950. At first this site was
admirable; just beyond the City walls in a large unenclosed space
it was able to hold as many animals as farmers cared to send there.
But with the growth of London beyond the walls the market site was
encroached upon and partly built over. It was surrounded by shops
and houses and to reach the place the animals had to be driven
through increasingly congested streets and thoroughfares. Also as
London grew it required more meat so increasing numbers of livestock
had to be driven into a diminished space. Between 1732 and 1830
the number of cattle recorded at Smithfield rose from 76,210 to
159,907 and sheep from 514,700 to 1,287,070. (1) In addition, the
improvement in breeds of livestock by the later date increased the
weight and size of the animals shown at Smithfield by an indeter-
minate amount. (2) The combined effect of these changes was to
render Smithfield totally inadequate to deal with the volume of
livestock needed to provide meat for the population of London well
before the end of the eighteenth century. (3)
  By the early nineteenth century the markets at Smithfield, held
on Monday and Friday of each week, were scenes of indescribable
confusion. In 1808-9 a memorial signed by 177 farmers and graziers,
ninety-nine salesmen and butchers and thirty inhabitants of

Smithfield was presented to the Privy Council. This document
alleged: (4)

That the ancient market-place at Smithfield is much too small to
contain the live cattle necessary for the supply of the
immensely-increased and increasing population of the metropolis
and its environs; - That the cattle often bruise and lame, and
sometimes trample upon and kill each other, by being confined
for hours together in a crowded state in the market; and some of
them are maimed and or bruised in a shocking manner by the
waggons, carts, or drays driven through Smithfield during market
hours; - That the buyers cannot go between or among the beasts
in their very crowded state at market, to examine them, without
danger of sustaining serious bodily injury.

The market covered 6 acres and 15 rods of land, and this included
roads and public thoroughfares. The whole place was also
surrounded by business premises associated with the meat trade like
slaughterhouses, triperies, bone-boiling houses and gut-scraperies.
On particularly busy days, such as the last market before Christmas,
the whole market, which was calculated to hold 4,100 oxen and
30,000 sheep besides calves and pigs, would be crammed to over-
flowing. The streets around were also full of animals blocking up
all access to and egress from the market. In 1854, the last year
the Christmas market was held on the old site of Smithfield, 6,181
cattle alone were recorded as having been exhibited; the year before
there were 7,037 on display. In these congested, noisy conditions
cruelty was almost a necessity to drive bewildered and frightened
animals through the market to the places they were sold and then
out again. The damage this alarm and the beatings of the drovers
caused to the livestock was a frequent source of complaint among
farmers and butchers alike. (5)

The situation at London's wholesale meat markets was little
better than at Smithfield. Here again the root of the problem lay
in inadequate premises. London had two chief dead meat markets:
Newgate Market and a smaller one at Leadenhall Market. Joseph
Fletcher described both these places in 1847 as 'places disgraceful
to any large city at the present day'. (6) They were, besides
being markets, also great slaughtering places. As the selling space
for meat was limited and inadequate, the slaughtering had been
relegated to premises beneath the markets. Cattle and sheep were
killed and skinned in dark, filthy cellars some of which at times
contained fifty to a hundred sheep crowded into the smallest
possible space. In some of these places water was not even
provided so it was impossible to keep the premises remotely clean.
They were so over-crowded that the butchers slaughtering the
animals did not have room to work properly.

The growth in the supplies of country-killed meat after 1850,
though it did not add to the pressure on the slaughtering space,
made the working conditions in both markets very much worse. There
are very strong indications that the dead meat market at Newgate
was already operating at full capacity as early as 1849. The
market had an area of only 2 roods and 45 perches. At the end of
the Napoleonic Wars there were only thirteen dead-meat salesmen
employed in the market. By 1849 this had increased, along with the
trade, to 200. The market had only one entrance for vehicles, and

that was only 18 feet wide, and four entrances, varying from 16 to
6 feet wide, for pedestrians. (7) Business at this market was an
indescribable scene of confusion. Vans and carts were crammed into
the street, unable to pass each other or get into the market, so
they were unpacked in the street surrounded by crowds of salesmen.
Conditions inside the market were so foul and oppressive, and
without sufficient space to handle the meat properly, that a large
quantity was spoilt for want of air and space to hang it. (8)

Joseph Gamgee's investigation of the conditions at Newgate in
1857 showed they had not improved in the decade following Fletcher's
report or since Wynter described it. According to Gamgee: (9)

its smallness altogether unfits it for the enormous business of
the day; while the vast number of its dark little shops, or
rather holes offers great facility to the hiding (of) bad meat,
which in the day is perfectly visible and when brought out under
a gas illumination on Saturday night does not show its true
colours, and finds purchasers in the poor and hard working
population.

Associated with this market he found the inevitable sales of bad
or diseased meat, which were an integral part of the meat distribution and butchering business in the 1850s and 1860s. On one early
morning visit when he saw great quantities of meat entering the
market in railway and other vans, the large salesmen were opening
business and they had, almost without exception, excellent meat to
offer. But in many of the small shops of the petty traders in the
market he witnessed a great deal of very bad meat offered for sale:
'stinking legs of mutton, sour smelling fragments of slipped calves,
large quantities of beef and pork only fit to be buried', sold quite
openly without the least attempt, or need, by traders to disguise
their business. (10)

Indirectly associated with these inadequate premises were
insufficient arrangements for policing the market and preventing
the sale of this bad meat. The whole of Joseph Gamgee's account of
the London wholesale meat markets at this time is full of fruitless
searches for the relevant official to take action against wrong-
doers. Even when the official was located and the rotten meat
pointed out to him it was not certain that he would agree to take
action against the offender. This happened to Gamgee on one
occasion in Newgate Market. The inspector, a Mr Robert Pocklington,
on being informed that putrid beef, unfit for human food, was on
sale at 1½d. per lb (the usual wholesale price of beef in 1857 was
between 4¼d. and 7¼d. per lb), and being shown it, refused to agree
with Gamgee that it was unfit, and declined to take an action on
his own initiative against the seller. Pocklington was himself a
retired meat trader from the market and it seems likely that his
reluctance to act was prompted by feelings of sympathy towards his
own trade, and hostility at any intervention from an outsider.
Gamgee concluded that because of his very advanced age he was
destitute of those special qualities which an efficient market
inspector should possess. (11)

The state of the meat and livestock markets inevitably affected
London's meat supply. The cruelties at Smithfield attendant upon
the beatings and goadings necessary to pack the animals into the
confined space damaged both hides and flesh. At various times

estimates of these costs were offered. In 1809 it was alleged that the loss sustained by the owners of cattle at Smithfield was £40,000 and the value of stock exhibited was not less than £5,000,000. (12) In 1828 the value lost on meat was put at £100,000, or around ten times the amount collected in market tolls. Another estimate in 1852 put the cost of the deterioration in the quality of stock to the farmers who sent to Smithfield at around £500,000. (13) Even allowing for the fact that these are only 'guestimates', the persistent way in which they are reported over a series of years is an undeniable indication that losses were sustained. It was said by persons in the trade that the grazier would be unable to recognize his cattle four days after they had left him, and that the greatest injury was not sustained during the rail journey to London, which might be several hundred miles, but in the short distance from the London termini to Smithfield and in the market itself.

At one time it was believed that the railways would soon put an end to these abuses by the transport of dead meat. Their effect was to increase the area that London could draw on for supplies of meat. The carcase trade was already in existence before the railways. In the early nineteenth century the catchment area for meat, as opposed to livestock, did not extent much beyond a radius of 70 miles from the city. Thus supplies were sent by road to salesmen at Newgate from Essex, Surrey, Hampshire, Berkshire, Bedfordshire, Buckinghamshire, Hertfordshire, Huntingdonshire, Oxfordshire, Wiltshire and Gloucestershire. The trade was also widely spread within these counties; for instance, from Berkshire consignments came from Reading, Newbury, Workingham, Thatcham, Wallingford, Wantage, Abingdon, Swallowfield and Hungerford. Similarly, from Surrey, Hampshire, Oxfordshire and Wiltshire meat was sent from four, six, nine and seven places respectively. But by 1850 supplies from Surrey, Hampshire, Berkshire, Oxfordshire and Wiltshire were greatly reduced and those from Bedfordshire, Buckinghamshire, Herefordshire, Huntingdonshire, Gloucestershire and Essex were reported to have undergone a lesser reduction. At the same time the total consignments to the dead meat market had increased and new areas and towns were sending the bulk of consignments. The greatest increase in supplies was from Scotland, Berwick, Newcastle, Durham, Liverpool, Bristol, Hull, Lincolnshire and Yorkshire. In addition supplies from Europe were also received as early as this from the Dutch ports and from Bremen and Hamburg. (14) The growth of the railway traffic of meat in the 1830s and 1840s was such that in 1855 a Departmental Committee examining the state of the London meat markets reported that: (15)

> The establishment of communication by means of railways and steam boats between the metropolis and every part of the United Kingdom has essentially altered the character of the meat market. While the increased supply of live cattle has hardly been in proportion to the progress of the population, the trade in meat has acquired a remarkable impulse.

The number of sheep and lambs sent to Smithfield showed a definite decline. In 1842-5 an average of 1,704,000 sheep passed through Smithfield each year; by 1850-3 the figure had declined to 1,620,000, (16) despite the continued increase in demand for lamb

and mutton. In 1854 Andrew Wynter suggested that the falling off
in the number of sheep sold at Smithfield was 'solely because they
now come to town in the form of mutton'. As for the beatings and
violence which accompanied the driving of cattle to Smithfield,
Wynter prophesied that 'Country slaughtering will in time, we have
little doubt, deliver the capital from the nuisances which grow out
of this horrible trade'. (17)

2   OBSTACLES TO REFORM IN LONDON

At various times objections to the state of affairs at Smithfield
and Newgate had been expressed, and attempts had been made to reform
the situation. (18) The opposition to reform came from a number of
groups who had a vested (financial) interest in leaving things as
they were. For the purposes of analysis three main groups can be
identified. First, there was the Corporation of the City of London,
backed by local traders and publicans who derived income from the
business of the market, supported by the surgeons and trustees of
St Bartholomew's Hospital, the Foundling Hospital, and the Highgate
Roads Trust who also derived revenue from the market site. (19)
The second group opposed to any change were the meat traders themselves, that is the cattle salesmen, jobbers, meat salesmen and
butchers who conducted their business from these places. The final
group also had a special business interest in the Smithfield market.
They were the bankers, or money-takers as they were called, who
handled all the financial transactions within the market.

The position of the Corporation with regard to Smithfield was a
peculiarly delicate one. In 1851 the population of the City of
London reached its peak at 130,000. Thereafter, the demographic
growth of the metropolis was outside the City proper, in the
administrative region of London, which already had 2.2 million
persons in 1857, and in Middlesex. In succeeding censuses the
population living within the City fell while the administrative
county rose from 2.6 million persons in 1861 to over 3 million in
1871. (20) Therefore by 1850 it is likely that more people were
supplied with meat from Smithfield who lived outside the jurisdiction of the City Corporation than its inhabitants. But the City
still controlled and derived a profitable revenue from the market.
Furthermore they were able to exercise restrictions over the
establishment of new markets within a certain distance of London.
In 1833 work on an alternative market to Smithfield was begun near
Ball's Pond, Islington, by a private individual. The proposal
aroused strong opposition from the Corporation who saw one of their
sources of income threatened. The initiator of the new market,
John Perkins, required a private Act of Parliament to establish the
place and this was opposed by strong City interests. In the event
the Corporation spent almost £7,000 on lobbying against Perkins
before the Act was passed and the market opened in 1836. (21) The
new market obtained support in the agricultural press and the
'Quarterly Journal of Agriculture' urged farmers sending livestock
to London to insist, on pain of dismissal, that dealers acting for
them use Islington and not Smithfield. (22) The market, however,
did not gain a lot of support from the meat trade which still clung

to Smithfield. In 1836 Perkins attempted to obtain another Act to close Smithfield with compensation for the Corporation but here they were successful in stopping him. As there was not enough trade to support Islington, Perkins then offered to sell his market to the City but they refused this offer and Islington was forced to close. (23) Although the market at Islington had much in its favour - at 22 acres it was some four times larger than Smithfield as well as being easily accessible - the combined opposition of the Corporation and traders was powerful enough to deny it success.

The losses that farmers suffered through the maltreatment of their stock when sent to Smithfield were never taken into account in the discussions over the market. This was because farmers were in a very weak position to exercise any sort of control over the way their animals were sold in London. In some of the larger provincial markets in 1850 farmers still brought fat animals in and personally conducted their sale. Although there was nothing to prevent the farmer selling in London from doing this, it was customary for him to consign his beasts to a salesman. The size of the market and the nature of the trade meant that the salesmen, who were always there, knew the butchers, dealers and contractors for meat, they were well acquainted with the nature of the trade and could tell if prices would rise or fall. Generally they were able to get the best bargain for the farmer. If a farmer conducted his own sale he would have to sacrifice at least a day, and probably more, if he lived any distance from the capital. Sometimes anxieties were expressed about the honesty of the salesmen. In fact there was a law which provided that 'no salesman, broker or factor employed in buying for others, shall buy for himself in London or within the bills of mortality, on penalty of double the value of the cattle bought and sold'. (24) However, it was freely admitted that this law was sometimes evaded.

In the mid-nineteenth century there could have been as many as three intermediaries involved, either directly or indirectly, in the transaction whereby livestock passed from farmer into the hands of the London butchers. The cattle salesman was responsible for transporting the animals from the farm to London and disposing of them wholesale. Sometimes he did business with several farms to collect a worthwhile number. From him the animals could either pass directly into the hands of small retail butchers who slaughtered only for themselves, or else they were sold to carcase butchers who slaughtered and then disposed of the meat to the retail outlets. Sometimes these outlets would be butchers, some-times caterers like the London eating houses and hotels. Also involved were a small number of banking businesses, the Smithfield money-takers, who were responsible for remitting back to the farmers and graziers the money received by the salesmen from who-ever they sold the stock to.

The cattle salesmen conducting business at Smithfield were usually commission salesmen who charged a fixed rate for the animals they handled, irrespective of the prices realized. Around 1850 this commission was 4s. per head for cattle and 6d. to 8d. per head for sheep. (25) These men were responsible for collecting or arranging for the collection of the stock from the farms. They also employed drovers on their own account to transport the animals to Smithfield.

Smithfield was not the only market in the London area for selling fatstock. Some of the commission salesmen also did a business at the markets around London like Romford in Essex and Southall in Middlesex.

The money-takers, centred in and around Smithfield, were more settled in their business location than the commission salesmen, thought even here individuals did a branch business at the outlying markets. (26) Within Smithfield there were seven firms that provided services as money-takers. They operated in the following way. Sales of livestock were effected in the market. Purchases were made by butchers (whether retail or carcase) from the salesmen. However, the butchers did not pay the salesmen directly. The salesmen had accounts with the money-takers and the butchers paid their bills for the animals involved at the money-takers' offices. These in turn charged a commission based upon the numbers of live-stock involved - 6d. a head for beasts, 4d. for calves and between 1s. 4d. to 1s. 6d. per score for sheep, and in cases of small lots 1d. per head for sheep. They then transferred the money paid by the butchers to a bank chosen by the farmers, either in London or in the country, on information supplied to them by the commission salesmen. (27) The money-takers never dealt in or purchased live-stock on their own behalf; their interest in the business was simply as financial intermediaries. For their part in the transaction the cattle salesmen received their commission from the farmer. In all cases the amount of money in the commission was fixed in advance and did not depend on the prices for which the animals were sold.

The money-takers also carried on a banking business in addition to their market activities. On many occasions, though, the divisions between the separate branches of their businesses were probably indistinct. It was not common for them to give credit to the butchers, as the majority of London meat retailers had only small businesses. If accommodation was given it was for no more than a few days, and only after consulting a trust list of reliable customers. (28) Also, unlike the butchers, the money-takers were wealthy men on account of the size of their business and the money passing through their hands. One, in 1847, thought that a capital of £11,000 per annum would not be enough to cover the business his firm conducted; he estimated that between £30,000 and £40,000 passed through his hands in a week. Their business required a great deal of correspondence, in the region of 360 to 390 letters a week, with banks in other parts of the country as well as City banks in Lombard Street. (29) The main objection on the part of the money-takers against moving the Smithfield market to a suburban site was a reluctance to operate too far away from their traditional premises in Lombard Street. Although this objection was not a serious one, the bankers were wealthy and influential men to add their voice to that of the Corporation against any sort of change.

Not all the banks engaged in these operations conducted their businesses in exactly the same way, but there was at least a common core of practice, imposed partly by the exigencies and personnel of the trade. Nor were all firms equally important. Of the seven firms of money-takers, the four largest ones did three-quarters of that group's total business. (30) In theory it was possible for the farmer or grazier who felt he could get a better

deal by acting on his own behalf to by-pass the commission salesmen
and money-takers. If he wished to he could make his own arrangements to convey his stock to London and, although he would have to
employ an official drover within Smithfield, he could act as his
own salesman and make his own arrangements with his customers about
payment. However, the former system did have the merit of
convenience, especially if the farmer only sent twenty or so beasts
or a few score of sheep to market at a time. In this case it was
unlikely to pay him to have a day away from his regular business
merely to sell so few animals. Again many customers at Smithfield
were small retail butchers who only bought a single beast or
perhaps half a dozen sheep. If these dealt with a salesman and a
money-taker, the money from numerous small customers could be
remitted in one transaction and with consequently diminished risk
of loss. Also from the evidence given by witnesses to the Select
Committee appointed in 1847, it appeared that the majority of the
business in the market was handled by professional salesmen and
money-takers and that the independent farmer marketing on his own
behalf was an exception.

In certain cases jobbers also operated in Smithfield. Unlike the
commission men they bought the animals outright before they appeared
in the market and so depended on the selling price for their profit.
Sometimes the jobbers would travel round the farms to make their
purchases and sometimes they would attend provincial markets where
they bought animals for London.

The position of the London retailer was comparatively weak
beside that of the various wholesalers in the meat trade. In other
parts of the country, especially beyond the large towns, the
retailer exercised many of those functions which, with the growth
in the size of the London market, had passed into the hands of
other parties. In the countryside the meat trade was far less
specialized. There the average retailer was required to have a
close knowledge of prices, be a shrewd judge of livestock and a
skilled butcher, as his profit margins depended on his success and
ability in all three operations. But in London many of the butchers
were men with too little capital to purchase live animals at
Smithfield or, after 1855, from Islington. These men obtained their
supplies from the carcase butchers, or wholesale dealers in dead
meat, in Newgate, Whitechapel and Leadenhall markets. In the summer
months the wholesalers would purchase livestock in Smithfield and
have it slaughtered for sale. In the cooler months there was a
greater supply of country-killed meat and they purchased this to
supply the smaller retailers of the metropolis. (31)

The result of this system, under which London's meat passed
through the hands of a number of intermediary traders on its way
from farmer to consumer, was effectively to insulate the City
Corporation from a large part of the criticism over the way it ran
its markets and to make it very difficult for external groups to
force proper reforms. The Corporation's reaction after the failure
of John Perkins's attempt to open a rival livestock market in the
1830s was to push through improvements to the existing market
between 1836 and 1838, at a cost of £29,665, to enlarge it and
thereby enlarging the nuisance. (32)

The agitation over the nuisance of the livestock market at

Smithfield in the early part of the nineteenth century was part of
a more general question concerning the reform of local government
within the metropolis. (33) The exclusion of London from the
provisions of the Municipal Corporations Act of 1835 meant that by
1850 London was without anybody responsible for co-ordinating
public services within the whole metropolitan area. Within the
area of the City of London the Corporation of the City of London
had jurisdiction but this body was sadly in need of radical reform
itself. As a result the government of the metropolis was divided
between the City Corporation and the livery companies of the City,
seven boards of commissioners for sewers, nearly a hundred for
paving, lighting and cleansing boards, about 172 vestries, Poor
Law guardians (since 1834), and a host of bodies dealing with the
police and law courts. (34) Jurisdiction over the city food
markets was largely a matter for the Corporation of the City of
London, with whom control of these markets became a struggle for
private rights, not for municipal duties.

The struggle that took place over the removal of the Smithfield
livestock market from the centre of London was symptomatic of the
difficulty of obtaining reforms when opposed by powerful and often
unscrupulous vested interests in the City of London. Attempts were
made to get the market moved to somewhere more spacious and
convenient from 1802 onwards without any measure of success.

To prevent the removal of the market the opponents of reform
entered into a substantial publicity campaign to demonstrate the
advantages of keeping it on its present site. No one, however, was
prepared to argue that if the market remained in the centre of
London it was not in need of serious reconstruction, so the
controversy over the market was conducted by two sides. There were
those wanting it moved from the centre to a less congested site,
preferably near to a railway station so that the animals would be
transferred from the trucks to the market pens with the minimum of
trouble. And opposing this point of view were the proponents of
the school of thought that had triumphed in 1838 and who still
wanted to drive horned cattle along Oxford Street in 1850 and to
retain the livestock market on its existing site but further improve
the accommodation there. (35)

Much of this controversy was conducted before, and for the
benefit of, the Parliamentary Select Committee and Royal Commissioners set up by the government to examine the Private Bills put
forward by various interests concerning Smithfield. During the
deliberations of these bodies it emerged that the problems London
faced with regard to livestock were common to all expanding cities.
Witnesses appeared before the 1850 Select Committee to report on
the experiences of a number of important provincial centres.
Wolverhampton, Shrewsbury, Bristol and Liverpool had all to re-site
their livestock markets in less congested areas in the years before
the middle of the nineteenth century. (36) Birmingham, too, had
faced a similar situation but that town had re-sited its Smithfield
some thirty-five years previously. In some of these cases the
original decision to move the markets into the quieter suburbs did
not remain a long-standing one because the pattern of urban growth
meant these areas rapidly became thickly populated. However, the
problems of congestion and nuisance in moving animals to and from

these places was considerably alleviated by the decision to site the new markets near to the railway stations. Also in some of these towns the old livestock markets had been street ones and the problems of congestion had been considerably eased by the decision to have the markets enclosed.

The opponents of the proposal to move the London Smithfield attempted to counter this evidence by producing witnesses who gave unfavourable reports on the effects of moving the livestock markets from the centres of other towns. At the same time the Corporation undertook lavish expenditure, prompted by interested parties, on propaganda to prevent the removal of the market. It was alleged that much of this money was spent improperly by the Corporation from various sources of income and that the precise nature and items of the expenditure were never publicly disclosed. It seems highly likely that this allegation was true. The Corporation had access to a great deal of money from wills and trusts for which it was under no obligation to publish any sort of accounts. According to J.T. Norris, a builder in Aldersgate who had long agitated for a change of site for the livestock market, (37)

> money was spent on the purchase of pamphlets written by doctors and men of that sort who had leisure and wanted work setting forth how healthy and beneficial the presence of cattle in the centre of the metropolis was. Those books were sent out gratuitously. There was a model made, and it was lectured on, and nothing was left undone that could be done.

In the end success was finally achieved by the other side when an Act of 1851 established the market on a more suitable site. (38) However, the removal of the market from Smithfield was so strongly resisted by the Corporation that it was only done as the result of a Bill put forward by the government and opposed by most of the City interests. The new cattle market, covering 15 acres of a 75 acre site and leaving ample room for expansion, was established in Copenhagen Fields between Islington and Camden Town near to Perkins's market site. The new market was called the Metropolitan Cattle Market Islington and was in every way superior to its predecessor: it was opened by the Prince Consort on 13 June 1855.

The opening of this market considerably eased the problems of sending livestock into London for sale. The Metropolitan Cattle Market was near to the railways, indeed it was connected with the Camden station, owned by the London and North Western Railway, so that it was possible to drive animals straight from the cattle trucks into the market. This was a great improvement over the site of Smithfield which was some distance from the nearest unloading point for the railways. The removal of the inconveniences attached to sending cattle to London prior to 1855 helped to maintain the numbers sent at the same level after that date.

3   THE DEAD MEAT TRADE WITH LONDON

The prophecies and hopes for the expansion of the dead meat trade with London were not realized in the decade after 1854. There is good evidence that the trade in country-killed meat to London, especially meat sent by rail and sea, grew at a slower rate between

1854 and as late as 1870 than it had prior to the first date. The
reasons for this slow growth were not technical factors such as the
lack of cold storage facilities. This can not be important as an
explanation as there was no cold storage in the initial period of
the dead meat trade. The slow growth can be explained by a number
of other reasons. Among these are factors in the regional economies
of certain livestock producing areas that limited the extent of the
dead meat trade, and also the relative costs of transporting live
animals and dead meat by rail. In addition the growth of the trade
was inhibited by inadequacies in the distribution system after the
meat reached London and the fact that the condition of the London
livestock market was greatly improved after 1854, but the dead
meat markets were neglected for over a decade longer.

There is no annual series of figures for the amounts of meat
carried into London by the railway and steamship companies. In 1853
it was put at 37,187 tons by Wynter. (39) In an attempt to estimate
the supply of dead meat railed to London in the mid-1860s G.R. Hawke
recently arrived at a figure of 50,000 tons per annum. (40) A
further estimate for the year 1859 is made here using sources not
employed in either of the preceding ones.

In 1859 Robert Herbert, who wrote reports on the meat supplies
of London between 1858 and 1869 for the Royal Agricultural Society,
reported that during the year ending June 1859 the quantities of
country-killed meat shown in Table 3.1 were received at Newgate and
Leadenhall markets. (41) Herbert also provided a range of dead

TABLE 3.1 Country-killed meat received at Newgate and Leadenhall
markets

	Beef	Mutton	Lamb	Veal	Pork
No. of carcases	22,000	98,700	34,500	3,250	227,200

weights for the different breeds of sheep and cattle on offer at
the Metropolitan Cattle Market. No contemporary estimates of
calves, lambs or pigs exist so Herbert's sheep and cattle weights
have been supplemented by the earliest estimates of other writers
in Table 3.2. If these figures are used to convert the preceding

TABLE 3.2 Dead weight per head in lb

	Cattle(a)	Sheep(a)	Calves(b)	Lambs(b)	Pigs(b)
Heaviest	800	100	112	42	149
Average	730	86	101	33	129
Lightest	664	56	90	24	90

(a) 'Journal of the Royal Agricultural Society of England', 1859,
    vol.XX, pp.475-6.
(b) R.H. Rew, Memorandum on some Estimates made by various Author-
    ities on the Production of Meat and Milk, 'Journal of the Royal
    Statistical Society', vol.LXV, 1902, p.675.

numbers of livestock into meat the estimates shown in Table 3.3 are
obtained. It will be seen that even if the heaviest estimates are

TABLE 3.3 Estimates of domestic dead meat sent by rail and sea
to Newgate and Leadenhall markets in 1859

			Tons			
	Beef	Mutton	Veal	Lamb	Pork	Total
Heaviest	7,857	4,406	162	647	15,113	28,185
Average	7,170	3,789	147	508	13,084	24,698
Lightest	6,521	2,468	131	370	9,129	18,619

taken the maximum amount is still under 30,000 tons in 1859. It is
interesting to see that the most important single type of meat was
pork. Herbert numbered among his 227,000 carcases some 90,000
from the west of England, chiefly imported from Ireland alive then
slaughtered to continue their journey to London as carcases. (42)
Given the tendency to send prime cuts of meat to London, from the
heaviest part of the animal, this may be a good reason for using
the heaviest dead weight estimates as conversion factors. Given the
approximate nature of all these estimates, they still appear to fall
within roughly similar margins of error, even if Herbert's does
appear a little low. (43)

As London was not immediately adjacent to any livestock-producing
areas, this growth in number could only be supplied with meat and
livestock imported from outside the region. The only significant
exception to this in the 1850s was pork. In addition to the
imported supplies above, a considerable proportion of the pork
consumed in London was 'town made', or at least produced in its
immediate suburbs. This appears especially to have been the case
in those districts where a large number of Irish settled. In 1854
Shepherd's Bush was called 'the pigsty of the metropolis' and almost
every house there was said to have had a pigsty. Kensington was
another area where the Irish population incongruously maintained the
habits of another society and another economy. (44)

In 1887 P.G. Craigie calculated that 45,000 tons of meat were
required for a year's supply for a million persons twenty years
earlier. (45) If we take the various estimates of the total amounts
of dead meat sent to London at various dates between 1850 and 1867
and use Craigie's figures for the number of people they would have
supplied, we can estimate approximately the relative contribution
they are likely to have made towards feeding the metropolitan
population. According to these figures, shown in Table 3.4, the
dead meat sent to London in 1865 was feeding the same proportion of
the population as in 1850, that is approximately 36 per cent. The
figure of almost 50 per cent for 1867 must be regarded as abnormal
because the cattle plague restrictions on the movement of livestock
artificially inflated the dead-meat trade that year. If the amount
of dead meat sent to London did not increase dramatically after
1855 it is equally certain that the numbers of livestock showed no

TABLE 3.4 Dead meat consumed by population of London, 1850-67

Year	Dead meat to London (tons)	Persons supplied (millions)	Population of London (millions)	% of London's population fed by dead meat
1850 (a)	40,000	0.88	2.45 (e)	36
1859 (b)	30,000	0.66	2.76 (e)	24
1865 (c)	50,000	1.11	3.10 (e)	36
1867 (d)	70,000	1.55	3.19 (e)	49

(a) A. Wynter, The London Commissariat, 'Quarterly Review', vol. XCV, no.CXC, 1854.
(b) R. Herbert, The Supply of Meat to Large Towns, 'Journal of the Royal Agricultural Society of England', 2nd series, vol.II, 1866, and calculations based thereon.
(c) G.R. Hawke, 'Railways and Economic Growth in England and Wales, 1840-1870', 1970.
(d) Based on 'Return relating to the past and present supply of dead meat to this Country, and the Metropolis', P.P., 1867-8, LV, p.489.
(e) Interpolation of the census figures, P. Deane and W.A. Cole, 'Abstract British Historical Statistics', London, 1962, p.20.

sudden decline. The numbers of cattle sent to the London market were well maintained and even rising in the first half of the 1860s. Table 3.5 shows that there was a fall in the number of sheep exhibited but not to any great extent.

TABLE 3.5 Cattle and sheep exhibited at Smithfield, 1850-4, and at the Metropolitan Cattle Market, Islington, 1855-64

Year	Cattle	Sheep	Year	Cattle	Sheep
1850	281,282	1,658,330	1858	315,764	1,463,235
1851	294,909	1,660,850	1859	298,509	1,352,440
1852	314,804	1,630,480	1860	322,327	1,570,090
1853	328,645	1,630,550	1861	315,770	1,496,860
1854	313,636	1,616,560	1862	332,692	1,498,500
1855	300,286	1,552,920	1863	351,429	1,498,270
1856	293,709	1,442,250	1864	374,621	1,544,460
1857	302,549	1,391,960			

Source: 'Return relating to the past and present supply of live and dead meat to this Country, and the Metropolis', P.P., 1867-8, LV, pp.9-10.

In some measure the supplies of livestock at the Metropolitan Cattle Market were maintained by imports from the Continent. The precise extent of this trade is difficult to measure prior to 1864 in the absence of comparable statistics. (46) However, according to one source, the proportion of foreign cattle and sheep and lambs at Smithfield in 1850 was 20 and 8 per cent respectively. (47) In 1864, 42 per cent of the cattle and 23 per cent of the sheep and lambs at Islington were foreign animals. (48)

Leaving aside the growth of imports of foreign livestock between these dates, the general picture of the nature of the London meat supplies between 1850 and 1864 is one of remarkable stability. There was some increase in the total numbers involved but there was no great expansion of dead meat at the expense of livestock. At the end of 1865 the whole meat and cattle trade came under the scrutiny of the Royal Commission on the cattle plague. The feature of the trade that appears to stand out up to 1865 is that the railway traffic carrying live cattle had increased in recent years, whereas the amount of meat carried by rail had not done so. Two of the witnesses appearing before the Commission were William Cawkwell and James Allport, traffic managers of the London and North Western and the Midland Railways respectively. Though neither of these men at this time submitted any figures for the amounts of dead meat carried by their companies, both agreed that they had not increased recently. (49)

4   PROVINCIAL TOWNS

In the 1850s and 1860s there were a number of towns which acted as marketing and distributing centres for the fatstock farmers of their region. Aberdeen fulfilled this function for the north east of Scotland, Edinburgh did the same for the south east and Glasgow the west of Scotland. In England, Leeds, bounded on three sides by agricultural districts, was an important livestock market for the whole of Yorkshire. Northampton had a fatstock market for the graziers of that district, and Norwich was the marketing centre for the fatstock of East Anglia. Lincoln and Derby served the Fens and part of the east Midlands respectively. Leicester had a huge fat-stock market, situated in the middle of England's richest grazing district. But after the cattle and sheep had been sold by the farmers in these places, the methods of distribution for their purchases adopted by the dealers and butchers in these places showed a considerable variety.

Broadly, two distinctions can be made. The traffic from some towns was sent chiefly in the form of dead meat, and in every case the destination of the product was London. Other towns, however, sent very little or even no dead meat. They specialized in the live cattle trade. From these towns the destinations of the cattle trucks were more varied. Some would go to London but others to large centres of consumption elsewhere, like Birmingham and Manchester. Towns that sent dead meat were Aberdeen, Edinburgh and Leeds. Towns that concentrated heavily on the live cattle trade were Leicester and Norwich. The towns of Derby and Northampton seem to have occupied an intermediate position within this spectrum. (50)

It must be emphasized that the ability of a town to send dead meat to London did not depend upon the local availability of fat-stock. The determining factor was the presence of local industries

able to utilize the by-products of the slaughterhouses - the offal
and bones, the hides or fleeces - which inevitably exist wherever
animals are killed for food. The town of Leeds was such a place.
In 1861 it had a population of over 200,000 and was a growing centre
of industry. It also had a well appointed market with six or seven
large slaughterhouses nearby capable of handling between 200 and
300 head of cattle a day, as well as sheep and pigs. (51) This
town also had an important leather industry to handle hides. In
1851 the leather industry in Leeds employed a total of 4,138 persons
and it was the second tanning town in the country. (52) Also the
West Riding woollen industry in the towns around Leeds was a ready
market for any fleeces. In addition Leeds itself had a substantial
working-class population within the town to consume the cheap edible
offal produced. Similarly, Edinburgh and Glasgow were large centres
of consumption with populations of 203,000 and 420,000 respectively
in 1861 to process and consume the by-products of the cities'
slaughtering establishments. Even Northampton, specializing in boot
and shoe manufacture, had an industry for which a by-product of the
slaughterhouse was an essential input.

In the grazing and feeding districts of eastern England the
industries to consume these by-products simply did not exist. (53)
During the first six months of the year heavy supplies of stall-fed
bullocks reached London from the Norfolk fattening districts. In
1866 it was estimated that 12,000 of these animals were sent to the
Metropolitan Cattle Market between January and June. More animals
came from Essex at the same time. These supplies were principally
despatched from Norwich and Colchester. In the autumn months the
grazier took over from the yard feeders and the cattle from the
pasture districts of the Fens were sent from Lincoln and
Peterborough.

These towns had neither the slaughterhouses nor the industries to
handle a large dead meat trade with London. They may have had
sufficiently large populations to consume the edible by-products but
this was only a part of the problem. Additional tanneries, gut-
scraperies, soap-works, and boiling-houses would need to have been
established to utilize the other remnants. Such industries would
have had to be established in an essentially non-industrial region.
East Anglia lost its woollen industry in the eighteenth century when
this manufacture passed to Yorkshire. Also eastern England lacked
the population and additional industries to support the establishment of more tanneries, etc. In 1861 Norwich had a population of
75,000 but there was no comparable town within a radius of 100
miles. Leeds, on the other hand, was surrounded by a number of
smaller industrial centres, all within easy reach.

The lack of markets near at hand was a factor which discouraged
farmers from doing their own slaughtering and sending meat to London
by rail. Farmers engaging in this practice found it impossible to
dispose of hide, rough fat, skins, etc., for local consumption on
any scale. Therefore they lost the value of this part of their
animals. In evidence before the Cattle Plague Commission a London
meat wholesaler reported that he had known several farmers who had
tried killing their own cattle and sending the meat to him by rail,
but had abandoned the practice and gone back to doing business with
cattle salesmen. (54)

The decisions of farmers and cattle dealers to market fatstock either as live animals or as dead meat were influenced by a comparison of the costs involved. These costs consisted of two major components: first, the rates charged by the railway companies for carrying livestock and dead meat; second, any differences between the prices of livestock and dead meat when they reached their final market.

The railway companies charged considerably higher rates, weight for weight, for the carriage of dead meat than they did for live-stock. They explained this differential in the following way. (55) Dead meat and live animals required quite different transport services. The live animals walked in and out of the cattle trucks unaided and once at their destination they were supervised by drovers employed by London traders and the railways had no further responsibilities or costs. But dead meat came in hampers, warehouse facilities were provided at the station, the meat was weighed and then loaded onto the trucks. When they arrived in London the trucks were immediately unloaded and the meat transferred to the railway company's vans and despatched to the market. In terms of both labour and capital employed the dead meat traffic was more costly than livestock. Also the railway companies had to take more trouble to see that the dead meat arrived in time for the day's markets, as delays and consequent loss of freshness cost consignors money and the railways claims for compensation.

However, the live cattle traffic was not universally popular with the railways. In the 1850s railway companies saw this as the least remunerative of all their forms of freight business. Low rates of carriage were charged in order to win and keep custom, as in the case of the competition with the steamships from Aberdeen. The animals needed a certain amount of attendance en route, though the consignors often complained the beasts were given little or none. Railways made the greatest profits by running loaded wagons wherever possible, but cattle trucks were unsuitable for any other merchandise and always returned empty from their destinations. This made the wagons expensive to run because there was no profit to be made from return cargoes and the engines pulled empty trains away from the London termini. In contrast, the dead meat wagons could always be filled with other general merchandise for return journeys. Finally, the cattle trucks had a relatively short amortization period because of the rotting caused by the urine and manure. (56) The railway companies probably regarded both the cattle traffic and dead meat traffic with disfavour. Each comprised items that were difficult to handle, both were labour-intensive and both came in relatively small quantities. Therefore the railways were unable to make large profits on either of these. Instead they preferred their freight traffic in the form of bulky and homogeneous goods that required little handling and sorting and which came in large enough quantities to make complete train loads. The prime example of this was the mineral traffic.

The argument in favour of a homogeneous product also applied to the person sending goods by rail. It was unprofitable for a provincial dealer to conduct a dead meat trade with London from a distant town and send both meat and offal by rail, as the price of the latter on arrival was not sufficiently high to pay carriage

costs and salesmen's commission. There was, however, a ready
market for the by-products of livestock slaughtered in London, and
prices there were in most cases higher than in the provinces. The
only exception was fleeces which fetched equally high prices in the
provinces and at certain times of the year better prices. In this
case farmers had the animals shorn at home and sent to London as
live meat. In October 1866 the station-to-station rate for a fully
fattened bullock (weighing 7 cwt on average) from Aberdeen to London
was 25s. and for a ton of dead meat the rate was 65s., including
delivery. (57) On this basis the margin was slightly in favour of
the dead meat trade. But the offal, which accounted for over 30
per cent of the weight of a live animal, cost the same to transport
as the most expensive cuts and only fetched 45s. in Aberdeen in
1871. Other rates quoted about the same time do not show even a
slight margin in favour of dead meat. Robert Herbert estimated it
would cost nearly 80s. to send an 800 lb bullock 200 miles by rail
or sea as dead meat, (58) and that a bullock's offal was worth 50s.
in London. In the case of the Aberdeen trade the problem of
despatching low cost parts of the animal by rail was overcome by not
only disposing of the offal within the city but also by keeping the
cheaper parts of meat to be consumed there. The consignor was
entirely free to choose what parts of the animals he would send: he
did not always send complete sides of beef. (59) As profits on the
most expensive cuts were highest they paid the cost of carriage
with the least difficulty.

These factors helped to restrain the level of the dead meat trade
to London. In their nature they were external factors and did not
depend on the state and conditions of the meat trade in London.
But internal factors within London, of an institutional nature, also
helped to limit the growth of this trade in the late 1850s and early
1860s.

While the removal of Smithfield solved the problem of the London
livestock trade the problem of the dead meat market remained
unsolved. There were proposals to establish a dead meat market on
the Smithfield site but this was opposed by interests within the
City Corporation and St Bartholomew's Hospital. The last group
argued that any building on the site would be detrimental to the
health of their patients. Ultimately these views prevailed with a
committee set up in 1855 to make proposals for utilizing the vacant
space at Smithfield and also to investigate ways of providing London
with an adequate dead meat market on a convenient site. The
committee agreed that Newgate was too small to provide an adequate
central meat market; it agreed with the meat traders that Islington
was unsuitable because it was too far from the centre of demand;
and it deferred to the wishes of St Bartholomew's by recommending
that the site of Smithfield be turned into a park! (60) In the
years immediately following not even this limited proposal was
adopted and the Smithfield site rapidly deteriorated into a derelict
wasteland. In 1860 the Corporation reluctantly obtained an Act of
Parliament to establish a dead-meat market at Smithfield, and
another Act in 1861 to close down the inadequate premises at
Newgate, which still remained the main meat market, once the new
meat market opened. But the reform of the dead-meat markets at
Newgate and Leadenhall were subject to further delay because the

nuisances at these places were largely hidden in a way that was impossible with Smithfield. Therefore it was not till 1868 that a new and adequate dead meat market for London was finally established. In the meantime this deficiency helped to restrict the growth of the dead meat trade to London.

CHAPTER 4
TRADE IN DISEASED MEAT, 1840-64

By 1850 concern was expressed about the conditions under which the
wholesale markets for meat were conducted. In this matter the
anxiety was felt on two fronts. The first was for the sale of
rotten meat which was positively unfit for human consumption. The
second was over the sale of diseased livestock for food purposes.
These two questions were closely related as the majority of meat in
1850 was wholesaled as livestock to retail butchers who slaughtered
the animals on their own premises. In 1850 the standard of veterinary knowledge among those reponsible for meat and livestock
markets was not very high, so there was a general ignorance of the
dangers of feeding the carcases of diseased animals to the population. The concern over these conditions was concentrated in the
large cities. They were the final destinations of large amounts of
diseased meat and livestock. There was also a great deal of concern
over the size and conditions of the urban livestock markets which
were very often too small, or otherwise inadequate, for the purpose
they had to serve.

1 THE GAMGEE FAMILY

In the mid-nineteenth century there was as much complacency over the
state of the meat trade as there was about many other aspects of
public health. The initial responsibility for changing prevailing
attitudes on this subject belonged to one family - the Gamgees.
They were an exceptionally talented family, and the male members all
followed veterinary, medical and scientific careers. The father,
Joseph Gamgee, was born in Essex and qualified as a veterinary
surgeon at the Royal Veterinary College, London, in 1824 but he
spent most of his working life in Italy. During that time he
married and had three sons. The eldest son, Joseph Sampson,
qualified as a veterinary surgeon like his father, but took up
human medicine and became a prominent surgeon in Birmingham. The
second son, John, was born in Florence in 1830 and after beginning
his training for human medicine, qualified as a veterinarian in
London in 1852. The third son, Arthur, also took medical qualifications and followed a career in biochemistry.

The leading part in the agitation over the meat and livestock trade was taken by John Gamgee. He was, like his brothers, an extremely astute man who argued from experience based on sound factual observations, at a time when many others relied on prejudice or at best flimsy experience. After qualifying he spent the next three years (1852-4) in Europe, where scientific education and the standards of veterinary practice were probably more advanced. He was certainly able to broaden his professional experience in this way; like his brothers he was an excellent linguist and able to converse fluently in several languages. After he returned to England he set about the work of reforming veterinary education in Britain. In 1857 he founded the New Edinburgh Veterinary College where he trained a new generation of students in the latest know-ledge on animal health. (1) It was during this time in Edinburgh that he also conducted his campaign against the unhealthy practices common in the meat trade.

As a student in London, John Gamgee had first visited the London dairies where cows were kept to supply milk to the metropolis. In these places he first witnessed the disgusting practices incidental to the sale and consumption of diseased cows. It was from these premises that he saw how the most filthy products of cattle disease were hashed up with other meat, equally unsightly and unpalatable, to provide the raw material for sausage making. When he took his investigations further he discovered that it was not only the health of the poor that was menaced by diseased meat. He saw carcases of sick animals cleaned, and the signs of disease cut away, and then sold to butchers who could not kill enough cattle themselves each week for their own trade. In this way steaks and joints of meat that were at best decidedly unwholesome, and even dangerous to eat, found their way to the tables of the middle and upper classes in London. (2) Also, he found that the sale of meat from diseased animals pervaded the whole of the meat business right from the farmer up to the retail butcher.

In his exposure of this trade and his attempts to reform it John Gamgee was joined by his elder brother, the physician, Joseph Sampson. The Gamgees were specially able to comment on these abuses. Joseph Sampson, like John, had also spent some time in Europe as a young man. He had been Principal Medical Officer of the British-Italian Legion during the Crimean War and on his return to England Assistant Surgeon to the Royal Free Hospital. In 1857 he was President of the Medical Society of University College. With their combined knowledge of animal and human pathology this pair were in a powerful position to identify disease among meat and animals and to advise on the effects of the unhindered sale of such refuse to the public.

The brothers opened their campaign in 1857 with a series of very forceful letters to the press. The veterinarian, John Gamgee, wrote to the most important Scottish newspapers exposing this menace in various Scottish cities. These letters appeared in the 'Glasgow Herald', the 'Aberdeen Herald' and the 'Scotsman'. They were also collected together and published in the form of an open letter to the Lord Provost of Edinburgh detailing the extent and the dangers of the practice of selling this meat in the capital. (3) At the same time Joseph Sampson published his open letters to the Home

Secretary, Sir George Grey, revealing the conditions in the London meat and cattle markets. (4) In addition John Gamgee published his own monthly journal, the 'Edinburgh Veterinary Review', between July 1858 and November 1865. This journal, besides containing a lot of technical publications on veterinary subjects, also included articles and addresses which reveal a detailed picture of livestock farming and the state of the meat trade, as well as stressing the urgency of reform. (5)

John Gamgee's general argument was as follows. A lot of the animal disease present in Britain after 1850 (though not all) could be explained by the free importation of livestock from Europe. Once this disease was introduced into the country it was allowed to spread virtually uncontrolled via livestock fairs and markets - in fact the whole distribution system for livestock ensured that imported disease was communicated to most places in the British Isles. By 1850, disease was so prevalent that infected animals were sold as a matter of course for human food: if they were not then there would have been a measurable shortage of meat.

2   MEAT AND PUBLIC HEALTH

The Gamgees' work on animal disease was carried on in the comparative ignorance of the 1850s and 1860s. But given the state of knowledge at the time they were among the most enlightened of observers. They also made limited claims as to the extent of their knowledge and urged the need to learn more about all diseases. The brothers were certainly aware of the deficient state of medical knowledge on the transference of disease from animals to man. Joseph Sampson wrote in 1857: 'public health, as a science, calls for more extended enquiry into the laws governing the health and diseases of man as affected by the health and diseases of animals'. (6) In the 1850s the sources of all disease were still a matter of debate, but three theories competed for acceptance. First, there was the germ theory; second, the theory that disease was subject to spontaneous generation, and finally there was the view that they originated in miasmatic hazes arising from decaying matter. Although later scientific discoveries were to confirm the first and disprove the two latter versions, the evidence available in 1850 was not overwhelming on this subject. The idea that epidemic diseases were transmitted by contagion and caused by micro-organisms was not exactly new in the middle of the nineteenth century. It had been put forward in the sixteenth and defended at various times in the seventeenth and eighteenth centuries. But it had fallen to a low ebb in popularity by 1840. Epidemiological experience with yellow fever, typhus and cholera where quarantine had proved supremely ineffective supported the claims of the anticontagionists.

The scientific observation of bacteria goes back to the seventeenth century and they were studied in the eighteenth and nineteenth centuries. However their pathogenic potentialities were not suspected, still less proved, before the middle of the nineteenth century. Much of the early work in what was later to become known as bacteriology (7) was carried out in Europe. As early as 1835 the Italian, Bassi, had shown that silkworm diseases were caused by

minute fungi and were contagious. However, observations of this
sort were primarily practical before 1850 and they only developed
into a cohesive body of scientific knowledge after the 1860s.
Among the early observations the animal disease of anthrax - which
is transmissible to man - had been studied and the presence of the
anthrax bacillus in blood of animals dying from the disease had
been seen in 1849 by Pollender and Caisimir Davine and by Pierre
Rayer in 1850. But the pathogenic nature of this bacillus was not
finally demonstrated and understood until Robert Koch made public
the results of his researches in 1876. Also it was not until 1877
that Louis Pasteur turned from twenty years of research on the
processes of fermentation and disease in silkworms to the study of
diseases in the higher animals. (8)

However the work against disease, especially in the large cities,
did not depend on accurate knowledge of their specific causes and
aetiology for its prosecution. The sanitary movement was well
under way before the great discoveries of bacteriology. The slums
of large cities with their chronic over-crowding, bad water, lack
of sewerage, adulterated food, represented reservoirs of infectious
diseases and epidemics which menaced not only the poor but all
sections of society. By the mid-nineteenth century the death rates
in places like Manchester, Liverpool and Birmingham had reached
such alarming levels that the possibilities of reform became a
concern of Parliament. The driving spirit of the English sanitary
movement was the lawyer, Edwin Chadwick, and his particular vehicle
for reform was the General Board of Health, established in 1848.
In fact this body was wrong in its assessment of the cause of
disease. The General Board of Health operated on the erroneous
'filth' theory of disease and believed that the invisible miasmatic
hazes arising from the heaps of decaying matter which were found in
abundance in all great cities, rather than contagion or micro-
organisms, were the cause of epidemics. For this reason the General
Board of Health conducted its vigorous campaign against filth and
stench. While this was never a complete approach to the problem,
it went far towards eliminating many causes of disease and disease
carriers like rats and lice. (9)

The interest in the conditions surrounding the sale and processing of meat was part of the more general anxiety about urban public
health. The facts are well known. The Registrar General's
Quarterly Returns gave the statistics of disease and mortality.
These statistics were the work of Dr William Farr who started to
work in the Registrar General's office in 1839, and they were given
more urgency by his famous letters on mortality which accompanied
the rather dry figures. Abstracts from the returns, as well as
passages from Farr's letters, were reprinted regularly in such
journals as the 'Journal of the Statistical Society' and the
'Journal of the Royal Agricultural Society' in the 1840s and 1850s.
The high death rates of the large towns, in comparison with rural
areas and the country at large were apparent to informed observers.
In 1845 the mortality rate in Manchester and its suburbs was
fifteen times as great as the mortality in Anglesea for the same
year. Again mortality was higher in the worst parts of the great
towns than in their most salubrious neighbourhoods. In 1847, in a
passage which exemplifies the miasmatic explanation of disease,

Farr observed: (10)

It is well known ... and it is proved satisfactorily by the facts ... that the excessive mortality from disease ... observed in towns is occasioned by animal or vegetable poisons ... depending on accumulated filth, crowding in dwellings and workshops, the closeness of courts, imperfect supplies of water, and the want of efficient sewers ....

The precise degree of influence which the various agencies have in causing the high mortality in towns, is not easily determined. Opinions differ as to what fraction of the suffering and death is to be set down to the want of water or of sewerage - crowded lodgings, narrow streets, ill-ventilated workshops - the destitution of skilful medical advice - the neglect of children - doses of opium and overflowings of quackery - slaughterhouses and rank churchyards.

These conclusions are general because the report of the Registrar General was based on the information in reports to his office from the local registrars. Particular instances of these conditions are easily found in the literature on any of the large industrial centres and on London. Unwholesome arrangements for marketing meat made up just one aspect of the unhealthy urban environment in the middle of the nineteenth century. They were certainly not the major cause of the high mortality rates. However, as the handling of meat and animal by-products could be classified as an offensive trade, the meat markets tended to be crowded into the poorer districts of towns and cities, thus worsening the situation for both. In the same year (1847) the two dead meat markets for London were described in a paper read before the Statistical Society of London as: 'places disgraceful to any large city at the present day'. The author went on to explain why this was so. He blamed it on the fact that they were great slaughtering places as well as great markets. But because these two markets, at Newgate and Leadenhall, were surrounded by other buildings and crammed into a space too small for the proper transaction of business, the slaughtering had to be carried out underground, in a still more cramped area beneath the markets. In these dark and filthy cellars sheep and cattle were herded and killed and flayed in the dark. The numbers of livestock that were crowded into these places made any attempts at maintaining cleanliness or hygiene impossible. (11) The influence of these terrible premises upon public health was deleterious in two ways. In the first place a large number of persons were forced to work and conduct their daily business in these filthy conditions. Second, as London grew, an increasing number of people were supplied with meat from these sinks of garbage.

3   REGIONAL EXTENT OF THE TRADE

The information on the state of the meat trade gathered by the Gamgees between 1857 and 1865 was a strong indictment of the whole system. They also demonstrated that this was not a purely local problem centred on the areas that supplied a few large towns, and in those towns themselves. The problem was, as they always main-

tained, a national one. Between them, their writings revealed an
alarming picture of the sources of urban meat supply and the methods
of distribution in the middle of the nineteenth century. They
contained incontrovertible evidence that animals found to be
suffering from disease were slaughtered for food and the diseased
parts removed before the rest of the beast was exposed for sale.
To ensure these practices went undetected some of the transport,
sale and slaughter of livestock seems to have been conducted with
a secrecy more appropriate for the distribution of contraband.

In all districts the same laxity seems to have applied. Aberdeen
was an important centre of meat distribution. Animals fattened in
the country were sent either by rail or steamer, or else as meat by
rail, to the London market. After visiting Aberdeen in the autumn
of 1856 John Gamgee spoke of 'witnessing as much heedlessness
regarding the sale of diseased meat as anywhere else in Great
Britain'. At that time the city possessed no special slaughterhouses within its limits for preparing carcases for the London
trade. Most of the slaughtering was done by butchers with premises
in the suburbs. But most of these men carried out the actual
killing of animals and dressing of carcases on their own farms,
which were some distance further from the city. Butchers took the
farms to give them somewhere to keep their purchases until the
market was ready to receive them, or they were ready for the market.
These places, however, also had a second important function. The
comparative privacy of the farms enabled the butchers to prepare the
carcases at their leisure, cut away and conceal any signs of
diseased meat, and send the finished articles into Aberdeen to be
consumed in the city, or despatched by rail to the metropolis.
Aberdeen was not entirely heedless in the matter of inspection and
attempts were made to enforce some regard for hygiene. The city did
have a meat inspector, but he was overworked with other duties. It
was the inadequate measures of control that were responsible for the
ease with which unwholesome meat brought into the city was able to
evade detection. Gamgee asserted that diseased meat was taken into
the city at night to escape the vigilance of the inspector.
According to him the police and night watchmen were either bribed to
turn a blind eye or else tricked. He even believed that meat was
carried in at night on carts with wooden axles for silent running.
(12)

Statements such as these cast a slur on local honour and, as was
to be expected, Gamgee's assertions elicited vehement denials from
the two individuals most intimately concerned, in the following
edition of the 'Herald'. John Watson, Superintendent of Police,
ridiculed the idea that carts with wooden axles were used in
Aberdeen at all, for any purpose. This form of transport was said
to have disappeared from use over forty years before. Also he
indignantly denied that the police were in any way to be found at
fault. The meat inspector, Mr D. Mellis, also agreed with Watson
that carts with wooden axles had been unknown in Aberdeen for at
least half a century. He also said that Gamgee's account of the
mechanics of meat distribution within the city was wrong:

Whether Aberdeen does or does not afford unusual facilities for
the traffic in unwholesome meat is not for me to say, but that
the butchers in the suburbs are the parties in whose stalls the

diseased meat is chiefly sold I most emphatically deny; and how
the diseased animals can be either driven or transported in carts
to the farms of those suburban butchers, and then removed to
town is to me a mystery, seeing those butchers have no farms.

However, Mellis did not deny that diseased meat was sometimes
sold in Aberdeen, as well as in other towns. But he did not believe
that Aberdeen was a special centre of such trade. As to the extent
of the practice he could make no estimate, though he did say that
its discovery was attended with so much difficulty that he believed
if Gamgee had to bring these cases to court he would find it hard
to prove them. (13)

Mellis may have been interpreting the term 'suburban' in a very
literal sense, but there is no doubt that it was common for the
leading Aberdeen butchers to have farms in the county. Reference
to the Aberdeen Post Office Directory for 1858-9 gives the number
of persons described as 'fleshers' as eighty. The majority of
these lived in the town, but there are nine names with home
addresses outside Aberdeen, some of them, like William Barron who
was listed as living at Stoneytown farm, residing in places that
sound decidedly rural. The largest family of fleshers in Aberdeen
at that time was the Williamsons, with six representatives,
including two sets of father and son, occupying stalls in the
Aberdeen market. This family had various homes outside Aberdeen
city. Three resided at a place called Wester Kinmundy, Skene,
which is 7 miles from the city, another one at Cairnfield, Old
Machar, 3 miles away, and the remaining two lived just beyond the
city among the grazing properties of the rural suburbs. In addition
to the nine fleshers carrying on a trade in the town and living
outside, there were another three living just on or outside the city
boundaries.

It might be argued that the mere fact butchers had private
addresses beyond the city is not evidence that they had farms; these
places may just have been country residences with no agricultural
land attached. But the Aberdeenshire cattle breeder, William
McCombie, writing ten years later, put special emphasis on this
difference between butchers in Aberdeen and elsewhere: (14)

The butchers in other cities are generally only purveyors, and
never dispute the honours of the show-yard with the grazier or
breeder. They buy their weekly supply at the weekly markets;
but many of the chief Aberdeen butchers do not depend upon the
market for their supplies, but feed large lots of fine cattle and
sheep themselves to meet emergencies, upon which they can fall
back .... They are not only great purveyors themselves, but
they supply a good proportion of the Christmas prize animals to
the chief butchers of London, Birmingham, Liverpool, Newcastle,
York, Darlington, Edinburgh, Glasgow, etc. The names of Martin,
Stewart, Knowles, etc., are celebrated not only in Great Britain,
but in France .... For several years, Mr. Skinner, Woodside, has
sent ... animals to the Christmas market (in London). He is one
of the greatest senders of dead meat, and he also feeds a large
lot of bullocks.

According to McCombie's estimate there were 500 senders of dead
meat, butchers and jobbers in the city and county of Aberdeen.
Allowing for his enthusiasm and possible exaggeration, the city

directory reveals nothing like this number. This would support the thesis put forward by Gamgee that the distinction between farmer and butcher in Aberdeen and district was not a clear one. Possibly some butchers did not appear in the city directories (which were always notoriously incomplete publications) because they thought of themselves as more farmer than flesher.

Also McCombie records an occasion when he had a bullock showing signs of pleuro-pneumonia. It was in a byre with ten others that were showing no symptoms. Accordingly he immediately sent them live to London, with instructions to his salesman there to inspect the carcases after they were slaughtered and to report back to him. This was done and the salesman confirmed that all the beasts had more or less infected lungs. As McCombie made no secret of this, it is an indication that it was normal trade practice. As confirmation he records the case of another farmer in Morayshire who had a byre of cattle slaughtered under the same circumstances and with the same result! (15)

The practice of secretly carrying diseased meat into town, noted by Gamgee when he visited Aberdeen, was also prevalent in England. (16) It was such a common nuisance in Leeds that in 1858 the corporation appointed a meat inspector to put a stop to it and generally supervise butchers' shops and slaughterhouses to stamp out abuses of the trade. Although by 1863 this inspector thought he had been successful in stopping smuggling and reducing the consumption of diseased meat in Leeds, he was aware that the general traffic in diseased cattle and carcases was still a flourishing business around Leeds and other towns. There were in Yorkshire a large number of butchers who made this their principal business and employed men to travel about the countryside to purchase the carcases of diseased animals from farmers and dairymen, etc. If animals died of pleuro-pneumonia on farms outside the limits of the borough there was no way the Leeds inspector could prevent their carcases being dressed and sold for food; all he could do was to prevent them coming into town for sale. In these cases the meat was bought by a butcher and sold in another town where the civic authorities were less vigilant. (17) This was a common occurrence in the absence of any national system of inspection and frequently applied to the meat and livestock traffic in the nineteenth century. When one local authority set up a system of control to prevent trade abuses these malpractices were not stopped but merely went round the obstacle passing into other channels which offered no hindrance.

The inspector at Leeds admitted that as far as he was concerned. the system of inspection was not satisfactory. He had no veterinary or medical qualifications himself. His former occupation was that of butcher and although he was sufficiently experienced to tell if meat looked wholesome he had no further guidance in this matter than personal experience. He was also critical of the general state of knowledge on the subject among the medical profession - a complaint which must have applied equally in most other places. He argued that had he only one professional man in the town able to speak with authority on the matter, Leeds could have been far more successful in stamping out the diseased meat trade. Also the Leeds authorities were forced to come to an arrangement that partially condoned but

still controlled the trade. For two years after the inspector was
appointed any animal that was diseased and brought into the borough
was seized as unfit for human food. Then, after representations
from the trade and discussions between the Town Council and leading
butchers, it was decided to allow farmers and butchers and any
owners of stock to bring to the slaughterhouses in the borough any
animal known or suspected of being diseased. Any person who did
this had to give notice to the meat inspector who would then examine
the animal (after death) and decide if it was fit for food. (18)
But the inspector only had his own judgment and experience as a
butcher, to rely on when he came to any decision. It was a motto
among butchers, 'remove the spleen and the carcase appears sound'.
As the inspector would only condemn on appearance he had no
evidence on which to act in those cases where carcases had been
skilfully dressed to deceive, however strongly he may have suspected.

Edinburgh, like all major cities, received its supplies of
diseased meat from two major sources: the city dairies, and farms
which were all distances from the city. Those cows from the
dairies that died in Edinburgh were taken outside the city boundaries to a farm at a place called Corstorphine where they were
cleaned up, and diseased parts removed, etc., and then brought back
into Edinburgh for sale as human food. In this way the carcases
were prepared for the butcher free from detection by the inspectors
in Edinburgh who had no jurisdiction outside the city. Eventually
the matter was brought to their notice, and though they could not
prevent the business conducted at Corstorphine they did prevent
this meat entering the city. Diseased beef was not the only product
emanating from this farm. The owner also kept a herd of pigs which
were fed on the diseased offal and the parts of the cows too far
gone for sale as meat. In this way some disease and certainly some
parasites were re-cycled into the pork from the farm. The prohibition on the entry of this meat for sale in Edinburgh did not put
the premises at Corstorphine out of business; instead they changed
their market and, as in other areas, the trade ran into other
channels that offered no hindrance.

The new market selected for the disposal of this meat was
Glasgow. The system of inspection there was more lax. In the
city's three slaughterhouses animals were killed without the possibility of a visit from an inspector because there were none appointed to oversee these places. There was an inspector of markets who
sometimes condemned carcases offered for sale that were obviously
rotten or otherwise unfit for consumption. This man, like many
others in his position, was not competent to judge beyond the most
obvious cases. According to Gamgee: 'The Inspector has no knowledge
of disease, except what he may have acquired as a Private in the
Dragoon Guards, or during his earlier lifetime when engaged on a
farm.' (19)

Both Edinburgh and Glasgow were, like all large towns, also
recipients of an unquantifiable amount of diseased meat sent to
them by train. Occasionally farmers and butchers in the country
were prosecuted for sending unwholesome flesh to town markets by
rail, but all agreed the majority of these offences went undetected.
The skilful preparation of the carcases of animals that could not

walk to the train to be transported live was the work of farmer-
butchers. In some cases the worst carcases were salted down to
avoid inspection but some were so bad that they rotted in the salt
tubs. This traffic was not confined to rail and Glasgow received
a lot of doubtful provisions by sea from Belfast, Londonderry and
other Irish or Scottish ports. (20)

4   THE EXTENT OF DISEASE

If one accepts that the trade in diseased meat, which was carried
on in the 1850s, was a normal and significant part of the general
meat trade, then two related questions need to be asked. In the
first place it is necessary to know what proportion of the nation's
farm animals were suffering from disease at any period of time.
And, second, what proportion of the meat passing into consumption
was likely to have originated from diseased animals.

The extent of animal diseases and the losses these gave to
farmers is, in the absence of any census of farm livestock before
1867 and any central record of animal disease before 1870, impossible to quantify with precision. The only evidence is estimates
made mostly for the 1860s by sanitary reformers - of whom John
Gamgee was the foremost example. He argued that prior to the 1840s
annual losses among farm stock from disease were between 1.5 and 2.5
per cent. In the 1860s he quoted losses between 5 and 11 per cent
per annum. (21)

In a study of the cattle in Kincardineshire, Scotland, carried
out in 1857, Gamgee found that out of a total of 26,449 cattle in
the county losses, from all causes, came to 2,017 head or 7.6 per
cent. (22) In 1863, according to figures supplied by the secretary
of the Hungerford Farmers' Club, the losses among sheep on twelve
farms ranged from 4.6 to 29.5 per cent and averaged 10.8 per cent
for the whole sample. (23) In Scotland in 1860, the statistics of
the Highland and Agricultural Society indicated that the average
losses among stock of all kinds amounted to 4.89 per cent. From his
own extensive experience Gamgee felt that an average mortality of
5 per cent was not too low a figure to apply to losses among all
kinds of farm stock in the three kingdoms. (24)

Mortality, of course, was not the same thing as the prevalence of
disease. It was often the custom to send animals that were already
affected to be slaughtered before they died on the farm. These
animals were not included among losses of farm stock as the farmer
received a price for them, though sometimes it was a reduced one.
One step which farmers took to protect themselves from loss was to
insure their animals with various cattle insurance societies
established after 1844. None of these institutions had a very long
existence because it was impossible to fix the level of premiums
they charged according to any sound actuarial principles. The
longest survivor up to 1863 was a proprietory organization called
The Agricultural Cattle Insurance Company which lasted for seventeen
years between 1845 and 1861. The companies mostly came to grief
during the periodic outbreaks of pleuro-pneumonia which ravaged
various districts from the 1840s. Although the prevalence of
disease in a district encouraged more farmers to insure their stock

and boosted the insurance societies' income it also meant that the
rate of fresh claims eventually exceeded any additional income.
The actions of the insurance societies also encouraged the spread of
disease.   These organizations made it a condition of insurance that
as soon as animals showed any symptoms the local inspector for the
company was called in to identify the animal and diagnose the
disease.   The societies usually guaranteed the owner three-quarters
of the market value of the animal on the day before any illness was
detected. (25)   On finding an animal diseased the inspector would
either have it treated, if he thought it would live, or if he
expected it to die would have the animal slaughtered on the farm and
the carcase sold, or send the beast to market for slaughter.   In
this way the insurance societies minimized their expenses because
the value of the animal at market, or the butcher's price for the
carcase, could be deducted from the amount of compensation paid to
the farmer. (26)   At the same time this practice encouraged the
distribution of diseased meat for food and contributed to the
number of infected animals in the livestock markets, thereby
promoting the spread of disease.

Livestock markets were the chief means of passing on disease.   As
every farmer with half-fat animals in the early stages of pleuro-
pneumonia sought an immediate sale for his beasts cattle marts were
nests of infection where disease was transmitted to healthy animals.
They also caught disease in the cattle trucks which were employed
indiscriminately by the railways for the transport of all animals,
whatever their condition.   In the 1860s it was estimated that 25 per
cent of the stock sold in London at the Metropolitan Cattle Market
was diseased in one way or another.   A similar state of affairs
existed in both the Edinburgh and Glasgow markets.   The position at
Glasgow was so bad that farmers in Lanarkshire fattening cattle
boycotted any livestock purchased there. (27)

These assertions would seem to indicate that something between 20
and 25 per cent of farm livestock were diseased.   In certain areas,
when epidemics of pleuro-pneumonia or foot-and-mouth were raging,
the numbers were greater.   Farmers living near to large towns who
purchased store animals in town markets or at cattle fairs were
particularly vulnerable.   In favoured districts where they were able
both to breed and to fatten their own animals the incidence of
disease was much less.

Within the town dairies the extent of cattle disease was greatest.   In these places pleuro-pneumonia was particularly prevalent
and mortality from all causes was put at 30 to 40 per cent. (28)
Tuberculosis in town dairies had first been noticed in the 1830s.
At that time many of these premises consisted of crowded and
insanitary sheds and presented every impediment to the health of
stock kept in them. (29)   In the 1850s the reforms carried out by
city Medical Officers of Health had many of these places cleaned up,
but the incidence of disease rose as pleuro-pneumonia became the
scourge of town dairies from the 1840s.   Prior to then it was common
for the town cow-keepers to have their dairy animals for two or
three years, keep them on pastures for a couple of months prior to
calving, and then return them to the town to continue with the milk
supply.   But the large number of deaths from pleuro-pneumonia made
this system unworkable.   Instead the dairymen purchased fresh

animals in the town markets, kept them for so long as they showed no
sign of disease, and sold them to the butcher as soon as they were
ill but before they began to show any great loss of condition.
Although the number of cows kept in the town dairies did not
increase after 1840, the higher replacement rates probably doubled
or even tripled those annually purchased to provide milk in any
town. (30) In this way the increasing supplies of railway milk,
substantial even before 1860, (31) were accompanied by an increase
in the total of town-kept dairy animals. Also the demand for
animals in town dairies was satisfied only by importing animals from
the countryside which forced up the price of stock. From an average
of two to three years the life of a town cow dropped to four or five
months. This also meant fewer calves were available for future
breeding and was a contributory cause of the rising price of meat in
the 1850s and 1850s.

Any attempt to estimate the quantity of diseased meat sold by
butchers is, like the attempt to quantify the proportion of diseased
livestock, largely an exercise to discover the extent of conceal-
ment. Only a part of this meat ever passed through the urban wholesale markets. For instance, some military contractors would buy
diseased carcases from farmers at a discount and then obtain the
contract price for sound meat agreed by government officials. Also
much diseased offal and other rejectamenta was purchased by pie and
sausage makers where it was minced and mixed up with a further
quantity of meat that may have been quite sound, although the final
product was as unwholesome as if all the ingredients had been
tainted in the first place.

The figures presented by urban authorities suggest that a very
small proportion of meat passing into human consumption was condemned as being unfit for human consumption. In the five years from
1861 to 1865 Dr Henry Letherby, the Medical Officer of Health for
the City of London, condemned a total of 418 tons of meat in the
London wholesale markets which was diseased, putrid or otherwise
unfit for food. In comparison with the total amount of meat
consumed in London in 1859, which was around 160,000 tons, this
quantity was puny. But Letherby did not consider that the amount
his officials seized reflected adequately the extent of the trade.
In a letter to the Cattle Plague Commissioners in October 1865 he
said: (32)

> It does not represent the actual amount which passes into the
> shops of the lower class of butchers; for not only does a good
> deal of meat escape the notice of the inspectors but, in
> consequence of our vigilance in the city, and the almost total
> absence of inspection outside the boundary of the city, there is
> a regular trade in diseased meat immediately beyond the city. I
> regard this as a very serious evil; for it is not only the means
> whereby unwholesome meat reaches the poorer classes but it is a
> hardship, in a certain sense, to the butchers within the city,
> who justly complain that they are closely watched, and are at
> any moment liable to a legal prosecution for that which their
> neighbours can do with impunity.

Also for Leeds the number of animals submitted to the meat
inspector to decide whether they were fit for food is trifling in
comparison with the total livestock trade of the town. At an

average market which was held weekly there were 600 fat cattle and
between 3,000 and 4,000 sheep and lambs on display. In the years
1861-4 the inspector examined the numbers of stock of all kinds
shown in Table 4.1, including pigs and calves. (33) These were
animals whose owners suspected or knew they were diseased. The fact

TABLE 4.1 Stock examined in Leeds, 1861-4

	Total submitted for inspection	Rejected	Passed
1861	798	305	493
1862	1,055	382	673
1863	-	598	-
1864	1,414	547	867

that Leeds had an inspector meant the situation was not typical of
most towns and his existence deterred many owners from bringing
their diseased animals into the town. The cattle dealers living
outside the borough had no need to worry about the rigours of the
Leeds system of inspection which, as the inspector himself admitted,
only caused one in six cattle with pleuro-pneumonia to be condemned,
and in the case of other diseases one in three. Rather than risk
these financial losses the dealers preferred to send the meat by
rail to a market where better prices could be realized than in Leeds
and with less risk of detection, therefore tons of diseased meat
went by rail to London. (34)
     Some information about the size of the diseased meat trade in
Manchester in the 1850s was revealed in the evidence given before
the Select Committee on the Adulteration of Food, which sat in 1856.
R.J. Richardson, the officer of the Local Board of Health for the
Newton Heath district of the city, revealed that a similar state of
affairs existed there. Newton Heath had sixteen slaughterhouses
and, of these, three specialized in killing and preparing diseased
animals. However, this was an improvement as there had been seven
engaged in this business when Richardson was first appointed. As
it was, in 1856 the three premises handled twelve cows and twenty-
four to twenty-five calves a week while the respectable establishments killed ten to twenty cows. The three still openly and
avowedly carried on their business despite frequent visits from the
Board's inspectors, who were themselves practical butchers. These
men would condemn the meat from cows that were suffering from a
variety of pathological conditions. As Richardson explained to the
committee: 'Some are called ticked; some have the milk fever; some
have worn-ith-tail; some are graped; (35) others are broken-up old
cows'. The meat that was obtained from these beasts was referred
to in Manchester as 'slinked' beef. That which appeared unwholesome was transformed into sausages and polonies, etc., as these
were always effective disguises for this ingredient. But the
better looking firmer pieces of the carcases would go on sale in
the retail shops as joints of meat in the normal way. Prosecution
was a fairly regular affair but the fines were so low that they

offered no real deterrent. Nor was the publicity from the court
cases a sufficient protection for the public. In Manchester the
system of weekly credits granted to the poor by tradesmen tied
them to the same shop and forced them to return week after week
despite seizures of bad meat. (36) For these reasons then the
diseased meat trade was maintained at a high level which the system
of inspection was powerless to reduce.

The estimate made by Gamgee was that as much as 20 per cent of
the meat eaten in the United Kingdom in the 1850s and 1860s came
from animals that were considerably diseased. Under this heading he
included contagious diseases, the two most prevalent being foot-and-
mouth and pleuro-pneumonia; anthracic and anthracoid diseases; and
parasitic diseases, where the living animals was colonized by lower
animal forms. (37) Although in modern terms the understanding of
these diseases was primitive, and sometimes mistaken, it was known
that some of these conditions, certainly animals parasites and
anthrax, were communicable to man. In other cases it was recognized
that it was unpleasant to eat certain diseased meats.

5 OBSTACLES TO REFORM

The attempts made to abolish these abuses in the 1850s and 1860s
were very largely frustrated. There were two causes of failure.
In the first place there was a very strong opposition against any
proposals from farmers, cattle dealers, meat salesmen, dairymen and
butchers. The majority in the meat trade were convinced they would
inevitably face ruin if Parliament passed any effective measures to
prevent the spread of disease among cattle and other livestock or to
stop the sale of bad meat. In the second place the complacent
attitude of the government proved a serious obstacle to any hope of
reform. This was partly through want of knowledge as to the real
extent of disease in the countryside and the size of the trade in
these animals.

The very uneven enforcement of such controls as existed was a
great assistance to this trade. By the early 1860s most large towns
had some vestiges of supervision to prevent the worst of insanitary
practices regarding the distribution and sale of food. But the
uneven enforcement of controls left many loopholes whereby the
unscrupulous individual could, if not escape detection, at least
avoid any legal interference in his business. Most large towns in
England used the Nuisances Removal Act of 1855 to employ inspectors,
others had private Acts of Parliament which allowed the town council
to employ persons to report on all offensive trades and businesses
carried on within the borough. But not all places enforced these
measures, especially the smaller country towns and the rural districts. In these places the diseased meat butcher was largely
uncontrolled, though some larger towns like Wakefield in Yorkshire
did give information to the local authorities of neighbouring towns
from which diseased meat had originated. (38)

Even when a town decided to implement the Nuisances Removal Act
and to appoint an inspector for slaughterhouses and meat markets,
this was no guarantee that there would be any great improvement. In
the early years after the Act was passed there was a marked reluc-

tance to appoint qualified men to these positions. In part this
was because the local authorities were not disposed to spend a
great deal of the ratepayers' money on these posts. As a result
tailors, weavers, butchers, policemen, coachmen, butlers and men
of all trades were selected for duties which were regarded as of
minor importance, and calling for little judgment or specialist
knowledge for their performance. Very often these jobs were
regarded as sinecures for worn-out men who had failed in other and
not very exalted callings, who obtained them with a little
influence among vestrymen or the municipal authorities. Not
unnaturally, such appointees were unable to further the cause of
sanitary reform or suggest means to control the spread of contagious
diseases. They were unable to trace out, because they did not
understand, the parasitic diseases which were so important in
relation to meat inspection. Nor could they recognize the first
signs of insidious disorders, which should have been in themselves
sufficient to warrant the exclusion of stock from crowded fairs and
markets.

Sometimes when the municipal authorities followed a vigorous
policy of inspection and seizure the disgruntled meat traders went
to almost unbelievable lengths to defeat the intentions of the
municipality. A typical example occurred in the spring of 1863
at Worcester. The inspector for the city seized several head of
cattle which were exposed for sale in the city market while suffering from foot-and-mouth disease, and condemned the lot to be
destroyed. In this case the loss fell upon the farmers, but the
whole incident gave such offence to many dealers, graziers and
butchers who were in the habit of attending the market that they
endeavoured to establish a market of their own outside the boundaries of the city and hence beyond the jurisdiction of the in
inspector. Unfortunately the field chosen by the traders was
contiguous to the ground being prepared for that year's exhibition
by the Royal Agricultural Society. Not unnaturally, the Council of
the Society did not relish the prospect of prime specimens of the
nation's most valuable breeding herds being assembled nextdoor to
what amounted to a market specially for the sale of diseased
animals. (39)

Indifference to the state of the meat trade was an attitude of
both central and local government. It does not seem that the early
work of the Gamgees had very much effect against this indifference.
Indeed, both men were years in advance of their time when they
started their campaign in 1857. In general their allegations and
accounts of conditions under which meat was sold were greeted with
apathy or disbelief, not least by those local officials who were
charged with the supervision and inspection of the markets in the
towns they visited and criticized. It is symptomatic of the apathy
shown in these places with regard to John Gamgee's original allegations that the 'Aberdeen Herald' did not even bother to publish the
letter he sent them when it was first received. It only appeared
in their columns after the publication of his open letter to the
Lord Provost of Edinburgh, with a rather unconvincing explanation
from the editor that the letter 'accidentally did not reach us
previous to its publication in the pamphlet'. (40)

This attitude, however, was not the sole preserve of the Aberdeen

press. Shortly after John Gamgee's assertions had stirred up such
debate, some cases of individuals bringing diseased meat into
Aberdeen came to light. Perhaps the Aberdeen court was a little
more casual than other places in the way it dealt with these cases.
The Sheriff adopted the unusual practice of allowing the defendants
to appear before him in private in his own room in the court house,
with only the Sheriff's clerk and the Procurator Fiscal present.
Even the appearance of witnesses for the prosecution or defence
counsel for the accused was dispensed with at the hearing. No
doubt hoping to redeem its reputation after public interest had
been aroused over the sale of diseased meat, though by no thanks to
itself, the 'Herald' sent a reporter to the court on the day
appointed for the cases to be heard. When he arrived at the building the 'Herald's' man found it extremely difficult to discover in
which court room the cases were to appear. This was not surprising
when he discovered exactly where the cases were to be heard, and
after he had with some further difficulty obtained access to the
Sheriff's room. Secrecy such as this deprived the public of any
protection the press might have been able to give through revealing
the names of offenders, a fact which aroused caustic comment in
the columns of the 'Herald'. (41)

Eventually the publicity given to the allegations made by the
Gamgee family, together with the reports of court cases and the
comments of the medical press, succeeded in making government take
notice of conditions in the meat and livestock trade. In 1862 the
Privy Council agreed that an inquiry should be made and asked John
Gamgee to carry it out. In the 1850s the Contagious Diseases
Prevention Bill of 1848 had been extended a number of times, but
remained very largely a dead letter. Also, this measure was only
concerned to prevent imports of diseased animals. Gamgee's investigation was designed to examine all aspects of the question and
report on the influence both of importation and the home trade in
spreading diseases. He was also instructed to give in his report
any statements credibly made to him about the injurious effects
upon man from the consumption of the flesh or milk of diseased
animals. In order to collect the information he was authorized to
visit the principal markets and slaughter-places as well as any
districts where he believed disease was particularly rife. He was
also authorized to visit parts of Europe from where it was likely
that the livestock trade might result in imports of diseased
animals. (42)

It is not surprising that this investigation confirmed the
allegations that Gamgee himself had been making for a number of
years. He also made a number of recommendations to prevent the
importation of livestock disease from abroad such as proper
veterinary inspections at the ports and quarantine measures to
prevent imported livestock from coming into contact with domestic
animals. In addition he advocated a policy of veterinary inspection at all livestock markets throughout the country to stop
diseased animals being exposed for sale. In much of his work on
this subject Gamgee was in advance of his time and his advice was
not acted upon.

In 1863 Edward Holland brought forward a new and improved
version of the Contagious Diseases Prevention Act, no doubt

impressed by the experience of the Royal Agricultural Society when
preparing for its annual show at Worcester that spring. Holland,
however, was persuaded to withdraw his Bill by the promise that
Parliament would promote similar legislation the following session.
In 1864 two Bills, the Diseased Cattle Bill and the Cattle and Meat
Importation Bill, were put forward by Sir George Grey and Mr George
Bruce. If these measures had been passed they would undoubtedly
have imposed some control over the largely unrestricted trade in
diseased animals and meat. That they were not was the result of
the opposition that these measures encountered from graziers,
dealers, butchers and importers alike. (43) Any measure that
attempted to place restrictions on the importation of foreign
animals was easily represented as a conspiracy against free trade
and a disguised attempt to reimpose agricultural protection. Prior
to 1865 and the experience of cattle plague this was an insurmount-
able parliamentary handicap. But even if these measures had been
passed it is doubtful whether they could have been satisfactorily
enforced. In 1863 the Royal College of Veterinary Surgeons revealed that there were in the United Kingdom 1,018 qualified veterinarians. This number was grossly inadequate to care for the farm
stock, let alone attend to the markets and sea ports. It was
estimated that for every qualified man there were five or six
unqualified quacks. (44)

There was very little incentive for farmers to employ veterinarians in a situation where disease was so prevalent and where the
rapid disposal of infected stock was the most economical course to
adopt. Most veterinarians were to be found in big cities and
devoted most of their time to the care of horses, where the
financial rewards were much greater. Farmers did their best to
avoid infection of their herds and flocks, but once this failed
they preferred to keep the secret to themselves and not to
advertise it by calling in a veterinary man who could, anyway, do
nothing in the case of foot-and-mouth or pleuro-pneumonia. By the
1860s, with a rate of mortality three, four or even five times
higher than a generation earlier, there was little grumbling.
Farming and the cattle trade had adapted themselves to the new
conditions and everyone seemed to act on the adage that 'the least
said the soonest mended'. (45)

There is evidence that urban dairy-keepers, like farmers and
dealers, adjusted their business methods to take account of the
high mortality of stock and still show a profit on their operations.
A dairy cow gave its greatest quantity of milk in the two months
after calving, thereafter the quantity of milk diminished. Therefore a herd of cows within two months of calving represented a
greater income for their owner than a larger number of animals
which had calved between three and six months previously. According
to Gamgee, in the 1860s a cow in an Edinburgh dairy would yield a
profit of 5s. to 6s. a day within eight weeks of calving and only
3s. to 4s. thereafter, so on this basis a herd of fifty cows newly
calved was equivalent to over eighty cows which had calved between
three and six months previously. (46) In addition fifty cows
needed less fodder and less labour than eighty, therefore the
dairyman obtained this milk with lower overheads, and the reduction
in the quantity of purchased inputs and wages meant that unit costs

were also lowered. In this situation the urban cow-keeper learnt
that the largest profit was gained when the stock was not kept too
long. It was not unusual for them to buy newly calved animals,
keep them the eight weeks or so when they gave the most milk and
then return them to the town market when diseased, for sale as
butcher-meat, and purchase fresh animals as replacements. Part of
this transaction involved definite deception, as a butcher purchasing stock directly from a dairyman would have good reason to suspect
they were diseased and so he would offer a lower price than if he
bought them in the market where a higher price would be paid for
allegedly healthy stock. Under this system the profits of the
urban dairyman were maintained and even increased. In Edinburgh
the dairymen claimed that nobody had known how to make money out
of cows before the disease came among them. A further indication
of the extent of mortality (chiefly from pleuro-pneumonia) in the
town cow sheds was the fact that the insurance companies refused to
do business with them.

The trouble taken by farmers, dealers and dairymen in this trade
was also matched by the retailers. All of the work preparing
carcases of diseased animals was carried out in small private
slaughterhouses, scattered over the cities as well as outside, and
too numerous to superintend. In London Gamgee reported there were
places where meat was 'polished'. This consisted of killing a good
fat ox at the same time a number of lean and diseased animals were
killed. Boiling water was at hand and when the lean animals were
skinned their flesh was rubbed over with the fat from the healthy
ox, and hot cloths were used to keep the fat warm and distribute it
over the carcase giving it an artificial gloss. In this way the
meat was disguised so as not to appear totally deprived of fat. In
Edinburgh the same authority had seen the carcases of sickly lambs
dressed up in the same way with the fat from healthy sheep. (47)

The economic incentives to carry on the diseased meat trade were
powerful and probably increasing in the 1860s. Meat prices had
moved upwards from the early 1850s, which was a reflection of a
general shortage. In turn this shortage was partly the result of
losses caused by disease.

Also this part of the meat trade can be understood, though not
excused, as an attempt to avoid personal losses caused by circumstances beyond the power of the individual to reform. Farmers, cow
feeders, urban dairy owners, cattle dealers, meat salesmen and
retail butchers acting alone could do nothing about the general
prevalence of animals disease in the livestock population. When
disease was not widespread a farmer could probably afford to bury
the occasional diseased cow or a few sheep and allow the receipts
from the rest of his animals to cover these isolated misfortunes.
But when 20 or 30 per cent of herds and flocks were affected this
involved too great a proportion of a working farmer's capital for
him to sacrifice without showing a loss. Therefore the farmer
adapted his operations to cope with the changed conditions and
wherever possible disposed of diseased animals for the highest price
they would fetch, which meant selling them for human consumption.

If these animals were sold to a dealer or if they were
slaughtered by the farmer himself, the railways offered the ideal
method for their distribution. The railway companies had no

interest in whether the meat they carried was sound or not. Nor was there any proper system of inspection at the stations from which it was despatched or at the depots in the large towns where it was received. London was the favourite market for this trade and it was made attractive by its size as well as the inadequacy of any system of inspection. Also Glasgow and Edinburgh were convenient places to dispose of doubtful meat. Birmingham was another large town that suffered from this nuisance, though the railways were not the only means used to carry it there. In April 1863 the Town Clerk reported that in the borough diseased and unsound meat was discovered in slaughterhouses, markets, railway stations, and public house yards where country carriers brought their carts. It was also found in houses and premises where saveloys, faggots and sausages were made as well as in all types of shops where meat was offered for sale. Given the fact that Birmingham, with a population of 296,000 in 1861, had only one inspector, under the Nuisances Removal Act of 1855, engaged full time in looking for diseased meat, it is not surprising that so much escaped detection and that its presence was so widely distributed throughout the meat trade of the city. The solitary inspector was not very successful in uncovering much of this trade as 5 tons of meat was seized in 1861 and 4 tons in 1862. As usual, there were known to be places near the boundary of the borough where diseased parts of carcases were cut away to avoid detection. Also a lot of this meat was boiled and brought in secretly in cans and barrels at all hours of the day and night. (48)

It is unlikely that this trade existed much before the late 1840s. According to Youatt, in the 1830s, besides the sheep and cattle, etc, at Smithfield, the London food supply also included 'a great quantity of dead meat sent up from the country'. Youatt said that generally speaking this meat was wholesome and fairly and honestly slaughtered, although he acknowledged that it was said that the flesh of some animals which had not come by their death at the hands of man occasionally found its way into Newgate Market. (49) But he did not give the impression that the traffic in diseased meat was ever a regular part of the butcher's trade at that date. Also, where abuses did exist - as in the conditions at Smithfield, or the state of the London dairies and milk trade - Youatt took pains to point these out. (50) This evidence supports the statements of the Gamgees and others in the 1850s and 1860s that the meat trade was not geared to handle diseased produce as a matter of course prior to the 1840s.

CHAPTER 5

FOREIGN IMPORTS AND THE DOMESTIC SUPPLY, 1840-64

In the years immediately after 1850 two questions came to dominate public thinking and discussion over Britain's meat supply. The first, which was part of the concern over public health in the mid-nineteenth century, was the expression of anxiety over the sale of rotten and diseased meat in the markets and shops all over Britain, especially in urban centres. The extent of this abuse in 1850 was undoubtedly widespread, and although work was started to establish a qualified and competent public health inspectorate to combat this it is doubtful whether much was achieved prior to 1865. The other subject of interest was the question whether Britain's supplies of meat were in fact adequate to feed the population.

The concern over meat supplies was part of the general concern about the adequacy of Britain's food supplies. According to estimates made by the statistician, Mulhall, for the decade 1850-61, the first in which meat imports were brought into the United Kingdom in any quantity, the average production of beef, mutton and pork in England and Wales, Scotland and Ireland was 1,047,000 tons or 84 lb per head per annum; this was supplemented by an average import of live cattle furnishing 44,000 tons, making in all a yearly supply of 87 lb of meat per person. In the decade 1861-70 annual home production of meat had risen to 1,078,000 tons and imported meat to 131,000 tons. Together these supplied 90 lb per head of the population. (1) As it was, the anxiety over feeding the population was never realized because of the availability of imported food supplies. In the case of meat, imports were making an increased contribution to the total consumption of the United Kingdom by 1870. Over the two decades after 1850 domestically produced meat supplies rose by less than 3 per cent, whereas supplies of imported meat rose by 197 per cent. In the first decade imported meat accounted for 4 per cent of the total supply; by 1861-70 it accounted for 10 per cent. At this time imports consisted mainly of continental cattle with some quantities of sheep and pigs. At the same time it must be emphasized that imported meat supplies were a minor part of total consumption, and that the greater growth of this item took place after 1870.

1   IMPORTS OF MEAT

Livestock imports were supplemented before 1870 by imports of
relatively small quantities of dead meat, prepared in various ways
to withstand putrefaction. Potential overseas supplies of meat
already existed in 1850 but the problem of geographical distance
precluded the possibility of exporting this meat to Great Britain.
At this time both Australia and New Zealand had a large surplus of
livestock, with an animal population far in excess of humans. In
these two countries the surplus was most serious in the case of
sheep which were used chiefly as a source of wool; secondary
products were the tallow from the carcases and fertilizers from
their bones. A similar situation applied to South American cattle
which were valued only for their hides, fat and skeletons, (2) the
flesh being wasted or disposed of at nominal prices.
   Early methods of preserving meat for export in these countries
were mostly confined to canning experiments. Various canning
projects had been tried in Australia in the 1840s. In 1846 a
cannery was set up at Honeysuckle Point, near New Castle, New South
Wales. In 1847 tins were sent to London where they found a ready
sale and the Admiralty took supplies. However, the 1851 gold
discoveries raised the price of meat at Honeysuckle Point to such
an extent that the business became unprofitable and the plant was
closed in the early 1850s. Not much was heard about Australian
meat for the next dozen years or so, until in 1865 Robert Tooth
began making meat extract at Yengaree, New South Wales, and Tooth's
Extract of Meat Company (London Bridge) imported its first lots in
1866. (3)
   Canned meat was also imported from Europe before 1865. In 1839
a Hungarian Jew called Goldner, residing in Britain, bought the
rights to an improved method of sealing cooked meat into airtight
canisters. He set up in business as a meat contractor for the
British Navy and supplied them with this product from premises in
this country, processing English animals. After a while, finding
the price of British beef animals too dear, he looked for a cheaper
source of raw materials. Being an eastern European by birth he
knew that the plains of Moldavia were a region containing vast herds
of cattle with inadequate local markets to absorb the meat produced.
There he found meat cost nothing as the hides, hoofs and horns sent
to Constantinople for export paid the entire price of the animals.
Wishing to take advantage of the lower British import duty after
1842 he established a factory at Galatz on the Danube from which
the British Navy was supplied with something over 2,700,000 lb of
meat. Most of Goldner's products were quite satisfactory as to
quality. However in 1846 some of the canisters were found to
contain rotten meat and others revealed offal and other objection-
able matter, probably deliberately placed in them by disgruntled
workers at the factory. In the scandal that followed this discovery
there was a revulsion on the part of the British public against
preserved meats and the Navy Commissioners cancelled the contract.
However, it was pointed out that the product itself, if properly
processed and the process strictly supervised, was quite satisfactory and wholesome. (4)
   Prior to 1842 import duties kept the trade in meat to a minuscule

level. After the freeing of this trade most of Britain's imports
came from the USA and consisted very largely of salted meats,
tallow, lard and cured products. As late as 1865 the packing
industry in Chicago was dependent upon the London and Liverpool
markets to absorb its surplus hog products. (5) From the available
information it seems that US pigmeat was exported to the United
Kingdom in two ways prior to 1865. In the first the meat was sent
as barrelled pork in a brine pickle. The other way of sending the
meat was in a dry state. In this case the meat was taken from the
Chicago packinghouse, rubbed in salt, loaded onto the railcars and
sent to the coast. At the ports the meat was then packed away in
the hold of a ship as it was between layers of salt. By the time it
reached Liverpool or London the meat was fully cured and ready for
consumption. If it was not sent loose then the meat was put in
rough, inexpensive wooden boxes between layers of dry salt. (6)
Sometimes this dry meat was referred to as 'bacon', but it is not
known whether it was smoked at any stage.

Apparently the dry meat, in particular, faced certain marketing
and distribution problems once it arrived in the United Kingdom.
These stemmed from the fact that the product was not entirely
suited to local tastes. US pigs were fed largely on a diet of
maize, also known as Indian corn. This had the effect of producing
a carcase which had a large amount of fat and a great deal of soft,
pink, fatty flesh. However, in England the preference among bacon
and pork eaters was for as little fat as possible. So, by virtue
of this excessive fat, US pigmeat fetched lower prices in English
markets than domestically produced meat. The US meat was also very
salty. This was a necessity forced upon the exporters in order to
preserve it on the voyage across the Atlantic. But the British
public, in general, preferred its bacon to be mild cured. So US
bacon laboured under the double disadvantage in the British markets
of being both fat and salty. As a result US bacon in the 1860s
sold in the English market for 6d. or 7d. a lb retail whereas
English and Irish bacon sold for 2d. or 3d. a lb more. Naturally,
the US meat found its largest sale among the poorer classes of
consumer.

Increased quantities of pigmeat were exported from Cincinnati and
Chicago during the early 1860s when the Civil War closed the
Southern markets to the Northern meat packing businesses. A large
amount of this increased export found its way to the ports of
Liverpool and London. During 1861-2 a large proportion of the hogs
packed in Chicago were cut for the London and Liverpool markets.
In Britain and Europe they helped satisfy the growing demand for
cheap food. The cheapness of pork products as compared with other
meats and the ease and economy with which it could be handled, cured
and transported to Britain brought the meat steadily into demand,
despite the fact that it was not as palatable as could be desired.
To some extent the wholesale provision merchants of Liverpool were
able to increase its consumption by exploiting regional variations
in taste. They found that the Irish consumer, living on a lower
income than his English counterpart, did not mind the saltiness and
greasiness of the US product if he paid 2d. or so per lb less for
it. But Ireland was also a large bacon producer and a net
exporter to the rest of the United Kingdom. So in the 1860s the

dictates of economic rationality were responsible for the curious situation whereby Liverpool wholesalers imported Irish bacon for distribution in the city and the district beyond and re-exported US bacon in the reverse direction, to Ireland. The Irish preferred to send their produce to England where it fetched the highest prices and to consume lower priced US bacon at home. (7)

Both consumer preference and price considerations made the export of US hog products more attractive than beef exports in the 1850s and 1860s. The pickled pork that was exported was sent in barrels of 200 lb of meat. There was also some differentiation of product. The different grades of cured pork came from different sizes and conditions of animal. The first quality, called 'clear' pork, was made from the largest animals and the sides of meat had the ribs (inferior parts) removed. The next quality, called 'mess' pork, contained entire sides and rumps in the barrel. The lowest grade was called 'prime' and came from the lightest pigs and contained more inferior parts of the flesh. (8) As far as taste was concerned it was said that the pickled pork was not so salty as US bacon.

In the case of beef exports apparently both costs and taste counted against them at this time though they were made and some received in Britain. As far as expense was concerned, it was not possible to export beef in the dry state as it was with pigmeat, so the only available product was the more expensive barrelled pickled beef. But the British public absolutely refused to consume the US pickled beef on account of its extreme saltiness. The beef that was received in Britain did not go to the civilian consumer, who refused it even when it retailed for as little as 3d. per lb. Instead, it was all purchased by the government for the Army or as Naval stores. Similarly, salted meat which had been received from Australia and South America before 1865 proved to be a considerable drag on the market on account of its unpleasant taste and, in the case of South American meat, its unsightly appearance. In 1865 the only regular exports of South American beef were made in the form of Liebig's beef extract. In 1847 Baron Justus von Liebig published the details of reducing meat to a concentrate. This consisted of boiling lean meat and then evaporating the gravy until a hard cake of beef extract was formed, 1 lb being obtained from about 32 lb of raw meat. (9) The nutritional content of the product was probably not very great, however it was easily trans-ported, and in 1863 and 1865 plants to produce the extract were set up in Uruguay. This, too, was used by the Army as well as being sold to the civilian poor to make soup. (10)

About 75 per cent of all US exports of salt meat in the 1860s were received in Liverpool and the remaining 25 per cent in London. This, however, does not provide a true indication of the pattern of distribution and consumption of this meat in Britain, as a lot of the meat received at Liverpool was sent by rail to London. (11)

Although the total imports of dead meat into the United Kingdom grew from 84,717 cwt in 1842 to 1,644,226 cwt in 1864 (see Table 5.1), the contribution that this made to the nation's total meat supplies was insignificant. Between 1850 and 1860 the per capita amount involved stagnated at less than 3 lb. Even in 1864, when the amount of dead meat had been somewhat artificially boosted by

TABLE 5.1 Imports of dead meat into the United Kingdom, 1842-64

Year	Beef	Bacon & Ham	Pork
	cwt	cwt	cwt
1842	30,033	520	54,164
1843	60,724	488	27,118
1844	106,768	36	30,848
1845	87,844	54	39,706
1846	177,172	2,960	72,789
1847	117,694	90,530	235,899
1848	121,980	219,033	234,132
1849	149,962	396,447	343,275
1850	135,414	352,401	211,254
1851	117,384	192,118	154,800
1852	124,693	81,436	95,555
1853	183,285	205,677	152,731
1854	192,274	423,510	160,898
1855	230,755	241,494	204,326
1856	187,838	372,793	156,266
1857	151,174	366,934	88,752
1858	196,685	196,685	89,765
1859	219,589	107,251	163,330
1860	262,194	326,106	173,325
1861	152,635	515,953	136,416
1862	189,761	1,345,694	227,758
1863	288,369	1,877,813	170,751
1864	346,821	1,069,390	228,015

Sources: 'Journal of Agriculture', vol. 18, October 1851, p.180;
'Statistical Abstract of the U.K., 1848-62', P.P., 1863, LXVII;
W. MacDonald, On the Relative Profits to the Farmer from Horse,
Cattle and Sheep Breeding, Rearing and Feeding in the United
Kingdom, 'Journal of the Royal Agricultural Society of England',
2nd series, vol. XII, 1876, p.8.

US bacon and hams diverted to the British market by the Civil War,
it only provided 6 lb per head of the population. The major part
of this meat was salted in one way or another and came from North
America. A very small amount of fresh beef and pork was brought

from Europe on the 48-hour steamers from Hamburg in the 1860s, but
like the domestic long distance dead meat traffic this was strictly
a winter trade.   In 1864 out of 346,821 cwt of beef and 228,015 cwt
of pork the fresh meat constituted only 43,961 cwt and 38,603 cwt
respectively.   The indications are that the per capita consumption
of imported meat was greater in London than in the country as a
whole.   Writing in 1856 George Dodd guessed that: 'Limiting the
range to the port of London, there appears to have been about ...
6,000 tons of foreign bacon and hams imported annually in the last
six or eight years.' (12)   With the Greater London population at
2,685,000 in 1851 (13) this would allow for a per capita consumption 5 lb in the metropolis, excluding imports of salt beef and
pork.   This is not the only indication that more meat was consumed
per head by the population of London than in the United Kingdom as
a whole.

2   LIVESTOCK IMPORTS

Imports of livestock to supply the British market began at the same
time as imports of dead meat, when the free trade budgets of Sir
Robert Peel largely freed this trade from restrictions in July 1842.
Although the import of stock was allowed the animals were still
subject to import duties ranging from 20s. on oxen down to 5s. on
swine.   These duties remained in force for some four years and were
not finally removed until 1846.
   The import of livestock started as soon as the prohibition was
lifted, and the first foreign sheep and cattle appeared in the
London market at Smithfield in July 1842. (14)   All the livestock
imported into Britain in this period came from Europe.   They were
supplied by a variety of countries and were exported from Spain,
Portugal, France, Belgium, Holland, Schleswig, the north German
states, Denmark and Sweden.   However, because of the European overland traffic in livestock some animals came from much further afield
than is suggested by their port of shipment.   The growth of this
trade before 1865 was not spectacular and foreign stock did not make
an important contribution to the nation's food supplies.   The trade
grew very gradually at first.   In 1845 imports were less than
17,000 oxen and 16,000 sheep.   There was a substantial rise in the
next two years, after the removal of customs duties on livestock
imported for food, which was accompanied by an increase in domestic
meat prices between 1845 and 1847 of 20 per cent (see Table 5.2).
After 1847 the numbers of cattle declined and the number of sheep
was virtually the same in 1850 as in 1847.   In the 1850s the growth
of imports was again unsteady.   Imports do not appear to have
responded strongly to price changes.   For instance, in January 1850
it was reported at Smithfield: 'Letters from Rotterdam and other
principal shipping ports abroad state that notwithstanding the low
prices ruling in this market, the supplies ready for shipment are
heavy, especially those of sheep, and that large numbers will be
forwarded hither.' (15)   After 1853 and until 1858 total numbers
fell off despite the general upward movement of prices.   This can
be seen most clearly in the case of sheep imports: between 1851 and
1859 only twice did the annual changes in the number of imports move

TABLE 5.2 United Kingdom imports of cattle, sheep and pigs and
London prices of inferior beef and mutton, 1842-64

Year	Cattle (oxen, bulls, cows, calves)	Beef	Sheep and lambs	Mutton	Pigs
	no.	d. per 8 lb	no.	d. per 8 lb	no.
1842	4,264	41	644	42	410
1843	1,521	33	217	37	381
1844	4,889	31	2,817	35	265
1845	16,833	34	15,957	40	1,590
1846	45,043	32	94,624	44	3,856
1847	75,717	42	142,720	48	1,242
1848	62,738	38	130,583	45	2,119
1849	53,449	31	129,266	37	2,653
1850	66,462	32	143,498	36	7,287
1851	86,520	32	201,859	35	15,599
1852	93,061	29	230,037	34	10,524
1853	125,253	32	259,420	35	12,757
1854	114,338	38	183,436	39	11,077
1855	97,527	40	162,642	42	12,171
1856	83,306	35	145,059	42	9,916
1857	92,963	36	177,207	41	10,678
1858	89,001	35	184,482	37	11,565
1859	85,677	40	258,580	39	11,084
1860	104,569	41	320,219	46	24,452
1861	107,096	40	312,923	42	30,308
1862	97,887	38	299,472	44	18,162
1863	150,898	44	430,788	48	27,137
1864	231,733	45	496,243	51	85,362

Sources: (a) Livestock imports: 1842-67, 'Return relating to the
past and present supply of dead meat to the country and the
metropolis', P.P., 1867-8, LV; cattle, p.3; sheep, p.4; pigs, p.5.
        (b) Prices of meat: 1842-51, 'Journal of Agriculture',
vol. 18, October 1852, p.573 (lowest prices of cattle and sheep,
per 8 lb at Smithfield); 1850-8, R. Herbert, Statistics of Live
Stock and Dead Meat for Consumption in the Metropolis, 'Journal of
the Royal Agricultural Society of England', vol. XXIV, 1863, pp.207-
8, 456-7 (inferior beef and mutton, per 8 lb); 1859-64,

'Agricultural Statistics 1879', P.P., 1878-9, LXXV, Table 27, p.
109 (inferior beef and mutton, per 8 lb).

in the same direction as changes in the previous year's mutton
prices. For cattle imports numbers followed the previous year's
price changes in only half the years in this decade. It would seem
that other factors were exercising a more powerful effect on livestock supplies from Europe than the movement of meat prices in
England. The drop in sheep numbers between 1853 and 1856, for
instance, was thought by Dodd to have been 'attributable in all
probability in some way to the (Crimean) War'. (16)
    The most important port of entry for these livestock was,
naturally, London and the largest number of imports were slaughtered
and consumed there. But in addition to London, livestock importers
also used other ports. Originally they were free to land animals
where they liked, but after the British customs officials
discovered, in the course of their investigations into the import
of livestock disease, that there were over a hundred places where
they were landed, including isolated creeks and inlets which might
receive just two or three animals, the trade was restricted to
certain ports where it might be subjected to some minimum supervision. (17) In addition to London the east coast ports of England
became important centres for receiving European cattle - this was a
natural development as most were shipped from northern Europe and
the Baltic ports. In the last six months of 1863 the majority of
sheep and cattle imported into London came from Amsterdam, Bremen,
Dordt, Hamburg, Harlingen, Medemblik, Rotterdam and Tonning. (18)
These ports were naturally suited to serve places like Lowestoft,
Harwich, Hull, Hartlepool and even Newcastle. For instance, as an
alternative to London, Lowestoft in Suffolk was developed as a port
for the reception of Danish cattle from Jutland and Schleswig
Holstein. In March 1851 it was decided at a meeting of the
Lowestoft Harbour and Railway Company to form a subsidiary, the
Northern Steam Packet Company, for this purpose. By May 1851 the
company had three sea-going vessels for the carriage of livestock,
and at Lowestoft it built a shed for servicing the ships' engines
as well as a lairage capable of holding 200 head of cattle. The
advantage of this route over the direct one to London was the
shorter sea journey from the Continent. Lowestoft is the most
easterly port in England and in the 1850s this reduced the time of
a sea journey over that to London by more than 24 hours. In this
way the animals arrived at Lowestoft in a better condition than if
sent direct to London, especially in winter weather. The company
then used the Eastern Counties Railway to send the animals on to
London. In this way they arrived at market more quickly and in
better shape than by any other route. (19) In 1854 this service
was in operation and despatching Danish cattle between Tonning and
London. (20) Cattle for the London market were also landed at
Harwich and they were even sent to London from as far away as Hull.
But the port of Hull could also furnish foreign cattle for
consumption in the industrial towns of Yorkshire.
    The quality of many of the sheep, cattle and pigs imported from
Europe was very much below that of domestic animals and this
further reduced the contribution they made to the United Kingdom's

meat supplies. The best animals came from Holland and Denmark.
There are indications that the opening of British ports to European
livestock in 1842 caused profound changes in the agriculture of
some, but not all, European countries. Before that date both
Denmark and Holland specialized almost exclusively in dairying.
Thereafter there was a trend towards increased emphasis on beef
production for the British market which was accompanied by an
improvement in the weight and quality of their livestock, especially
cattle. From other countries the quality of animals on offer in
London was very poor indeed. In 1859 German sheep were described
as being 'in wretchedly bad condition - in fact completely rotten'.
(21) In 1861 cattle from the northern departments of France,
averaging 11 years old 'without a particle of good or consumable
food on their backs' and which had been evidently worked for
several years, were noticed at Islington. Buyers were generally
astonished that their owners had even bothered to try and find a
market for them in this country. Spanish cattle were also
described as being generally as 'light as cork' and even though
they were better formed than French beasts they quite often 'died
badly', that is yielded less meat and internal fat, etc., than
might have been expected from their external appearance when live,
and so only experienced buyers were disposed to purchase these
animals. (22)

The generally inferior nature of the European beasts imported
into Britain is indicated in their average weight. For many years
after their admission, this was not more than 480 lb per beast
whereas in 1839 the average dead weight of British cattle was 700
lb. By 1859 there had been some considerable improvement and the
average dead weight of imported beasts was 584 lb, though by this
time the average dead weight of domestic cattle had risen to 730
lb. Although this was a smaller improvement than for foreign cattle
it is to be expected as there was less room for improvement in
British breeds. (23)

Although most of the imported animals were for killing there was
some business done with store animals for further fattening. It
seems that this was most likely when farmers in Europe were forced
to export stock in a half-fat state because of shortage of fodder at
home. These animals might either be bought by British butchers at
a low price and killed as they were, or sometimes sold to graziers
who would give them further feeding and hope to make a profit by
the speculation. In most cases this was not a paying proposition.
In 1861 Robert Herbert reported that several thousand sheep from
Germany had been bought for grazing near London (on the Essex
marshes) but that after a month's run they had been returned to the
market without gain to the purchasers. (24) Similar experiments
with Dutch cattle often ended with no profit. One problem facing
the farmer in such an enterprise was the possibility of undisclosed
disease. If these animals were bought and turned out he was faced
with the losses of a high mortality as well as the likelihood of
infecting any other stock he had already. By the 1860s this had
been given sufficient publicity for farmers to know of the danger,
so the use of imported European animals for stores was not likely
to have been very important in terms of numbers of stock involved.

The largest number of livestock imports was seen after 1860, and

they were particularly heavy in 1863 and 1864. In those years,
after a generally rising trend of British meat prices from the mid-
1850s the price of meat in Britain was high enough to suck in a
record number of livestock from European sources. Between 1859 and
1864 London received over 70 per cent of the pigs and foreign cattle
and over 85 per cent of sheep and lambs imported into the United
Kingdom. The greatest numbers of cattle came from Holland and
Denmark; Holland, Germany and Denmark sent the bulk of sheep; and
Holland, Germany and France the majority of pigs. The main
personnel behind these transactions were European livestock dealers
and cattle salesmen - 'German Jews' as one journal ungraciously
identified them. (25) But this description was not entirely
accurate as English cattle dealers also made journeys to Europe to
purchase livestock, either on their own account of in partnership
with continental businessmen.

Even in 1864 when the number of imported stock reached its highest figure since importation had been permitted, these animals only
made a very small contribution to the supplies of meat from domestic
animals. Although the first official estimate of domestic farm
stock was not made until 1867, in 1862 John Gamgee gave an unofficial estimate of the herds and flocks in the United Kingdom. His
results are presented in Table 5.3 together with those from the
first two 'Agricultural Returns', for purposes of comparison.

TABLE 5.3   Estimate of livestock in the United Kingdom in the 1860s

	Cattle	Sheep	Pigs
Livestock in the UK in: (a)			
1867	8,731,473	33,817,951	4,221,100
1868	9,083,416	35,607,812	3,189,167
Estimated UK livestock in the early 1860s (b)	7,646,998	40,000,000	4,298,141
Estimates for the proportion and number slaughtered for food in the early 1860s (c)	25% 1,911,749	26% 10,400,000	100% 4,298,141
Imports into UK in 1864	231,733	496,788	85,362
Imports in 1864 as a proportion of the number of domestic stock slaughtered in the early 1860s	12%	5%	2%

(a) Agricultural Returns.
(b) J. Gamgee, Statistics of Loss Amongst Live Stock in the United
     Kingdom ..., 'Edinburgh Veterinary Review', vol. V, no. XL,
     August 1863, p.477. These figures are: cattle - England (1854
     estimates), 3,422,156; Scotland (1857 statistics of Highland
     and Agricultural Society), 974,437; Ireland (1862 statistics),
     3,250,396; sheep - estimate by Robert Herbert, no further
     details given; pigs - no details given.
(c) R.H. Rew, Memorandum on some Estimates made by various
     Authorities on the Production of Meat and Milk, 'Journal of

the Royal Statistical Society', vol. LXV, 1902, p.675.   The
estimates are: cattle - 1837, McCulloch;   sheet - 1837,
McCulloch;   pigs - 1871, Clarke.

Little can be said about the accuracy of Gamgee's figures other than
that they are an approximate indication of the number of livestock
in the United Kingdom in the early 1860s, and that they involve a
large margin of error.   Further early estimates of the percentage
of livestock annually slaughtered can be used to furnish an estimate
of the number of animals used to supply meat in the early 1860s.
The result of these calculations is to reveal that in 1864 imported
cattle, sheep and pigs were approximately 12, 5 and 2 per cent
respectively of those domestic animals slaughtered for meat.

3   DOMESTIC LIVESTOCK SUPPLY

The low per capita figures for meat consumption in the United
Kingdom and their failure to rise significantly prior to 1870
deserves some further comment.   When one considers the implications
of Mulhall's figures for the standard of living controversy, it
seems doubtful whether they can have more than a passing relevance
to the debate.   In the first place the various authorities who
have conducted this discussion have concentrated their attention on
a time period which begins between 1750 and 1800 and ends between
1800 and 1850, (26) according to which author and contribution is
selected.   As Mulhall's figures cover only the last twenty years of
this period, i.e. 1830-50, they can make no contribution to the
major part of the discussion.   But also recent debates have
concentrated on the comparison between wages and prices and have
not attempted to re-estimate the availability of foodstuffs.   This
is probably wise as only approximate values can be obtained which,
like Mulhall's, summarize the average position over decades and take
no account of the sharp fluctuations that could take place in
prices, wages, and the quantities consumed between individual years.
Again, the availability of foodstuffs is not the only thing that
should be borne in mind.   There is the question of fluctuations in
employment, the levels of rents, and the general quality of life
for the population at large to be taken into account.   But Mulhall's
meat figures show that the availability of this item of consumption
was no better in the 1850s than in the 1830s.   However this takes no
account of the availability of other items of food.   Mulhall's
summary of the consumption per capital of wheat, sugar, tea, beer,
rice and eggs in the United Kingdom between 1831-50 and 1851-70
shows that the quantities of all these commodities rose by a greater
amount than meat. (27)
   Low as Mulhall's estimates may seem, they are a little higher
than those made by a recent writer, when estimating the production
and consumption of meat in the United Kingdom between 1850 and 1880.
According to E.F. Williams: (28)
   By 1850 the total production of meat, i.e., beef, pork and
   mutton, in the U.K. had risen to about 900,000 tons providing
   about 72 lbs per head per year.   This was supplemented by importing animals to give a further 44,000 tons making a total of about

75 lbs per head of population yearly. In the next thirty years
the total tonnage had risen to about 1.25 million, giving a per
capita consumption of about 110 lbs, and it stayed at that level
until refrigeration was established.

Unfortunately this author does not give the sources for these
estimates, nor does he venture to show how the increase was distributed over the years 1850 to 1880. However it is likely that his
1850 estimate is a rounding off of Mulhall's with a rather approximate divisor for population.

Although in per capita terms the amount of meat that was
available to the population between 1840 and 1870 was around 87 lb,
we know that the distribution was very unequal. The poorer sections
of society would have received a lower share, and for some groups,
for example the agricultural labourer, meat would be a rarity par-
taken of, say, only once a week. Details of family budgets for the
years before 1880 are very scarce and they are not common even after
that date. But the examples which Burnett has assembled show a
consumption of meat ranging from 5 lb a week purchased by a semi-
skilled urban worker in 1841 who had a wife and three children, to
that of a Suffolk farm labourer with a wife and five children, of
whom three were working, who in 1843 apparently had nothing to
spare to pay for meat, and whose only sources of animal protein
were butter and cheese. (29) Consumption varied with region as
well as occupation. It is likely that the per capita consumption
of meat in Ireland was lower than for the rest of the United
Kingdom, and the position probably worsened during and after the
famine of the 1840s. One estimate of Mulhall's suggests that the
annual per capita consumption of meat from all sources at the end
of the 1880s was 118 lb in Great Britain but only 56 lb in Ireland.
(30)

The very slow growth in domestic meat supplies up to 1870 may
prompt the question whether British agriculture was somehow failing.
However, in this context it should be remembered that the output
from farming included other commodities besides meat, and there is
the possibility that there were certain constraints on increasing
meat production prior to 1870. We know, for instance, that the
production of animal feeding stuffs on British farms had to supply
two markets which were in some sense competing ones. Besides the
feeding of cattle, sheep and pigs, the British farmer also had to
devote some of his output of grass and cereals to provisioning the
growing number of horses in mid-Victorian Britain. Professor F.M.L.
Thompson has already revealed that the record of the number of
horses on British farms after 1867 provides a deceptive under-
estimate of this total. (31) Besides those employed solely as
agricultural movers there were those horses kept by urban and
country carriers, horses and ponies in the coalfields, those used
by the Army, as well as the number kept for hunting and sport by
the upper classes. Again these sources of demand must have grown
as the economy itself expanded. According to recent estimates by
the same author, the number of non-agricultural horses in Great
Britain rose from 487,000 in 1811 to 533,000 in 1851 and to 858,000
by 1871. The total number of horses (i.e. agricultural and non-
agricultural) almost doubled from 1,287,000 to 2,112,000 between
1811 and 1871. (32)

Again, part of the increase in the total domestic output of meat after 1870 was achieved by the use of imported inputs. Thompson's estimates of imports of fertilizers and feeding stuffs (see Table 5.4) show a far greater absolute increase between 1859-63 and 1887-91 than between 1837-42 and 1859-63. (33) As it is the total amounts of these commodities that are important when it comes to the numbers of livestock for which they may, either directly or indirectly, be used as a feeding supply, then this source appears more important after 1864 than before that date. In the 1880s and 1890s Fletcher refers to livestock farmers being able to increase their output with the aid of imported cereals, (34) an option that was not available to the same extent for farmers operating before the 1870s.

TABLE 5.4   Estimates of imports of fertilizers and feeding stuffs, 1837-91

Years	Imports of feeding stuffs (1,000 tons)	Retained imports of fertilizers (1,000 tons)
1837-42	132	73
1859-63	783	348
1887-91	2,403	654

We know that British agriculture was unable to keep pace with the growing demand for meat in the 1870s. The question is, how long before that date was it unable to keep pace with this demand which was fuelled as much by the rise in the level of wages after 1850 as by the increase in population. There is certainly no doubt that meat and livestock prices rose between 1840 and 1870. That they rose in relation to grain prices can be taken as evidence that there was an unsatisfied demand for meat, certainly after 1850 when real wages and money wages rose too. (35) Between 1839-42 and 1861-4 the average annual price of Cheviot wethers rose from 18s. to 25s. and Blackface wethers from 27s. to 33s., (36) which represented rises of 38 and 22 per cent respectively. In 1865 it was alleged that cows which sold for £10 or £12 in 1840 realized from £18 to £20. (37) Also a general rise in all livestock product prices has been noted. Collins and Jones show for the period between 1851-5 and 1866-70 that prices for beef, mutton, cheese and milk increased by an average of 28 per cent. (38)

Contemporaries were certainly expressing their concern about adequate supplies for the future in the 1860s. This anxiety showed itself in a number of ways. In 1862 and 1863 Dr Edward Smith presented his reports to the Privy Council on food of the depressed cotton workers of Lancashire and the poorer domestic workers of London and other places. In all cases these reports reveal diets that contained less than 1 lb of meat per week, in some cases very much less than this amount. (39) The Society of Arts also took an interest in nutrition. In December 1866 the first meeting took place of its Food Committee which was appointed to examine ways of augmenting and improving the nation's supply. At this its chairman,

Mr Harry Chester, observed that when he had delivered the centenary
address of the council in 1853 he had alluded to the need to devise
a means to bring fresh meat into the country from the colonies where
a surplus was known to exist. At that time he had asked why
Australia could export only tallow and wool from her sheep and not
the mutton itself to feed the masses. This was a matter in which
the society took an active interest from 1863 when it offered a
medal and a prize of £70 for the first practical invention that
could bring meat from the colonies in a raw state. But in 1866
Chester asserted that: 'The home supply of meat for the population
of these islands (is) not nearly sufficient for the due sustenance
of one half of the population'. (40)

    Some of the anxiety about meat supplies took the form of attempts
to publicize other substitutes, either in print or by example. The
'Journal of Agriculture' was notable for the former. From the mid-
1850s to the mid-1860s it received a number of communications from
readers, and published pieces, discussing the artificial rearing of
fish, especially salmon! In October 1857 this magazine published
an article on 'Hippophagy, or should we eat our Horses?'. And in
October 1863 there was an editorial article which debated
'Mycophagy; or, Should we eat Funguses?'. (41) These last two, like
the various debates on 'pisciculture', were a response to publications that had appeared outside the 'Journal of Agriculture', and
they presumably represent a wider even if still a rather specialized
interest. On the practical side, these attempts to popularize
substitutes for conventional meat mostly took the form of public
demonstrations to persuade the population to eat horse-flesh. In
1868 a Mr Bicknell gave a lecture before the Society of Arts on
the attempts that had been made to publicize this meat in France.
In it he recounted how a banquet had been held in Paris in 1865
where soup, roasts and sausages, all of horse-flesh, had been eaten,
and at which there was even a joint of donkey! In 1868, possibly
in emulation of this experiment, a much publicized dinner was held
in London at the Langham Hotel under the auspices of the Society
for the Propagation of Horse Flesh as an Article of Food. (42)

    Some of these ideas and projects no doubt reflected the
obsessions of philanthropically minded cranks. Nevertheless there
was certainly a core of hard-headed commercialism behind some of
the attempts to bring fresh meat into the country from overseas
sources. The evidence of rising prices and an unsatisfied demand
for meat in the United Kingdom gave impetus to much of the activity
that went into discovering a feasible method of transporting fresh
meat across the ocean from those countries with a surplus. Between
1850 and 1859 eleven patents were taken out in Britain for various
methods of mechanical refrigeration. But from 1860 the interest
and the number of patents rose accordingly. In the quinquennium
1860-4 ten were granted, in 1865-9 twenty, and between 1870 and 1874
no fewer than fifty-six patents were taken out. These figures,
moreover, probably understate the interest that was shown because
they cover only mechanical methods of refrigeration (i.e. by heat
exchange) and they take no account of the many schemes devised for
refrigeration by ice and salt or other freezing mixtures. (43)

CHAPTER 6
THE DOMESTIC TRADE, 1865-89

After 1865 the livestock trade experienced the first effects of
government interference by measures to contain the spread of
animal diseases. Before then it was possible for dealers to move
livestock anywhere in the United Kingdom and by any means of
transport without the slightest let or hindrance from the central
government. The measures adopted by local authorities prior to that
date to keep livestock markets free from visibly diseased animals
were only a slight impediment to trade. In the absence of uniform
local controls it was quite possible for dealers to circumvent the
restrictions of one local authority by taking animals for sale to a
market within the jurisdiction of a neighbouring authority. After
1865 the options available that enabled persons to conduct their
livestock businesses in this way were reduced. In the first place
central government measures, that were far more comprehensive than
anything initiated by local authorities, imposed severe restrictions
on the movement and sale of livestock in whole districts when
certain diseases were discovered. It is true that at times the
force of these measures was reduced, as it was still largely left
to local authorities to implement them, but from 1871 a central
veterinary inspectorate did much to ensure that they were observed.
Also the closing of a number of the smaller public markets on
public health grounds forced more of the livestock traffic into the
large markets where supervision was easier.

In addition, the dead meat trade increased in popularity. This
was particularly so with regard to supplying the London market. The
metropolis retained its position as the nation's most important
meat market and the provision of proper premises for the London
market in 1868 helped the growth of this trade. The meat trade was
also subject to more official intervention to control the sale of
diseased meats. But the public health Acts, under which this was
done, left a lot of freedom to individual Medical Officers of
Health as to how rigorously they interpreted and enforced the law.
Therefore this aspect of official regulation was as patchy as the
controls imposed to prevent the spread of livestock disease.

1   OFFICIAL INTERVENTION

The quick passage of the 1866 Cattle Diseases Prevention Bill
through Parliament between 12 and 20 February 1866 signified the
acceptance by the government of the necessity for positive control
of the livestock trade. The new Act embodied a number of provisions, the most important being the compulsory slaughter of all
diseased animals and the slaughter of animals in contact with the
disease at the discretion of local authorities. Also compensation
could be paid to owners from the local rates and the movement of
livestock itself was severely restricted. However, the effective-
ness of the Act was reduced because its administration was left to
local authorities. In certain cases these bodies were conscientious
in carrying out the various parts of the Act, but in others neglect
and indifference were widely in evidence. The business of enforcing
the law was placed with the justices at the quarter sessions for
the counties, the borough magistrate in towns and the Metropolitan
Board of Works for London. They were to hire inspectors to assist
them and report offenders, who were subject to a variety of fines.
At the same time the Privy Council continued to issue orders that
either modified or strengthened the powers of the original Act
when this was thought necessary. For example, under the Act there
was a total prohibition of the movement of livestock by rail, but
under an order of 27 March 1866 this was changed to the effect that
no movement was permissible by land, rail or water without a
licence. Again on 27 April the Cattle Diseases Prevention Act was
modified, this time by Parliament, to let imported foreign cattle be
shipped directly by rail to London and sold there for immediate
slaughter. On 10 August a further order in council provided a
penalty of three months in prison or a £20 fine for forgers of
licences because, by an astonishing oversight, no penalty had been
incorporated into the Act itself for offenders against this part
of it!
     In both the agricultural and the national press there was fierce
discussion and not a little complaint about the variety of measures
that were evolved to cope with the emergency. In Aberdeenshire it
was said the scale of compensation to stock owners was inadequate
and that this would encourage farmers not to declare the disease.
(1) Also the prohibition on railway traffic brought forward overwhelming complaints from all sections of the trade as well as the
railway companies themselves. The attitude in the localities to
the measures was infinitely varied. In general they were enforced
better in England than in Scotland, but the slaughter provisions
were not well enforced anywhere. The number of inspectors employed
was inadequate and very often their quality was seriously deficient.
As they were mostly recruited locally their loyalties were often
mixed and they acquiesced in the evasion of measures in which they
had little confidence or interest. Some local officials were
hostile to the Act and the orders, some where too lazy to undertake
the work and expense involved; others procrastinated hoping the
plague would spend itself before they were forced to act. (2)
Nevertheless, despite the imperfections in their operation, the
measures eventually succeeded in bringing the outbreaks under
control although it was not until 1867 that the country was

officially declared free of the disease. The greatest shortcoming
of the government's performance during this episode was probably
the failure to complement local diversity by central uniformity.
Measures which were in themselves quite satisfactory had they been
fully implemented were made less so by local delay and imperfect
enforcement and the absence of any effective independent inspectorate to monitor local action.

Following the anti-cattle-plague measures of 1866-7 which were
largely ad hoc restrictions and not subject to any real overall
control and supervision, the methods adopted after 1869 under the
Contagious Diseases (Animals) Act of that year represented a more
comprehensive and unified attack on the problem of disease. The
responsibility for supervising the control of outbreaks remained
with veterinary officers responsible to the Privy Council up to
1889, and after that to the Board of Agriculture which was established that year. Among the domestic livestock population the chief
endemic diseases that attracted their attention were in cattle,
pleuro-pneumonia and foot-and-mouth; in sheep, sheep-pox, sheep-
scab and foot-and-mouth; in pigs, swine fever. Also for the first
time separate annual records were kept of the fresh outbreaks of
certain diseases from various dates after 1869. Thus pleuro-
pneumonia and foot-and-mouth disease were recorded from 1870, swine
fever from 1879, and both anthrax and rabies from 1886. Under the
Privy Council, the Veterinary Department extended its activities
and this was reflected in the expansion of the number of officers
it employed and the increase in its annual budget. Within seven
years of its inception in 1865 it absorbed rather more than one
third of the total estimate for the Privy Council, and by 1877 its
annual estimate exceeded that of the Privy Council. In 1883 it was
renamed the Agricultural Department of the Privy Council and in that
year its estimate was £26,792 compared with £16,517 for the Privy
Council itself. In 1884 it had a senior establishment of ten
officers with various divisions of duties, and this remained more or
less the case until 1889. (3) With this complement of personnel
and an increased expenditure, the department was in a far more
powerful position to exert controls and supervision of the general
livestock trade for the eradication of disease than was the case in
1865.

In the 1870s and 1880s the armoury of measures available to the
department and to local authorities to stamp out disease was
gradually increased and these had the inevitable consequence of
encroaching upon the conduct of the livestock trade. Some measures
were, from the dealers' and farmers' points of view, less troublesome than others and some were more nuisance to one group than to
the other party. The progress of this control can be illustrated
with reference to one important cattle disease, pleuro-pneumonia.
From 1870 outbreaks of this disease, under the 1869 Act, had to be
notified to the Privy Council by local authorities. Also local
authorities were permitted to slaughter infected as well as contact
animals but were not compelled to do so. As compensation to their
owners was paid from local rates there was a marked reluctance to
put this into operation. As a result, out of a total of 25,238
cattle affected by the disease between 1870 and 1873 only 12,894
were slaughtered and 9,146 healthy contact cattle were also killed.

From September 1873 the slaughter of all cattle diagnosed as suffering from pleuro-pneumonia was made compulsory but still not the contacts, but also cattle in contact with the disease could not be moved or sold for 28 days. However, by themselves these measures were not very effective in reducing the extent of the disease. In 1872, seventy-one counties in Great Britain were affected and this was only reduced to sixty-seven by 1878. In 1878 under the Contagious Diseases (Animals) Act of that year the period of quarrantine for contacts was extended to 56 days and this seems to have been more effective as by 1880 the counties with the disease had been reduced to fifty-one. From 1881 to 1884 even greater success was achieved, not so much from the measures against pleuro-pneumonia, but following the severe restrictions placed on the movement of stock with the increased extent of foot-and-mouth disease in the country. With the success of these measures against foot-and-mouth, which severely hampered the livestock traffic in many parts of the country, the controls were eased at the end of 1884. The increase in the movement of livestock allowed from 1885 was also accompanied by an increase in the number of counties affected with pleuro-pneumonia from thirty-three in 1884 to forty-seven in 1887. Then in the early part of March 1888 an order was passed compelling local authorities to slaughter and compensate the owners of cattle in contact with the disease. However, from the time the order was in force to the end of 1889 the number of fresh outbreaks was not very greatly reduced and in 1889 the number of infected counties was forty-one. (4)

The lesson of this experience was that the unpopular restrictions on the movement of animals in the years 1880-4 had more effect in reducing the number of outbreaks of pleuro-pneumonia in Great Britain than the optional slaughter of diseased cattle, or even the compulsory slaughter of diseased cattle and those in contact with them by the local authorities. The same thing was revealed in the efforts against the disease, swine fever. Here the local authorities were not willing to incur the expense of the wholesale slaughter of diseased and infected pigs which they were empowered but not forced to do from 1879. However they could and did impose very stringent regulations over the movement and sale of swine from premises where the existence of the disease had been confirmed. In 1886 the Animals Order of that year allowed local authorities to make regulations with regard to the movement of swine into their district. This was a powerful measure of control as it permitted them, if they so wished, to regulate the movement of pigs from districts where the disease was prevalent for sale in clean areas. Although these regulations, like the ones for foot-and-mouth disease and pleuro-pneumonia, interfered very much with the ordinary course of pig marketing where adopted, they were much more successful than slaughter in preventing the spread of disease. (5) It was also true that as the measures were not compulsory, certain districts and localities where no controls were in force attracted an increased number of pigs through their markets from areas where the disease was prevalent. The effect of this 'patchy' enforcement of the available measures of control tended to confirm and probably strengthen the presence of disease in districts where the local authorities did not bother.

The activities of the Veterinary Department in recording disease outbreaks, and later on in tracing the contacts involved, positively confirmed that particular counties were centres of infection. Districts with large markets and an extensive cattle trade were more or less permanently infected with disease, not only pleuro-pneumonia but other conditions as well. Pleuro-pneumonia was revealed to be distributed over a considerable area of England and Scotland while Wales was largely free from it. In particular years, 1874, 1884, 1886, 1888 and 1889 there were no outbreaks recorded in the principality at all. This freedom was due to the fact that Wales was a breeding and exporting but not an importing district and very few cattle were ever taken into Wales from other parts of Britain. Conversely, in the feeding and fattening districts of England and Scotland, which received imports from other regions as well as from Ireland, disease was rife. Annual statistics of pleuro-pneumonia outbreaks in Great Britain from 1871 to 1890 revealed that the ten most seriously affected counties in England were, in descending order, Norfolk, Yorkshire (West Riding), Essex, London, Lancashire, Kent, Suffolk, Stafford, Northumberland and Middlesex. Most of these counties received imports of stock for fattening or other purposes. In the case of Lancashire, London and Middlesex these counties were between 1870 and 1890 engaged primarily in dairying (6) and it was among the cattle brought in for the city and suburban dairies that pleuro-pneumonia was particularly prevalent. Other places were affected with the disease because of marketing centres in their region. Thus the West Riding of Yorkshire was a badly affected county because of the stock brought in to and passing through the markets at Leeds, Huddersfield, Bradford, Halifax, etc. Also outbreaks in London and Middlesex were often traced to stock passing through the Metropolitan Cattle Market at Islington. In Scotland the five worst affected counties between the same dates were Midlothian, Fife, Forfar, Aberdeen and Lanark. (7)

However the officers found that the reports of the disease coming to their notice were not necessarily a reflection of its full extent in the country. Although owners were legally obliged to give notice of any cases, there were a number of ways this could be avoided. For instance if an owner failed to call in a veterinary surgeon to give a positive diagnosis he could plead that he knew nothing was amiss. Failure to seek professional advice might be through negligence, ignorance, or for more culpable reasons but was not grounds for prosecution. Often the department discovered when they traced an outbreak back to its source that the owner had several animals suffering from the same illness and a history of deaths among stock for some time previous to that. However it was not always possible to find the source of outbreaks. The reason for this was the exceedingly complicated nature of the livestock trade. Very often the same animals were exposed for sale in different markets and sale yards, in the possession of different owners. When questioned a dealer was very often unable to give any precise information about the origin of his animals. It was claimed that they had been bought in open market for ready cash from a person whose name and address were unknown. This vagueness did not always indicate a deliberate attempt to conceal information. It was

recognized that the ordinary cow dealer was, as a rule, an uneduca-
ted man who rarely kept any written record of his business
transactions. Even if auctioneers could give details of the stock,
and names and addresses of their owners, that passed through their
hands, positive identification of the origins of a particular beast
was usually impossible as animals rarely carried any brand or other
permanent identifying mark. The outbreak of pleuro-pneumonia in
the permanently affected counties usually followed some weeks after
the periodical movement of store or dairy cattle into those
counties from outside. Thus in 1889 the disease was positively
traced back to cattle passing through the auction marts at Brechin,
Warwick, Hellfield, Inverness, Peebles and St Boswells, as well as
the markets and fairs at Aberdeen, Banbury, Blackburn, Bolton,
Doncaster, Halifax, Huddersfield, Ingatestone, Kingston-on-Thames,
Leeds, London, Northampton, Otley, Rochdale, Romford, Rugby, Salford
Salford, Skipton, Southall and Wigan. (8)
    It was difficult to prove that dealers specialized in the
disposal of cattle from infected herds, as firm evidence would also
have constituted grounds for prosecution. For this reason persons
in the trade were less open about this side of their activities than
in the period from 1840 to 1865. According to the Chief Travelling
Inspector in 1889, the man responsible for tracing outbreaks of
disease to their source: (9)

> the majority of fresh (pleuro-pneumonia) outbreaks appears
> attributable to certain sale-yards and to a class of unscrupulous
> cattle dealers who carry on a regular trade in cattle (for the
> most part cows) purchased from persons who fail to report the
> appearance of the disease on their premises, and who, to escape
> detection, sell the diseased animals to butchers, and those
> animals not showing actual signs of illness are distributed by
> these well-known dealers over all parts of the kingdom.

The actions of central government over the livestock trade did
not extend to the meat selling section of the meat industry. Here
the initiative remained in the hands of local authorities who
operated under the Public Health Acts to stop the sale and to seize
unsound or diseased goods from butchers, wholesalers and meat
processors. After 1865 the extent of local authority intervention
in this field gradually became more comprehensive as these bodies
were made aware of the dangers of eating all bad or contaminated
foodstuffs, not only meat. The retail butcher felt the pressure of
local authority intervention in a number of ways. Regulations that
closed livestock markets and limited the movement of animals in
localities where disease was present inevitably restricted his
freedom to purchase the most suitable supplies for his trade. In
addition, the attempts made by local authorities to close down small
private slaughterhouses attached to butchers' shops and to
concentrate all the animal killing for a town into one large muni-
cipally owned abattoir was a threat to the way the retailer conducted his business operations. Finally, the more frequent inspection
of meat shops by the Medical Officers of Health, and the more
exacting standards of fitness for human consumption applied to the
product from the 1870s onwards, particularly after the passing of
the 1875 Public Health Act, was another encroachment upon the trading life of the retailer.

In all cases the purpose of regulation and control was to protect either the British farmer or the consumer. However, these ends were often regarded by members of the meat trade as being achieved at their expense. For instance the question of private slaughterhouses generated a considerable amount of anxiety and argument among the trade. The disadvantage of the private slaughterhouse from the public health point of view was simple. It was impossible to supervise and inspect the large number of these places found in a provincial town of any size. Birmingham, for example, was without a public abattoir as late as 1889 and had 300 private slaughterhouses supervised by just two inspectors. In the borough of Leeds there were 300 slaughterhouses scattered over an area of 33 square miles. (10) If the animals killed in these private premises were discovered after death to be suffering from disease it was an easy matter for their owners to follow the usual trade practice and cut away the parts that showed signs of disease and market the rest in the normal way. But in a municipal abattoir official inspection was much easier and consequently the chances of stopping such meat passing into human consumption were higher. In this case the losses from the seizure of such carcases fell on the owner and, if he was a typical member of the butcher's trade who purchased a single cow and one or two sheep and pigs each week, this represented a sizeable portion of his working capital.

The butchers were often critical of the qualifications of the local authority meat inspectors and also of the grounds on which they sometimes condemned whole carcases for destruction, when the trade felt that the sound parts could be sold to the public without risk. It should also be admitted that it was not only among butchers that some unease over the quality of meat inspection was felt. Anxiety was expressed in both medical and veterinary circles that inspectors frequently had no scientific training about the nature and causes of disease and were therefore unqualified to judge these matters. From 1875 to 1889 the inspector of meat in the city of Glasgow was a police constable. If he condemned a carcase and the butcher objected there was a recognized procedure where the case was considered by a sort of high court composed of two butchers and a police surgeon. This situation generally satisfied the trade, especially as only really badly diseased carcases were condemned. However the procedure was challenged and changed from May 1889 when two beef carcases, obviously tubercular, were seized and condemned. There was no dispute about the nature of their condition but only whether they should be regarded as totally unfit for human food. The case was heard in the Glasgow Sheriff Court and a number of witnesses were called for both sides, and from these the practices current in a number of important cities emerged. The picture was one that gave considerable grounds for disquiet. Witnesses for the prosecution established that the practice of total seizure of tuberculous carcases was followed in Edinburgh, Greenock and Paisley. Witnesses for the defence testified that only the parts obviously affected by the disease would have been seized in Leeds, Liverpool, Birmingham, Hull and the London borough of Holborn. Furthermore the witness from the last place, Dr Septimus Gibbon, was responsible for inspecting the Central Meat Market and he said that the greater part of the two carcases would have been passed for

human consumption at that place. Quite apart from the diversity of
practice there was also a division of opinion among those witnesses
who were Medical Officers of Health over purely scientific points.
Thus Gibbon revealed he believed that tuberculosis was the result
of environmental factors and he regarded the theory that it was
caused by a bacillus as nonsense, and this view was echoed by at
least two other medical witnesses. (11)

Leaving aside the question of who was right or wrong over the
medical and scientific points and whether sufficient time had
elapsed since Koch had first isolated and identified the tubercule
bacillus (in 1880) for his view to become generally accepted, the
diversity of scientific opinion was reflected in a practical way by
the lack of uniform action over the inspection of meat. In these
circumstances when the decision to condemn all or only part of a
carcase rested with the individual Medical Officer of Health, when
even the experts disagreed over the dangers of eating the flesh of
diseased animals, and when livestock markets and the movement of
stock were closely controlled in some districts and not at all in
others, it was not surprising that butchers complained they were the
victims of arbitrary officialdom. It was against this background
that the first attempts were made to form a national association of
meat traders in the late 1880s. However this was not solely a
reaction to developments on the public health front, as other causes
of anxiety also appeared on the agendas of meetings of butchers and
meat traders by the 1880s.

The National Federation of Meat Traders' Associations was founded
in 1888. Local associations, like the Leeds Butchers' Association
(founded 1852), had been in existence for many years. The National
Federation grew out of temporary confederations of meat traders
which had existed in Lancashire and Yorkshire to deal with matters
that arose from time to time. The emergence of a national body in
the 1880s was a consequence of two factors. First, it was related
to the rapid growth in meat supplies after 1881, accounted for by
increasing imports of foreign meat. Second, on the public health
front the growing number of regulations were having a direct effect
on the conduct of the meat business. Agitation for further reform
also threatened to alter the way business was transacted in the
future. The members of the meat trade, like other branches of food
distribution in the 1880s, reacted to these changes by banding
together for mutual defence. The National Federation was to act as
spokesman for the trade when dealing with governmental and other
institutions.

The federation represented both the wholesale and retail sides of
the meat business from its foundation and it dealt with the transport and distribution of both live cattle and dead meat. Lancashire
and Yorkshire remained the area most strongly represented in its
early history. This was because the meat trade in both counties had
aspects that aroused controversy. Thus Lancashire received both
Irish and US cattle and refrigerated meats. Yorkshire was a heavy
meat and fatstock exporting county, but it also received imports of
stores from other districts. Thus attempts to control livestock
markets had an important effect on butchers in both counties. Also
the Leeds association had recently fought off an attempt by the
corporation to close all private slaughterhouses in the borough

(without compensating their owners) and force all butchers to use a municipal abattoir.

The federation was, however, heavily weighted with organizations representing the retail side of the business. In 1888 it comprised sixteen local associations, of these thirteen were described as 'butchers' or 'retail' bodies, one was a 'butchers' and meat traders' association', another, the Yorkshire Confederation, and the last was the Dublin Victuallers' Association. (12) The Yorkshire Confederation appears to have been a regional affair, comprising more local associations of retailers.

The inaugural meeting of the federation was held at Dewsbury on 17 March 1888 and the following matters were listed as objects prompting the members' actions: (13)

Improved transit of cattle and sheep; responsibility for b uises and damage; reduction of railway rates; local regulations, movements of cattle, etc., conflicting regulations; Irish importations; communications on interesting matters; newspaper for the trade; Parliamentary representation.

These matters were to remain the concern of the federation in the following years. The call for a trade newspaper was answered less than two months later with the 'Meat Trades' Journal' which was founded on 5 May 1888.

2   THE LIVESTOCK TRADE

The situation already observed for the period 1840-64, where certain towns and districts were net importers of livestock and others were net exporters, was maintained during the next twenty-five years. But it is difficult to measure the relative importance of various districts, either as senders or recipients of fatstock. The obvious source for the answer to this question is the railway companies. As it was unusual for cattle and sheep to be driven any further by road than from the farm to the nearest railway station by the mid-1860s the majority of long distance fatstock traffic went by rail, the minority by sea.

However, the railway companies did not publish the figures for livestock, nor indeed for any other goods they carried, on a town-to-town basis. The situation was summarized by Robert Giffen, when he wrote about the railway statistics available at the end of the 1890s, in the following terms: 'There is no publication generally showing the districts from which the goods come and the districts to which they go, and classifying them under all the different descriptions....' (14) The only exceptions to this rule happened when statistics were furnished, during the course of a sponsored investigation, in order to clarify some point for the group of people charged with the investigation. Such an instance occurred in 1866 when the Cattle Plague Commissioners asked for, and the London and North Western and the Midland Railways gave, the numbers of livestock they carried to and from certain towns. This information was not comprehensive, even for these companies. For some of the towns the figures supplied were of livestock carried for just one month - September 1865. Although it is dangerous to base conclusions solely upon such incomplete information, especially as the movement of

livestock from certain areas was purely seasonal, some of this
evidence can be used to support the verbal statements made by
witnesses to the commission. Table 6.1 contains the details of the
livestock traffic to and from certain towns given to the First and
Second Cattle Plague Commissions.

    To measure the extent to which any one place was either an
exporter or importer of livestock the third set of columns expresses
the numbers despatched from the town as a ratio of the number sent
into the town. Thus if any town despatched as many of any livestock
as it received the figure in the third set of columns would be 1.0;
those towns where the figure is less than unity are net importers
and those where it is greater than unity are net exporters. In
certain cases, as in Kibworth (Leicestershire), it is impossible to
express this value for the export of cattle by the Midland Railway
as it carried none to that place. Here the letter 'D' denotes that
Kibworth was a despatching centre for cattle. Similarly, the 'R'
for cattle and sheep in the case of London shows that it received
these animals only. As only twelve pigs were sent from London via
the Midland Railway in September 1865 it would be inappropriate to
describe London as a distributing centre for pigs, and also misleading, as it is clear from other sources that London was a net
importer of all livestock. The ratios in the third set of columns -
which have been provisionally named as 'export ratios' - have a
further weakness in addition to the very partial coverage of the
original figures upon which they are based. This weakness is the
inability to distinguish between store animals and fatstock in the
figures given by the two railway companies. To some extent it is
possible to identify the existence, though not the precise extent,
of store animals in the movements of livestock from a particular
town with some reference to the local economy. Thus it is certain
that the export ratio of 3.01 of cattle for Liverpool included a
number of Irish stores which were sent by rail to East Anglia for
fattening on the Norfolk farms or else to be fattened in Herefordshire and the Midlands. However not all the Irish cattle coming
from Liverpool were stores. The London and North Western Railway
also did a trade in finished Irish cattle to the London market and
other places. Some of the export of cattle from Shrewsbury was
likely to be Welsh hill stock sent to the Midland grazing districts.
The large outflow of sheep from Carlisle would include an indeter-
minate number of stores to be finally fattened elsewhere.

    Although certain towns and cities were very heavy importers of
all sorts of livestock this does not necessarily mean that the
entire net import was slaughtered and consumed in that place.
Birmingham, which was not situated near a cattle feeding district,
had large numbers of animals brought in by rail from all parts,
including London. Dealers from Birmingham were accustomed to travel
to London to buy cattle at the Metropolitan Cattle Market at
Islington on a Monday, take them back to Birmingham on Monday
evening and sell them at the Birmingham cattle market held on
Tuesdays. In this way, although it was a net importer of livestock,
London also acted as an important distributing centre for animals.
In addition to Birmingham, stock were re-routed after passing
through the London market to destinations in Kent and towns along
the south coast of England. In 1865 it was estimated that out of

TABLE 6.1 Animals sent to and despatched from various towns in England in 1864 and 1865

	I Sent from			II Forwarded to			Export ratio i.e. I ÷ II		
	Cattle	Sheep	Pigs	Cattle	Sheep	Pigs	Cattle	Sheep	Pigs
(a) Month of September 1865									
Sheffield	27	299	168	977	3,247	1,472	.06	.09	.11
Derby	535	2,606	1,287	256	3,524	918	2.09	.74	1.40
Market Harborough	1,172	1,984	4	117	1,244	83	10.02	1.59	.05
Kibworth	681	1,094	–	–	67	–	D	16.33	–
Bedford	42	370	499	261	1,005	237	.16	.37	2.10
London	–	3	12	3,051	4,579	–	R	R	–
(b) Year ending 30 September 1865									
Leicester	18,766	26,495	1,290	11,823	55,930	18,990	1.60	.47	.07
(c) Year ending 31 August 1865									
Liverpool	67,300	147,964	107,883	22,375	195,515	5,961	3.01	.76	18.41
Manchester	11,437	51,282	3,660	73,524	242,841	65,987	.15	.21	.05
Leeds	1,398	10,085	10,138	3,154	326	6,754	.43	30.93	1.50
Carlisle	7,748	46,690	2,464	25,071	6,627	1,844	.31	7.04	1.34
Wolverhampton	2,960	12,482	10,141	16,561	48,732	53,399	.18	.26	.19
Birmingham	1,984	5,433	8,755	18,052	70,033	70,278	.11	.08	.12
Shrewsbury	6,693	15,535	10,512	4,350	19,572	7,269	1.54	.79	1.45

(a) and (b) Carried by the Midland Railway, 'First Report Cattle Plague Commissioners', P.P., 1866, XII, Minutes of Evidence, p.166.

(c) It is not clear if this traffic was carried by the London and North Western only or if it was shared with other companies. 'Second Report Cattle Plague Commissioners', P.P., 1866, XII, Appendix D, p.64.

an average of 5,500 cattle passing through the London market each
week around 20 per cent went to other parts of the country for
slaughter. (15)   The extent and complexity of the movements of
fatstock was revealed when the Cattle Plague Commissioners tried to
trace the spread of the disease from London to other parts of the
country. Although Edinburgh sent meat and livestock to London,
livestock bought in London were sent the other way to Edinburgh.
(16)

The animals taken to Birmingham came from other centres besides
London. Large supplies of Irish animals came via Liverpool and the
rest were made up from local markets and fairs. Also a large
number of foreign beasts found their way to Birmingham via London
and Liverpool. Taking the Irish supplies and the London and
Liverpool trade, fully 75 per cent of the cattle sold in Birmingham
came from these outlying parts. Being a farming area with no large
graziers, locally fed fatstock was barely sufficient to feed a
quarter of the population in the west Midlands. Birmingham itself
had around 300,000 persons, and Wolverhampton around 65,000 persons.
Then there were smaller places like Bilston, Dudley and Walsall, as
well as the rural population between all these places. Birmingham
was not the sole market for these towns - Wolverhampton had a
substantial livestock market - but the market at Birmingham made a
significant contribution towards supplying these more distant
places, as well as the city itself. Dealers and butchers would buy
cattle in Birmingham and then take them home to be slaughtered.
Birmingham had around 400 licensed slaughterhouses within the
borough. These were mostly very small affairs, attached to the
shops of individual butchers, but they were not adequate to kill the
meat for the outlying districts. The animals taken from Birmingham
were distributed throughout the town and 10 or 12 miles around.
These animals were driven out of the market to their ultimate
destination by road. A large number were sold to butchers from the
mining district of South Staffordshire, who kept the animals alive
for two or three days before killing them as they were needed. (17)

Wolverhampton was a net importer of all sorts of livestock, being
in a similar industrial and agricultural situation to that of
Birmingham. Manchester was another large industrial centre of
population which was forced to rely heavily on livestock imports.
Some of the large export ratio of pigs from Liverpool would be to
Manchester. Both cities had large working-class populations which
represented a sizeable demand for pork and bacon. A lot of the
pigs sent out of Liverpool were imported from Ireland and a proportion of these also showed up as imports into Manchester.

The fact that a certain town was a net importer of livestock
might disguise the fact that it was also an exporter of dead meat.
In Table 6.1, Leeds is a case in point. It had a cattle export
ratio of .43 which makes it an importer, although the amounts
involved are not very great. Leeds was also an exporter of dead
meat to the London market though this is not apparent in the table.

It is interesting that the trend for certain towns was not always
in the same direction for all three types of livestock. Leicester
was a net exporter of live cattle but imported sheep and pigs. One
suspects that a large proportion of the net inflow of sheep were
stores destined for the grazing districts of that county. The

heavy net import of pigs into Leicester is surely a reflection of a
local speciality trade - the manufacture of pork pies centred upon
Melton Mowbray? Being at the heart of an important grazing district
it had a very large cattle market, but the great bulk of the cattle
sold there were not for the supply of the population of the town.
There were no large scale cattle slaughtering establishments in the
town. Nor did it have any industries that used the products of the
slaughterhouse. The footwear industry of the county was only
small scale and local at this time (18) and did not become important
until after 1870. The farmers brought their cattle to the market
where butchers and cattle dealers from various other parts of the
country attended, and after these had made their purchase they sent
the animals to other towns and villages. In this way the cattle
markets at Leicester and, to some extent, Derby were merely collecting centres from which cattle dealers forwarded the animals to the
districts where they would finally be slaughtered. According to the
traffic manager of the Midland Railway his company carried the same
amount of cattle traffic from Leicester as it did into the town.
And on market days the cattle traffic from Leicester was very large.
Not all the fatstock produced in Leicestershire even found their
way to the county's main market. Sometimes the farmers sent their
animals to dealers, who had them loaded at small stations convenient
to the farmers and sent to London or other large towns, so by-
passing Leicester market. The cattle sent from Kibworth and Market
Harborough in September 1865 are examples of this traffic. In these
ways the cattle of Leicestershire were despatched by different
routes to London, Birmingham, Sheffield and Nottingham. (19)

After 1865 there is more precise information on one important
part of the domestic livestock trade, the shipment of animals from
Ireland. From 1861 there are annual totals for the individual
numbers of cattle, sheep and swine landed from Ireland (20) and
after 1876 much more detailed information on this traffic is available. From this date it is possible to discover the ports in
Ireland from where the animals left, the ports in England, Wales
and Scotland where they landed, and the numbers of store and fat
cattle, and calves, the numbers of sheep and lambs, and the numbers
of store and fat pigs involved in the traffic. (21) The numbers
of animals carried annually in this trade between 1864 and 1889 are
summarized in Table 6.2, with the exception of 1868 as no figures
could be found for that year.

The first point of importance about this trade is its steady
growth throughout the period. In 1865-7 an average of 1,225,471
cattle, sheep and swine were imported from Ireland each year. In
1886-9 the total number had risen to 1,812,495 per annum. Also
after 1876 the relative importance of fat and store cattle and swine
in this trade can be judged. Ignoring the classes of 'other cattle'
and 'calves' the ratio of store cattle to fat cattle in this trade
was approximately 5 to 4 and the ratio of store swine to fat swine
was approximately 1 to 12. The number of 'other cattle' -
presumably breeding animals - are a relatively unimportant part of
the trade but the numbers of Irish calves shipped to Great Britain
averaged about 50,000 a year. Unfortunately there is no way of
telling just how many of these animals went for veal and how many
were kept alive. The largest numbers of animals were exported from

TABLE 6.2   Livestock imported from Ireland, 1865-89

Year	Cattle			Calves	Sheep		Swine	
	Fat cattle	Store cattle	Other cattle		Sheep	Lambs	Fat swine	Store swine
1865		246,734				332,831	383,452	
1866		399,231				398,846	504,224	
1867		473,871				588,906	348,319	
1868								
1869		456,035		53,071		1,015,694	264,620	
1870		415,673		38,296		620,834	422,976	
1871		423,396		60,529		684,708	528,244	
1872		481,878		134,202		518,605	443,644	
1873		684,618				604,695	364,371	
1874		509,330		41,879		744,234	344,335	
1875		559,614		35,704		917,979	463,618	
1876	279,134	328,512	15,735	42,947	474,871	211,937	436,044	77,272
1877	246,698	356,249	7,706	38,788	431,129	199,645	508,912	76,515
1878	246,944	416,759	4,954	61,564	446,628	196,371	401,167	69,380
1879	247,897	320,244	6,845	66,384	506,621	166,750	371,079	58,584
1880	232,905	417,203	2,812	68,471	502,806	211,957	333,653	39,237
1881	279,125	250,899	3,701	37,832	415,703	161,924	349,532	33,463

1882	291,777	427,798	3,006	59,693	393,848	164,556	453,443	49,463
1883	229,603	278,518	1,819	46,927	312,108	148,621	433,793	27,224
1884	255,026	387,352	2,220	71,245	355,466	177,819	437,227	19,451
1885	243,348	342,938	1,884	52,300	430,410	198,680	370,639	27,925
1886	285,156	388,917	1,247	42,069	493,983	240,230	391,509	29,776
1887	331,119	302,878	2,283	32,973	321,644	226,924	438,155	42,756
1888	282,537	405,540	2,941	47,698	400,836	236,748	495,680	49,292
1889	248,362	372,682	1,432	47,367	373,313	240,374	428,103	45,448

Source: notes 20 and 21 to chapter 6.

the port of Dublin, with Cork, Waterford, Drogheda, Londonderry and
Belfast making important contributions to the trade. In Great
Britain Liverpool was the most important centre of reception for
Irish animals with Bristol, Holyhead, Milford and Glasgow as ports
of secondary importance.

By 1870 the Irish livestock trade was criticized on humanitarian
grounds. It was alleged that animals suffered from over-crowding
and unnecessary ill-treatment both on rail and sea journeys. The
worst cases of ill-treatment seem to have occurred among the cattle
shipped from Dublin to Liverpool. When they were assembled and
loaded on board ship in Ireland the process was attended with
frequent brutalities from the drovers to force the animals into the
hold of the vessel. There was no provision for feeding or watering
the animals either at the Irish ports or on the cattle boats. On
board ship the animals were subjected to gross over-crowding and
poor ventilation. In these circumstances injuries and even deaths
en route were not uncommon. When an animal stumbled and fell in
the holds it was in double danger of being suffocated or trampled
upon by its companions. Some of the boats appear to have been
properly fitted for their purpose and to have carried the animals in
reasonable comfort, but in others accommodation was makeshift and
unsatisfactory in almost every respect. (22) The evidence given on
conditions under which the cattle were carried and their general
fitness on arrival in England is contradictory. English livestock
dealers generally deplored the conditions both of the ships and the
animals. Ship owners and the railway companies who ran cattle boats
naturally presented an optimistic picture, minimizing cruelties and
suffering. Occasionally passengers on the ships, who may be
considered as impartial witnesses, gave evidence of what they had
observed themselves. Also the municipal and port officials were
able to give an unbiased testimony. According to Mr Joseph Lloyd,
the corporation inspector of meat and animals at Liverpool, there
was great competition among the steamship companies to get the Irish
cattle trade, especially among the railway companies. The
Lancashire and Yorkshire, the Midland, Great Northern, and London
and North Western Railway Companies all had their agents in Ireland
and were all anxious to get the livestock for their boats and their
lines. He implied that as these men were mostly concerned with
recruiting new trade they regarded the conditions under which the
animals were carried as unimportant once they had achieved this
objective. (23)

At various dates regulations were introduced to enforce certain
minimum standards on board Irish cattle boats and at the ports, but
it must be emphasized that government interference in this matter
was on a very minor scale prior to 1889. The veterinary inspectors
employed by the Privy Council were mainly interested in detecting
signs of contagious animal disease in Irish cargoes, not in supervising the general conduct of the trade. Nevertheless the
inspectors were ideally situated to observe this traffic and to
comment on the reasons for those aspects that gave grounds for
complaint. In most cases the evils that existed were preventable.
For instance, more care and attention could have been given to
building and fitting out vessels that would carry animals in
greater comfort. The injuries sustained by travelling animals

could have been reduced if the drovers, employed for the most part
on a casual and part-time basis, were properly instructed, licensed
and supervised so that they carried out their job without inflicting
unnecessary suffering on their charges. However, both these things
would have inevitably cost money to put into practice and this extra
expense at the ports and by the shipping companies would have meant
higher freights. A cause of injury that was not in the power of the
carriers to remedy was the fact that nearly 90 per cent of Irish
cattle in the 1880s carried horns, and serious injuries and suffering resulted from the way the animals gored each other. However
whether the practice of dishorning cattle involved cruelty and
suffering to the animals operated on was then a subject of
controversy. (24) However as the expense of the operation would
fall on the farmer or the dealer it was perhaps for that reason it
was unpopular. Finally a lot of the suffering resulted because the
owners of stock were not prepared to exercise any supervision when
the animals undertook the voyage to England. Usually they were sent
with no attendant, as if they were already so many carcases of meat,
and even when attended it was often by a man who was entirely
incompetent and frequently drunk for the whole of the journey. As
the Board of Agriculture's Chief Travelling Inspector concluded in
his report on this trade in 1889: 'It must always be a difficult
matter for the Government to protect the property of persons who
will take no measures to protect it themselves.' (25)

The treatment the animals received had a most definite effect on
the prices they fetched when they arrived in England. In 1869 it
was estimated that an animal which started its journey from Ireland
worth £15 would be worth £2 or £3 less when it arrived in England.
(26) Twenty years later one of the largest cattle dealers in
Ireland put the loss in value caused by horn injuries along at £$\frac{1}{2}$m.
(27)

In the case of stores the injuries sustained on the journey
merely resulted in lower prices, but their effect on fatstock was
more complicated and not only influenced the prices fetched by
animals, but also dictated the districts where they might be sold.
Most Irish fat cattle found their markets in Manchester or
Liverpool. Up to around 1860 London butchers made the journey to
Liverpool to buy Irish beasts. However, the animals had so
deteriorated during their journey from Ireland that, after a
renewed interest in consequence of the cattle plague regulations in
February 1866, the London butchers gradually gave up purchasing
Irish cattle. At this time the metropolitan demand for high quality
meat excluded the bruised and battered carcases of Irish beasts
from sale in the London shops. Instead these animals found their
market among the less discriminating customers of Manchester and
Liverpool. (28)

The transport of all livestock within Great Britain by the railway companies raised comparatively few protests and was generally
well conducted by the standards of the time. Part of the reason for
this was that the railway companies, unlike the port authorities,
employed staff who were engaged full-time to load and unload livestock at the stations and were trained to do this job in a skilful
and humane manner. The rigours of the railway journey alone for
Scottish and English beasts were not so severe as the sea journey

from Ireland. However the distance travelled by animals did involve some amount of strain and probably a loss of condition, in propor-tion to the journey time, on reaching market. Long rail journeys were certainly more hazardous and demanding for the animals than short ones. The furthest distance any animals were sent within Great Britain was from Aberdeen to London. This is a journey of 515 miles and the cattle were not watered or fed during the 36 hours it took. But many of the cattle sent from Aberdeen had already come some distance to the rail head. Many Aberdeen cattle attending a Monday market at Islington started the journey a week before at the various fairs and cattle markets of Morayshire and Aberdeenshire. There the animals were bought and collected to-gether by the dealers and they arrived in Aberdeen by Thursday. They started on the rail journey by 4 o'clock in the afternoon and reached London at 6 o'clock on Saturday morning. On a journey like this, lasting five or six days, it was comparatively easy for feeding and watering to be overlooked so that the animals reached London in a state of considerable dehydration. The railway companies did not provide food and water mainly, it seems, because it was believed that animals would lie down after drinking and would then be trampled on and injured by the others in the cattle trucks. For this reason they were unsympathetic to any suggestion that the cattle from Scotland should be fed and watered at Newcastle on the east coast route and at Carlisle for the west coast route. The general consensus among those interested in the Aberdeen trade was that where the animals were adequately fed and watered before and after the journey they suffered no great dis-comfort. It was argued that the first requirement was spacious trucks in which the animals would not be crowded. (29) Over-crowding was seen as the greatest cause of injuries to animals travelling by rail.

3   THE DEAD MEAT TRADE

This part of the meat business received an indirect boost after 1865 from the effects of the cattle plague restrictions. The cessation of the live cattle trade from February 1866 and its severe curtail-ment from April of that year until 1867 forced traders to devote greater attention to alternative methods of supplying the great urban markets. This effect was particularly noticeable in London where the grossly inadequate system of dead meat markets groaned and strained under the additional burdens placed on it from the spring of 1866. The conditions around Newgate Market at the height of the cattle plague restrictions strongly resembled pandemonium. Robert Herbert's report on the situation said: (30)

   No additions have been made to the number of meat markets in the
   metropolis; but the City authorities have stopped the traffic
   through Newgate Street till late in the afternoon to enable the
   railway companies' waggons to reach Newgate and Leadenhall. The
   scene of confusion, however, baffles description. Thousands of
   tons of meat remain for many hours in the waggons as the meat
   salesmen have not sufficient room in their shops for the
   arrivals, and the process of unloading can only take place after

the shops have been partly cleared by the purchasers.... There
can be no help for this state of things until after the new dead
meat markets are formed.

Despite these scenes there was apparently no question of the meat
distribution system for the metropolis breaking down during these
months. The ban only applied to bringing in domestic cattle by
rail; sheep and pigs could still be freely carried by the railways
and foreign livestock were still landed in London, but they could
not be moved inland. In fact, a cordon sanitaire was placed around
the city for a brief period with regard to the movement of cattle.
All the same, London still received a supply of live cattle from
Europe and domestic beasts in the Metropolitan Cattle Market were
replaced by foreign stock. The restrictions of February and March
1866 merely underlined the thorough inadequacy of the meat markets.
According to a statement made by Earl Cathcart before a council
meeting of the Royal Agricultural Society, when the whole meat
supply situation during the plague was discussed, by March 1866
Newgate was receiving 10,000,000 lb of meat a week which was said
to be double the quantity sent before the outbreak. (31)

Some high prices for dead meat were experienced at Newgate and
Leadenhall in March and April 1866 but these did not continue for
long, and fell sharply under the pressure of increasing supplies.
The greatest disruption appears to have been in local markets outside London which were not geared to the dead meat trade and where
it was impossible to bring cattle in by water. At one time meat
prices in 1866 were 25 to 30 per cent higher in these places than
they had been the previous year. (32)

Faced with the problem of arranging for the distribution of an
artificially expanded meat supply, all those engaged in the trade
had to adapt their methods to cope with the enlarged traffic. The
railways, in particular, were forced to pay greater attention to the
arrangements for handling carcase meat as there was no alternative
to the domestic beef trade for some weeks, before the restrictions
on the movement of cattle were relaxed in 1866. The congestion at
Newgate caused some of the large London butchers to employ agents
in various parts of the country for the purchase of meat which was
conveyed by the railway companies from the London stations direct
to their shops, so by-passing the wholesale market. The early
relaxation of the measures.was partly because the long distance
carcase trade was always more difficult to conduct in the war
months. The experience gained by handling this increased traffic,
coming from the Continent as well as from Britain, and the revela-
tion of the patently inadequate marketing arrangements in London,
finally persuaded the authorities to undertake a reorganization of
the wholesale meat markets.

The power to build a new market had rested with the City
Corporation since 1860 when they obtained the necessary Act of
Parliament. The complaints about the condition of the Smithfield
site since it was closed to livestock in 1855 had continued una-
bated. There was also some debate as to how suitable it was as a
site for the City's new meat market; it was centrally situated and
would only permit a limited expansion of capacity. In October 1865,
with still nothing done to develop the Smithfield site, the
inhabitants and churchwardens of the parish of St Sepulchre,

Smithfield, driven to desperation by the nuisance suffered for ten years from the derelict market site, petitioned the Home Secretary. Exasperated by years of delay, they urged him to transfer the responsibility for executing the job to the Metropolitan Board of Works. (33) But the lessons of 1866 did not go unheeded and the Corporation of the City of London at last took steps to implement what had long been proposed by numerous parliamentary committees, Royal Commissions and individual persons for over 100 years - the establishment of one central and adequate meat market for London. In 1868 the first section of what became the London Central Markets was opened on part of the site of Smithfield and the market at Newgate was closed soon after.

The new market at Smithfield represented a great improvement over the previous arrangements. It was not very large at just under 3 acres, but this was over five times the extent of the old Newgate site. Access to the new market was made easier by the fact that it was built over the goods station of the Great Western Railway and the underground works of the Metropolitan line. This coincidence was exploited by the architect who was responsible for the design of the new building. Beneath it there was an area of over 5 acres covered with sidings and goods platforms, and also equipped with ample cellarage and store rooms. As a result of existing agreements between the companies, the railway systems north and south of the Thames as well as those serving the northern and eastern counties had the use of these facilities. This meant that trucks of meat could be brought directly under the floor of the market by the companies carrying the largest amounts to London. From there they were easily unloaded and their contents sent up by hydraulic lifts, specially installed for the purpose, to the market area and meat salesmen's shops at ground level. (34) When the new market opened there were eight companies either with direct access to the platforms beneath Smithfield then, or who had entered into agreements to obtain this once the necessary engineering works were finished. These eight carried between them 48,822 tons, or over 80 per cent of the meat sent to London by rail in 1867. (35) The underground rail links relieved the road system around the market of some of the inevitable extra congestion that would have arisen if the expanded dead meat trade had relied solely on surface transport to convey it from the rail termini. The roads were used mainly to take the meat from the market after sale, and the bulk of the incoming traffic was kept off the streets.

Nevertheless it is doubtful whether the site of the new meat market was ever entirely satisfactory for its purpose. (36) Its selection represented a compromise of interests. It was the most acceptable location for the meat traders themselves who were anxious not to be moved from the centre of London to a suburban situation far from their old customers and other business connections. The retention of Smithfield for part of the meat trade went some of the way to pleasing the City interests. It meant that this section of the trade was retained under their control so that, with the ownership of the Metropolitan Cattle Market at Islington in their hands, they continued to derive an income from the London meat trade. But the geographical separation of the livestock and meat markets meant that animals slaughtered at Islington often made the journey to Smithfield as meat before they passed into the hands of the retailer. If the proposals of those reformers in the 1850s who wanted the meat market at Islington, next to the cattle market, had been adopted, this extra journey would have been avoided. In the case of supplies for hotels and eating houses in London this did not represent too large a diversion, but for the meat sold to suburban butchers it was probably inconvenient and certainly inefficient to take it from Islington into the City and out again.

Be this as it may, the market itself was an immediate success and its opening was followed by an important increase in the business done there. In its first year, 1868, the London Central Meat Market had 120,000 tons of meat pass through it and by 1876 it was handling 175,000 tons. (37) In 1875 it was necessary to extend the building to handle extra business and a new section called the Central Poultry and Provision Market was added in that year.

There is evidence of a change in attitude by some of the railway companies towards the dead meat trade. In their evidence before the parliamentary committee on the transit of animals in 1869 some of the companies appear to have favoured the carriage of meat rather than livestock. This view was taken by Seymour Clark, the general manager of the Great Northern. He reported that his firm was loading meat at practically all of the 197 stations along its lines. This company also preferred the meat trade, notwithstanding the extra carriage and handling of goods. It was argued that the company could get return cargoes for the carriages carrying meat, whereas cattle trucks were sent back empty from London to the stations where they had started. But the railway companies were not unanimously in favour of the meat trade. The goods manager of the Great Eastern seemed to prefer the livestock trade. This may have been because it served an area where there was less possibility of conducting an extensive rail-borne meat trade. Certainly the Great Eastern did a larger trade in livestock and carried less meat than did the Great Northern. Between 1861 and 1867 it carried 9 million cattle, sheep and pigs while the Great Northern only transported two-thirds of that number. On the other hand, the Great Northern carried 22,065 tons of meat to London in 1867 but the Great Eastern took only 11,081 tons. (38) But even the Great Eastern, which had no direct rail link with Smithfield, found the benefit of the new market in the quicker turn-round times for the road vans carrying meat from its stations to the market. (39)

The railway companies' willingness to encourage a further development of the long distance carriage of carcase meat meant that both they and the meat traders were prepared to improve handling arrangements and eliminate bottlenecks to make the trade a satisfactory one. Special care was required when sending meat by rail. Besides beef a good deal of lamb was despatched by train to London. Of the two meats lamb was the most perishable but it was possible to send it to arrive in better condition than beef. Beef suffered from a worse deterioration on the railway journey than lamb because of the greater weight of the pieces. This was because in the 1860s the railways mostly carried meat in hampers. It was possible to pack ten to fifteen sheep or lambs into a hamper and they would not arrive much the worse in London. But it was a different matter to pack four quarters of beef, weighing 10 to 15

stones each, into a hamper. The parcel was heavier than the lamb,
and it was difficult for the railwaymen to move around and lift.
In consequence of its unwieldiness it was subject to much knocking
around and bruising on the journey. In fact, beef travelled very
badly when cut into quarters and packed in hampers. A much better
result was obtained when whole sides were sent in properly designed
trucks with the meat suspended on hooks from the roofs. (40)

In addition to being certain it would arrive in good condition,
any person who sent meat by rail to a large market also had to be
confident that the system was capable of getting the product to the
customer with no delay. Whatever its drawbacks may have been, the
chief advantage of the fatstock trade with London was that the sale
of animals could be delayed for a few days in hope of a more
favourable market. At the Metropolitan Cattle Market two market
days were held each week, Monday and Thursday, and sellers could
hold stock over, keeping them at the lairage sheds on the site at
Islington until the next market day. When they sent live animals,
farmers and livestock dealers were aware that they did not put
themselves entirely in the hands of the butchers and dealers of the
town where they were to be sold. Dead meat, on the other hand, had
to find an immediate sale in the place to which it was consigned.
Its keeping qualities were no more than a further 24 hours once it
reached there, consequently, if the market was overdone with
supplies, the sellers were forced to take what price they could get.
One is struck by the relatively unorganized state of the distribution network for meat and animals before the 1880s. Mr James
Bonser, a London commission meat salesman accustomed to receiving
meat from Scotland, stated that he rarely knew before it arrived
what was being sent to him. Only occasionally he would receive
advice of a consignment the day before it arrived. Or did he have
any advice from his customers - butchers in the West End and other
parts of London - as to what they required. His firm neither
received any regular notice of what was coming nor informed its
suppliers of its future needs. (41) This practice was not unusual
and did not seem to present any particular problems. After the new
market opened the London salesmen had their own particular stalls
at Smithfield and all consignments sent by rail were to named
individuals, so delivery was a simple matter. Also the market
served an estimated population of 3,125,000 in 1865 rising to
4,000,000 by the second half of the 1880s. As this remained the
largest single market in the kingdom it was more difficult to over-
stock than any of the provincial cities. It was for this reason
that the bulk of the long distance trade remained concentrated on
the London market.

As a consequence of the changes in the 1870s, there was a
further decline in the importance of livestock as a source of
London's total meat supply. With the growth of the dead meat
traffic into London many butchers who had formerly slaughtered their
own livestock gradually abandoned the practice. In 1877 there were
5,000 butchers in London but there were only about 1,100 slaughterhouses, so that four out of every five butchers purchased dead
meat. There were scores of small butchers around Smithfield each
with private slaughterhouses that had been unused for years. Some
time after 1870 dead meat was in plentiful supply to the London

markets even in hot weather. The quantity from Scotland reached 60
to 70 tons a day throughout the summer months. Also Norfolk, which
before the cattle plague had only exported livestock, was sharing
its resources between animal traffic and the meat trade by the
1870s. One prominent livestock dealer who had been forced to
slaughter stock for the London market in 1866 maintained this trade
after the plague restrictions had been removed. Each week he killed
fifty cattle for the metropolitan trade in a converted railway shed
just outside Norwich. He got over the problem of a lack of local
industries to take the by-products by sending the whole carcase to
London and not just the meat. Although he grumbled about the
expense involved he was still able to maintain the trade on an all-
the-year-round basis at a profit. As this supply became more
regular butchers were able to guarantee that they could go to the
dead meat market and buy a suitable stock for the day's trade. In
the past, when the supply was irregular, the butcher had no choice
but to purchase live and slaughter for himself. (42)

Less meat was sent to provincial towns than to London and it
seems highly likely that they received a greater proportion of
home-produced meat supplies on the hoof than did the metropolis.
The precise extent of this difference is not clear, but it is
likely that the smaller size of provincial towns was a factor
limiting the trade. Also railway communication was easiest to and
from London as all main lines emanated from there, and this may
have meant it was more difficult to send meat across the country.
The long distance meat trade was geared so that a number of cities
like Aberdeen, Edinburgh, Glasgow, Leeds, Liverpool and Hull acted
as processing centres where live animals were received and
slaughtered and their carcases sent on to London. The only town
where the meat trade was organized in any way like that of London
was in Manchester. Within the meat distribution system of London
and Manchester carcase butchers held a position not repeated elsewhere. (43) In other parts of the British Isles the typical retail
unit was run by the small man who bought the animals and slaughtered
them himself. It seems likely that this is the reason why the
National Federation had its genesis in Lancashire and Yorkshire and
not in the metropolis. Provincial butchers ran their businesses on
more traditional lines than in London, and so had more to lose if
official regulations, as for example in the matter of private
slaughterhouses, altered the whole conduct of the trade.

CHAPTER 7

IMPORTS FROM EUROPE AND NORTH AMERICA, 1865-89

In the twenty-five years after 1864 there was a radical alteration
to the import trade in meat and livestock into the United Kingdom.
The meat trade was transformed by the application of technology to
the problems of transporting fresh meat over long distances. The
solution of these problems by the application of chilling, freezing
and cold storage techniques effectively enlarged the area from which
the United Kingdom drew its supplies of meat. In addition this
partially solved the problem of increasing the per capita meat
consumption of the United Kingdom, which was faced with a domestic
agricultural sector that was unable to raise output as fast as the
growth of population. Also the quality of these products was
superior to any previous imports of dead meat, all of which suffered
from varying degrees of unpopularity with consumers in the 1850s and
1860s. Refrigerated meat was nutritionally superior to the various
forms of salted or otherwise preserved meat that was imported
earlier. Therefore chilled and frozen meat helped to maintain and
increase the standard of diet in Britain by adding to the quantity,
quality and palatability of available protein. In these years the
imports of livestock, though increasing absolutely, suffered a
relative decline in the face of increasing imports of fresh meat.
Also the livestock trade was made subject to a greater degree of
government supervision and control which effectively reduced the
number of countries from which the United Kingdom could import
animals for food. The first occasion of this control followed the
traumatic experience of the cattle plague brought into this country
by a cargo of infected cattle carried from the port of Revel and
landed at Hull in the early summer of 1865. Thereafter British
governments, remembering the tremendous losses of farm stock, were
able to overcome their previous reluctance to interfere with this
branch of food imports and provide this measure of protection for
livestock farmers. This action was also made easier after the 1870s
when imports of refrigerated meat provided a viable alternative to
livestock imports and so restrictions on the latter did not provoke
earlier anxieties that they would be accompanied by an inevitable
rise in the cost of living.

1   GOVERNMENT CONTROL OF LIVESTOCK IMPORTS

Until 1848 there were no measures to inspect imported animals and
destroy those suffering from disease. In that year, after the
importation of sheep-pox among a cargo of German animals, an Act
was passed giving such powers to the port authorities. In 1854
attention was drawn to the spread of cattle plague from Russia into
Poland. In enquiries being made it was learned that the disease
had been spread by the movement of Russian troops in the Crimean
War. Apparently the armies kept herds of cattle to supply them with
meat and the disease was present in the Crimea. By 1856 this
disease had spread from Poland through Prussia and Mecklenberg to
Holstein, a district from which the English market was supplied with
cattle.
   This fact caused some anxiety to the Foreign Office. It was
feared that a serious epidemic might infiltrate the English market
with imported cattle. The Professor of the Royal Veterinary
College, J.B. Simmonds, was sent to Germany to investigate the
disease. He did not express any great anxiety on this account as
he believed that the measures taken on the Continent were sufficient
to stamp it out. (1) The Gamgees, however, did not share Simmonds's
complacency over the likelihood of its introduction into England.
Their 1857 pamphlets were in a large measure directed towards
publicizing the need for greater care and vigilance at British ports
receiving European cattle. They stressed the fact that it was not
enough to look for animals with obvious signs of disease. They were
well aware that cattle plague had an incubative stage of several
days' duration during which the animals would appear perfectly fit
but were also capable of infecting others. This point was of
particular importance as the journey time from the north German
ports of about 48 hours was considerably less than the incubation
period for livestock diseases. As an additional safeguard against
this they wanted to prevent cattle and sheep being landed unless the
shippers could produce a clean bill of health in the form of a
certificate from the British consul in the port of export, to the
effect that no contagious animal diseases were present in that
neighbourhood. (2) Unfortunately no significant action was taken
by the British authorities to tighten up the regulations regarding
the import of animals before 1865.
   This was an unfortunate omission as the mechanics of meat distribution between 1850 and 1864 made the transfer of disease from
imported animals to the domestic herd an extreme likelihood. The
majority of the livestock from Europe were landed in London. All
livestock sold publicly in London, whether domestic or foreign in
origin, went to the same market - Smithfield before 1855 and after
that date to the Metropolitan Cattle Market, Islington. At the
Islington market in the early 1860s there were no special arrangements to keep domestic cattle and foreign animals separate. Hence
the spread of infection from one pen of foreign animals to domestic
beasts was an easy matter. Not all cattle sold at this market were
slaughtered in London. It was the custom for dealers and butchers
from other districts to come to London, and purchase animals there,
which they sent home by rail. On the way to these destinations they
were a source of infection to other animals they might encounter at

railway yards and sidings. They would also infect the railway
trucks which might be used later to carry 'clean' stock. When they
reached their final markets they were again a possible source of
infection to farm animals in those neighbourhoods.

The first outbreak of cattle plague in Britain in the nineteenth
century (3) followed the arrival of the S.S. Tonning which docked
at Hull on 29 May 1965, landing a cargo of oxen and sheep from the
Baltic port of Revel. It seems that the animals on board had been
in contact with beasts suffering from rinderpest before they
embarked. The animals were shipped by two dealers - an Englishman,
James Burchell, and a German, John Honck. Burchell had actually
made the deal and from his own accounts had been put under some
pressure by the Russian authorities in Revel to buy some visibly
diseased cattle. These animals were not loaded on board, but as
they had been allowed to mix with the rest of the consignment prior
to embarkation the damage had been done. Burchell was anxious on
this account and his partner, John Honck, made special arrangements
for the cattle to be landed at Hull because he did not consider the
port authorities were very strict about inspecting animals that
landed there. Thereafter the animals became part of the domestic
cattle traffic of Britain as foreign animals could be moved inland
at that date without being subject to any sort of control. It was
symptomatic of the general complexity of the livestock trade at that
time that the whole cargo landed at Hull was split up and sent to a
number of towns in England. It is certainly known that cattle from
this consignment were sold in Wakefield, Manchester and London. (4)
However, it is not known if these were the last places where these
animals were sold before they were slaughtered as it would have been
quite possible for them to go to other markets where they could have
had contact with more cattle. As it was, the disease appears to
have been confined to London and it was only after the critical outbreak there that it was carried to other parts of the United Kingdom
by the movement of livestock out of the capital.

It was first conclusively diagnosed as rinderpest by John Gamgee
on 29 or 30 July, but reports that cattle had been dying in the
metropolis from an unknown cause had been circulating since the end
of June. Once the correct diagnosis was made and the disorder
recognized for what it was the Privy Council, which was the only
institution with powers over animal health on a national scale,
issued a series of orders in council designed to prevent the spread
of the infection. However, by this time, the action was too late.
There is evidence that infected cattle had been in the metropolitan
market on 14 June, and by 24 July there were in the whole country
eighty-two centres of infection when the Privy Council first acted
to stop the spread of the then unidentified pestilence. The early
controls of the Privy Council did not have much direct effect upon
the foreign cattle trade since they were intended to prevent the
infection from spreading within the United Kingdom, not at stopping
fresh imports of the malady. Even when the government appointed
Royal Commission on the subject had its first sitting between 9 and
20 October 1865 and was establishing the means by which the disease
had entered the country, no attempt was made to interfere with the
imports of European animals for food.

However, the seriousness of the disease soon became apparent with

the ease by which fresh areas of the country were affected and the
increasing losses suffered by town dairymen and country cattle
farmers alike. Early in 1866 the scale of financial losses persuaded the nation to accept the need for more comprehensive measures
and for the first time government was induced to establish effective
control over the movement of foreign livestock into and within the
United Kingdom. This was done under the Cattle Diseases Prevention
Act of 20 February 1866, which provided that foreign animals were
only to be landed at certain ports and they were not allowed to be
moved inland alive. However, exceptions were made later in the case
of London and cattle were allowed to be moved along defined routes
from the Port of London, Harwich and Southampton into the
metropolis. In June 1867 an order was passed providing for the
detention of foreign cattle at the landing place for 12 hours so
that they could be inspected for disease before they were moved
inland. A further order in October 1867, after the disease had been
controlled, restricted the number of ports where foreign cattle
could be landed. Prior to 1868 all measures affecting imports of
livestock were aimed to control cattle plague. In July 1868
attention was turned to sheep diseases. Because of the prevalence
of sheep-pox in Europe imports of sheep from Hamburg and from
Holstein were only allowed for almost immediate slaughter on
landing.

It was at last realized by this time that imports of livestock
carried with them the risk of introducing disease among British
animals. A constant debate took place upon the desirability of
banning these imports in order to protect the national herd. On one
side the farmers and some veterinarians argued for prohibition.
Ranged against them were the free traders and the proponents of
cheap food for the masses. Although the percentage of foreign meat
consumed in Britain in the 1860s and 1870s was not large, it was
argued that any interference with the trade would have a material
effect on prices. This view was taken by all parliamentary
committees called to investigate aspects of the livestock trade
between 1866 and 1877. Typical of this attitude was a statement
made in 1869: (5)

that any measure tending to place the foreigner in the smallest
degree at a disadvantage in our markets, as compared with the
home producer would be attended by a gradual but certain diminution of our supply of animals from abroad.

This attitude may have had a particularly strong appeal to
committees sitting in London, hearing evidence from traders and
persons based in London, as that city was dependent on imported
supplies to a greater extent than the national average. As over
half the imports of meat between 1867 and 1869 were represented by
live animals (6) it was considered impractical to enforce a general
bar on the imports of livestock from Europe. The compromise solution that was adopted after 1869 was strict control over the
conditions under which animals were allowed to be imported from what
were named 'scheduled countries'. The scheduled countries were
those where particular diseases were known to be endemic or where
there had been a recent outbreak of disease. Animals were only
allowed into Britain from these places for slaughter at the place of
debarkation within ten days of landing. They were not allowed to

be imported as stores for fattening or even be sent to inland
markets for slaughter. In this way, plus more stringent inspections at the ports and strict quarrantine measures, it was hoped
that the danger of cross-infection of domestic animals would be
minimized.

A complete prohibition on imports of livestock from particular
parts of Europe was imposed for limited periods. This was during
the reported duration of an outbreak of disease. It was lifted as
soon as the local representative of the British government sent
word that the outbreak had been eliminated. For instance, following
the 1865 outbreak of cattle plague the importation of livestock
from certain districts in Holland was prohibited during parts of
1866. Measures such as these were imposed with extreme reluctance.
There is also evidence that they were being lifted for certain parts
of Holland at a time when disease was still pretty general. (7) The
British government still aimed to have as few restrictions as
possible on the free movement of livestock from Europe to Britain.

Greater control over the importation of livestock first came in
1869 under the Contagious Diseases (Animals) Act. This measure
broadened the definition of contagious diseases to include for the
first time pleuro-pneumonia and foot-and-mouth disease. For the
first time specific countries were enumerated as scheduled
countries. Also a strict definition of the geographical boundaries
of the ports where animals from the scheduled countries were allowed
to land was given. In the years following, most European countries
from whence livestock were imported were placed on the schedule.
This was not always done permanently. After an area had been
reported free of a disease livestock from its ports would once again
be admitted into the United Kingdom free of any restrictions. There
were further outbreaks of cattle plague in Europe in 1869, 1872 and
1877. In 1872 and 1877 diseased animals were once again brought
into the country and on both occasions the disease spread inland but
was stopped by effective controls. It was generally felt by
veterinarians that the provisions for isolating imported animals at
the ports were unsatisfactory. Cattle plague was the most contagious animal disease and it was possible for that to be spread
inland by dung, hides or offal from diseased animals. At times the
Privy Council struck certain ports off the list of places allowed to
receive animals from the scheduled countries until the handling
arrangements at these places had been improved.

The system of slaughtering at the ports was strongly opposed by
all persons engaged in the livestock trade. Both foreign importers
and British salesmen argued that measures interfering with the free
transit of livestock would drive these animals to other markets in
Europe, reduce the home supply of meat and raise prices unduly.
By 1877 the rules regarding livestock imports were extremely
confused and liable to sudden change. Animals from non-scheduled
countries could land at any port, those from scheduled countries
only at certain named ports. If disease was reported in a country
hitherto unscheduled it was liable to be placed on the list of
scheduled countries immediately by an order in council. Also
certain kinds of livestock from a particular country might be
scheduled and other livestock from the same country be admitted
freely. It was argued that this uncertainty was itself a disturbing

factor for the trade. If an unscheduled cargo of animals was found
on inspection at the port of debarkation to contain disease they
had to be re-shipped and taken to another port for immediate
slaughter. This was said to render the exporter uncertain of his
market, not knowing where he might have to land his animals or the
conditions under which they would be offered for sale. These
things could have a material effect upon profits. As scheduled
animals had to be slaughtered and sold within ten days of landing,
if markets were already over-stocked this reduced the time the
animals would be held before prices recovered.

The largest market for scheduled animals was the Foreign Cattle
Market at Deptford in London. Prior to any restrictions all
foreign animals sold in London went to the Metropolitan Cattle
Market at Islington. The Deptford Market was by the Thames, very
close to where the cattle boats were unloaded. It was provided by
the Corporation of the City of London as a foreign animals' wharf
under the 1869 Contagious Diseases (Animals) Act, for the reception,
sale and slaughter of animals from where disease was known to
exist. This place was first opened to the public in December 1871.
These restrictions were disliked by exporters bringing livestock
from scheduled countries. They complained that when some countries
in Europe were scheduled and others were not, the animals from the
scheduled countries were placed in a less competitive position vis-
a-vis unscheduled animals. The Foreign Cattle Market at Deptford
was relatively small in the 1870s and only stocked with animals
from a limited number of countries. These arrivals tended to be
irregular and so the market only attracted a limited number of
buyers. This contrasted unfavourably with the market situation at
Islington where the livestock from the unscheduled countries were
sold alongside home-fed animals. This was a much larger market
with a wider selection of animals; it therefore attracted a greater
number of buyers. Prices at Islington were also higher. One
farmer, from Schleswig Holstein, calculated that he lost from 35s.
to £2 a head on cattle and 5s. a head on sheep if he had to sell
them at Deptford rather than at Islington. (8)

The years when the list of scheduled countries was increased saw
a rise in the number of animals sold at the Foreign Cattle Market
and a fall in the number of foreign animals sold at Islington.
This effect was evident between 1872 and 1877. In both years fear
of importing cattle plague from Europe led the Privy Council to
increase restrictions on imports. In both years increased numbers
passed through Deptford. In the intervening years, when restrictions were relaxed, the trade at Deptford declined and the
proportion of foreign animals exposed for sale at the Metropolitan
Cattle Market increased (see Table 7.1). This effect was not
apparent in the 1880s as by then scheduling was applied to the
majority of livestock imports.

The import of European cattle and sheep was conditioned by the
ease of distribution in this country, access to alternative markets
in Europe and the price differential between British and European
markets. In the 1877 outbreak of cattle plague in Germany, all
cattle imports from that country were stopped and were never
permitted to be resumed. Imports of sheep, however, were not as it
was believed they carried less risk of disease than cattle. They

TABLE 7.1   Cattle and sheep at the Foreign Cattle Market, Deptford, and percentage of foreign cattle and sheep sold at the Metropolitan Cattle Market, Islington, 1871-80

	Cattle		Sheep	
Year	No. at Foreign Cattle Market, Deptford	% of foreign animals at Islington	No. at Foreign Cattle Market, Deptford	% of foreign animals at Islington
1871		45.5		38.9
1872	38,426(a)	28.3	122,601(a)	41.5
1873	7,090	38.4	2,339	47.5
1874	7,175	38.9	114	39.4
1875	29,225	42.0	86,896	43.3
1876	21,860	41.1	38,714	47.4
1877	67,817	20.6	697,714	7.7
1878	60,675	27.6	699,911	7.1
1879	81,445	18.3	662,197	9.7
1880	120,196	21.5	658,899	9.0

Source: 'Agricultural Statistics', 1887, Table XXVI.
(a) First year open.

were admitted to Britain subject to the usual provision of slaughter at the port of debarkation. Continental regulations about the passage of animals over national frontiers were much more strict. As soon as cattle plague appeared in Germany the French closed their frontiers to both cattle and sheep. Deprived of the alternative market of Paris the German sheep continued to come to London, in spite of the restrictions of having to be killed at Deptford. Some time later in 1877 the French government opened their frontiers once more for German sheep and this resulted in a diminution of the supply to Deptford. The animals were diverted from London to Paris where they fetched a higher price. (9)

The failure of the numbers of animals passing through Deptford to fall in 1878 as it did in 1873 can be explained by the operation of the Contagious Diseases (Animals) Act of 1878. This Act said that animals were to be landed only at foreign animals wharfs for immediate slaughter, unless the central authority was satisfied that there was no danger of disease from the country concerned. Under this Act the 'scheduled countries' became the norm and free entry of animals was the exception. The controls over livestock imports under this Act up to the end of 1889 are summarized in Table 7.2. The Privy Council still retained the power to exclude absolutely animals from any country if it was believed that imports from these carried the risk of introducing disease. Prohibition was a piece-meal measure and was applied to each country as and when circum- stances merited. In the 1880s control became far stricter than it had ever been in the 1870s, as it was eventually realized that with

free entry there was an ever present danger of importing animal
disease.   Prior to 1878 free entry was the norm and restricted entry
the chief means of control.   After that date, under the 1878
Contagious Diseases (Animals) Act, restricted entry became the norm
and absolute prohibition on entry the chief safeguard whenever
disease was present in other countries exporting livestock to
Britain.

TABLE 7.2 Summary of restrictions on livestock imports to
31 December 1889

Prior to 1 January 1879 when the Contagious Diseases (Animals) Act
of 1878 came into force the principle of free importation from all
countries was the general rule.   However, when disease was confirmed
abroad or detected in a foreign cargo the Privy Council had the
power to prohibit or order the slaughter at the landing places of
all foreign animals imported from where diseases existed.   After
1865 the disease causing most concern was cattle plague, but under
the Contagious Diseases (Animals) Act of 1869 pleuro-pneumonia,
sheep-pox, foot-and-mouth disease, sheep-scab, glanders and any
other disease the Privy Council might specify were added to the
list.

AMERICA

Argentina	From 1 January 1879 importation allowed for slaughter only.
Canada	From 1 January 1879 importation free after inspection.
USA	From 1 January 1879 importation free after inspection. From 3 March 1879 cattle allowed for slaughter only. From 16 May 1879 swine allowed for slaughter only. From 23 May 1879 sheep allowed for slaughter only.

EUROPE

Belgium	Prior to 1879 cattle prohibited, sheep and swine allowed for slaughter only. From 12 May 1888 all stock prohibited.
Denmark	From 1 January 1879 importation free after inspection. From 22 September 1882 swine allowed for slaughter only.
France	From 1 January 1879 importation allowed for slaughter only. From 6 April 1883 all stock prohibited.
Germany	Prior to 1879 cattle prohibited; sheep and swine allowed for slaughter only. From 23 March 1889 all stock prohibited.

Holland	From 1 January 1879 importation allowed for slaughter only. From 1 September 1889 cattle and sheep (not swine) free after inspection.
Iceland	From 1 January 1879 importation free after inspection.
Norway	From 1 January 1879 importation free after inspection. From 18 October 1886 all stock prohibited. From 24 November 1886 importation free after inspection.
Schleswig Holstein	Cattle were allowed for slaughter only from time to time.
Spain and Portugal	From 1 January 1879 importation free after inspection. From 19 June 1881 importation allowed for slaughter only.
Sweden	From 1 January 1879 importation free after inspection. From 22 February 1882 swine allowed for slaughter only.

Source: 'Departmental Committee on Combinations in the Meat Trade', P.P., 1909, XV, Appendix IV, p.286.

2   THE TRANSATLANTIC CATTLE TRADE

As an accompaniment to the government's controls over livestock imports, though not necessarily because of them, there was a decline in the relative importance of European livestock imports. Europe's place in this trade was taken by North America and in the 1870s and 1880s an increasing volume of cattle were brought across the Atlantic from both US and Canadian ports, though chiefly from the former. In 1865-9 nearly all cattle, sheep and swine imported into the United Kingdom came from Europe. The first experiments in sending livestock across the Atlantic were made in 1868 when a few cattle were sent from the USA to Glasgow and London by Nelson Morris. (10) However, the trade was not an immediate success in the way the chilled beef trade was and the next consignment was not sent for another five years. In 1873 and 1874 further small experimental cargoes of cattle were sent from the USA and Canada and in 1875 and 1876 the numbers sent from Canada rose to 1,212 and 2,655 respectively, while the US trade stayed at a few hundred. However, in 1877 the USA was the chief exporter and it retained this leading position right until the end of the North American livestock trade just before the First World War. In addition to cattle some sheep were sent, mainly from Canada after 1875. However, this trade was never very important and the majority of sheep and lambs imported into the United Kingdom continued to originate from Europe. At times transatlantic exports of live pigs were tried but this trade never acquired a position of economic significance. In fact the whole trade in live pigs was a very small part of the total international livestock trade as it was far more convenient to transport these animals in the form of bacon and ham. With regard to value the cattle trade was by far the most important section of the whole livestock trade. In 1880 the total value of livestock imported from all countries was £10.24 million and of this £7.79 million was accounted for by cattle. Sheep and lambs were valued at £2.27 million and pigs were only worth £0.18 million. Therefore it is not surprising that most discussions of the international livestock trade by contemporaries saw the fortunes of the whole business largely in terms of what affected the size of the cattle trade.

The development of both the trade in chilled beef and live cattle from North America might at first seem inconsistent. A number of persons expected and some, like the groups who objected to the transport of livestock on the grounds of its cruelty to animals, hoped that the trans-oceanic livestock trade would be extinguished by the increasing volume of refrigerated meat carried. In its early years there were grounds on which the transatlantic cattle trade justified many of the complaints made against it on humanitarian grounds. In the years when cargoes were experimental, cattle were carried on board the ships in improvised and rather unsatisfactory accommodation, often housed in temporary sheds erected on the deck. (11) The voice of the objectors which continued as long as the trade itself, was an intermittent thing, occasionally excited by newspaper reports of accidents or extremely large fatalaties among animal cargoes, due either to bad weather or negligence. But as this trade grew, many of the humanitarians' arguments tended to lose their force. This was mainly as a consequence of the imposition of government regulations, on both sides of the Atlantic, governing minimum standards of accommodation and attendance for the animals on the voyage, which met many of the humanitarians' criticisms. However, there is no doubt that in the early years of the trade protests were very often fully justified. The cattle were carried in a variety of vessels: some were regular liners built expressly for the purpose; others were vessels belonging to regular lines which had been modified specifically to carry cattle; other ships used were the occasional vessels chartered specially by a line for the trade and, finally, there were the casual tramp ships. (12) In these last two classes of vessel the accommodation was of a temporary nature, and it was in these that the worst conditions were found. Properly fitted cattle boats carried the animals in better conditions and, consequently, had extremely low mortality rates. But in the early years of the trade conditions were very bad, with large numbers of animals crowded below decks with neither adequate space, nor attendance, a situation which caused the animals to suffer badly in rough weather. Sometimes they were carried on deck in a temporary shelter which, though rather better ventilated, was always in danger of being washed overboard in heavy seas, taking the animals with it. (13) But in response to public misgivings and government enquiries and inspection, the shippers were forced to improve such conditions. Also, from their point of view, with insurance and freight costs to be paid, it was ultimately in their best interests that the cattle arrived in Liverpool or London in a

fresh condition with unbruised flesh and having lost as little
weight as possible on the voyage.

The economic argument was also one which was used against this
branch of the cattle trade, hopefully as a pointer to its extinction. The reasoning behind this argument can be summarized as
follows. In 1877 it was estimated that it cost £7 to ship a live
animal from New York plus another 30s. attendance, etc., on the
voyage, or in all it cost approximately £8 10s. to bring a live
bullock to England. The cost of a dead animal, brought as chilled
beef, was only 30s. (14) In addition all the chilled meat could be
sold whereas a bullock contained approximately 45 per cent offal.
Hence the argument was that the low cost of transporting the cattle
dead would soon put an end to the live cattle trade. However, cost
was not the only consideration as the selling price per pound in
England of chilled meat and beef obtained from a bullock brought
here live was strongly in favour of the latter and enough to
compensate the importer for the extra cost of carriage and leave him
with a profit. Also live animals did not present the problem of
finding an immediate sale which often faced the early importer of
chilled beef. For instance, the ports chosen to land US cattle had
large populations to absorb this meat, very often without the need
for importers to search for markets elsewhere. As the meat was
very close in quality to home-fed beef the trader did not have to
encounter the same consumer prejudice that he found against the
chilled article. Although the first cargo in 1868 was sent to
Glasgow, London and Liverpool soon became the chief centres for
their reception, because these ports were already well equipped to
handle large numbers of European and Irish cattle, respectively, as
well as being adjacent to the south eastern and north western
centres of population which were ready markets for the beef.

Although the trade in cattle and other livestock between the
Continent and Great Britain had been subjected to increasing
restrictions imposed to control disease, the cattle trade with
North America was left free of restrictions because there was less
evidence of disease on that side of the Atlantic. This situation
was changed after the discovery of pleuro-pneumonia among a cargo of
cattle from the USA. As a result of this the Privy Council used the
1878 Contagious Diseases (Animals) Act for ordering the compulsory
slaughter of cattle from the USA at the port of debarkation within
ten days of their landing. This meant that the animals had to
remain at the special foreign animals wharfs established by the Act
under strict conditions of quarantine until they were sold, and then
they had to be slaughtered at the wharfs before their buyers were
allowed to remove the carcases. All this required even more costly
arrangements at the ports than the natural expansion of the trade,
under conditions of completely free entry, would have demanded.

At London the particular facilities for the reception of US
cattle already existed at Deptford, but in Liverpool, which had
only received Irish cattle before, fresh premises had to be provided. The first foreign animals' wharf built under the 1878 Act was
at Birkenhead. Here the extension of the landing premises such as
wharfs, lairages, etc., to handle the reception of the cattle were
put in hand even before the restrictions of the Act were enforced.
The preparation of a wharf was begun at Wallasey in November 1878,

and after the new restrictions were introduced from 1 January 1879
four lairage sheds, holding 1,000 head of cattle, and a slaughterhouse were added by March. But even these were insufficient to
handle the numbers landing, so two more sheds and three meat stores
were added by the end of the summer. Similar buildings were later
erected further along the Mersey at Woodside and these had the extra
advantage of a refrigerated cold store, added in 1882, capable of
holding 500 sides of beef. This last item was a gain both to
consignors and buyers and, from the point of view of hygiene, to
the consumer as well, especially during the summer months when a
succession of cattle ships arrived whose cargoes had to be
slaughtered quickly and, like the chilled beef, required an almost
immediate sale. To improve the efficiency of distribution, both at
Wallasey and at Woodside, the railway lines were extended into the
area of the foreign animals wharfs, terminating beside the store
sheds so that the trucks could be easily loaded with the sides of
beef. Also at Birkenhead, at the Alfred Dock, a third series of
buildings was erected intended for cattle coming from uninfected
countries (in the main Canada), not requiring quarantine and
slaughter. The total cost of these three installations was
estimated at between £40,000 and £45,000 over a period of five
years. (15)

Although the expansion of cattle imports from North America was
important, the requirement for their compulsory slaughter had more
far-reaching implications. Certainly it reduced the advantage which
the importers of live cattle had over those dealing with chilled
beef. As the animals had to be slaughtered within the stipulated
time, these dealers were in danger of running into similar problems
of over-stocked markets which beset the chilled beef importers.
Under these circumstances, the only really effective remedy was to
extend the cold storage accommodation to cater for this product as
well. But even with some cold storage facilities at the ports to
take care of the carcases (and in these early years it was still far
from adequate) there was now less justification for bringing in live
animals, and even though this trade continued to grow, and remained
important for thirty years after the passing of the 1878 Act, the
trade in chilled beef had a higher rate of growth and assumed
greater importance.

Although US cattle suffered the distributional inconvenience of
enforced slaughter at the ports, Canadian cattle could be landed and
sent inland alive before 1893. This led to the growth of a small
trade in store animals which was useful to farmers in parts of
Scotland and in Norfolk who would fatten these animals for a while
before selling them for consumption. However, as with European
cattle, the trade in imported stores never became numerically very
important. Nor is there any evidence that easier conditions under
which the import of Canadian cattle was permitted ever led to the
expansion of this trade at the expense of the USA. In 1878 imports
from North America comprised 68,903 cattle from the USA and 17,955
from Canada. By 1889 the US number had risen by 427 per cent to
294,391 and Canadian imports by 471 per cent to 84,588.

In many respects the characteristics of the trade in US cattle
differed from the European livestock business. As a rule,
provincial buyers did not attend the Deptford market to purchase US

cattle. All meat from the animals slaughtered at Deptford that found its way to Midlands and Northern markets passed through the hands of London butchers. Almost all the buyers attending Deptford in the early twentieth century had holdings at the London Central Markets, Smithfield. (16) In the 1870s it had been the custom for provincial dealers to buy foreign animals in the metropolis and to send them to their home towns by rail. Even though they had a preference for live animals, the presence of restrictions under the 1869 Contagious Diseases (Animals) Act did not deter them from this practice. European sheep, considerably lighter, and therefore cheaper than British animals, were consumed in Manchester, Birmingham, West Bromwich and Wales. During times when restrictions on the free movement of European livestock were in force, butchers and dealers from Manchester, Birmingham and Merthyr Tydfil still bought foreign sheep at Deptford, had them slaughtered there and their carcases sent by rail to these places. (17) On the other hand, US cattle were heavy enough and of high enough quality to find a ready sale within the markets of the metropolis in direct competition with meat from home-fed beasts.

In the 1870s there were a number of firms exporting US cattle to England and there were a number of firms in the European livestock trade. The personnel engaged in the two trades were entirely separate. The quality of US cattle was far superior to European and the two types of meat do not appear to have been directly competitive. US beasts were from stock improved by imports of British pedigree animals. Most European cattle were great ungainly bullocks with almost as much bone as meat. (18) Therefore the US imports competed directly with home-fed beef rather than European animals.

3   CHANGES IN EUROPEAN LIVESTOCK IMPORTS

In 1869 the organization of the European livestock imports was largely in British hands. The majority of ships carrying on the trade from both the Port of London and the outports were also British owned. The gross tonnage of ships of one large company involved in the trade with Europe, the St Petersburg Steam Ship Company, varied from 406 tons to 788, and the numbers of stock they could carry ranged from 200 oxen and 100 sheep for the smallest to 600 oxen and 300 sheep on the largest vessel. This company had a total of twelve steamers carrying animals between Holland, Portugal and France. Probably the average vessel regularly engaged in the livestock trade carried about 400 cattle on each voyage. This figure was subject to some variation and depended on how closely the animals were penned on board. It also depended on the sise of the stock and whether they were longhorn or shorthorn varieties. Thus the owner of the St Petersburg Steam Ship Company reckoned that one of his vessels of 780 tons gross would carry more than 500 Dutch cattle but not more than 400 of the longer German cattle or 400 Spanish (longhorn) beasts. The journey time also varied. The shortest voyage was from London to Holland which took about one day and the longest was from Oporto to London which took about four days normally. (19)

A great deal of uncertainty surrounded the trade in European
cattle and other livestock exported to the United Kingdom. In many
cases the precise country of origin of the animals was not known,
nor was it possible to discover this fact. For the most part they
were sent to England by foreign dealers resident in German towns
and consigned to salesmen in this country and sold by them on
commission. In 1866 the bulk of the cattle imported left for
Britain from the ports of Hamburg and Rotterdam. But these towns
were the terminal stations of a great network of main German railway lines and branch lines which ran into Hungary, Poland and
Gallicia and which by the late 1860s was expected to extend up to
the Bessarabian frontier. The Dutch ports alone sent 150,000 cattle
and 250,000 sheep at that time and these animals may have passed
through the markets of Austria and several of the German states
before they reached their port of embarkation. Again, cattle from
Hamburg may have stood in the markets of Magdeburg or Berlin. (20)
It was no accident that the earliest controls on imports of livestock were on supplies from these ports and countries which acted as
entrepots for the livestock traffic of Europe. In this way Belgium,
France, Germany and Holland were only allowed to send livestock for
immediate slaughter after 1879, and in the case of mainland Germany
this applied only to sheep and swine, cattle imports being prohibited since before 1879. (21) Restrictions on other countries which
were outside the mainstream of the European livestock traffic, that
is Iceland, Scandinavia and the Iberian peninsula, were not as
severe and were imposed at a later date since stock from these
places was less likely to have been exposed to infection from
diseased animals brought overland from other parts of Europe. These
restrictions were accompanied by a change in the geographical
emphasis of the European livestock trade after 1879. Prior to that
date Britain had received its main supplies from Germany and
Holland, after then Scandinavia became more important as a supplier.
Between 1870-4 the three Scandinavian countries of Denmark, Sweden
and Norway furnished Britain with an average of 28,350 head of
cattle per annum, but by 1880-4 this had risen steadily to 106,244.
On the other hand, the older European countries of supply, Germany
and Holland, which had provided an annual average of 134,000 head in
1870-4, registered a very slight increase in 1875 and 1876, then
dropped both absolutely and relatively as a beef supplier and annual
average imports between 1880-4 were only 68,190 head. Supplies from
Spain and Portugal rose slightly between the two sets of dates,
being an average of 38,140 per annum between 1870 and 1874 and
40,865 per annum between 1880 and 1884. In the next quinquennium
supplies of European cattle declined absolutely, and although the
largest drop was in the numbers from Spain and Portugal which only
averaged 17,800 between 1885 and 1889, Scandinavia still remained
the leading exporter with 84,560 and Germany and Holland came
second with 55,980. This change also reflects in part the different
response of these countries' agricultural sectors to the changes in
the world prices of agricultural products which were apparent by
1889. Scandinavian agriculture took advantage of the lowered cost
of imported animal foodstuffs which was reflected in lower grain
prices. As early as 1872 Danish exports of livestock exceeded grain
exports in value and by the 1880s Danish exports of livestock as

well as meat and dairy products were firmly established and Denmark
became a cereal importer. In contrast France and Germany adopted a
policy of tariff protection for cereal as well as livestock farmers
and so agriculture in these countries did not have to exploit overseas markets. (22)

From some parts of Europe exports of livestock to Britain were
seasonal, but from other parts they were sent throughout the year.
The countries that were able to export animals for twelve months in
the year were Spain, Portugal, Holland, France, Germany and Denmark.
In most cases these countries maintained their supplies because
different regions supplied finished animals at various times. For
instance, Germany was able to export for twelve months because
Prussia and south Germany provided fat cattle from January through
to July when Oldenburg took over to supply grass-fed beasts for the
English market in the autumn. The supplies from France included
stall-fed cattle more or less all the year round and in the autumn
grass-fed cattle came from Normandy. Again, Denmark sent its
heaviest supplies in the first six months and from Spain it was
only from the northern districts that exports came all the year.
One must be careful to distinguish between countries that sent
cattle reared and fed at home and those which dealt in transit stock
fed elsewhere. Germany and Holland sent both classes of beasts,
but Belgium, which also exported cattle to Britain throughout the
year, prior to 1877, sent mainly transit cattle from Germany and
further afield. Apart from the possible exception of Denmark the
trade from Scandinavia was mainly a seasonal one, although the
various countries complemented each other by sending at different
times of the year. Norway sent animals mainly from January to
March, although the trade was sometimes extended to April. Those
from Sweden lasted a little longer, from January to July, and
exports from Schleswig Holstein were an autumn trade where the
season lasted from July to November. (23)

The livestock exports from Scandinavia were not organized in the
same way as the trade conducted from Holland or the north German
cities. In the last case the ports were collecting centres to which
animals gathered from a number of countries in central and eastern
Europe were sent. Prior to the expansion of the railways the
heaviest arrivals had been in grass-fed beasts in the months from
July to Christmas. But the extension of the railway network since
about 1858 increased the catchment area from which supplies were
drawn and exporters received almost as many animals in winter and
spring as they did in the summer and autumn. (24) But the trade
from Scandinavia was only in beasts fed locally. Consequently,
this trade did not provide the same employment opportunities for
livestock dealers as those residing in the German and Dutch ports
and engaged in the export trade all the year round. Therefore the
Scandinavian livestock exporting business was organized by rather a
different class of men. Here the farmers themselves took more of
the financial responsibility for sending their animals to England
and exercised a greater personal supervision over the whole trade.
As an example the duchies of Schleswig and Holstein, which had more
in common agriculturally with Scandinavia than mainland Germany,
may be considered. From these places the cattle trade to England,
which only operated for four or five months of the year, was

organized in the following manner. The English shipping company
that carried the beasts used agents who contacted local farmers
before a cattle boat was due to arrive at the port of Tonning from
which all Schleswig Holstein cattle left. The agents knew the
precise capacity of each vessel in the trade and also how many
beasts a farmer wished to send to England each week, and they made
arrangements to fill the vessels accordingly. At an appointed time
the farmers took their cattle to the waterside and with the help of
their agent loaded them on board ship. They also paid the agent to
travel with the vessel and to engage attendants to look after the
beasts on the voyage, which normally took 38 hours but could be as
much as 72 hours in bad weather. At this stage the farmers took all
responsibility for the animals and also paid the shipping company,
so that all the latter did was to carry the farmers' property. The
cattle themselves were consigned to salesmen in England who met the
ship when it docked and took charge of the beasts. Quite often a
cargo of 400 animals would be consigned to as many as fifteen or
twenty salesmen. This reflected the past pattern of business where
individual farmers had dealings with particular salesmen. Once the
cattle were sold at the metropolitan market they became the property
of the purchaser and the salesman made his own arrangements to remit
the money to the farmer in Germany or Denmark, retaining for himself
his own commission. In this way it was in the interest of the
dealer to get as high a price as possible for the animals and the
farmer in Europe retained ownership until the moment they were sold.
If any accident befell the animals en route and it became necessary
to slaughter a beast the loss fell on the sender, the farmer. (25)

The absolute decline in importance of European livestock imports
in the face of increasing supplies from North America deserves some
explanation. Even before the absolute prohibitions on the imports
of European animals finally extinguished the trade, the numbers sent
were reduced under the system of slaughter at the ports. This,
however, is not a demonstration of cause and effect as exactly the
same rules applied equally to US cattle from 1878. For instance,
in 1887 P.G. Craigie observed: (26)

France was once an exporter of sheep to England ... in 1872, I
believe as many as 21,800 ...; but long before we ceased, in
1884, to take her animals at all, on account of the foot-and-
mouth disease, she had practically dropped out of the race.

The reason for the decline in imports from this source was the
failure of French agricultural output to keep pace with the growth
of population in that country. France was a large consumer of
mutton and in the 1880s was having to import around 600,000 head of
sheep per annum from her Algerian colonies besides importing a
larger number from other European countries. The same argument also
applied to other European states which formerly sent livestock to
Britain, for instance Germany and Belgium. In most cases the
countries of Europe were not as successful as Great Britain in
maintaining the ratio of their livestock to human populations
between 1867 and the end of the 1880s. Those countries that were,
like Norway and Denmark, for example, found ready markets with lower
transport costs in Europe, and so did not need to market all their
surplus animals in Great Britain. Therefore, in this sense, the
veterinary restrictions imposed to prevent the import of animal

disease, and even the later absolute prohibition on imports, were probably only hastening an inevitable decline in the economic importance of the European livestock traffic to Britain. This is not to deny the underlying necessity for those restrictions, without them the British livestock industry which provided the major part of total meat consumed would have been as defenceless against losses as it had been prior to 1865.

After the passing of the 1869 Contagious Diseases (Animals) Act the Privy Council controls over the landing of foreign livestock was a factor that distorted the volume of animal traffic handled by the various ports in the United Kingdom. From 1869 there existed two classes of ports able to handle foreign animals. The largest group were only allowed to receive stock from countries that had been declared free of disease. The authorities at these places had to arrange for adequate veterinary inspection of incoming cargoes by veterinary officers responsible to the Privy Council. After inspection stock landed at these ports was free to be sent anywhere in the United Kingdom without any further interference. This second class of port also received imports from countries where disease was absent, but in addition they had special sections set aside to handle livestock from the scheduled countries, that is those countries where animal disease was endemic. The sections of the ports set aside for this purpose had to be sealed off from the rest of the area and had to have slaughtering places as scheduled animals were not allowed to leave the ports alive. After 1869 the Privy Council gradually became more strict about the conditions of inspection at all ports and the quarantine arrangements at ports taking animals from scheduled countries. On occasion when it was not satisfied with the arrangements at a port it would withdraw that place from the list of ports able to handle foreign animals. This was an extremely effective sanction as the loss of this traffic and the prospect of wharfs and sheds standing idle in most cases was sufficient to force the authorities controlling the port to remedy any defects in order to regain the trade. Thus, under the Privy Council's 1873 Animals Order there were twenty-one ports which could take foreign animals and of these only nine were allowed to receive animals from scheduled countries. But by 1875 the list of ports in the first category had been raised to thirty-two and at sixteen of these stock from the scheduled countries could be landed. But as the arrangements at all these sixteen were not to the satisfaction of the Privy Council's officers, the 1877 Animals Orders reduced these to thirteen. (27) This strategy was employed continually by the Privy Council during these years. At times suggestions and persuasion were enough to get the authorities controlling the ports to improve the safeguards against the spread of imported animal disease, but if these failed sterner methods of coercion were used.

In the North Sea trade particular ports tended to receive con-signments from specific countries. Thus Newcastle, which was the most important provincial livestock port after Liverpool at the end of the 1880s, took most of its trade from Scandinavia. In 1888 out of a total traffic of 71,409 cattle and 57,115 sheep, 57,459 of Newcastle's cattle came from Denmark, 13,753 from Sweden and her quota of sheep imports included 45,719 from Denmark, 9,392 from Norway and 1,004 from Iceland. (28) Hull, however, shared with

London the shipments of stock received from Holland. As the Dutch
livestock trade was subjected to an increasing amount of supervision and restriction in the 1880s this inevitably had the effect
of reducing the importance of Hull as a livestock handling port.
These restrictions also affected London. In 1889 the London
authorities were alarmed when Liverpool became the leading port for
the reception of cattle, having 169,334 landed there in that year,
against London's total of 127,955. This was the effect of extending
the restrictions in force against imports from Holland and Germany;
it also had repercussions on the market at Deptford as it reduced
the numbers that passed through the market there. The relegation of
London to second position was a serious blow, in terms of reduced
revenue, and both the London and Deptford corporations endeavoured
unsuccessfully to persuade the government to remove the stringent
regulations in force against Holland and Germany. (29) Also the
number of sheep going to Deptford from Europe fell and the displace-
ment of this Dutch and German traffic in 1889 enabled Danish and
Swedish shippers to extend their sheep exports to Newcastle. In
1888 London received over 77 per cent of the United Kingdom's
entire sheep imports, but in 1889 only 51 per cent were received
there. However, as in the 1860s, there was a considerable traffic
of livestock landed at the outports which was sent to London. In
1888 the port of London received 34 per cent of the foreign cattle
landed at all ports in the United Kingdom. In addition to this a
large proportion of the stock landed at Falmouth, Portsmouth,
Southampton and Bristol ultimately found its way - alive or dead -
to the London market. Taking this trade into account it was
estimated that 40 per cent of the foreign cattle received in the
United Kingdom really passed through the London market. (30)
    Changes in the sources of livestock imports between 1865 and 1889
away from Europe in favour of the USA and Canada were accompanied by
changes in the relative importance of the ports that received them.
While the trade was mainly in European animals, London and the east
coast ports of England were the most convenient places to land
supplies. After North America became the leading exporter of livestock to Britain in the years after 1884 the west coast ports, in
particular Liverpool, handled the majority of this traffic and
London and the outports on the east coast declined both relatively
and, in some cases, absolutely.

4 DEAD MEAT

In these years there was an absolute and relative increase in the
importance of dead meat imports as a part of the United Kingdom's
total foreign meat supplies. In 1867-9 an estimated average of
60,300 tons of meat was imported annually as live animals and
56,500 tons as dead meat. Thus 52 per cent of total meat imports
were accounted for by the livestock trade. By 1885-6 the meat
obtained from live imports had more than doubled to 125,000 tons
per annum but imports of dead meat had risen six-fold to 334,900
tons and accounted for 73 per cent of meat imported. In the 1860s
and 1870s dead meat imports comprised mostly bacon, ham and salt
pork with smaller amounts of fresh beef and pork and various kinds

of unenumerated canned meats. The exploitation of new sources of
fresh meat in Australasia and North and South America did not have
the effect of diminishing the relative importance of Europe as a
supplier of dead meat before 1889. This was because already only
minor amounts of dead meat were imported from Europe in the 1870s.
In the quinquennium 1870-4 Britain's total imports of dead meat
averaged 133,890 tons per annum but of this only 20,620 tons, or
just 15 per cent, came from Europe. The major supplier at this
time was North America which sent various kinds of pigmeat. By
1885-9 total dead meat supplies imported had risen to 351,960 tons
per annum but of this supplies from Europe at 51,680 tons still
stood at 15 per cent of the total. (31) The important change in
the structure of imports was in the range of products available,
thus fresh (refrigerated) beef was added to the various pig products
imported from North America, and fresh mutton and lamb were added to
the canned meats which had hitherto comprised the small supplies
from South America and Australia. Also, North America maintained
its relative importance as a supplier of meat imports by 1889. In
the period 1870-4, 93,880 tons per annum or 83 per cent of non-
European imports of meat came from North America: by 1885-9 the
corresponding figure was 251,810 tons or 84 per cent. Therefore in
this period there was no radical geographical shift in the regions
that supplied dead meat to the United Kingdom. Instead there was a
diversification in the type of product supplied and a large absolute
increase in the amount of these products sent, an increase in which
all continents with a surplus available for export were able to
participate. The most notable changes were within regions and were
associated with shifts in the amounts of meat individual countries
were able to export. The best example of this was in Europe. In
the 1870s the largest European imports of pigmeat came from Germany,
but after 1887 that country lost its leading position and thereafter Denmark became the most important European exporter of bacon
to Great Britain. (32)

It is not possible to make an exact comparison of changes in the
various kinds of meat coming to Britain in this period. This is
because prior to 1882 and 1890 the source of all import figures, the
'Annual Statement of Trade', included certain categories of
unenumerated meats which do not specify the animal origins of these
imports, though they do give the country of origin. Although
unenumerated meats only comprised about 5 per cent of the total
annual imports of dead meat it is impossible to be sure how much
was beef or mutton or pork, even though the country of origin does
give some guide. In fact most of this meat was either mutton or
beef. This was because prior to 1882, when frozen mutton imports
first became important enough to merit a separate category, the
small amounts of European fresh mutton, mostly sent from Germany or
Holland, were not separately recorded. Again, the relatively small
amounts of tinned beef and mutton, mainly sent from the USA and
Australia, were not distinguished separately before 1890. In this
last case it would have been impossible for the customs officers
who kept a record of imports to discover the animal origins of this
meat as it arrived at and passed through the ports in sealed cans
which prevented any inspection of their contents. However, an
approximate indication of the importance of beef, mutton and pigmeat

can be obtained from the enumerated categories of dead meat imports
which comprise about 95 per cent of the total. Taking Craigie's
figures once again, for 1867-9 pigmeat in one form or another
accounted for 77 per cent of the enumerated imports and the rest was
beef. By 1885-6 the relative importance of pigmeat had declined a
little to 73 per cent of the total, beef had declined to 17 per cent
and mutton made up the remaining 10 per cent. (33) Therefore there
does not seem to have been any radical shift in the composition of
dead meat imports. The overwhelming importance of pigmeat among the
imports of dead meat compensated for the unimportance of swine among
livestock imports where they were a scarcely appreciable part of the
total. On long voyages pigs were always easier to transport dead
rather than alive and as the USA continued to have a large surplus
of hog products available for export, this explains the preponder-
ance of pigmeat in the total United Kingdom dead meat imports.

The first extension of non-European supplies of meat were imports
of chilled beef from the USA in the late 1870s. (34) The trade in
frozen meat from South America and Australasia did not begin until
the 1880s. In 1889 the United Kingdom imported approximately
63,780 tons of chilled beef from the USA against only 50,290 tons of
frozen mutton from South America and Australasia. It was not until
after 1890 that imports of frozen meat became more important than
the chilled imports from the USA.

It has to be emphasized that neither with regard to the products
supplied, nor the conditions under which it was organized and
conducted, was the trade in refrigerated meats sent to Britain ever
a homogeneous one. The frozen Canterbury lamb which came to Britain
in increasing quantities from New Zealand after 1880 was a far
superior product to South American frozen lamb and mutton. And
similarly, the chilled beef which arrived in Britain from North
America was a better quality product than either South American or
Australian frozen beef. These differences in quality were partly
the effect of the differing climatic conditions and economic circumstances of the countries where the meat was produced, and partly the
different methods used to preserve it for transportation from those
countries.

Refrigerated meat is preserved in two ways: by chilling and by
freezing. But when any meat is refrigerated to prolong the time it
can be kept fresh an inferior article is produced. This is because
although refrigeration arrests the bacterial processes of decay it
also brings about chemical and physical changes in the meat which
detract from its appearance and taste. Frozen meat is kept at a
temperature of between $14^{\circ}F$ and $18^{\circ}F$, but between the temperatures
of $31^{\circ}F$ and $25^{\circ}F$ large ice crystals form between the muscle fibres
of the meat and this process ruptures some of the small vessels of
the flesh. When the meat is thawed this gives it a sweaty, dis-
coloured appearance and it loses a certain amount of moisture,
making it less juicy when cooked. This effect is more noticeable
in large carcases like beef, as having a greater bulk than mutton
and lamb they take longer to pass through the critical range of
temperature where the large ice crystals are formed and the damage
done. But meat can also be chilled, that is, kept at a temperature
of $30^{\circ}F$ which is just above its freezing point, and this means that
the ice crystals do not form in the carcase. The problem of the ice

crystals can be overcome by rapid freezing, but this is a twentieth-
century innovation which was not available to nineteenth-century
refrigeration engineers. (35)   Therefore the frozen beef, mutton and
lamb available in the nineteenth century was less palatable than the
chilled beef which came from the USA, and this partly accounted for
its lower price.

It may be asked why it was necessary to freeze meat sent from
Australasia and South America but only to chill beef from North
America. The reason for this was the longer time taken by the
voyages from these places to Great Britain which also involved
crossing the Equator. Under these conditions it was necessary to
freeze the Australasian and South American products to keep them
fresh. This was not always to be so: and after 1900 improved refrigeration techniques permitted chilled beef to be brought from South
America as well, but this development took two decades, and in the
early years of the trade in refrigerated beef the North American
product carried a quality advantage.

Because the trade in North American chilled beef preceded that in
frozen meat it is possible to examine the problems facing the trade
in refrigerated meat during the early stages of its development.
Some of the difficulties faced here were again common to the food
trade as a whole that was starting to rely on increasing quantities
of highly perishable imported foods to feed the growing urban population of Britain. These early difficulties took the form of,
first, arranging for railway companies to carry the new product in
a satisfactory manner and, second, overcoming the shortage of
proper storage facilities for these highly perishable foods while
they were awaiting sale. Also the early importers of this product
had to overcome a certain amount of prejudice against the article,
both from the consumer and some parts of the meat trade.

The trade in chilled beef did not begin properly until 1875 when
T.C. Eastman sent the first cargo of chilled beef from New York in
October of that year. (36) The beef arrived in good condition and
the trade very quickly developed. By 1877 the trade was regarded
as substantial, 444,043 cwt of chilled beef being landed at British
ports in that year. The early extension of this trade was more
rapid than that for cattle. By January 1877 there were eight firms
in the chilled beef trade (37) as opposed to four carrying US
cattle. The ports of departure and landing were very much the same
for both trades. New York was the chief one with additional cargoes
being sent from Philadelphia and Boston, as well as some live cattle
sent from Quebec. There was also an overlap of firms and
personnel between the two trades. For instance, in January 1877
Lehman Samuels and Brother of New York shipped both beef cattle and
chilled beef from that city. (38)

However, in their early years both these trades were subject to
difficulties. When James MacDonald visited the USA in 1877 to
report on the situation in that country he found that the chilled
beef trade had expanded so rapidly, under boom conditions in its
early months, that there was now too much competition to make the
business healthy for those engaged in it. By the spring of 1877
the average arrivals of chilled beef at Liverpool were equivalent to
1,000 animals a week. The market was becoming so over-stocked that
the US exporting firms were forced to take a loss. Some members of

the trade were already saying that some thinning out of numbers
would be a good thing and this process had already claimed one
victim with the bankruptcy of Lehman Samuels and Brother, largely
because of their heavy and continuous losses in the export trade.
(39)

The losses made in the trade had their origin on both sides of
the Atlantic. In the first place, there had been heavy purchases
of cattle for export, either live or dead, which had forced up the
price in the USA by something like 1d. per 1b. At the same time,
the heavy demand for transatlantic shipping space raised freight
costs, even though this was not by a very large margin. And then,
because the markets were over-stocked in London and Liverpool, the
prices the shippers had to take on the English side were forced
down. This situation had an acute effect on the shipper with
chilled meat to dispose of. (40)

With some exceptions most people in the meat trade in Britain
were slow to realize the importance of the refrigerated meat trade
in terms of its potential development. The Select Committee
investigating the import of livestock in 1877 still thought, at
least in terms of the immediate future, that most supplies would
arrive on the hoof. Nevertheless, they heard the evidence of
persons engaged in the US chilled meat trade, and these witnesses
all testified that they thought the trade was capable of considerable expansion. In its report the committee observed: (41)

> With regard to the importation of dead meat from America, ... the
> evidence shows that there are hardly any limits to the amount of
> meat which can be imported from that country; that in cool
> weather the meat can without difficulty be delivered here in
> perfect order, and that with greater care in the packing, and
> with better arrangements for storage here, it could be brought
> over in the hottest months. American meat already forms a useful
> supplementary supply to the meat markets of this country, and in
> no very distant future will probably constitute a most important
> addition, ... But the trade is at present in too uncertain and
> experimental a condition to justify reliance upon it for an
> unfailing supply.

Much of the prejudice shown against this meat before the
committee was by men who were already established in one branch or
another of the meat and livestock business in Britain. Of the ten
witnesses who commented adversely on the taste, condition or the
general quality of US chilled beef six were cattle salesmen, four of
whom certainly dealt in imported animals; three were practising
butchers including one who was the Master of the Butchers' Company
in London. The only adverse witness who appeared at first sight to
be neutral was the chief meat inspector at Liverpool but he was in
this job partly on account of his twenty years' experience in the
trade as a butcher. The credentials of the ten witnesses who gave
favourable reports on the quality of the US imports were rather
more varied. Four were salesmen or importers of this commodity but
one of these also sold English meat. Another four gave occupations
or addresses which indicate that they were either farmers of else
representatives of the agricultural interest. Of the remaining two,
one was a steamship agent whose vessels carried European livestock
to Britain and the other was a City alderman. (42) There is little

doubt that those who gave adverse comments on the chilled meat
viewed the product with a certain amount of personal apprehension.
Herman Gebhardt, a German cattle dealer doing business in London and
a pioneer of the European livestock trade, stated that if large
quantities of US beef were imported it would have the effect of
stopping the supplies of live animals from Germany and the rest of
Europe. One of his critics, the City alderman Thomas Rudkin, who
had also been a member of the City Markets Committee for twenty
years, thought that this would be an immense public boon because it
would rid the country of livestock disease and would also have the
effect of generally reducing the price of meat in Europe. (43)

It is doubtful if the committee were very much impressed by the
adverse comments of the meat trade against the quality or the freshness of chilled meat. However, they were aware that this new
product did face certain problems of distribution within Britain.
Given the novelty of this trade and the nature of the difficulties
the cautious attitude of the committee in making any forecasts about
its future is understandable.

From its start in October 1875 the grade grew steadily. This
marked the beginning of a development that revolutionized the dead
meat trade. For the first time it was possible to send meat quite
independently of prevailing weather conditions. The flow of
unrefrigerated meat from Europe in the 1860s had been confined to
the cooler months of the year and had always disappeared in the
summer. After the introduction of the chilled meat trade the flow
of US fresh meat to Britain continued to grow throughout the summer
of 1876. There were natural fluctuations in the trade from month
to month but these were not in any way determined by the weather, as
Table 7.3 shows.

TABLE 7.3 Chilled meat (beef) sent from the USA in the early
months of the trade, October 1875 - April 1877

Month	1875	1876	1877
	cwt	cwt	cwt
January		1,446	22,968
February		2,607	44,229
March		2,696	59,892
April		11,214	76,564
May		9,036	
June		10,179	
July		10,446	
August		12,188	
September		21,889	
October	321	24,283	
November	321	37,446	
December	1,196	33,700	

Source: 'Report of the Select Committee on Cattle Plague and
Importation of Livestock', P.P., 1877, IX, Q 4508. (Up to September
1876 the only port sending meat was New York. From October 1876
Philadelphia also sent meat.)

The meat consigned to Glasgow was imported by Messrs John Bell and Sons and they were the sole agents of T.C. Eastman for the distribution of his meat in Britain. Bell's made their first attempt by offering the meat for sale to retailers in Glasgow, as there they had the best contacts among the meat trade. However, if they found that the Glasgow market was over-stocked and prices were too low they looked further afield. The first market they tried was Edinburgh, but if this was not satisfactory it was possible to send the meat on by rail to London to find its way through the wholesale market at Smithfield. Even after the long sea journey to Glasgow and handling in that city the meat was usually still fresh enough to stand the extra delay of the journey down to the capital. Glasgow and John Bell's did not retain their pioneer monopoly of the trade for very long and in a few weeks other individuals entered the trade to send consignments to other places in the United Kingdom, and the port of Liverpool soon became the centre of the trade. (44)

The machinery of distribution in the early stages of the trade was an ad hoc affair. Cargoes were sent mainly to Liverpool but landings were also made at Southampton, Bristol and Glasgow. For the Bristol trade the US exporters, who were the patentees of the refrigeration process, hired space on board a company's vessel trading between Bristol and New York. The refrigeration rooms were installed in the ships and the representatives of the patentee had charge of the cargo on the voyage. The shipping firm however did have a further interest in the cargo as the US shipper asked the managing owner of the ships to act as agent for the disposal of the meat once it arrived in Bristol. Of the early cargoes sent to Bristol some of the meat was sold in the city and some was sent to London for sale. (45)

A certain amount of anxiety was felt about the freshness of the meat after the transatlantic journey. In the 1870s the refrigerating equipment on board the ships was relatively unsophisticated. There was more than one process in use and different shippers each had their own. Refrigeration engineering was not sufficiently advanced to actually manufacture ice on board the ships. The low temperature was achieved in two ways. In the first method ice was taken on board the ships at the start of the voyages and placed in tanks to melt. The cold water and ice so produced was then pumped through pipes in the refrigeration rooms. In this way a temperature not varying beyond $34^{\circ}F$ at the lowest and not more than $37^{\circ}F$ at the highest was maintained. (46) The other method involved using fans to pass a current of air over ice. The cold air was then passed into the refrigeration rooms where the meat was hung on hooks allowing sufficient space between each piece for the cold air to circulate properly. Both these methods had the disadvantage that they required the carriage of a substantial quantity of ice in addition to the meat. Also if a ship was slowed on a voyage by bad weather there was the danger of the ice running out before it reached the port. Despite these hazards the losses in the early months of the trade seem to have been remarkably small. One US businessman in this trade put his losses through meat being condemned as unfit on arrival at 7 per cent. This figure compares with one of 7.5 per cent for live cattle reported as being lost on

the voyage from the USA in 1876 as a result of injury or exhaustion
on board the ship. (47)

In the early weeks of the trade the US beef had a considerable
'novelty' following among the consuming public. One store in
Liverpool at Compton House in Tarleton Street was besieged with
customers the first morning the meat was on sale. The rush was so
great that a policeman had to be employed to keep the street and
the shop clear. Despite the store having laid in a substantial
supply, the demand was so brisk that the entire stock was sold by
3 o'clock on the first afternoon. This state of affairs lasted for
some weeks, until the public had got used to the article. To some
extent retail butchers were prejudiced against the article but
equally some bought it to sell alongside English meat. It was also
sold by traders who were not even butchers; in the poor neighbourhoods of Liverpool, like Marybone, it was sold by greengrocers.
(48)

In its early years, the import of chilled US beef was carried out
under what were far from ideal conditions. While the meat was still
in mid-ocean the agents in England for the exporting firms would do
all they could to arrange for its immediate disposal on arrival.
This was made necessary by the absence of any cold storage facilities at the ports. Failing this they could take advantage of a few
days' grace to keep the meat on board the ship in the refrigerating
rooms until a customer was found, but this was strictly limited by
cost and the ship's turn-round time. When customers were found the
meat was immediately dispatched to different parts of the country in
unrefrigerated railway vans with only a few air holes in the front
to provide a draught through to the meat inside, a practice which
gave the contents a good chance of arriving at their destination
covered in soot and coal dust. (49)

In the 1870s and 1880s the chilled beef trade in Britain consoli-
dated its position and improved its distribution network. In one
respect this was made easier by the entry of Australasian and South
American frozen mutton and lamb onto the British market after 1880.
As these meats also needed cold storage they provided an extra
incentive for the engineering industry to produce the necessary
equipment for low temperature storage plants. The first cold store
opened in Britain appears to have started in 1877. This was run by
a company called the Fresh Preserved Meat Agency. In fact this firm
was controlled by one man, Daniel Tallerman. He was in many ways an
innovator in the food trade and made several attempts to pioneer new
products and handle their distribution between 1877 and 1890. He
was interested in imported chilled meat because this seemed to him
to have a promising future if the initial difficulties of the trade
could be ironed out. In 1877 his firm had premises in London at
Upper Thames Street under Cannon Street railway station. It is
known from later accounts of these premises that they were large and
Tallerman on his own evidence was recorded as having paid £2,000 per
annum rent for them. However, the enterprise did not prosper. The
reasons for its failure are rather obscure. According to Tallerman
it was opposed by the butchers in London, who presumably acted as a
body to boycott his goods. However, that alone does not seem to
constitute a sufficient reason for his lack of success, as other
firms handling chilled meat were able to arrange for its sale and

TABLE 7.4 Origins of United Kingdom livestock imports, 1865-89

	Cattle		Sheep and lambs		Swine	
	North America	Europe	North America	Europe	North America	Europe
1865	–	283,271	–	914,170	–	133,280
1866	–	237,739	–	790,880	–	76,541
1867	–	177,948	–	539,716	–	48,164
1868	88	136,600	–	341,155	–	33,769
1869	–	220,190	–	709,843	–	69,488
1870	–	202,172	–	669,905	–	95,624
1871	–	248,611	–	917,076	–	85,562
1872	–	172,998	–	809,822	–	16,100
1873	402	200,400	–	851,116	–	80,978
1874	273	193,589	–	758,915	82	115,307
1875	1,511	262,173	–	985,652	33	72,137
1876	3,035	265,886	1,865	1,039,464	38	43,520
1877	14,058	184,601	23,395	850,660	806	19,228
1878	86,858	163,918	85,699	806,426	18,279	37,632
1879	101,001	144,646	191,914	752,974	19,747	32,619
1880	204,467	182,572	145,284	795,837	13,111	38,080
1881	146,369	170,562	115,306	819,838	1,773	22,510
1882	80,023	261,055	127,787	996,604	–	15,670
1883	208,191	264,005	183,368	932,747	1	38,862
1884	200,731	222,128	91,684	853,358	17	26,420
1885	206,350	164,936	51,513	699,373	57	16,465
1886	181,134	136,658	99,894	939,071	70	21,281
1887	159,983	133,787	36,500	934,904	3	21,962
1888	204,639	170,192	46,542	909,668	–	24,509
1889	378,979	173,581	74,547	603,411	–	25,324

Source: 'Annual Statement of Trade', P.P. North America includes Canada and the USA. Europe excludes the Channel Islands.

distribution. Part of the reason may be that Tallerman came into
the meat trade as an outsider. He was also interested in other
projects at the same time, in particular a scheme which required
hiring a stall in the Central Markets at Smithfield for the sale of
home-produced meat on behalf of the British farmer! (50) It seems
likely that Tallerman's difficulty stemmed from organizing too
many business projects simultaneously without sufficient practical
experience.

After this initial start, the provision of cold stores for
chilled meat became caught up with the general expansion of cold
storage for frozen meat in the 1880s which is described below.
Also, although Tallerman's business foundered, it seems the cold
store itself was a success and in the 1880s it was taken over by a
New Zealand firm importing frozen lamb and mutton.

The marketing of the US beef in Britain was left in the hands of
British salesmen. By the 1880s the majority of these men were based
in London or Liverpool. Under these arrangements the US firms in
Boston, Philadelphia or New York had no control over the way their
meat was sold. The prime requirement of this trade remained one of
speed. After the meat was taken from ship or from the store it
tended to become soft with drops of condensation covering the
surface. This sweaty appearance made the meat look less appetizing
than home-killed beef and so the salesmen handling the product had
to work harder to push a sale. Again, any delay in putting the
produce onto the market, or any delay in selling, caused the meat to
deteriorate in quality and so fetch a lower price. (51) As this
meat had a less prolonged storage life than frozen meat it was vital
not to allow arrivals of separate consignments to pile up at the
ports before being released onto the market. The problem of markets
over-supplied with arrivals of chilled beef was not entirely solved
even with the provision of adequate cold storage space in Britain.
Using nineteenth-century refrigeration techniques chilled meat had
only a limited storage life of around 35 days as opposed to a
storage life of up to a year for frozen meat if kept carefully.
Therefore, chilled meat arriving in Britain in the 1880s had to be
sold within two weeks of its arrival even with adequate cold storage
accommodation in this country.

CHAPTER 8

THE DOMESTIC MEAT TRADE, 1890-1914

1 OFFICIAL REGULATION

The scope of official supervision of the meat and livestock trade
was considerably extended between 1890 and 1914. This action also
exerted a powerful influence over the way this branch of food
distribution evolved before the First World War. The Veterinary
Department of the Board of Agriculture remained the chief agency
responsible for co-ordinating the measures aimed to eliminate outbreaks of livestock disease, although enforcement at the local
level was with the co-operation of local authorities and the police
force. The activities of the department which had the greatest
effect on the movement of livestock and the conduct of markets
concerned four diseases. These were foot-and-mouth, swine fever,
sheep-scab and pleuro-pneumonia. Perhaps the disease anthrax should
be added to this list, but although it was present in the country
throughout this period and was one which the department took action
against, the nature of the disease and the form of this intervention
did not greatly affect the livestock trade. The disease of pleuro-
pneumonia ceased to be a problem after 1898 when the last outbreak
in Great Britain occurred. Foot-and-mouth was eliminated from the
country in 1886 and was not continually present thereafter.
However, it did reappear in 1892-4, 1900-2, 1908 and again between
1910 and 1913. In spite of their intermittent nature, these outbreaks tended to cause a great deal of interference with the livestock trade in the districts where they occurred, simply because
the disease is highly infectious and easily conveyed to fresh
subjects, and so stringent controls over the movement of stock were
necessary to contain it. The control of sheep-scab was mainly a
matter of seeing that the animals were dipped in areas where outbreaks were reported in order to kill the mite that infested their
fleeces and gave rise to this condition. The control of swine fever
inevitably meant severe restrictions on the movement of pigs in
infected areas. This disease was perhaps the most difficult to
control, partly because of the short life (not more than six months)
of most of the pig population which meant animals were often
rapidly moved to market before the authorities could trace outbreaks
to their source. Also the organism causing the disease was not

recognized till 1903-4 and it was not realized that it remained alive in the flesh of animals long after death. As some owners fed their swine on swill containing pigmeat, collected from hotels and workhouses, etc., this was a source of fresh outbreaks. The department also unwittingly helped to re-cycle the disease itself by the practice of selling the carcases of pigs compulsorily slaughtered to reduce the cost of compensation paid to their owners. Between 1894 and 1915 it received £800,000 for such carcases, which indicates that a substantial amount of 'salvage' work was being undertaken. (1)

After 1889 the department gave some attention to the question of tuberculosis in cattle, and its relationship to the same disease in humans. This was a matter of some considerable controversy in the 1890s and the first decade of the twentieth century. The argument was over whether man was capable of being infected by the bacillus responsible for the disease in cattle. This was because by the late 1890s three types of organism were separately identified as causing the disease in birds, in cattle and in man. The settlement of this dispute had important implications for cattle feeders and dairy farmers. If the organism causing the disease in animals was also pathogenic to man, then both the meat and milk from tuberculous cattle should plainly not be consumed. Moreover the tuberculin test, which was available from 1891, was capable of detecting infected animals with about 90 per cent accuracy. As far as the meat industry was concerned this was largely academic as the presence of the disease in carcases was apparent to the naked eye. Also it was the practice in particular localities to condemn badly diseased carcases as early as the 1850s, before the causal agent of the disease was identified. (2) The difficulties arose over carcases which revealed the animal not to have been badly affected with illness and which had perhaps showed no symptoms during its lifetime. Was it sufficient merely to remove the affected portions as some authorities advocated or, as others believed, should the whole carcase be condemned? Again, if the first course was adopted what exactly was a 'badly diseased carcase'?

Because of the lack of agreement over the nature of tuberculosis a number of Royal Commissions were established to investigate the relationship between the human and animal forms of the disease. (3) From the point of view of the historian the first two of these, which reported in 1895 and 1898 respectively, reveal most about the actual machinery and procedures adopted for inspecting meat. This is because they heard the oral evidence of witnesses. But from the scientific point of view the last Royal Commission, established in 1901, was the only one to provide definite answers. Its task was to investigate whether the disease in animals and man was the same, whether reciprocal infection was possible and, if this were so, how it occurred. The work of the commission took ten years to complete as, instead of listening to the conflicting opinions of expert witnesses, it conducted its own investigation by setting up an experimental station. Interim reports were issued in 1904, 1907, 1909 and the final report in 1911. The 1907 report concluded that considerable disease and loss of life, especially in children, could be attributed to the consumption of milk from tuberculous cows. (4) On the question of meat it was generally agreed that dangers existed but the opinion was that they were less than in the case of milk. In some quarters, the attitudes taken by certain local authorities after the case in Glasgow in 1888 were criticized on the grounds that they were over-severe. (5) It was argued at the time that it was not necessary to condemn the whole carcase of an animal which was suffering from tuberculosis, but where the disease was not widespread. The wholesale destruction of all meat from tubercular animals insisted upon by some Medical Officers of Health was held to have been a panic reaction. In the 1890s there was a strong body of opinion among medical men and scientists in favour of condemning only emaciated tubercular cattle and salvaging for the butcher the sound parts of any beasts that appeared only lightly afflicted. From 1898 up to the outbreak of the war the official attitude remained the same and inspectors were recommended only to seize the carcases of animals with advanced tuberculosis. This condition was however quite closely defined to reduce any uncertainties. In other cases, where the disease was not advanced, only the tuberculous portions needed to be condemned.

The formulation of this recommendation was the result of the report of the 1898 Royal Commission. It observed that the same situation as existed before 1890 was still in operation. (6)

As to the amount and distribution of tubercular disease which justifies the seizure and condemnation of a carcase as unfit for human food, the widest discrepancy prevails in opinion and practice. Chaos is the only word to express the absence of system in the inspection and seizure of tuberculous meat, and it has, in our opinion become necessary that regulations should be formulated for the guidance of those who are concerned in dealing with this subject. (7)

However, even after 1898, action was still in the hands of local authorities operating within the public health Acts. Tuberculosis did not formally become the concern of the Veterinary Department of the Board of Agriculture before 1914 because the disease was not added to the list including swine fever, foot-and-mouth disease, etc., that were scheduled under the diseases of animals Acts. There were two reasons for this failure. First, tuberculosis in cattle was mostly a chronic disease and so did not present the same urgency for action. Second, the thorny question of compensation arose if the disease were scheduled and infected animals were compulsorily slaughtered. This happened when the Board of Agriculture issued its Tuberculosis Order of 1909 with provision for slaughter in certain cases. It was opposed because compensation was to be paid out of the rates and the storm of protest this aroused from local authorities was so strong that the order was withdrawn without being allowed to operate.

Part of the resistance to scheduling tuberculosis was dependent upon the uncertainty about the extent of the disease, which would determine the amount of compensation to be paid to owners of livestock. In the early 1890s the Veterinary Department's officers decided to record the presence of the disease in the carcases of animals slaughtered under the pleuro-pneumonia regulations. Although these beasts could not be regarded as a normal sample of the cattle population they give the only indication of the prevalence of tuberculosis. In 1891 it was discovered that 12.22 per

cent of the cattle slaughtered for this disease were tuberculous.
Also there was a regional variation in the extent of tuberculosis.
In Midlothian 22.5 per cent of the slaughtered cows were tuberculous
and in London 15.53 per cent. (8) In the following year 20 per cent
of the Midlothian cattle that were slaughtered had tuberculosis and
in London the proportion was 25 per cent. There was more disease
detected in 1892 than in 1891. (9) This information was useless for
determining its precise extent but it gave grounds for the anxiety
that the bill for compensation might prove to be unacceptably large.

The complementary nature of meat and livestock inspection was
demonstrated by the outbreak of foot-and-mouth disease in June 1912.
On 27 June the meat inspectors of the corporation of Liverpool at
the Liverpool abattoir found that feet and tongues of animals that
had been slaughtered showed lesions which were identified as foot-
and-mouth disease. The animals then being slaughtered had been
exposed for sale at the Stanley Market on 24 June before being sent
to the abattoir. The number of animals sold at this market was very
large and composed principally of Irish imports. The usual practice
was for the Stanley Market to be held on Mondays and for animals
sold there to go to the Salford Market which was held on Tuesdays.
Thereafter a number of the animals were moved to Leeds, Wakefield,
Derby and Nottingham, and passed through their markets later in the
same week. On the day in question at the Stanley Market about 1,100
cattle and about 9,000 sheep had been on sale. As it was established from the carcases at the abattoir that the animals had the
disease when they passed through the Stanley Market the chances that
it would be carried to Salford Market, and thereafter to some if not
all of the other markets, were very great indeed. Further enquiries
revealed that the dealer who had sold the cattle found in the
Liverpool abattoir had exposed 62 cattle and 168 sheep at the
Stanley Market the previous Monday and that these animals had come
from the environs of Dublin.

The Board immediately issued an order prohibiting the landing in
Great Britain of animals from Ireland until further notice, though
this was soon amended to allow animals to land for immediate
slaughter. Also the movement of animals within the Liverpool districts was prohibited on 29 June as the disease was discovered on a
farm in the city among cattle purchased from the same dealer. It
was also definitely ascertained that animals from the Stanley Market
had been moved thence to Salford, Stoke, Longport, Nottingham,
Derby, Wakefield, Leeds, Halifax and Oswestry. The tracing of all
such animals was immediately undertaken by the Board's inspectors.
Later outbreaks of the disease near Carlisle and in Northumberland
revealed that the diseased animals had been carried on board the
S.S. Slieve Bloom to Liverpool and that animals from this boat had
also been landed at Holyhead and taken from there into Cumberland
and Northumberland.

The disruption caused to the normal pattern of the livestock
trade by these outbreaks was considerable. Besides the Stanley
Market and the Liverpool area, restrictions on the movement of live-
stock had to be imposed in Cumberland, Lancashire and North
Cheshire, Yorkshire (East and West Ridings), Northumberland and
Durham. Further outbreaks that year were detected in Surrey,
Leicestershire, the West Country, Hampshire, Sussex and Flintshire,

and restrictions applied to the livestock trade in those places.
The duration of the measures depended on local circumstances and
the number of outbreaks. When an outbreak was confirmed the movement of stock either into or out of the district was prohibited;
the district being approximately a radius of 15 miles from the
affected premises. At an early date this was modified where
necessary, so as to provide for the meat supply of any large town
that came within the district. Thus fatstock were permitted to be
moved in for slaughter only and often by specified routes, for
example by rail and then straight from the station to the slaughterhouse and by-passing the livestock markets, which were closed under
the disease regulations in any case. Even the journey from the rail
yard to the slaughterhouse had to be authorized by a licence.

Although the severity of the regulations used by 1912 caused
complaints from some parties, they could be justified on the grounds
that they were necessary and effective in halting the spread of the
disease once its presence in a district was confirmed. Also,
reasonable measures to reduce the extent of any private inconvenience were taken. When it was realized that the disease was likely
to appear in Yorkshire, and before the first outbreak in the county,
the Royal Agricultural Society was informed. This was because its
annual show was due to be held in Doncaster in the first week of
July 1912 and the warning enabled the society to tell exhibitors
that, if an outbreak was confirmed in the neighbourhood, it might be
found necessary to prohibit the movement of cattle, sheep and goats
from the showyard. (10) This was a great advance over the official
attitude almost fifty years earlier in 1864, when no government
measures were taken to prevent a market for diseased animals being
established nextdoor to the society's showyard at Worcester. (11)

The Swine Fever Act of 1893 was passed to give the Board of
Agriculture powers to eliminate this disease from Great Britain,
starting in November of that year. Its successes against pleuro-
pneumonia probably encouraged the Board to undertake a new campaign.
It also received a certain amount of support from agricultural
organizations and some promise of co-operation from pig owners,
breeders and local authorities in districts where the disease was
widespread. But the measures employed against the disease also
caused severe disruption of the pig trade in the areas where they
were used. As it was more or less permanently established in
districts with a high density pig population the Board's measures,
which included prohibition on the movement of animals and the
closure of markets in infected areas, caused the maximum of inconvenience to the largest number of persons. Therefore, in many
instances the private and public response to the Board's efforts was
either indifference or determined and organized opposition. (12)
This attitude from persons in the pig trade was a constant feature
of the Board's endeavours to control swine fever before 1914. The
reaction was an understandable one, as the Veterinary Department
frequently acknowledged in its annual reports. Swine fever was a
troublesome and also expensive burden on the industry as a whole.
But the methods used against it caused a great deal of personal
inconvenience, and perhaps financial loss as well, to those individuals unfortunate enough to earn their living from the pig trade in
a district where swine fever was rife. It was therefore necessary

to consider whether the cure was a greater expense to the industry
than the disease itself. The official view was that the exercise
would prove worthwhile in the long run. However, when success
proved elusive and the campaign started in 1893 turned into a long
war of attrition with no end in sight, (13) the disillusion felt by
farmers and traders became deeper.

Some districts had a high incidence of swine fever because their
local economies depended on imports of pigs from elsewhere. Thus
imports of Irish store swine into the west coast areas of England
and Scotland were often blamed for outbreaks in these places. Most
dairying counties needed store animals to consume their milk
surpluses. In Cheshire there was generally a rise in the number of
outbreaks in the early summer months when pigs were moved in from
outside the county to cope with the seasonal rise in the milk output. The same problem existed in Ayrshire. Normally the disease
was not so prevalent in Scotland as in England and Wales because the
pig population was smaller and more thinly distributed over the
country. However, in the dairying areas of south west Scotland
there was a high concentration of swine, and stores brought in from
both Ireland and northern England were an important source of
infection. An outbreak of the disease in an area which exported
pigs to other districts contained the threat of subsequent epidemics
elsewhere. For example, swine were sent from Suffolk to all parts
of Great Britain so, following heavy outbreaks of the disease in
that county in 1906, the store traffic was stopped. If it had been
allowed to continue unhindered it would almost certainly have spread
the disease still further. In some parts of the county it was not
practical to ban the movement of pigs entirely. In Wiltshire the
bacon curing industry required a constant input of fat pigs. Any
government measures that prevented this would have been counter-
productive as they would have crippled the bacon curing factories
and also have destroyed the market for producers of bacon pigs.
For this reason the traffic of fat swine from producer to market was
subject to less interference than the flow of stores from rearer to
feeder. (14)

The general antagonism towards measures of control applied only
to the restrictions on the movement of animals and the closing of
markets. The slaughter of infected pigs and possible contacts was
universally popular within the industry. The reasons for this
difference are not hard to discover. In the first case owners and
traders received no financial compensation for any inconvenience
they suffered, but when herds were killed owners were always adequately compensated. Even if the animals did not have swine fever
some farmers still found it worthwhile to contact the authorities.
In 1900 the Veterinary Department complained that: (15)

> owners of swine frequently inform the Police of cases of illness
> among their pigs even though they are well aware that the
> animals are suffering from some malady other than swine-fever,
> such owners being apparently (motivated) by a desire to obtain
> gratuitous veterinary advice and the burial of carcases at the
> cost of the State.

As late as 1913, when there were 2,573 confirmed outbreaks, the
number of suspected ones reported was 14,044, so the rate of
confirmation was only 18.3 per cent. (16)

The conditions under which many owners kept their pigs also helped to maintain the disease. Any yard or hovel, no matter how insanitary or how many pigs had died there from swine fever in the past, was often considered a good enough place to house them. The Board's policy of slaughtering animals in contact with the infec- tion, which was tried at certain times in selected districts between 1894 and 1914, may actually have discouraged owners from taking precautions to keep their herds free of disease. This was because the payment of compensation was regarded as a guarantee of insur- ance against loss. It was also suggested that in certain circum- stances it was very much in the interests of dealers in (store) swine to spread the disease among the stock of their poorer clients. Some dealers allowed considerable credit to those who regularly bought pigs from them to fatten. But the price of fat pigs was subject to very violent fluctuations caused by the pig cycle. During times when prices were bad and the profits of pig feeding low or non-existent, a dealer's only chance of recovering the money due to him would be to know that on or about a particular date the debtor would be in receipt of a certain amount of ready money, and to press him for payment at about that time. So the distribution of suspected swine among such clients would, if slaughter were resorted to, afford the dealer a better chance of receiving his money than might otherwise be the case. Of course it was another thing to prove that this had been done intentionally, but the department's officers reported that the way in which the disease was spread by certain dealers made them strongly suspicious that such unscrupulous motives were behind their business transactions. (17)

One measure to assist in the prevention of all disease was the requirement that markets where livestock were regularly sold should be cleaned and that the floor should be constructed of material like concrete or ashphalt which could be easily hosed down. A number of local authorities had already made such improvements by 1902, partly on their own initiative and also with the encouragement of the Board of Agriculture. As a result practically all market places and sale yards where weekly sales took place and the bulk of those at which fortnightly sales were held had been provided with surfaces capable of being washed by water. Under the Markets and Sales Order of 1903 places where sales were held more frequently than once in eight days had to meet this requirement and the order came into force in October 1904. The delay was to give market authorities ample time to comply with the new requirements. Under a further order in 1910 the new requirements were extended to all places where sales took place at intervals of less than fifteen days, as from October 1911. Besides providing an extra precautionary measure against livestock disease, the orders had the incidental effect of improving, in many respects, the conditions under which livestock were exposed to public sale in Great Britain, both regarding the general comfort and well-being of the animals, and also the conven- ience of persons frequenting the markets. (18) As most fatstock passed through these markets on their final journey to the butcher any improvement made to the places where they were exhibited for sale was bound to benefit the quality of the meat offered to the public.

2 FATSTOCK MARKETING

In the 1880s agricultural writers gave some attention to the manner of selling domestic livestock at markets. This was part of general interest in improving the marketing methods for United Kingdom farm produce as one response to the threat from foreign and colonial imports. Also the way that all fairs and markets were conducted, not only those dealing with agricultural goods, caused a certain amount of discontent in various parts of the country. The complaint here was that these establishments were run mainly for the benefit and profit of the market owners, and little attention was paid to the interests and needs of the buyers and sellers doing business. An enquiry into the reasons for this discontent was conducted by a Royal Commission on Market Rights and Tolls which was appointed in July 1887. This body was charged with the duty of collecting evidence from both sides, and reporting what alterations might be desirable in the existing law relating to markets, having due regard to the interests of the persons concerned.

Even before the Royal Commission reported, one alteration had already been made in livestock markets. Under the Markets and Fairs (Weighing of Cattle) Act of 1887 all authorities of cattle markets were directed to provide 'weighing machines and weights for the purpose of weighing cattle'. Although these machines were erected throughout Great Britain they were unpopular both with market owners, compelled to incur an expense for which they saw no need, and with farmers, who were accustomed to purchase and sell animals by judgment of eye rather than by weight. When the assistant commissioners visited the markets they found that weighbridges were often inconvneiently situated and sometimes the machines were too small to take cattle easily. Market authorities did only what they had to in order to comply with the letter of the law; weighing machines were unattended, often inaccurate, and generally inadequate for the requirements of the market. To remedy this particular situation the commissioners made a recommendation in their final report. It was that the markets required to have machines for weighing cattle should be furnished with suitable and sufficient accommodation for these and that the question of suitability and sufficiency should be determined by the Board of Agriculture after inspection. A further recommendation was that it was desirable to collect market prices of meat, and in particular the prices of cattle per stone live weight, in the manner that corn prices were collected, at certain markets selected by the Board of Trade. (19)

The collection of live weight cattle prices was closely linked with the adequate provision and proper administration of weighing machines at livestock markets. Indeed, the absence of the latter in earlier years made the former a feasible proposition only in the 1890s. The absence of official series for the market prices of meat has already been commented on in an earlier chapter. Although there are unofficial price series, the fact that they were not based on the actual weight of cattle caused practical complications for the farmer if he used them as a guide. Most of the meat prices quoted in the press were per stone live weight as given by salesmen and butchers to the newspaper market reporters. (20) They were in fact the prices which purchasers said they paid for the different

classes and qualities of animals sold in the markets. The accuracy
of their figures, however, depended on two things: that they were
right about the actual weights of the animals and also the proportion of the live weight that was represented by the weight of meat
after slaughter. If a purchaser underestimated the live weight of
an animal then the price he paid to the seller, if the transaction
was per stone live weight, would understate the amount he paid for
each stone. Again, if the purchaser underestimated the amount of
meat he would get from an animal, even though its total live weight
was correctly estimated, then the price he paid for each live weight
stone of meat would be understated. The ultimate check was made by
the butcher because, unlike the farmer, he had the chance of weighing the carcase after slaughter. However, it was possible to know
with considerable accuracy, by weighing them alive, what the animals
would weigh when dead and the hides, offal, etc., were discarded.
This was done in the manner of a scientific experiment with a
sufficient number of animals of varying weights and conditions first
weighed alive and then the carcase meat and offal were separately
weighed after death. From the records obtained it was possible to
compile tables which would allow the person unitiated in the finer
points of judging fat cattle to be able to estimate from the live
weights the amount of carcase meat a beast would yield.

When it came to the farmer judging the weight of fatstock and
matching his judgment against that of the butcher and professional
dealer, the farmer was at a disadvantage. This was inevitable.
The dealer or the butcher spent his life in estimating the weight of
stock. His eye and judgment were his stock in trade and by long
experience they became very efficient. The average farmer, however,
attended a livestock market only on those occasions when he had
stock to sell, which were comparatively few in relation to the
number of attendances put in by the professional traders. At
various times a number of tests were carried out by agricultural
writers to ascertain how accurately the individuals concerned with
their sale and purchase were able to judge the weight of fatstock.
The results were always in favour of the butchers who consistently
underestimated the meat on an animal when they saw it live. For
instance in 1879 Sir John Lawes asked several competent traders to
his farm at Rothemstead to give an opinion of the weight of five
Hereford bullocks. The total carcase weight after slaughter came to
454 stones (21) 5 lb but the estimates of the experts varied from
431 stones for the lowest to 455 stones for the highest and averaged
445 stones. However, Lawes's own estimate of the total carcase
weight, derived from the live weights of the animals, was 455 stones
7 lb. (22)

Another agricultural writer to carry out similar tests was
Westley Richards. His were conducted at several markets in England
and Scotland. Like Lawes he demonstrated the wide margins of error
between the estimated live weight of an animal and its estimated
dead weight and its actual dead weight on the butcher's block.
Moreover he showed that farmers were worse judges than butchers in
that they underestimated the carcase weights of animals by an even
greater amount. As sellers of livestock it was argued that this
worked against their interests as it meant they would go into the
transaction expecting a price lower than the highest the butcher

was prepared to pay.

The two recommendations of the Royal Commission, for the better provision of facilities for weighing cattle and for the collection of live weight prices at markets, were put into effect by the Markets and Fairs (Weighing of Cattle) Act of 1891. This Act extended the requirement to provide weighbridges to auction markets and gave the Board of Agriculture the power to decide if they were satisfactorily maintained, etc. In addition the Board also collected and published, in official form, the live weight prices in a certain number of scheduled markets in England, Wales and Scotland from 1892. The official figures also included the numbers of livestock weighed as a percentage of the total cattle passing through some of the scheduled markets. This last series does not suggest that farmers were concerned to know the weight of their cattle before striking a bargain. In the fifteen towns in England making returns in the years 1893-5 only 2.73 per cent of the cattle sold in those markets passed over the public weighbridge. By 1899-1901 there was some improvement as by then the figure was 6.49 per cent. In Scotland farmers seem to have been either more enterprising or else less willing to trust their own judgment. In the six markets in that country for which figures were published, the number of cattle weighed in the same sets of years was 26.83 per cent and 31.14 per cent respectively. (23) However, the practice did become more popular as time wore on. By 1911-12 twenty-five English markets returned the numbers of stock weighed and for these they amounted to 30 per cent of the fat cattle and 14 per cent of the stores in these two years. In Scotland, however, the figures for fat cattle were much higher. In the ten Scottish markets making returns in 1911 and 1912, 80 per cent of the fat cattle entering were weighed, although only 2 per cent of store beasts were. (24)

A number of estimates of the loss to Britain fatstock producers through their inaccurate knowledge of prices and carcase weights were made by agricultural journalists. Westley Richards argued that there was an average loss to the farmer of 45s. per animal on fatstock sold. Using James Caird's figure of 2.1 million cattle sold annually for slaughter, he arrived at an annual loss, in the mid-1880s, to the beef producing sector of agriculture of £4,725,000. Therefore Richards argued that: 'A weighing machine is as necessary an implement on a stock farm as a plough on an arable farm if any accurate knowledge of the size, growth and value of stock is to be obtained.' (25) However, it seems doubtful if farmers had weighed their animals before sending them to market that their total receipts as a group would have increased very much. If they were more knowledgeable about the carcase weights of their animals, then presumably the meat traders would have adjusted their wholesale live weight prices downwards to compensate for any possible increased purchasing outlays at livestock markets. The only alternative available to the trade would have been to accept a lower margin of profit, which was not likely to occur. (26)

It is hard to know what effect imperfect knowledge of prices had on the British farmer. If he relied on the press reports and sent his animals to market believing that the current price was so much a stone there was a chance that he would be disappointed by the sum he received. His position in the transaction was illustrated by Sir

John Lawes's evidence to the Royal Commission in July 1888. (27)

If I send to the London market and look at the quoted prices for that meat in the paper, I find that instead of my animals weighing 55, 56 or 58 per cent, as I know they ought to weigh, they only weigh perhaps 50 or 51 per cent. I know with absolute certainty that the figures are misleading and incorrect.

In this case Lawes was certain of his ground because his knowledge was backed by carefully kept records; but the vast majority of farmers did not have this information. Weighing livestock yielded the best dead weight estimates for good quality animals fed to a certain standard of fatness. However, near many towns, particularly in the English Midlands, there is reason to believe that the spread of intensive dairying before 1914 meant that a large number of the animals sold for beef were of low quality, indifferently bred and poorly reared. (28) Any profits made from the sale of this cow beef constituted only a portion of the total profits of dairying enterprises. Consequently, when dairy animals were dried off and fattened up for the butcher the profits provided little incentive for the farmer to worry very much about such niceties as the percentage of carcase weight to live weight. When they were sold their owner probably made a rough calculation of the price he needed to obtain in order to cover rent, feeding costs, etc., and to recoup part of his initial outlay. But they had also provided a revenue, and presumably a net profit, during the time that they had been giving milk. Therefore the dairyman was content to name a particular sum he wanted for his cows and to leave it at that. In Scotland, where the influence of dairying was not felt so widely, the general quality of beef animals was higher. Also the market situation of the farmer who only fattened bullocks was different, as he made all his profit on the one occasion when his beef animals came to market. Given the English farmer's comparative reluctance to use the market weighbridges, which were free of charge, the lower quality of animals involved may explain why a more informal marketing strategy was adopted in England than in Scotland.

By 1914 there were a number of channels through which home-grown meat passed into consumption (see Figure 8.1). In rural areas it was still possible for retail butchers to buy single and small lots of animals direct from the farmer. Country butchers could also make their own purchases in the local markets of most small provincial towns. In both these cases the retailer dispensed with the services of the wholesaler by performing those functions himself. This arrangement was only possible where the sources of supply were close at hand and also where the small local retailer had his own slaughterhouse.

In most parts of England there existed a two-tier system of auction sales. The first of these were held either on the farms or the auctioneer's property. Occasionally they were attended by local butchers, but a large number were held at small villages and hamlets in which there was no local demand for fatstock, and the majority of buyers were jobbers and dealers from the large towns. Therefore, the sales were merely channels which went to feed the main markets. Usually they were held one or two days before the market day of the big town and they were mostly conducted within a radius of 15 miles from them. After the 1890s these small sales increased in number,

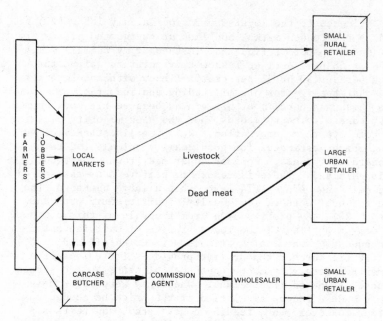

FIGURE 8.1   Distribution of home-produced meat, 1890-1914

and although prices were lower than in the large town markets, their
benefit to the farmer was the saving in time and expense for him to
attend the latter. (29)

These arrangements made the chain of distribution to the large
towns inevitably more complex than to the country areas. Sources of
supply were too distant for retailers to make their own purchases at
the farm gate. Also the continued success of urban authorities in
the removal of small slaughterhouses on the grounds of public health
debarred an increasing number of urban butchers from livestock
purchases. These conditions conferred positions of special importance on the commission agents and carcase butchers in supplying
British-grown meat to large towns. The distinction between these
two groups was that commission agents only handled dead meat sent to
them by rail from the country: carcase butchers bought animals
either in the rural or urban markets for slaughter. The large urban
retailers and chains of butchers' shops bought their meat from
carcase butchers and commission agents as both sold large lots.
Smaller urban retailers, buying mostly single animals at a time,
purchased from a wholesaler who was another intermediary, between
them and the commission agent or carcase butcher (see Figure 8.1).
(30)

Therefore the extremes, in terms of numbers in the distribution
network, applied to the small retailer. In country districts the
chances were that none, or perhaps only the auctioneer, stood
between the producer and retailer. But the small retailer in the
large town was often at the end of a chain that passed through at
least three hands: carcase butcher, commission agent and wholesaler.

3   TRANSPORT OF DOMESTIC MEAT BY RAIL

In the 1890s and right up to 1914, when home-produced meat was
transported to distant markets in carcase form, it was always taken
there in small consignments. This feature of the domestic trade was
in sharp contrast to the way the distribution of imported meat was
conducted. In the latter case individual consignments were very
much larger. This difference was responsible for a certain amount
of acrimony between the various competing business interests
involved in the distribution of home-produced and imported meat.
As the railway companies carried both articles they found themselves in the invidious position of having to justify to the home-
producer the rates they charged to carry imported meat. (31)   The
burden of the home-producers' complaint was that the railways
charged the importers of foreign meat less to carry this product
than they charged the British farmer. The allegation obtained support from those butchers who only sold British meat and were
affected by the competition from retailers selling the various sorts
of imported meat.

In 1895 the whole question of the so-called preferential railway
rates given to importers of foreign goods was settled by the
Southampton case. (32)   In this the Mansion House Association
(inspired thereto by the London Docks Company, rendered uneasy by
the competition of the Port of Southampton) alleged that the London
and South Western Railway Company were giving undue preference to
foreign traders and subjecting home merchandise to undue expense.
This, they argued, was a contravention of the Railway and Canal
Traffic Act, 1888. The Act stated that 'no railway company shall
make any difference in the tolls, rates, or charges made for, or any
difference in the treatment of home or foreign merchandise, in
respect of the same or similar services'. The association alleged
this provision was infringed by the railway company carrying a
number of imported items, among them fresh meat and bacon, from
Southampton Docks to London at lower rates than they charged for the
same commodities sent from inland stations along the line.

The case was heard by the Railway and Canal Commission. The
company based their defence on the fact that the differences between
home and foreign consignments justified the different rates. They
showed that home produce sent from the fifteen inland stations along
the line represented only a comparatively small total weight,
usually in consignments of just a few hundredweights, whereas
foreign produce sent from Southampton was tendered in large quantities, representing very substantial individual consignments. In
the case of the fresh meat carried to London by the railway, it
showed that it had received 357 tons of home-produced meat in no
fewer than 1,566 individual consignments, the average weight of each
consignment being less than 5 cwt. In contrast it received over the
same period 10,638 tons of foreign meat in 286 separate consignments; the average weight of each consignment was almost 38 tons.
Home-produced consignments of meat were either packed in hampers or
hung on hooks, occupying much space on the vans, and were liable to
injury. The foreign meat was far more easily handled. It came
frozen and was loaded into the wagons tier upon tier so that each
wagon carried its maximum load.

The comparisons between foreign and British bacon and hams
carried by the railway reveal a similar order of difference.
Foreign bacon and hams were secured in strong wooden boxes which
weighed about three to the ton. The boxes were included in the
total weight on which carriage was charged. This method of packing
allowed the trucks to be fully loaded, the average truck load being
more than 4 tons. The boxes rendered their contents practically
free from liability to damage during handling. The boxes could be
unloaded by cranes which was labour-saving. The average train load
of foreign bacon and ham sent from Southampton to London was over 18
tons. Home-produced ham and bacon would sometimes arrive at the
stations en route for London wrapped in canvas; frequently they were
protected by no more than brown paper. Because of the inadequate
packaging the contents were liable to damage by rough handling, dirt
or damp. The consignments had to be loaded and unloaded by hand so
labour costs were high. The railway did offer special low rates for
home-produced bacon and ham in 1 ton lots from Southampton and
Winchester to London, but no consignment of such a size was ever
tendered at either station. The average weight of home-produced
consignments of bacon and hams was 2 cwt and 3 quarters: the average
consignment of foreign bacon and hams was more than 130 times this
size. Even the clerical costs were higher for home-produced consignments. The foreign loads had just one invoice to cover many
tons, which were pre-packed and weighed and sent to a single
consignee. British consignments often had to be checked and weighed
at the stations where they were received and as they were often
split up among several consignees one load required several
invoices.

On this evidence the commissioners found that the different
rates were fully justified. In the case of fresh meat they did
require the company to make some minor modifications to the rates.
But they upheld the principle that lower rates for large consignments that were cheap and easy to handle, than for consignments sent
in small and irregular lots involving much trouble and working
expense, did not constitute an 'undue preference'. If British
farmers and dealers between Southampton and London could have sent
the same bulk that the foreign suppliers did, they could have had
the same rates. Part of the disadvantage regarding home-produced
meat sent along the London and South Western Railway Company's lines
stemmed from the fact that meat was sent from any one of fifteen
stations on the way to London. Inevitably this gave the company
very small individual loads. Unlike the meat trains from the docks,
these loads were sent at irregular intervals which necessitated
loading the meat into individual wagons and, because the cargo was
perishable, the wagon had to be put into the next passenger train
along the line.

Even when home-produced meat was sent regularly from a town by
goods train it was still likely to be more expensive to handle than
imported meat. The meat sent from Aberdeen to London was a case in
point. (33) In 1904 an anonymous correspondent to 'The Times'
complained that meat trains from Birkenhead to London charged 25s.
per ton, whereas the Aberdeen meat dealers were charged 70s. a ton
to send their meat to London. In fact, the rate charged from
Aberdeen was only 67s. 6d. per ton, but the services the railway had

to provide for meat from the two towns were in no way similar.
    The trains from Birkenhead were loaded right from the start and
they ran straight to their destination. The so-called 'special meat
train' from Aberdeen in fact only carried about 50 per cent meat;
the remainder of the load was made up of fish, livestock and general
merchandise for stations situated between Aberdeen and London.
Although the Scottish meat consignments were regular, those sent
from Aberdeen represented only small lots compared with those sent
from Merseyside. An analysis of the meat traffic from Aberdeen to
London for a fortnight in November 1904 and a fortnight in June 1904
revealed that out of 561 consignments sent in the four weeks, there
were only six between 2 and 3 tons, 136 were between 1 and 2 tons
and that 419 were less than 1 ton.
    In fact the rate charged to the Aberdeen farmers and dealers was
not in any way disadvantageous. The ordinary rate for fresh meat
from Aberdeen to London was 100s. a ton. The rate of 67s. 6d. was
itself a special rate for lots of meat not less than 3 cwt, so that
small traders could take advantage of it as well as large. When
account was taken of the greater distance from Aberdeen to London
than from Birkenhead to London, the ton-mile rate, which was the
cost to the consigner, was identical, as Table 8.1 shows. Consider-

TABLE 8.1 Fresh meat to London

From	Miles	Rate per ton	Rate per ton-mile
Aberdeen	523	67s. 6d. (owner's risk, any quantity over 3 cwt)	1.55d.
Birkenhead	194	25s. (large consignments)	1.55d.

Source: E.A. Pratt, 'Railways and their Rates', London, 1905, p.152.

ing the greater trouble in collecting, consigning and delivering so
many small consignments from Aberdeen, compared with the complete
train loads sent from the Mersey, it is likely that earnings per
ton-mile were much lower on the meat service out of Aberdeen than
for that out of Birkenhead or Liverpool. Certainly the meat trains
left Aberdeen less frequently than they left the Mersey. The
'special' meat trains left Aberdeen each evening, except Friday,
whereas the London and North Western Railway Company ran meat trains
from Liverpool to London every day (with rare exceptions), and on
Mondays and Thursdays - the heaviest days for the traffic - the
company generally ran three, and never fewer than two such trains.
The actual consignments of US meat from Liverpool to London by the
London and North Western Railway during 1904 were close on 45,000
tons. (34) During the twelve months ending 30 September 1904, the
Caledonian and North British Railway Companies between them
forwarded around 6,750 tons of fresh meat direct to London.
    In all cases the difference between the consignments of home-
produced meat and those of imported meats carried by rail was
between small and large loads. Thus, the farmer in Cheshire who
sent only a few hundredweights of dead meat from a wayside station
could not take advantage of the 25s. per ton charged to the

importers for the train loads from Liverpool and Birkenhead. Often
he did not tender enough to take advantage of the 40s. per ton
charged for 3 ton lots.

Given the dispersed nature of British agricultural production,
the problems in merely assembling a bulk load of English and
Scottish meat in one place were extremely great. E.A. Pratt records
attempts which were made from time to time to achieve this end.
They were all characterized by a lack of success. For instance,
attempts to start combined bacon farms and curing factories in
Norfolk and Suffolk, on the Danish model, had they been successful,
would have ensured large enough quantities of meat for the railways
to offer the same rates they gave the continental bacon off the
ships at Harwich. (35)

Another attempt to achieve the same object of large consignments
of domestic meat was made in Scotland, this time at Glasgow. When
the English railways originally conceded their 25s. a ton rate for
meat from Liverpool to London the Caledonian Railway Company, in an
attempt to encourage companies to land foreign meat at Glasgow,
offered the shippers a special rate of 45s. per ton to London for
20 ton lots, compared with the normal rate of 70s. a ton for meat
sent to London from Glasgow. The trade grew for some years and was
accompanied by complaints from the Scottish dealers in domestic meat
that they paid higher rates for Scottish beef than the other dealers
did for US beef. The railway companies gave the usual reply in
these circumstances: if the dealers could supply 20 ton lots of
Scottish meat they could have the same rates as the importers of US
meat. One of the local dealers managed to do this. He sent 20 ton
lots of Scottish meat to London at the 45s. rate. But in London he
was handicapped by the fact that there were no refrigerated stores
where he could keep his supplies when the market was over-stocked.
Only the persons in the imported meat business, who were geared to
handling bulk consignments, possessed cold stores. The machinery of
distribution for the domestic meat trade was only able to deal with
small lots. When only one dealer brought forward large consignments
it was impossible to accommodate him within the existing machinery,
and it was certainly not profitable to invest in cold stores for 20
ton lots of domestic meat when the foreign cold stores were carrying
stocks of many hundreds of tons. Consequently, the Glasgow dealer
was forced to abandon his enterprise. (36)

4   THE PURCHASE OF LIVESTOCK BY THE RETAIL TRADE

One question which came to concern the traders dealing in domestic
cattle had no counterpart among the persons dealing with US cattle
and foreign meat. This was the matter of responsibility for
diseased animals purchased from farmers in good faith by dealers
and butchers, and subsequently found on inspection to be unfit for
human consumption. The National Federation of Meat Traders waged a
fight from its beginning for adequate compensation arrangements for
the trade. The topic was referred to in various forms at every
A.G.M. up to 1914, and no satisfactory arrangement which applied to
the whole trade was arrived at.

The traders, like all other bodies subject to a degree of

official supervision, complained about the quality of meat inspection. They alleged that the inspectors, appointed by local authorities under local by-laws or the Public Health Acts, were unsatisfactory. It was frequently asserted that these men were untrained
and ignorant of the normal appearance of various meats. Because of
these deficiencies meat that was in fact quite sound was summarily
condemned and ordered to be destroyed and the unfortunate trader
was prosecuted. In the absence of independent 'expert' witnesses
it is difficult to tell how far these complaints from the butchers
were justified. The standards of the inspectors varied between
local authorities. Although the meat inspector of one town would
pass an article, it was no guarantee that the inspector of another
area would pass an article in a similar condition. Consequently
certain towns and boroughs gained a reputation within the trade for
being particularly harsh towards its members.

The greatest arguments over animal disease within the trade were
caused by tuberculosis in cattle. The matter became a hardy peren-
nial at the annual conference of the National Federation of Meat
Traders' Associations before the First World War. The 1906
conference adopted a resolution recording its 'most emphatic protest
against the harsh and extreme action of certain Metropolitan and
Provincial Local Authorities in ordering criminal prosecutions under
the Public Health Acts of 1875 and 1891 in relation to the seizure
and confiscation of meat for alleged tuberculosis, which had been
bought in good faith'. It was also decided to report all cases of
harsh and extreme action by local authorities regarding seizures by
the Local Government Board and if necessary to have the question
raised in Parliament. (37)

In this matter the butchers and meat traders as middlemen were
not only in conflict with the local authorities, but also with the
farmers. In their dealings with the local authorities there was
little that the butchers as individuals or the trade as a whole
could do. In 1899 the National Federation formed a Legal Defence
Fund Account which was called into action to fight, among other
things, cases against local authorities for 'unjust' meat seizures.
It also attempted to petition Parliament and the government in the
way just referred to on other occasions for some sort of legislative
protection. However, it was always agreed that these measures did
not bring about the desired effect. In their dealings with the
farmers the meat traders tried for more positive results. At the
1897 conference the first consideration was given to demanding a
warranty from the seller of stock, whether at an auction or on a
farm. When dealing with farmers the meat traders were undoubtedly
in a stronger position than when they faced the government. The
meat traders in an area were fewer in number than the local farmers
and were often the only local outlet for their stock. Farmers who
sold their stock locally were reluctant to send to markets further
afield. It was therefore possible for the buyers to combine to
exert oligopsonistic pressure on the farmers to enforce their own
conditions of sale, and to protect themselves against any loss from
purchasing animals that were subsequently found unwholesome.

The ability of the meat traders to extract the required guarantees from the sellers of livestock depended upon the ability of the
various local associations to take concerted action. The question

of warranties reached a crucial stage between the years 1908 and
1910. At the National Federation conference of 1909 a warranty was
demanded for all vendors on a national scale. In 1907 a London
butcher bought three cattle at Islington for £21 each. One of
these, on being slaughtered, was found to contain tuberculosis and
to be unfit for food. The carcase was voluntarily surrendered to
the inspectors and destroyed, the butcher receiving nothing for his
outlay. He applied to the farmer from whom the animal was purchased for compensation, but was refused. The meeting of the
National Federation at Portsmouth in August decided to take this
case to the High Court. The outcome of the test case (Newbury v.
Perowne) was not helpful to the trade. The Lord Chief Justice gave
a verdict in favour of the farmer because the purchaser had not
specifically asked for any guarantees when he bought the animal.
He suggested that the only help for the butchers was to demand or
enforce an expressed warranty for each animal they purchased for
human food. The meat traders were also aggreved by the verdict
because the National Federation had undertaken the heavy expenditure
of £300 on the case from their defence fund. (38)

At its next biannual conference the federation took action on the
judge's recommendation to demand a warranty. After 1 September 1908
any animal bought at any auction, private sale or fair by members of
the National Federation had to be guaranteed 'to be free from any
infections or contagious disease and warranted to pass the inspection of the Medical Officer of Health or any qualified veterinary
surgeon after slaughter'. (39) This demand immediately brought the
butchers into conflict with the farmers' associations. (40) The
debates between the butchers and farmers took up the autumn of 1908
so the ultimatum on the warranty was deferred until 1909. However,
national agreement with farmers' organizations was not possible so
it was decided that express warranties should be extracted and
enforced by local meat traders' associations. Also where associations had difficulty in securing this the federation arranged the
purchase and consignment to them of warranted cattle from farmers in
other areas. The warranty was conceded in a number of areas during
1909 and in other parts of the country partial indemnity was secured
or insurance schemes were put into practice. This practice gained
hold in the years following, especially after the war, and buyers of
cattle were gradually protected from losses in this way. (41)

In certain areas, insurance schemes of some description had
existed among purchasers of stock for many years before the matter
was made public. (42) For instance in north east England it was
the practice of the farmers at the sales to return to the buyers of
stock 1s. per head as luck-money. The custom has already been
mentioned elsewhere, (43) and it proved possible to adapt this
ancient practice, with a little ingenuity and imagination, to suit
the requirements of the twentieth century. This was achieved in
quite a simple way. The butchers used the luck-money to form their
own insurance scheme - the Newcastle, Gateshead and District
Butchers' Cattle Insurance Society. In 1907, 16,683 bullocks and
heifers bought in the North East were insured in this way. Of this
number 13,728 were thought to have been slaughtered in Newcastle and
forty-three claims for compensation had to be paid because the
animals had tuberculosis. This came to around one animal in every

300 which, according to the meat inspector, was probably an under-
statement of the incidence of disease. On these forty-three carcases the butchers were allowed two-thirds of their value from the
compensation fund and they received the amount obtained from the
market value of the hide and tallow from the carcase. These claims
cost the insurance fund £441 18s. 4d. At the end of 1907 the fund
paid its members a dividend of 5d. in the shilling and retained
£53 2s. 2½d. as a float for 1908. (44)

On the likelihood of detecting diseased meat the inspector freely
admitted that the chances were very strongly in the butchers'
favour. At that time Newcastle was a city of around 300,000 inhabitants. The slaughterhouses were small and scattered over a wide
area, which made the detection of diseased carcases by the
authorities a difficult matter. Newcastle had 132 slaughterhouses
in each of which an average of two beasts were killed weekly.
However, the risk of loss was always a deterrent for the small
butcher. In Newcastle even with the insurance fund some of the
smaller tradesmen, rather than run any risk of loss, preferred to
purchase ready dressed meat wholesale from the larger butchers. It
was admitted that this branch of the trade was growing rapidly in
1909 and tending to reduce the extent of small scale slaughtering
by butchers on their own premises, (45) even though this type of
retailer still predominated in the north east region before 1914.

Although the National Federation's publicity-conscious membership
gave a lot of attention to the question of tuberculous cattle
through the columns of the 'Meat Trades Journal' and also the
national press, the body did not speak for the entire trade. At one
meeting in London between the farmers and meat traders, held in
December 1908, to discuss the matter of a cattle warranty, some of
the farmers' representatives taunted the federation with the charge
that it was unrepresentative as it only spoke for a minority of
butchers. (46) The allegation was undeniable as the federation had
an estimated individual membership in 1891 of 1,000, rising to
11,000 in 1911. (47) But with the exception of London, where it was
also strong in 1908, the federation was probably strongest in those
parts of the country where retail butchers who purchased and
slaughtered livestock themselves made up the majority of the trade.
It was in these districts, of course, that the butchers' demand for
a warranty from farmers was most keenly expressed, because there the
question had the greatest bearing on the business lives of federation members.

In London the question could not have had the same urgency
because in that city the small retailer who did his own slaughtering
was in a minority. The decline of the retail butcher with his own
private slaughterhouse in London has been mentioned already, and was
under way in the 1870s. (48) It was estimated that at that time
there were 1,500 private slaughterhouses scattered around the
metropolis. By 1895 the number was down to about 700 and in 1906 it
was reported that there were only 315 left. These establishments
were strongly attacked in some quarters on the grounds of the filth
and nuisance that they caused and since 1883 an organization called
the London Abattoir Society had been in existence with their entire
suppression as its object, and the centralization of all slaughtering in London, under humane and hygienic conditions. (49)

In the twentieth century butchers representing the federation point of view tended to blame the retailers' uncertain position and liability to pecuniary loss when purchasing live animals as the chief reason for this change in London. It is true that the inspection of meat in the metropolis was made more exacting and the penalties for possessing unsound meat were, by the twentieth century, more severe there than in some other parts of the country. (50) But this alone is not a complete explanation of the relative unimportance, and the further decline in the position, of the small butcher who did his own killing within the structure of the London meat trade. As far as London was concerned the period between 1890 and 1914 saw the continuance of the trend begun in the 1850s. This was the increased reliance on the carcase trade to supply the London market with both domestic and foreign meat.

Livestock in London were offered for sale at two places. Domestic cattle and sheep were sold at the Metropolitan Cattle Market in Islington. Some foreign animals could also be sold there but only from those countries where it was considered that there was no risk of disease. Gradually, under the various Contagious Diseases (Animals) Acts, they could only be exposed for sale at the Foreign Cattle Market at Deptford where they did not come into contact with domestic animals. Until 1890 the numbers of foreign and domestic cattle coming into London had been about equal (see Table 8.2). Thereafter the number of foreign beasts grew at the expense of the domestic so that in the decade 1901-10 about 70 per cent of the cattle sold in London came from overseas; that is mainly from North America. The cattle sent to the Islington market fell in number in the 1870s from an annual average of 180,558 between 1872 and 1875, to 51,227 per annum between 1911 and 1913. Although the foreign cattle at Deptford rose from 94,783 per annum between 1886 and 1890 to 199,619 per annum between 1896 and 1900, this did nothing to increase the choice available for the small butcher who wanted to buy beasts to slaughter himself, as all the cattle at Deptford had to be killed before they left the market. The imports of foreign sheep declined after 1900, but so did the numbers of domestic sheep sent to Islington. Therefore, for both cattle and sheep supplied to the London market, there was a diminishing number available to be purchased by the small independent metropolitan retailer who wished to do his own killing before 1914.

The London market was, to a greater extent than in the country at large, supplied by foreign meat. The decline in the number of home-fed animals sent to Islington was attributed to the following causes: (51)

    (i)   Heavy railway company charges for the carriage of live animals.

   (ii)   The growth of local livestock markets within a small distance of London.

  (iii)   The absence of any compensation to owners of carcases seized as affected with tuberculosis where admittedly the presence of disease was not apparent while the animal was alive.

  (iv)   The ever increasing development of the chilled and frozen meat trade.

Although it is difficult to rank these causes in order of import-

TABLE 8.2   British and foreign sheep and cattle sold in London, 1872-5 to 1911-13

Average of years	Years	Home Metropolitan Cattle Market		Foreign Metropolitan Cattle Market		Foreign Foreign Cattle Market		% of foreign animals	
		Cattle	Sheep	Cattle	Sheep	Cattle	Sheep	Cattle	Sheep
4	1872-5	180,558	870,887	107,375	653,173	220,486	552,887	41.45	44.77
5	1876-80	179,253	789,200	68,179	210,464	70,399	551,487	43.60	49.12
5	1881-5	148,983	588,298	34,279	44,788	118,594	684,594	50.30	55.43
5	1886-90	142,674	684,820	46,678	81,560	94,783	508,282	49.30	46.26
5	1891-5	102,521	810,074		52,513	141,972	102,324	66.06	16.04
5	1896-1900	84,685	602,201			199,619	276,691	70.21	31.40
5	1901-5	73,507	519,452			169,719	67,722	69.78	11.57
5	1906-10	59,063	368,640			143,136	1,968	70.79	0.53
3	1911-13	51,148	289,386			44,338	1,990	46.43	0.68

Source: 'Departmental Committee on Combinations in the Meat Trade', P.P., 1909, XV, Appendix XII, no. 5, p.303. 'Agricultural Returns', 1911-13. 'Annual Statement of Trade for 1913', P.P., 1914, LXXXIII, p.99.

ance, it is unlikely that the third reason was more important than
the combined effect of the other three, especially as the decline
was under way well before the tuberculosis question attracted public
attention. It was the increased variety of meat supplied to London
from all sources which robbed the live cattle market at Islington of
its former significance. This applied not only to cattle but to all
kinds of livestock. Frozen mutton from Australasia after 1880 came
to replace the supplies of domestic sheep at Islington as the main
source of mutton sold in London. Associated with the decline in the
numbers of livestock sent to London was the decline in importance of
the big Christmas cattle market at Islington which was first noticed
in the mid-1890s. (52) Another symptom of the diminished importance
of Islington within the London meat supply system was the fact that
the market lost money. Prior to its removal from Smithfield in 1855
it had made an annual profit of around £6,000 but thereafter it had
lost about that sum annually. In 1892 the revenue at Islington came
to £27,793 and the expenditure totalled £41,212. Part of this loss
was on account of the competition from Deptford and the segregation
of the two markets meant an inevitable duplication of facilities
which had not existed prior to 1869, when Deptford was opened. In
the 1890s while Islington was losing money Deptford was making a
profit, and in 1892 the revenue from the Foreign Cattle Market was
£51,981 and the expenditure was £37,071. (53) As a market for swine
Islington had been long over-shadowed by the pig market at Finchley.
(54) The imports of Danish bacon reduced the importance of this
market as a supply centre for London by the twentieth century.
Imports were not the only reason for this, as restrictions over the
movement of domestic pigs to control swine fever hampered the pig
trade and helped to reduce London's dependence on home-fed animals
for its supplies of pork and bacon. By 1907 only 20 per cent of the
beef and mutton sold at the Central Meat Markets was domestic in
origin and virtually none of the pigmeat. (55)
    Finally, the position of the independent retailer within the
structure of the London meat trade was gradually eroded over time.
It has already been observed that the average wholesaler was a
larger trader than the average retailer and possessed greater
reserves of capital. Because of this the flow of credit in London
was from the wholesale to the retail section of the trade. (56) In
this way wholesalers gained control of a large number of retail
outlets through the agency of bad debts. In 1896 it was alleged
that the wholesalers at the Central Meat Markets had come to own
hundreds of shops after insolvencies. (57) When this happened, even
if the ex-owner were retained as the manager of the shop, the
establishment lost its former freedom to purchase live animals as
the new proprietor would naturally supply it exclusively with
carcase meat from his own stock. Even when there was no formal
ownership of retail outlets by the wholesalers, their activities
restricted the number of animals at Islington for the independent
butcher to purchase. This was because a lot of the animals exposed
for sale there were consigned by farmers, graziers and country
wholesalers to agents and salesmen in London. But many of the
London livestock salesmen also had stalls in the Central Meat
Markets. This created some problems as there were rules in both the
Islington and Central Meat Markets that forbade individuals from

selling to themselves. Nevertheless it was still possible to evade
the letter, if not the spirit, of these rules by members of the
trade selling to each other. In any event, the effect of this
situation was for the meat wholesalers to increase their share of
livestock purchases at Islington and for them to perform the
slaughtering before the animal passed to the retail butcher.

From the point of view of public health the meat traders' opposition to municipal abattoirs was certainly retrogressive. The
small slaughterhouse was often inconveniently sited and inadequately
equipped. The public abattoir had in its favour the advantages of
scale plus the fact that proper inspection of meat could only be
made if slaughtering was centralized, as even the most conscientious
inspectors found it impossible to visit the numerous small establishments of a large town regularly. In their opposition to the
municipal authorities the butchers were able to appeal to the
sentiment which had existed in the 1880s and was still strong in
Edwardian Britain. It represented the small scale trader as being
locked in a struggle for his very existence with forces threatening
to exert a powerful monopoly. The argument was similar to the one
employed in other branches of food distribution. In the case of the
meat traders dealing in home-produced meat these forces were the
large scale importers, the railway companies and the municipal
authorities.

The reaction of the meat traders was combination through the
National Federation. It is no accident that it was founded at a
time when the imported meat trade was undergoing a radical transformation both in importance and organization. In 1890 total meat
imports from all sources, including both livestock and dead meat,
were 30 per cent of total United Kingdom consumption. By the five
years 1910-14 imports accounted for 42 per cent of total consumption. (58) Like all the other associations of small traders the
National Federation was essentially conservative in its outlook.
Hence its opposition to what it deemed as unfair competition. At
times it even joined with the Grocers' Federation, the arch bastion
of the old order, to lobby for common objectives. In 1911 the Shops
(No. 2) Bill raised a storm of protest. The butchers along with
other traders objected to the enactment of a compulsory working week
of 60 hours for all trades. It was argued that this would cause
serious loss, delay and great confusion to the perishable foods
trades. The federation conference also voiced the archaic and mistaken belief that the arbitrary interference for the first time with
adult labour which the Bill contemplated was inimical to the
interests of both employers and employed. On a more progressive
note they also protested that the Bill continued to legalize Sunday
opening. (59)

The National Federation also gave its support to moves towards
training within the trade. In 1906 there were correspondents within
the trade press who were pressing for the introduction of a scheme
of education for the meat trade because of the lack of experience of
many traders. In 1908 the subject was discussed at the A.G.M. in
Manchester. It was revealed there that the local associations were
quite uninterested in the subject: none of them had ever applied to
the National Federation for a lecturer on technical instruction.
The first recorded course of technical lectures on the meat industry

was held the following year at the College of Agriculture in
Edinburgh with an audience of around 150. At the end of the course
an examination was set and the best candidate received, in accordance with current practice, a silver medal. The contents of the
course covered: the history of the trade; the development of cold
storage; the merits of public abattoirs versus private ones;
diseases in meat; sausage making and pickling beef. The beginning
of the course may also have been influenced by the start of
practical training for meat inspectors by the Royal Sanitary Insti-
tute in 1899. (60) However, such courses were not widely available
as training for members of the meat trade. Though it is difficult
to see what use knowledge of the history of the meat trade would be
to a practical butcher, no doubt the parts of the Edinburgh course
on cold storage and other technical matters were of some use to
entrants to the trade. The most important aspect of the butcher's
training, however, still depended on the acquisition of skills that
no amount of technical education could impart. The small butcher,
purchasing and slaughtering for himself, remained the norm in the
home-killed meat trade. After he had fulfilled the requirements of
hygiene and evaded the attentions of the meat inspector, the profit-
ability of his business depended on his own decisions. He needed to
anticipate customers' preferences for particular types and cuts of
meat. These were liable to vary widely, and sometimes illogically,
according to changes in prices, the availability of substitutes and
variations in the weather. The extent of his profits on each
carcase also depended very much on his skill as a butcher in cutting
the joints and as a salesman in persuading customers to purchase the
less popular pieces. As the historian of the retail trade has
observed: 'Up to 1914, however, the skilled butcher selecting and
buying livestock on the hoof, slaughtering, and retailing remained
the dominant figure in the home-killed trade ....' (61)

CHAPTER 9

IMPORTS FROM EUROPE AND NORTH AMERICA, 1890-1914

1 LIVESTOCK FROM NORTH AMERICA

Just as the imports of meat and livestock from Europe diminished
between 1864 and 1889, so the North American beef and cattle trade
declined after 1900. For the transatlantic trade the contraction
was more severe, so much so that the business became virtually
extinct by 1914. Before this occurred, however, these imports from
North America had gained a special position within the British
market by virtue of their high quality. This applied particularly
to the US and Canadian cattle landed mostly at Liverpool, but also
in smaller numbers at other ports along the west coast. North
American animals acquired a reputation for good quality because
there was a steady improvement of farm livestock on that continent
from the middle of the nineteenth century onwards. This was largely
done by importing pedigree stock from Scotland and England. In
addition the US exporting firms were careful to send a good class of
animals for sale in Britain. The attitude towards this trade was
explained in 1899 by John Clay, an important figure in the US cattle
industry. (1)

> We go to the parent country, buy in Aberdeen their best short-
> horns and Angus cattle, from Hereford and other parts of England
> we import the best white-faced blood .... The Europeans do not
> get our best cattle because New York and Boston still claim
> these, but the exporter buys a grade close to the top. He wants
> nothing else. This influence on the markets has been far reach-
> ing and all powerful when we come to guage quality .... One of
> the well springs of our prosperity rises in our export trade,
> and among its various branches our livestock products form no
> mean proportion .... Our live cattle exports alone last year
> exceeded in value £6,250,000 while our meats and dairy products
> had an aggregate value of £37,500,000, a seventh of the total
> value placed upon our exports of domestic merchandise in the
> calendar year 1899.

The bulk of the export cattle belonged to the 'good' and 'choice'
grades of steers and they weighed between 1,200 and 1,500 lb.
Comparatively few 'prime' steers were wanted, as the only time there
was an active demand for these beasts in Britain was for the

Christmas market. At other seasons the lighter weights, from 1,200
to 1,400 lb, were more in demand, and a good beast for export
weighed somewhere around 1,350 lb; the ideal requirement being
neither the best nor yet the cheapest grade of fat cattle. There is
also evidence that there was some regional variation within the
British market with regard to the type of animal preferred. Cattle
destined for the London market were invariably of better quality
and finish, as well as heavier, than those purchased for the
Liverpool and Glasgow markets, as the latter towns preferred to take
a cheaper, plainer grade. (2)

Though US cattle now had to be slaughtered at the port of debarkation, Canadian cattle were still allowed to be landed and sent
inland alive. This led to the growth of a trade in store cattle
which, though not numerically important, was found useful by
graziers in parts of Scotland and in Norfolk who would fatten the
beasts on for beef. The live entry of Canadian cattle lasted until
1892 when pleuro-pneumonia was discovered at Dundee among a cargo
of cattle from Montreal, and so from 1893 the same regulations
applied to cattle from Canada as from the USA, that is, compulsory
slaughter at the port of debarkation. (3) However, these regulations did not reduce the numbers of Canadian cattle which were still
imported, and seem to have had little impact at all on the trade.
The majority of the agricultural interest in Britain was in favour
of this move and it was supported by the Royal Agricultural Society,
the Central Chamber of Agriculture and the Smithfield Club. The
only strenuous objectors were the comparatively small numbers of
farmers who had made use of Canadian stores for fattening.

Although the cruelty objectors to the transatlantic cattle trade
were as vociferous after 1890 as they had ever been, they did not
have any influence in preventing it. There is little doubt,
though, that their complaints helped to improve the conditions under
which the animals were carried. This was reflected in a steady fall
of the numbers of animals reported dying on the voyage and also in
a reduction of the numbers sustaining injury. By 1892 mortality was
no more than 0.6 per cent of those carried. (4) But the North
Atlantic cattle trade only accounted for a small proportion of the
livestock carried by sea to Britain. In 1893 of the 2,655,976
imported into Great Britain from all countries, 2,253,200 came from
Ireland, and in comparison with this the North Atlantic trade with
a mere 345,428 was a relatively minor affair. (5) The worst
casualties occurred with the Irish trade, which was subject to far
less supervision than the transatlantic as it was part of the
domestic trade of the United Kingdom. It was here that the humanitarians and the Royal Society for the Prevention of Cruelty to
Animals needed to devote most of their attention.

As far as the US exporter was concerned, the business of shipping
live cattle was inherently risky. In the 1890s, it was calculated
that a difference of some 3d. to $3\frac{1}{2}$d. per lb between the Chicago
buying and English selling prices (6) was enough to enable the
exporter to recover his outlay and make a fair profit. The prices
in the two countries tended in the long run to adjust themselves in
this relation. A difference of more than $3\frac{1}{2}$d. per lb would
stimulate purchases for export in Chicago, and a decline of more
than 3d. per lb at Liverpool or London would make exporting a losing

business. The exporter's business was one involving some uncertainty and risk, as he was generally forced to engage his shipping
space some months in advance of when he would need it, and if prices
fell he would have to choose between sacrificing his freight or
shipping at a certain loss. (7)

This situation obtained late in 1892 and in the early months of
1893. At that time export cattle in New York, from Chicago, cost
from 3d. to 3¾d. per lb live weight (including their cost of transport to Great Britain), which meant about £18 per beast. These
animals were selling in London at Deptford market at 4¾d. to 5½d.
per lb (estimated dead weight, which accounted for 56 per cent of
the live weight), or £16 per beast. (8) In these circumstances the
decline in live imports was not long in coming, and while imports of
dead meat remained at their previous levels the number of livestock
fell, as Table 9.1 shows.

TABLE 9.1 Imported into the United Kingdom

	Number of cattle	Value of livestock (mostly cattle)	Dead meat (all sorts)
January-April 1892	142,150	£2,769,893	£6,909,729
January-April 1893	81,627	£1,513,574	£6,847,695

Source: 'Agricultural Gazette', new series, XXVII, 15 May 1893,
p.462.

The cattle and beef export situation was further complicated by
the level of home demand in the USA, but at this time the over-
riding factor was the price obtainable on the English market. In
1897 two-thirds of the cattle shipped to England had been bought in
Chicago, at prices of 2d. to 2½d. per lb. That year the price of
US cattle on the Deptford market ranged from 5d. to 5¾d. per lb, so
the margin appears frequently to have gone below the 3d. necessary
to make a profit. From this behaviour it would seem reasonable to
assume that the exporters, to keep their hold on the English trade,
were prepared to do some of their business at a sacrifice. But it
must also be remembered that by this date the large firms which
controlled the live export trade did a big packing and dressed meat
trade in the USA, as well as being in control of the export of
chilled beef, so presumably they could afford to conduct one branch
of their trade for a time without return in order to retain the
goodwill of their customers. (9)

Part of the reason for its survival in the twentieth century can
be explained by the agreements reached between the importing firms
to avoid wasteful competition and to share markets. In the first
instance this was a reaction to the losses sustained in the live
cattle trade in 1892-3. (10) There were some complaints from outsiders that the associated companies monopolized the carrying space
aboard the cattle boats and kept outsiders from participating in the
business. But by this time cattle carrying had become a specialized

business, requiring considerable expenditure to fit out a vessel for this purpose. These firms, who had large capital resources, were obviously in the best position to meet these expenses, and so they had greater facilities for the cattle trade, both from US and Canadian ports. (11)

Despite the fact that losses were at times experienced, the trade in imported cattle continued to expand to around a half million a year about the turn of the century. It did so in the face of intermittent criticism and downright opposition, as well as the disadvantage which the 1878 Contagious Diseases (Animals) Act had placed on it. Its expansion continued even after the lack of cold storage, particularly in the provincial towns, was quickly remedied after 1890. (12) With all these developments, the North Atlantic cattle trade was still able, in favourable times, to show a good return for those engaged in it, for despite the transport costs and handling charges, they could still find a sale for US port-killed beef at a higher price than the chilled meat would fetch.

As can be seen in Table 9.2, this article was able to command a price somewhere between that of the first and second qualities of home-fed English beef. Of course, the port-killed US meat was never good enough to compete with the best home-fed Scottish beef, but it

TABLE 9.2   Prices of English, and US and Canadian port-killed beef, 1905-9

Year	English				US and Canadian port-killed	
	1st quality per cwt		2nd quality per cwt		1st quality per cwt	
	s.	d.	s.	d.	s.	d.
1905	50	6	46	6	48	0
1906	49	6	46	0	47	6
1907	51	6	48	0	51	0
1908	54	0	50	6	53	6
1909	54	0	51	0	53	6

Source: 'Agricultural Returns'.

did compare favourably with a sizeable proportion of the English beef that was sold. Furthermore, when cut up and displayed by English butchers it was very difficult, if not impossible, to tell it from the genuine home-produced article. This was never the case with chilled beef. The process of chilling invariably led to some discolouration and US butchers cut a carcase differently from English butchers, so its origins would be apparent to the experienced eye.

This closeness in quality between port-killed and home-fed beef led to some butchers fraudulently selling Birkenhead- and Deptford-killed beef as English. The practice aroused frequent outcries from British farmers that they were being exposed to unfair competition and that the British public were also being cheated. These fears had always been present since the first (and sometimes over-

exaggerated) reports about the quality of the US cattle imports had
appeared in the British press in the late 1870s. (13) But complaints about this form of competition first became marked around
1887 and 1888, after the fall in meat prices in the mid-1880s.
Farmers' committees and their MPs began to agitate for legislation
to control this fraudulent sale of US beef, and in 1890 the Central
Chamber of Agriculture, in London, took up the case and pressed for
an Act of Parliament making it compulsory for all foreign meat,
whether imported alive or dead, to be marked as such. (14) Indeed,
between 1893 and 1894 there were three Bills before the House to
provide for the marking of foreign meat, and the question came up
again in 1897 in the wider context of marking all foreign agricultural produce sold in Britain.

   Competition from the imported animals was most heavily felt in
the neighbourhood of the great ports where they were landed. This
was especially serious for the farmers near the lairages at
Liverpool. Mr James Kay, President of the Lancashire Federation of
Farmers' Associations, told a House of Lords Select Committee in
1893 that there was a demand for the marking of foreign meat from
farmers around Accrington, Darwen, Bolton, Rochdale, Bury,
Rossendale, Preston and Chester. He and the other farmers in this
area had noticed how difficult it was to get local butchers to come
to their fatstock sales when they knew the same butchers went to the
foreign lairages at Birkenhead where over a thousand head of cattle
were slaughtered daily: they had come to the conclusion that the
money which used to be spent with them in the past was now going on
foreign meat at Birkenhead. (15) Five years later a farmer from the
Wirral told a House of Commons Select Committee that the live US
beasts were sold at the lairages in Birkenhead for less than it cost
him to produce and market a similar grade of animal. The same
witness confirmed that the full brunt of the competition from this
class of imports was being borne by the farmers in the vicinity of
the ports: 'We cannot get the same price per pound that people in
the country get. So we have to compete against the lairage more
than the Midland counties.' (16)

   The importance of adequate cold storage at ports receiving
imports of live cattle after 1878 was demonstrated by the plight of
Newcastle some twenty years after the passing of the Contagious
Diseases (Animals) Act of that year. Under the Act, US animals
would only be landed at those ports which were able to satisfy the
authorities that they had sufficient arrangements for quarantine
and slaughtering. By 1898 there were only seven ports in the
United Kingdom that satisfied this requirement and were allowed to
accept such cargoes: these were London, Manchester, Liverpool,
Bristol, Hull, Glasgow and Newcastle. Over the years all these
ports had, with the sole exception of Newcastle, provided cold
stores to hold the meat from the animals if it could not be sold
immediately after their slaughter. The lack of cold stores at
Newcastle meant the livestock trade of that port fell, whereas at
the others it increased. In 1883 around 90,000 foreign cattle and
70,000 sheep were landed at Newcastle but by 1898 the numbers of
cattle had fallen to 3,608 and the sheep to zero, whereas Liverpool
handled 87,037 foreign cattle and 49,752 sheep in 1883 and 254,547
foreign cattle and 283,025 foreign sheep in 1898.

Some decline in the relative importance of Newcastle as a centre
for the reception of imported animals was perhaps inevitable as the
emphasis was switched from Europe to North America as a source of
supply. In 1890, when the European trade was on its last legs, the
US shippers expressed interest in developing Newcastle as an
alternative to Liverpool. They were prepared to put the yards at
the port in a condition to satisfy the more stringent demands made
by the Privy Council for the receipt of US cattle at their own
expense. Dealers in Newcastle showed interest in this proposal and
asked the US consul there to investigate the situation and provide
them with more information. (17) However no mention of cold stores
was made at this time. This may have been because the cattle landed
at Newcastle were Scandinavian animals, which could be moved inland
and exposed for sale at the Newcastle livestock market alongside
domestic beasts. As this option was not open for US animals, and
as the local dealers would not be involved in the distribution of
the carcase meat from the port-killed US cattle, it may explain why
no further interest was shown in the proposal. The Newcastle cattle
market itself served a population of about a million persons, but
only about a quarter of this number lived in the immediate vicinity.
The meat supplies for the majority in the outlying districts were
taken thence on the hoof. As long as this was possible the imported
cattle sold at Newcastle were at no competitive disadvantage vis-a-
vis the domestic animals they were sold alongside, and the presence
or absence of cold storage in the town was of no importance. In the
next few years Newcastle did not remain without cold stores and
there is evidence that the town had its share of the general
construction of this type of plant in the provinces in the 1890s.
(18) But there is no record of cold stores being erected specifically at the docks to handle incoming cargoes of livestock or meat.

In the twentieth century it was found that Newcastle and its
immediate neighbourhood (with a population of 247,000 in 1901) could
only absorb imported beef at a rate equivalent to about 200 animals
every week or so. One cattle boat, however, could carry as much as
three times that number. The lack of cold stores also meant there
was less scope for transporting the beef to markets any distance
from Newcastle. This problem was most acute in summer months.
Unless the carcases are cooled soon after slaughter, beef deterior-
ates rapidly in hot weather. The problem presented itself in July
1895 when two cargoes, each of 600 cattle, were landed in Newcastle
within a few days of each other. Total demand was not much in
excess of 400 beasts and the hot weather and lack of sufficient cold
storage prevented the remainder from being kept in Newcastle or sent
to other markets without risk. As a result, the importers had no
choice but to 'cash' all the animals in the town for what they would
fetch and lost around £1,200 on the two cargoes. (19)

The decline of the cattle trade from North America was shared by
the chilled beef trade and both had the same cause. The explanation
can be found in conditions in the USA and not in competition from
other sources of supply within the British market. The growing
population of the USA and rising real incomes in that country meant
that domestic demand was able to absorb nearly all the beef production of the USA. As population grew many of the ranges formerly
given over to cattle raising were broken up and devoted to more

intensive systems of farming, particularly cereal-growing. The
result was that in the decade 1900-10 beef cattle production in the
USA actually declined 18 per cent, although the increase in population during the same period was 20 per cent. (20) The concomitant
rise in the price of beef at home meant it was no longer worthwhile for the US firms to ship either cattle or beef to the United
Kingdom. The decline was not unexpected. In 1909 R.H. Hooker,
the chief statistician working for the Board of Agriculture and
Fisheries, concluded that the USA was approaching the end as a
supplier of imported meat to Britain. Instead he looked chiefly
to the countries in the southern hemisphere to supply the nation's
imported meat in the future, to South America for beef and to
Australasia for mutton and lamb, (21) the point being that these
countries did not have large urban populations, like the USA, to
consume their meat production at home.

With profits squeezed, one reaction from the firms exporting live
cattle to the United Kingdom was to pay closer attention to the
processing of the animal by-products left after slaughter, as these
could make the difference between profit and loss. In this, the
firms were aided by the English local authorities that owned the
wharfs where foreign animals were landed and did not want to see
them standing idle. This tendency can be seen in the arrangement
between the Manchester Corporation and the US firm of Morris and
Company in 1907 for the former to provide special accommodation in
connection with the slaughtering establishment attached to the
foreign animals wharf in that port, for the storage and treatment of
animal by-products. The Manchester lairages had been opened in
1896, the same date as the Manchester Ship Canal, when the imports
of US beasts were approaching their limit. As the cattle ships to
that port passed through the canal, the Manchester Corporation had a
double interest in maintaining the traffic using the waterway: it
collected the tolls, and it wished to preserve the revenue it earned
from the foreign animals wharf, which it owned. But even without
help from the local authorities, the importers were taking a greater
interest in the industrial processing side of the business. At
Birkenhead, Swift and Company and Morris and Company jointly owned
the National Oil and Hide Company. (22)

These efforts by British local authorities to maintain the situation had only a temporary success. They were ineffective as
attempts to reverse the trends of the international meat trade. The
cessation of this flow had important, and even distressing,
consequences for the local economies of the ports concerned. In
April 1910 it was reported that there had been practically no work
at the Foreign Cattle Market for the previous six months. As each
animal landed there earned some £5 or £6 by such things as drovers
charges, butchery, and also the processing of by-products, the end
of the trade had a profound effect on the labour market in
Greenwich. Similar effects were noticed at the other ports that
dealt with foreign livestock. It was alleged that unemployment
among the drovers, slaughtermen and butchers at Deptford, Woodside
and Glasgow was so serious that it had led to some emigration of
these personnel from all those places. Many of those who stayed
were added to the thousands who regularly haunted the docks before
the First World War in the hope of finding some casual employment.

It was argued that this was a powerful reason for ending the embargo on the landing of Argentine cattle, which had been in force since 1903. (23) However, the government did not adopt this response because of the risk of importing animal disease. As a result the extinction of the trade was seen in the autumn of 1913 (See Table 9.3). The monthly livestock trade reports which appeared in the 'Journal of the Board of Agriculture' ceased to quote North American port-killed (or North American chilled) beef prices after October of that year, and the foreign animals wharfs at London and Liverpool were practically empty in the months before the war.

TABLE 9.3 United Kingdom imports of livestock from North America and Europe, 1890-1913

| Year | Cattle(a) | | | Sheep and lambs(b) | | Swine | |
| | North America | | Europe | North America | Europe | North America | Europe |
	US	Canada					
1890	384,639	121,312	133,657	46,544	289,829	1,086	2,950
1891	314,895	108,289	78,032	42,170	281,423	-	540
1892	392,934	98,239	6,058	18,572	45,918	3,802	24
1893	248,892	82,925	41	3,589	36,034	137	1
1894	381,932	82,323	3	333,760	76,276	-	-
1895	276,533	95,993	120	667,560	85,695	319	-
1896	393,119	101,591	34	350,527	75,167	-	-
1897	416,299	126,495	-	250,516	12,797	-	-
1898	369,478	108,405	-	189,091	28,086	450	-
1899	321,229	94,660	-	184,960	22,650	-	-
1900	350,209	104,839	-	178,579	24,217	-	-
1901	405,704	88,211	-	368,162	15,432	-	-
1902	324,431	93,674	-	288,260	4,943	-	-
1903	301,760	190,812	-	254,677	16,623	-	-
1904	401,249	146,598	-	372,639	9,601	-	-
1905	414,906	148,714	-	178,335	4,749	-	-
1906	398,887	160,688	-	98,480	4,879	-	-
1907	344,461	125,752	-	103,069	2,532	-	-
1908	259,700	122,086	-	76,385	2,515	-	-
1909	205,449	113,583	-	8,131	-	-	-
1910	138,387	78,691	-	427	-	-	-
1911	155,817	42,239	-	47,673	-	-	-
1912	39,987	6,800	-	15,430	-	-	-
1913	10,093	1,755	-	501	-	-	-

Source: 'Annual Statement of Trade', P.P.
(a) Omitting imports from the Channel Islands, Iceland and Greenland.
(b) Omitting imports from the Channel Islands, including Iceland and Greenland.

2   NORTH AMERICAN CHILLED BEEF

The North American beef and cattle trade reached its peak just
before the turn of the century, both in terms of absolute size and
of the relative importance of its contribution to the imported beef
supplies of Great Britain. Along with its growth in size the
organization of the trade had undergone a complete transformation
since the 1870s. The number of businesses engaged in the trade had
been somewhat reduced and the previous unrestricted competition
between the firms exporting meat and animals to Great Britain had
been made a thing of the past by the rise of the giant concerns in
the meat industry within the USA. Just as circumstances had
favoured the extension of these firms' control over the US domestic
market, they also allowed them to gain a large measure of control
over the exporting business, with a system of subsidiary companies
in Great Britain, which reflected the policies of the parent firms
in the USA. (24)

Instead of the risky business of selling to commission agents,
which prevailed in the 1870s and early 1880s, the firms went more
directly into the meat wholesale business and acquired a number of
stalls in the Central Markets at Smithfield, beginning with Swift's
purchase of the Corner Stone Tavern in 1891. (25) The reason for
this change was the dissatisfaction on the part of the importers
with the services provided by the established wholesalers who
handled the chilled beef. They complained that English firms over-
charged for their services by returning false weights for the meat
passing through their hands, and some US firms sought proof by
weighing the meat themselves. (26)

Along with the various agreements made between themselves to
limit competition, the US firms sought to dictate to the English
companies handling their business at Smithfield the exact terms on
which they would continue to do so. It had always been the custom
for English wholesale purchasers to claim an allowance of 1 lb on
each quarter of beef for 'wastage' when cutting up carcases. The
US firms announced in October 1894 that henceforth any English firm
handling their product should cease this practice. They also forbade these salesmen to make any of the traditional allowances to
their trade customers. The Smithfield traders objected to being
told how they should deal with the retail side of trade as, in the
past, they had more or less dictated their terms to the British
farmer for handling his meat. The ensuing conflict between the US
companies and the London wholesalers lasted into 1895. The
Americans exerted pressure by stopping supplies to those salesmen
who allowed the 1 lb rebate. It was a radical departure from the
pattern of business in the past for any suppliers to try to dictate
the conduct of the trade. In this respect the US companies were in
a far stronger position than the British farmer who sent only a few
beasts to London at infrequent intervals. Whereas the latter had
to accept the customs of the jobbers and wholesalers, the former,
who were dealing in hundreds of carcases a week, could dictate terms
to the wholesalers and determine the character of the trade. But
although the US firms were able to abolish the rebate system among
those companies who continued to act for them, the move was bitterly
resented by the Smithfield interest. (27)

In this way North American firms secured greater control over the disposal of their beef. But they were able to exercise this in other ways and not all of their meat passed through the wholesale markets; the firms had arrangements with various retail organizations in London and the provinces, to supply them direct with port-killed and chilled US beef. To do this they acquired numerous wholesale depots scattered up and down the land, but particularly concentrated in those districts that had the greatest density of population. For example, in 1908 the Morris Beef Company had twenty-three separate branches in the United Kingdom. In terms of geographical coverage this selling organization was more comprehensive than any possessed by any firm in the frozen meat trade. The one with the largest number of branches in that business was the River Plate Fresh Meat Company, which only had them in fourteen centres. (28) The Morris Beef Company's wholesale outlets were most numerous in the south of England and around London. With branches in Southampton, Croydon, Kingston, Brighton, Hastings, Tunbridge Wells, Ramsgate, Dover, Canterbury and Windsor, their network covered practically the whole south east corner. To serve the Midlands there were two branches, in Birmingham and Northampton. Lancashire was covered from Manchester and Liverpool, and Yorkshire from branches in Leeds and Bradford. In the north east of England the firm was established in Newcastle and Grimsby, while the west country was covered from Bristol, Plymouth and Torquay. Finally, Morris had branches in the two major Scottish cities. (29) The control exercised by the North American firms did not extend further forward into the retail business. Their provincial branches were strictly wholesale and the actual selling to the public was mostly undertaken by the traditional sort of small scale butcher. Given the high quality of US beef it was probably easier for the retailer to combine the sale of this article with domestic meat than to incorporate lower quality products like frozen beef or mutton into a home-produced trade. The situation in the early years when supplies of chilled beef sent by several firms arrived simultaneously no longer applied from about the mid-1890s. Within limits, the firms engaged in the business were able to arrange that supplies of beef were not released onto the market in such quantities as to depress the price unduly. But the limits of this practice were still set by the storage life of the chilled beef once it arrived in port, so, in this respect, the frozen meat from South America and Australasia was still far less vulnerable to the low prices of an over-stocked market. Moreover, the large US firms were also powerful enough to negotiate special rates with the railway companies in Britain for the bulk carriage of their produce, a matter that was always a source of grievance to British farmers who had to pay high inland transit rates on the small quantities they sent.

Although consignments of foreign meat were always large when compared with domestic ones, they had quite different characteristics depending on whether the meat was chilled or frozen, or if it was fresh meat from US cattle slaughtered at Birkenhead. Frozen beef from South America would be piled onto the trucks with fore and hind quarters on top of each other until the truck was full. In this way 4 tons 10 cwt could be put in one truck. Chilled beef

was more susceptible to damage en route and so more careful
attention had to be paid to loading it. In this case only between
3 tons 5 cwt and 3 tons 6 cwt could be loaded into a truck. Fresh
meat - live cattle from the USA slaughtered at Birkenhead - had to
be suspended on hooks from the roof of the trucks. This limited
the carrying capacity to only 2 tons 10 cwt per truck. (30)
    Even the size of the trains varied for different types of meat.
The loads of fresh meat were always sent from Birkenhead by the
Great Western Railway. The meat train to London comprised, on an
average, twenty-six wagons. Each train therefore represented about
65 tons of fresh dead meat. The chilled and frozen meat was always
dispatched from Liverpool, usually by the London and North Western
Railway, but the Midland and other companies also handled considerable quantities. The meat trains to London run by the London and
North Western Railway contained an average of fifteen wagons.
Table 9.4 presents a comparison of the varying weights of train
loads of different meats sent to London, together with the costs of
sending these different amounts.

TABLE 9.4 Comparison of the loads and costs of different types of
imported meat sent by rail from Liverpool to London in 1904

Type of meat	Load per truck	Average no. of trucks per train	Load of meat per train	Cost per train at rate of 25s. per ton
Fresh (Birkenhead killed)	2 tons 10 cwt	26	65 tons	£81.25
Chilled	3 tons 5 cwt to 3 tons 6 cwt	15	48 tons 15 cwt to 49 tons 10 cwt	£60.94 to £61.87
Frozen	4 tons 10 cwt	15	67 tons 10 cwt	£101.25

Source: E.A. Pratt, 'Railways and their Rates', London, 1905,
pp.135-6.

    Meat was also carried by rail direct from Liverpool to the
provincial centres of consumption. Meat carried to these places
was usually charged at a higher rate than for London. One reason
for this was that the meat for the provinces gave more trouble than
that for London. The Provincial consumer of beef and mutton was
more discriminating than the London customer. The provincial
markets got the best qualities from any shipment. Whereas the
consignments for London went straight from the steamer to the railway wagons, those for the provinces had to undergo a process of very
close inspection and selection. Although this work was all carried
out by the importers or their representatives, as it was done in
the railway company's loading sheds, it necessitated an increase in
requirements both for accommodation and railway labour. Another
reason for higher proportionate rates for provincial meat was that
the railways could not make up through train loads as for London.

The average truck load of frozen or chilled meat sent to London
came to 3 tons 10 cwt, the average truck load of the same sent from
Liverpool to the provinces was 1 ton 18 cwt. Also there was a
better chance of return cargoes to fill the meat vans sent from
Liverpool to London than there was for those sent to the provinces.
(31)

By 1900 the transatlantic beef and cattle trade was controlled by
the firms Armour and Company, Swift and Company, and Morris and
Company. These three had branches under the same names trading in
the United Kingdom. In the USA they also controlled the National
Packing Company, which had an English subsidiary called the Hammond
Beef Company which dealt in dressed beef and live cattle. (32)
These four firms were the backbone of what was known in the USA by
others in the trade, and by government watchdogs and investigators,
as 'the Trust Companies'. The purpose of the trust was to eliminate
what it considered to be wasteful competition among its members,
though just how much its behaviour served the public interest was
a matter of fierce controversy, on both sides of the Atlantic. Less
important than these four, both in the USA and the United Kingdom,
were the Cudahy Company and Messrs Schwarschild and Sulzberger,
whose United Kingdom representative was Archer and Sulzberger.
Both of these worked in association with the trust at some time or
another; Cudahy in a loose association and Schwarschild and
Sulzberger only prior to 1903.

The entry of trusts and combinations into the North American meat
export trade was a relatively late phenomenon when compared to the
progress of these bodies in other branches of the food trade. In
1903 meat was not included among the items of exported foodstuffs
whose production was controlled by trusts, cartels, syndicates, etc.
There were only five items of food with which these organizations
were connected and they were flour, sugar, glucose, eggs and
chocolate. (33)

After 1903 the combination, both in Britain and the USA, became
less close. In the USA Schwarschild and Sulzberger disagreed with
the trust in 1903 and thereafter conducted their business on both
sides of the Atlantic as completely free agents. With the diminution of supplies of cattle and beef from the USA to the United
Kingdom there was less need for such close co-operation between the
companies on the eastern side of the Atlantic as the United Kingdom
trade was now of less importance to the US firms. Also, the growing
shipment of chilled beef from the Argentine to the United Kingdom
after 1900 meant that the North American firms no longer held a
practical monopoly of the trade in this product and so co-operation
among themselves became increasingly irrelevant as far as chilled
beef was concerned. Furthermore, the acquisition by the trust firm
of Swift of an establishment in the Argentine led to a conflict of
interests which was to further weaken this aspect of the trust's
activities. (34)

The falling off in this trade led to some misgivings in Britain.
One allegation made was that the rise in beef prices in 1908 which
took place in Britain was the result of the trust firms' combining
among themselves to raise the price artificially by holding back
supplies for the market. However, the Departmental Committee on
Combinations in the Meat Trade which reported to Parliament in 1909

found there was no evidence to support this allegation. It was true
that the trust practically controlled supplies of North American
beef but this article was only a part of the foreign meat on sale
and it was certainly not a large enough portion for any group
controlling it to influence meat prices as a whole. Also, as the
trade was beginning to diminish in importance when the committee
undertook its investigation, there was even less evidence of, or
reason for, combined operations among members of the trust than
there had been when the trade was at its height. Indeed, the rise
in prices which had prompted the committee's investigations was no
more than a warning that supplies of imported meat, from all
sources, were ceasing to grow at the rate at which they had done
prior to 1900. (35)

Although a lot of attention was devoted to the chilled beef
trade at the time, it is important to note that pigmeat was the
largest item of meat imported from North America, in terms of
weight (see Table 9.5). In all years more bacon was supplied by
the USA than imports of chilled beef from that country. To this
must be added imports of hams from there also, as well as the rather
smaller quantities of Canadian bacon and ham. In the decade 1901-
10 the annual value of pigmeat products imported into the United
Kingdom varied between £17.3 million and £20.1 million, not
including imports of lard. Over 70 per cent of this was supplied
by North America. Between the same dates the value of imports of
beef and cattle varied from £6.6 million to £9.8 million, or
roughly a half that of pigmeat. The latter does not appear to have
been handled by the same firms that dealt in beef. In 1904 the
Morris Beef Company described itself as 'Importers of American
dressed beef, pork, poultry and provisions', and Armour's also
listed the same commodities on its trade advertisements. (36) But
the majority of US and Canadian pigmeat came to this country as
bacon with hams taking a secondary place. Imports of fresh pork
from North America were quite a minor item and only accounted for a
few thousand hundredweights each year. Instead of being handled by
the trust firms the North American bacon and hams sold in this
country were in the hands of a separate group of businesses.

This was because the chain of distribution for cured pig products
(i.e. bacon and hams) was totally different from the one existing
for fresh meat (i.e. beef, mutton and pork, whether chilled, frozen
or unrefrigerated). Whereas the last three were the sole stock in
trade for the ordinary retail butcher, the former two were merely
one branch of the grocery trade, often sold in the same shop alongside eggs, cheese, butter, lard and tinned meats under the general
heading of provisions. Therefore the retail outlets and contacts
used by the trust firms to dispose of their imported beef were not
appropriate for ham and bacon and very little of these passed
through Smithfield in London. Because imports of provisions
included a high percentage of standardized grades of commodities
with a predictable quality, wholesale dealings could be conducted
through the machinery of a produce exchange. Such an institution
existed for dealings in butter, cheese, lard, tinned meats, bacon
and hams. It was called the Home and Foreign Produce Exchange,
Ltd., and it was situated in London. The membership of this company
included all the large firms of importers, dealers and wholesalers

TABLE 9.5 Principal meat imports from North America and Europe, 1890-1913

Year	Beef US(a)	Bacon Denmark	Bacon US	Pork Canada	Pork Holland	Hams US	Hams Canada
	cwts	cwts	cwts	cwts	cwts	cwts	cwts
1890	1,693,148	465,866	2,934,465	292,420	25,994	1,094,383	108,848
1891	1,747,578	580,868	2,675,054	151,109	90,114	1,116,441	83,680
1892	1,951,887	671,882	2,895,951	239,121	92,808	1,131,279	114,198
1893	1,489,949	711,854	2,177,293	193,773	120,147	920,961	57,780
1894	1,775,538	766,828	2,561,203	254,203	133,526	1,075,270	50,576
1895	1,649,473	1,013,930	2,649,482	268,886	245,726	1,203,157	81,707
1896	2,074,644	1,222,114	2,751,518	456,723	244,344	1,285,976	169,276
1897	2,242,063	1,026,552	3,592,635	290,283	226,215	1,603,533	119,133
1898	2,301,956	1,017,520	4,087,389	535,879	222,672	1,851,520	117,428
1899	2,756,458	1,210,612	4,088,546	453,773	344,346	1,823,965	150,698
1900	2,867,238	1,094,626	3,956,527	529,864	389,184	1,602,453	196,182
1901	3,180,291	1,060,909	4,244,329	398,697	377,061	1,730,536	125,867
1902	2,290,465	1,255,627	3,283,855	462,487	353,398	1,312,779	163,930
1903	2,693,920	1,496,101	2,893,507	665,249	527,269	939,169	197,497
1904	2,395,836	1,723,884	2,806,108	829,883	448,154	1,042,732	196,732
1905	2,232,206	1,471,687	2,755,233	1,191,390	306,379	1,022,855	292,173
1906	2,426,644	1,463,880	2,775,919	1,190,524	318,296	1,045,718	254,495
1907	2,417,604	1,806,934	2,280,644	1,192,401	429,324	832,042	296,949
1908	1,432,142	2,051,148	2,541,945	1,004,126	384,004	900,795	321,463
1909	856,216	1,809,053	2,189,053	443,386	378,376	1,073,569	53,593
1910	477,147	1,794,416	1,306,921	411,935	366,197	665,775	37,621
1911	174,350	2,122,087	1,817,835	615,807	370,345	887,303	62,295
1912	6,111	2,318,708	1,698,347	387,401	264,050	819,997	74,525
1913	1,462	2,334,945	1,803,371	243,522	4,188	760,567	90,082

Source: 'Annual Statement of Trade', P.P.
(a) Fresh beef, i.e. mostly chilled.

trading in these goods throughout England. Although this exchange was located in London and concentrated on the provision business in the south of England, its influence was felt further afield as businesses in Liverpool - which imported and consumed a large amount of North American bacon and hams - were also members of the London exchange. (37)

In some respects this trade had greatly altered since the 1860s. The most important change was made in the methods of curing. By the twentieth century most US bacon and hams were very mild cured and much less salt was used in the process than a generation or so earlier. This produced a more palatable and therefore higher priced article but it also gave it a much reduced storage life. Instead of being able to keep their stocks for a number of weeks, or even months, importers now handled an item that required almost immediate consumption, even with cold storage. This caused no problem as cargoes were sent from North America at regular intervals so that the same quantities arrived throughout the year and the trade had nothing of a seasonal character. The importers were also saved the expense for long periods of storage on this side of the Atlantic and the wholesale trade merely had to ensure that supplies were equalized with the level of regional demand.

There are indications that US bacon was particularly popular in the north of England and that the US curers had taken the trouble to prepare a product suited to local tastes. For instance, there was a range of names applied to bacon and hams, according to how the carcase had been divided, that suggested particular regional associations. Thus there was one cut called 'Cumberland', another 'Yorkshire', as well as others called 'Stafford', 'South Stafford', 'Wiltshire' and 'Welsh Wiltshire' (sic). (38) Of these the Cumberland and Yorkshire types, which were cut so that they included more of the cheaper parts of the carcase, were particularly popular in the north of England. In the poorer parts of Liverpool 'Cumberland' hams weighing 20 to 30 lb were sold, while in the better neighbourhoods of the same city the demand was for the same type of cut but weighing from 30 to 40 lb. In general the north of England was prepared to take rather more fat on its bacon and hams than was required in the south. In London, where the demand was so large by virtue of its size, all types of bacon and hams were consumed, though lighter weights were most popular. (39) As US and Canadian pigs were mostly fed on a diet which produced more fat on the carcase than English, Irish or European pigs, the product was generally well suited to the northern towns. In addition, most of the US bacon imported into this country was landed at Liverpool. There is also evidence that the custom noticed in the 1860s where US bacon was shipped from Liverpool to Ireland and Irish bacon was shipped in the other direction for the English markets (40) still existed in the twentieth century. In most years the flow of this item across the Irish sea was more or less equal: the cheaper US bacon was imported into Ireland and the finer Irish bacon found a market at a much higher price in England. (41)

The importance of imported supplies in the pattern of meat consumption for individual towns could vary greatly and it is not always safe to generalize about the reasons for these differences any more than it is to do so about the variety of regional tastes

and preferences for different types and qualities of meat. As far
as beef was concerned the indications are that markets further from
the ports were more self-contained and drew more on local supplies
than those of the large cities with easy access to the lairages.
In general it was cost and convenience that determined from what
areas a particular town would draw its supplies of meat. Evidence
given before the Departmental Committee on Combinations in the Meat
Trade reveals that in 1907 80 per cent of the meat sold in Dundee
was home produced, 90 per cent in Newcastle, and in Norwich almost
100 per cent, whereas over 50 per cent of the beef sold in
Manchester was foreign (either chilled or live imports), and in
London over 80 per cent of the meat sold at the Central Markets at
Smithfield was foreign. (42) In the years 1876-80 meat produced in
the United Kingdom made up 86 per cent of the meat handled at
Smithfield. This large fall in the proportion of home supplies
within a generation was also accompanied by a complete change in the
methods of the market.

The failure of foreign imports to dominate supplies in certain
areas, however, appears to have been due more to the abundance of
local supplies than to any difficulties over transport. The strong
geographical bias which the sale of imported meat had in favour of
London, the Midlands, and parts of Lancashire around Liverpool, has
been explained by local preference. It has been noted that in
Yorkshire, the northern counties, the south west, Wales and
Scotland, the butchers refused to sell imported meat except as a
last resort. (43) However, the areas where the foreign meat was
sold had larger concentrations of urban population than the areas
where the foreign meat was less in evidence, and these latter areas
generally specialized in the fattening of livestock. (44) Taken
together, these two factors indicate that the public in these areas
could afford to be selective in their purchases of meat because
local supplies were adequate to meet the level of demand. In the
more densely populated areas supplies of home-fed meat were
insufficient to satisfy the higher demand, and there it was cheaper
to sell the imported meat than to have home-fed brought in from
outside the region. Furthermore, it seems that the failure of
foreign imports to dominate supplies in certain areas can be
explained by the adequacy of local supplies, rather than any purely
physical difficulties over transport. In the case of Norwich this
was known to have been so, not only from the evidence of a
representative of the US meat firms but also because the Norfolk
buyers of store cattle had ranged as far afield as Yorkshire,
Westmorland, Cumberland, Lincolnshire, Northamptonshire and
Leicestershire in their search for animals, and had also received
Irish stores from Liverpool. (45)

3 THE EUROPEAN TRADE

The extinction of the livestock imports from Europe came in the
1890s. In 1890 cattle imports were only allowed from Holland,
Sweden, Denmark and Norway. In 1892 the trade from the first three
countries was stopped and an insignificant import was still allowed
from Norway until 1897 when that too was finally ended. Imports of

sheep from Europe continued rather longer and did not end until
1908 (see above, p.165). However the numbers involved were insignificant after 1891 and only in the years 1894-6 did they exceed
75,000 annually. After the trade in sheep from Holland was stopped
in 1892, the remaining imports from Europe came only from Norway,
Denmark, Iceland and Greenland. Imports from Norway were ended at
the same time as the cattle trade from that country. (46)
Accompanying the fall in livestock imported from Europe was the
final demise of the sea ports on the east coast as centres of the
livestock trade, a process that had started in the 1880s. The only
place in the eastern half of England to retain any importance in
this trade was London with the Foreign Animals Market at Deptford.
Between 1901 and 1905 the only ports in Britain receiving foreign
animals were, in ascending order of importance, Liverpool, London,
Glasgow, Manchester, Bristol, Hull, Cardiff, Newcastle and
Southampton. (47)

As a consequence of these changes, by the twentieth century the
only contribution that Europe made to the British meat supply was
through imports of Danish bacon and a much smaller quantity of
fresh meat, mostly pork from Holland. The conduct of the Danish
bacon trade was rather more impersonal than any of the other kinds
of imported meats since prices were regulated from Copenhagen and
not in London. Also for this article, as with Irish bacon, very
little business was handled by wholesalers and most was imported
directly by retailers. (48) Danish bacon had its largest sale in
London and the south of England where it competed closely with Irish
as to quality and price. The Danish article had less fat than the
US bacon, and as consumers in the southern part of the country were
alleged to dislike any kind of fat meat the imports from Europe had
the greatest share of the market in that region while US bacon and
hams dominated the market for imports roughly north of the Trent.
In 1896 most of the bacon housed in the cold stores at Manchester
came from Canada, the USA and Ireland. Very little was sent there
from Denmark because the price in that market was not high enough.
(49) The geographical distribution of sales was, however,
extremely sensitive to relative price changes. For instance, in
1902 the supplies of US bacon sent to Britain declined as a
consequence of the cyclical fall in the number of pigs in the USA.
This caused a shortage of bacon in the north of England and prices
of imports rose from £2 7s. 1d. a cwt in 1901 to £2 12s. 9d. in
1902. The result of this was that a part of the Danish (and
Canadian) bacon that was normally sent to London was diverted to the
northern markets and consequently there was a shortage throughout
the country and a generally higher level of prices as the price
effects were communicated to domestic supplies. (50)

The ability of the Danish producer to supply an article which
competed successfully with English and Irish bacon depended very
much on the close co-operation between the pig producer and the
curing establishment. In co-operative ventures, which dominated the
Danish industry as early as 1896, the bacon factories were owned by
farmers' associations and run by a council of the members. The
parties agreed to deliver all their saleable pigs to the factory for
a fixed term, usually of seven years. In this way the factory
manager was guaranteed a constant input and the farmers could be

sure of a permanent market. The greatest difficulty lay in guaran-
teeing an economic price to farmers. For the factory this was not
so difficult because if the supply of swine was falling off, the
manager could purchase from non-members of the co-operative at a
price fixed weekly by the council, and this price was brought to
the attention of members. Quality control was ensured by strict
grading and payment for the different grades was agreed by the
factory manager and the council. Further quality control was sometimes enforced by prohibiting the farmers from feeding their animals
on fish offal and fish cake, which had a bad effect on the flavour
of the flesh, and also not allowing a diet containing more than 50
per cent of maize, as this produced too much fat in relation to lean
meat for the finished article to command the highest price. At the
end of the year any profits were distributed among the members in
proportion to the weight of pork they each delivered to the factory,
after setting aside an appropriate amount for reserves. (51) The
English and even the Irish bacon industry lacked this intimate
association between producer and factory and so the curer was unable
to exercise the same degree of close control over the article
delivered to the factory and hence the quality of the final product.
Also the (unknown) extent of farm curing resulted in a completely
non-standardized product for that portion of the industry's output.
Finally, the Danish system offered the farmer a certain degree of
protection from the violent price fluctuations of an industry with
intensely cyclical characteristics. The fact that the producers
involved owned the factory itself made possible some redistribution
of an equalization of income between times of low and high prices.
In Britain the industry was not so important within the whole
agricultural sector and therefore did not receive the same degree of
organization and attention. (52)

   Imports of fresh meat from Europe were, on a national scale,
rather insignificant. However, they did make a measurable contribution to the London meat supply and they comprised one of the
categories of meat sold at the London Central Markets, Smithfield.
Between 1906 and 1908 there were five categories of home-produced
and imported meat which together made up the total supplies passing
through Smithfield. These are shown in Table 9.6. The disappear-

TABLE 9.6 Home-produced and imported meat passing through
Smithfield, 1906-8

Beef	(	40 per cent US beef
	(	10 per cent home-fed beef
Mutton	(	25 per cent Australasian mutton
	(	10 per cent home-fed mutton
		15 per cent continental pork and mutton
Total		100 per cent

Source: 'Departmental Committee on Combinations in the Meat Trade',
P.P., 1909, XV, Appendix XII, Nos 2-4, pp.302-3.

ance of home-produced pork from the London trade by the twentieth
century was principally an effect of the stringent regulations for
the control of swine fever. The continental supplies that filled
this place were neither chilled nor frozen. In this respect the
trade was similar to the imports of beef and mutton that were a part
of the metropolitan meat supply in the 1860s. (53) The animals were
mostly killed at the Channel ports in Europe and from there
dispatched directly by fast steamer to the port of London. In this
way the European exporters avoided the prohibition imposed on the
entry of live animals under the Contagious Diseases (Animals) Acts.
Even so the carcases were still inspected at Smithfield and the
results were not always satisfactory. According to the meat
inspector for the market, commenting on the general condition of the
pork carcases that arrived from Ostend: 'We find them suffering from
all kinds of disease, lung disease, typhoid, measles, and goodness
knows what.' (54)

However, despite the presence of disease in some of the carcases,
there is evidence that the European fresh meat trade generally aimed
to supply the high quality market. This applied particularly to the
carcase trade in mutton from Holland. Most of it was actually
produced in that country, though some originated from Germany. At
the Central Markets, Smithfield, this meat was in steady demand
from butchers whose customers required high quality meat, and as it
compared very favourably with the best mutton produced in Britain,
for instance that from Scotland, it also commanded some of the
highest prices. (55)

CHAPTER 10

FROZEN MEAT

The switch from predominantly European to largely trans-oceanic
supplies of imported meat after 1880 was accompanied by new problems
of storage and distribution. The freezing and chilling works of
North and South America, Australia and New Zealand and the refrigerated ocean freighters were essential features of this trade, but
the provision of efficient cold storage in Britain was equally
important. In the two decades from 1880 the firms that imported
fresh meat into Britain faced the task of building up a national
distribution network for their wares. This network had two important components. The first requirement was either part-time agents
or full-time employees to organize the trade and seek retail outlets. The second was plant in the form of cold stores to ease the
problems of distributing the stocks within this country. As the
volume of imported fresh meat grew there was an inescapable need for
cold storage space if the problems of glutted markets and ruinously
low prices were to be avoided. The rather crude refrigerated
transit vans provided by some railway companies in the 1890s were
also an adaptation of this technology to overcome other difficulties
of distribution.

1 COLD STORES

Cold stores in Britain were provided by a number of different
organizations, most of them having some prior connection with the
meat trade, either directly as importers or indirectly like dock
companies. They were also provided on an unplanned and ad hoc
basis as and when the need for them seemed apparent. As with the
first stores, already mentioned, for chilling meat from slaughtered
imported US cattle, (1) the early cold stores were confined to
London and Liverpool which received the largest quantities of
refrigerated meat. As the quantities of fresh meat sent to other
ports increased cold stores were erected there; then as the distribution network was extended to include inland provincial towns cold
stores were finally established in these places. The whole process,
however, was very gradual. For instance few provincial towns had
cold stores for meat before 1890. The unplanned development of this

side of the business may have been one of the reasons for the
relatively slow introduction of frozen meat into some areas at this
time. For the 1880s and 1890s there is evidence of under-capacity
and high demand for storage space. When the industry did react to
this situation and provide larger numbers of cold stores during the
boom in domestic investment in the second half of the 1890s this
deficiency was quickly remedied. (2) Probably the remedy was too
quick and too effective as there were complaints of over-capacity
in the cold storage world after 1900.

The first effective cold store for frozen meat opened in London
was a dockside installation owned by the London and St Catherine
Docks Company. This store was situated in part of a converted
warehouse and was originally intended for the Australian meat trade.
It consisted of a large vault some 500 feet by 70 feet and could
hold 500 carcases of (56 1b) sheep. This was in 1882. As the trade
grew the size of the store was increased by taking over more of the
warehouse till by 1886 it was sufficiently large to hold 59,000 56
1b carcases. The next development was carried out by the East and
West India Docks Company which provided stores upon two floating
hulks, the 'Seawitch' and the 'Robert Morrison'. The combined
capacity of these two vessels was a further 15,000 sheep carcases.
(3)

In the early installation of cold stores, both in London and the
provinces, the dock companies took the leading role. This development was viewed as a profitable extension of their services to their
clients. It was also advantageous for the importers to be able to
store the meat as close as possible to the point of discharge from
the ship. In this way the meat, at least in theory, was less likely
to be damaged by a long journey from ship to store. In practice,
of course, ideal conditions for the transfer of meat from ship to
store did not always apply. This was so in the older docks,
principally London and Liverpool, where the meat had to be loaded
first on a lighter and from there to a wharf. The arrangement was
not ideal because of possible damage to the meat through double
handling and also from any delay in transferring it to the cold
store. However, in the absence of wharfside unloading of the ship
it was the best method and dock stores minimized the extent of the
journey from ship to store. Therefore in the 1880s the development
of cold storage as a public service was pioneered by the dock
companies. However, despite their early start they were not able
to keep pace with the growing volume of imported frozen meat and
this encouraged the establishment of cold stores on alternative
sites.

The first attempt to establish an 'up town' cold store in London
- i.e. a store away from the docks - was a failure. In 1883 a
group of meat traders from Smithfield attempted to form a company
for the purpose of building a store under part of the market, but
their plan never became operational and the company, the Dead Meat
Storage Company, was dissolved in 1890. In the meantime a second
company of Smithfield traders, the Central Markets Cold Air Stores
Ltd, was formed in 1884 and they took over the idea of building a
cold store in the vaults of Smithfield. Although the store did
become operational it was never a great success, possibly because
the site was not entirely suitable given the technical limitations

of refrigeration engineering at the time. The company was wound up
in 1901.

The first successful up town cold store for frozen meat was built
in 1885 by Messrs Nelson Bros, a firm directly engaged in the New
Zealand frozen lamb trade. In 1884 this firm began to send meat to
London from its Tomoana works at Hawkes Bay. Like the other cold
stores at this time, the Nelson Bros' premises were not custom
built. Their store was located in the arches under the Cannon
Street railway station. However, the situation was not as inconvenient as it might at first sound. Also Nelson Bros were not the
first firm to use this site to store meat. In 1878, Daniel
Tallerman's company, the Fresh and Preserved Meat Agency, had
established a cold store there, from which it distributed chilled
North American beef. (4) Under the station a central arch ran
from Thames Street to the river and from it other arches ran at
right-angles. At the river end of the central arch was a landing
platform and the carcases were unloaded here and put into trucks
which were pushed along to the smaller arches, each of which had
been insulated and fitted out in order to store the meat. When the
time came to release the meat it was pushed in the trucks up to the
Thames Street end of the main arch. From here the meat was easily
loaded into vans for Smithfield or else into railway company vans to
be taken directly to other railway stations and thence to the
provinces.

Unlike the Smithfield attempts, the Thames Street cold store was
an immediate commercial success. In the short run the company
found it lowered their costs for storing meat and this effect was
transmitted to other importers still using the dock companies'
stores. As Nelson's trade grew the Thames Street premises became
inadequate for their purposes. In 1889 they opened a second
freezing works in New Zealand and the additional carcases needed
more storage space than the Thames Street store allowed. In 1892
the company opened their own riverside custom built store in
Commercial Road, Lambeth. The store had a capacity of 250,000 56 lb
carcases and was at that time the largest cold store in the British
Isles. It was on five floors and the meat was unloaded from the
barges and moved about the store by mechanical hoists. In addition
there were mechanical cutting machines for separating the carcases
when smaller parts and joints were required. (5)

In the early 1880s the difficulties facing the distribution of
frozen meat in the provinces were as great as in London. In
addition to the lack of cold stores, there were no reputable retail
outlets through which to channel the product to the consumer. The
towns presented smaller markets than London and were consequently
easier to over-supply with meat. Many had also traditionally drawn
their meat supplies from local farmers so in these cases the seller
of frozen meat was confronted by a strong consumer preference in
favour of the domestic product. Faced by these unfavourable
conditions the frozen meat suppliers concentrated the bulk of their
early efforts in the sea port cities.

As in London the first cold stores in the outports were provided
at the docks. (6) The first provincial up town store was erected
in Williamson Square, Liverpool, in 1883. This enterprise was
headed by Thomas Borthwick, an Edinburgh man who had started in

Liverpool and Manchester as a livestock agent twenty years earlier.
Borthwick was quick to see the possibilities of the frozen meat
trade and opened depots in Manchester, Glasgow and Birmingham to
handle the trade. He specialized in the sale of Australasian meat
(he was selling agent for the New Zealand Loan and Mercantile
Agency Ltd in 1883) and concentrated on pioneering the product in
the provinces in the 1880s. It was not until 1892, when this trade
was established, that he transferred the head office of his importing and wholesale distribution business from the provinces to
London. (7)

The Williamson Square premises were a public cold store which
could be used by all traders on payment of the storage rates. The
next provincial up town store was also a public one, this time a
municipal enterprise erected shortly after by the Manchester
Corporation near the city's meat market. (8)

In both London and the provinces cold storage accommodation was
generally inadequate throughout the 1880s. In 1888 there were only
eight cold stores in London with an estimated capacity of 300,000
56 lb carcases. In addition there was space for a further 100,000
carcases at Liverpool. (9) Imports of frozen mutton and lamb
amounted to 888,509 cwt and frozen beef imports were 45,022 cwt. In
addition 784,429 cwt of chilled beef was imported in that year.
Thus the country's total cold storage capacity was only 21 per cent
of frozen meat imports and 12 per cent of total refrigerated meat
imports. Put another way, the cold storage capacity in 1888 was
equivalent to eleven weeks' supplies of frozen meat or only six
weeks' of all sorts of imported fresh meat.

The rates charged for cold storage dropped between 1883 and 1891
as additions were made to the available space. It is difficult to
measure the reduction precisely as the cold store keepers charged
varying rates from the outset according to the size of the consignment handled. The rule employed was to charge lower rates per unit
of weight for larger 'parcels' of meat containing a greater number
of carcases than for small parcels of just a few carcases. This was
because each parcel had to be kept separate and the particular
labels or other marks on the carcases had to be identified when it
was withdrawn from store. The effect of this was to increase the
handling costs of smaller parcels of meat. Also, as the trade grew
and the average size of the cargoes increased, the definition of a
large parcel needed to be revised upwards. In the early years the
store owner made two separate charges, the first was for carrying
the meat to the store and an initial rent, usually for one week,
and the second was the actual rent for the carcases for any period
of time thereafter. Also in the early years there were several
conditions as to minimum charges stipulated by the store owners.
In the very early days of cold storage the rate charged was around
¾d. per lb per period of 28 days, the equivalent of 140s. per ton.
This rate was drastically reduced through the 1880s till in March
1891 the London cold store owners introduced what was called the
'management rate' of one-ninth of a d. per lb per 28 days or
20s. 9d. per ton.

The first fears that cold storage capacity was likely to exceed
requirements were expressed for Liverpool in May 1899. In that
month the North Western Co-operative Cold Storage Company Ltd opened

new premises at Redfern Street with a capacity of 270,000 cubic
feet - equivalent to 85,000 56 lb carcases. (10) By 1901 the
situation had grown more serious and the cold store owners had
banded together to form the familiar type of trade society - in this
case the Liverpool Cold Storage Association. In addition to
competition among themselves the cold store companies also faced
further competition from ice making companies, who had also formed
their own association in the city. In the event the efforts of
both organizations were only partially successful. The Cold Storage
Association did prove a restraint against the most cut-throat
general rate-cutting among the main body of the trade. But like
the ice association its main problem was with outsiders who would
not join and therefore would not accept any control over the level
of their rates. (11)

The problem of under-capacity in the cold storage industry
appears to have disappeared first in the provinces. During 1899
practically no addition was made to the number of refrigerated
stores in London, and only one or two in the provinces, started
during the previous year, were completed. In London there was
some scarcity of accommodation at times, but in the provinces there
was a superabundance of space throughout the year. In London the
expansion of business in other frozen goods besides meat, that is
mainly butter, rabbits, fruit and furs, was responsible for any
scarcity of space. One difficulty facing cold store owners was the
unpredictable level of arrivals, which made it hard to say how much
cold storage space was necessary. In July 1899 the London arrivals
of frozen meat were the equivalent of 800,000 56 lb carcases; in
February they were only a quarter of this number. (12) It was as
difficult to provide satisfactory cold storage as it was to provide
satisfactory marketing for such irregular arrivals. At the same
time, owing to this uncertainty and the need at all times to have
enough space to allow for the prompt unloading of meat ships, the
cold stores at the Victoria Docks were being extended by the dock
company.

Against this background of reported over-capacity, excessive
competition and rock-bottom cold storage rates it is hard to understand accounts of the persistent extension of capacity, both in
London and the provinces during the early years of the twentieth
century. For example Weddel's 'Review' for 1900, 1901, 1903 and
1904 reports the building of new cold stores both in London and the
provinces. (13) Part of the reason may have been an ill-founded
optimism by company promoters as to the prospects for future
expansion of demand for cold storage space, but this seems unlikely.
In 1900 the first meeting in London of the Cold Storage and Ice
Association was very sparsely attended and one trade journal
gloomily noted the fact. (14) An alternative interpretation would
be that comparatively few members of the industry felt any need for
the protection of a trade association. A little later the 'Cold
Storage and Ice Trades Review' editorial articles between 1901 and
1903 complain about reckless company promotions and claim that cold
storage rates had reached their lowest possible levels. However,
the very persistence of the first complaints indicates that there
was no shortage of fresh investment in this branch of the food
industry after 1900. Also, if profits had been as low - at times

non-existent - as the editorial writers claimed then presumably
there would have been a wholesale reduction in the number and
capacity of cold stores as they succumbed to bankruptcy. No such
reduction took place. At the end of 1900 there were twenty principal cold stores in London with a capacity of 1,648,000 56 lb
carcases: in 1912 the number of operational cold stores for the
capital had risen to twenty-nine with a capacity of 3,032,000
carcases. (15)

The thesis that the supply of cold storage accommodation was
equal to demand after 1900, with isolated examples of excess
capacity in particular towns in individual years, is given additional support from the quantities of natural ice imported into the
United Kingdom between 1865 and 1914. Natural ice was principally
obtained from Scandinavia and was brought into the country on a
substantial scale from the 1860s. In the absence of mechanical
refrigeration this material was used in the food trades as an aid
to preservation. In many respects it was not an ideal product. At
times questions were asked about its purity and whether the lakes
from which it was cut were liable to contamination. In addition,
it was a very difficult material to handle in transit.

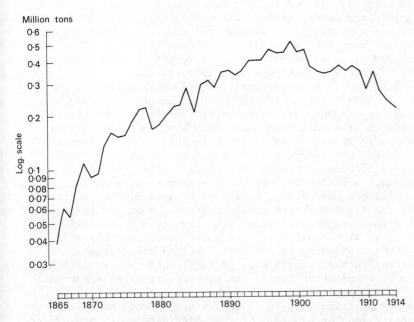

FIGURE 10.1 United Kingdom imports of ice, 1865-1914

In spite of these objections, imports of ice grew steadily from
38,605 tons in 1865 to 224,837 tons in 1878. The depression of the
late 1870s checked this growth from 1879 to 1881. Thereafter the
trend of imports was upwards in the 1880s and 1890s but at a slower
rate of growth than in the 1860s and 1870s. The peak for ice

imports was reached in 1899 at over half a million tons. The continued growth of imports in the 1880s and 1890s, alongside the establishment of the refrigeration engineering industry and cold stores in the United Kingdom, seems to indicate an unsatisfied demand for such services. The falling off in imports of natural ice after 1899 coincides with the complaints from some sections of the industry that the rate of growth had slowed down and that profit margins had been reduced. Among the London cold store owners an unofficial agreement had existed since 1899 and this was generally adequate to prevent the worst excesses of unrestrained competition. This agreement was sufficient to maintain the 'management rate' of one-ninth of a d. per 1b or 20s. 9d. a ton except for a brief period at the beginning of 1906. After this time of three short months of civil war among the store owners when goods were accepted at as little as 10s. a ton, the agreement was restored and the 'management rate' was once again enforced. Also, after 1898 the dividends paid by cold store owners declined. In 1909 the average ordinary dividend of twenty of the principal cold storage companies in the United Kingdom was slightly over 5 per cent. (16)

By 1900 the structure of the cold storage business was heavily weighted in favour of public cold stores all seeking business wherever it could be found. In 1912 only six of the twenty-nine London cold stores were privately owned by meat importers and their combined capacity of 259,000 56 1b carcases made up only 8.5 per cent of the storage space available in the capital. The private cold stores had a guaranteed trade and the cost of their services was part of the operating expenses of the meat importing firms. No such guaranteed trade existed for the public cold stores. In London their reliance on meat was less complete than in the provinces, but the scope for diversification was limited. Goods like fruit, rabbits (from Australia), butter, cheese and furs did provide additional trade for store keepers but frozen and chilled meat remained their staple commodity, both in London and elsewhere. The temptation to reduce rates in order to obtain more trade was reinforced by the peculiar technical requirements of cold store management. The optimum solution was to fill a store entirely with just one product and then to keep it at a single temperature. In these circumstances overheads were lowest because of the assistance rendered by the already frozen goods in keeping down the temperature; a half-full store required more engine power to maintain the temperature than did a full one. The worst possible combination was to have a store containing frozen meat, chilled meat, fresh fruit, and some of the chambers unfilled. As these goods all required different degrees of coldness and the empty sections also needed to be cooled, fuel consumption was heaviest.

However the plentiful supply of cold storage space after 1899 was a factor that eased the problems of the distributor. To some extent he was able to avoid the worst market fluctuations that resulted from irregular arrivals at the ports. Also the public benefited from lower storage costs which contributed towards cheaper meat. The only really serious shortage of space before 1914 was in 1909 when unusually heavy supplies of South American beef congested the cold stores. (17) As this was the result of a trade war between the firms operating in South America that was aimed at

altering the shares of trade they currently held, it does not
destroy the thesis that cold storage space was adequate to the
trade's requirements.

2 DIFFERENCES BETWEEN AUSTRALASIAN AND SOUTH AMERICAN METHODS

From the start there were marked differences in the distributional
arrangements in Britain between the importers or South American and
Australasian frozen meat. These variations originated in the way
the freezing companies were constituted and managed in the countries
where the meat came from. Also a rather different sort of relationship between the farmers who produced the animals and the companies
that exported the meat evolved in Australia and New Zealand from
that in South America. In many instances in Australasia the farmers
had close connections with the freezing plants and in some cases
owned them; very often the exporter was working directly for the
farmer who had fed the animals and still owned the meat when he
undertook a meat shipment to Europe. In South America there was
always a rigid distinction between the farmer and the exporter. The
freezing companies only purchased the livestock from farmers; at
that point the agriculturist's interest in the meat finished and the
freezing works undertook the export on their own behalf only.
    The initial exports of South American frozen meat came from the
Argentine and the freezing firms were located in one region, along
the estuary of the River Plate. Admittedly this was an area of
coastline that extended for some 100 miles, but these works were
nowhere near so geographically dispersed as the Australian works or
even those in New Zealand which were located on both islands. In
addition there were considerably fewer firms engaged in the meat
freezing and exporting business from South America than from
Australasia, and the size of their plant and the scale of their
operations was considerably larger. Also the industry was based on
a single established banking and commercial centre, in the city of
Buenos Aires.
    The pioneering work of the River Plate meat trade was carried out
up to 1885 by five separate concerns, though by the early 1890s this
number had been reduced to three. Of the successful companies two
were British and the third was registered under Argentine law. The
first firm to export South American frozen meat was a British one,
the River Plate Fresh Meat Company Ltd, which shipped 7,500 frozen
sheep to London in 1883. This firm was established in 1882 by an
English businessman connected with South American banking and railways, George W. Drabble. The company had no previous experience of
the meat trade, though it started with a capital of £100,000 put up
by the directors. (18) Two other firms which followed in this
trade, both Argentinian, La Compania de Carnes Congeladas (1883) and
La Congeladora Argentina (1884), each failed to make a success of
the business. The former ceased to operate by the early 1890s when
it passed into the control of the three successful companies who
kept the plant closed to eliminate competition. The latter firm
suffered almost instantaneous extinction.
    The two other River Plate firms were, like the River Plate Fresh
Meat Company, both successful. In 1886 the firm of James Nelson and

Sons, cattle salesmen in Dublin, Manchester and London built the Las Palmas works at Zarate and formed a company called Nelson's River Plate Meat Company (in 1889 changed to Nelson's (New) River Plate Meat Company) to supply the parent firm in England with frozen meat. In 1893 the firm was registered in Argentina as the Las Palmas Produce Company, the family in England holding all the shares. This firm had the advantage of the existing network of distributive contacts in the British meat trade possessed by James Nelson and Sons. The final firm to enter this trade was the Compania Sansinena de Carnes Congeladas which in England became popularly known as the Sansinena Company. This firm was already engaged in the manufacture for export of tinned meat in the early 1880s and in 1885 they built a freezing works from which to export mutton to Great Britain. Although the Sansinena Company did not have a pre-existing network of British contacts they were able to take advantage of the Nelson ones by making their first English shipments to James Nelson and Sons in January 1887. In the following months they took a close interest in the marketing of their product in Britain and opened a Liverpool office in 1887 and one in London the following year. (19)

Whereas there were relatively few companies exporting from South America, the Australasian trade was characterized by a large number of separate establishments engaged in the same sort of business. In 1899 there were seventeen freezing works in Australia and twenty-five in New Zealand, while the number in South America still remained at three. (20)

Australia, the pioneer of the frozen meat exporters, did not retain the lead given by her early start and her other two competitors forged well ahead. The development of the freezing industry in Australia was not undertaken on such a scale as in New Zealand. This was partly due to the periodic droughts that Australia was subject to which reduced the surpluses available for export at irregular intervals. Also it was partly caused by the distances separating the sheep breeding districts from the shipping ports. The features of geographical distance and widely dispersed pastoral settlement had the effect of increasing the number of separate freezing works required in each State as it was often impossible to transport sheep (and to a smaller extent cattle) any greater distance to a series of large centralized freezing works. As a result the early freezing works were all coastal, at the point of shipment, and linked by rail to the interior livestock producing areas. In Australia the freezing of mutton was only a secondary agricultural enterprise; the main source of agricultural income came from the sale of merino wool. Only the surplus sheep were exported, mainly when world wool prices were particularly depressed.

In the case of New Zealand the frozen meat industry arrived just in time to put farming on a paying basis. In that country the surplus of livestock was so great that sheep had little value apart from their fleece. In 1880 the flocks of both islands amounted to almost 13 million animals and the human population was under half a million (21) persons. The success of the Australian consignment aboard the 'Strathleven' in 1880 encouraged a number of farmers' groups in New Zealand to take preliminary action to form companies to undertake meat refrigeration. These enterprises were started by

farmers in conjunction with land, mercantile and finance companies.
In the early 1880s farming was so depressed and farmers were themselves so indebted that the pastoral industry was in fact largely
in the hands of these companies. Without their financial assistance there would have been little chance of establishing the frozen
meat trade on agricultural capital alone.

Taken alone, the entrepreneurial combination of several groups
of farmers working in co-operation with a number of land and
finance companies is not sufficient to explain the large number of
separate freezing companies which characterized the New Zealand
meat trade. However, it was a feature of the industry which was
further encouraged in the early years by the readiness of profits
and the comparatively low cost of entry into the business. Unlike
the Australian trade the New Zealand export of frozen mutton grew
steadily each year from its beginning in 1882 to 1895 and only
suffered one setback in the quantity exported before 1900, in 1896
(see Table 10.8). At the same time the prices the meat fetched in
Britain remained high enough to make the trade a paying one, at
least for some of the shippers. Critchell and Raymond report that
the first drop in New Zealand lamb prices, caused by an over-
supplied market, came in 1889. (22) Other evidence reveals that
some firms were facing difficulties as early as 1887. (23) In the
early 1880s the refrigeration plants were primitive affairs and
their capacity only needed to be small both on account of the
limited cold storage capacity afloat and the small extent of the
trade in England. For example, the second company formed to export
frozen meat from New Zealand was the Canterbury Frozen Meat Company
with a capital of only £20,000 in 1881 and an original works with a
daily killing and freezing capacity of only 250 to 300 carcases of
mutton. Not until after 1890 did the market value of mutton in
England fall sufficiently to force all New Zealand companies to look
closely at the economics of their business and to pay stricter
attention to things like overheads, unit costs and distribution
arrangements in Britain, (24) but by that time there were already a
large number of firms established in the trade.

The matter of distributing their products in Britain raised
fewer problems for the River Plate meat firms than it did for the
bulk of the Australasian companies. This advantage cannot be
explained in terms of a superior South American product. In the
case of all meat, the only general guide to quality which can be
used is that of price. On this basis the quality of South American
mutton and lamb was below Australian, and considerably below the
quality of mutton and lamb originating from New Zealand. In 1885
New Zealand mutton at Smithfield was $5\frac{1}{4}$d. per lb, Australian mutton
was $4\frac{3}{4}$d. per lb and South American mutton $4\frac{3}{8}$d. per lb. (25) When
the freezing industry in South America was started the sheep avail-
able offered an unpromising future for the industry. At that time
the Argentine national animals was characteristically a Spanish
Merino or Rambouillet, justly celebrated for its wool but certainly
not for its mutton, (26) producing a light carcase that compared
most unfavourably with the well grown meaty carcase of mutton from
a cross-bred New Zealand animal. Despite attempts (which were
successful) to improve the Argentine breed by crosses with imported
pedigree rams from Britain, New Zealand mutton always remained

decidedly superior to South American.

In the years between 1883 and 1902 the distribution arrangements of the Australasian meat companies were often compared, not at all favourably, with those adopted by South American firms. Because of the restricted entry into the River Plate trade before 1888 the South American firms were able to undertake greater extensions in the size of their plants and to increase the whole scale of their operations as meat exports grew. In Australia and New Zealand the rapid entry into the trade caused by high British prices of mutton in these early years, and the low cost of sheep in the colonies, offered less scope for individual firms to take advantage of the economies of scale. The small number of South American concerns also enabled them to avoid the danger of competing among themselves for the purchase of cattle and bidding up the prices paid to the farmers. In Australia and New Zealand the blurred distinction between agriculturist and processor in the form of the 'farmers' companies' inevitably caused some conflict of interest. So long as farmers had a stake in the freezing companies, and so long as there were more than a small number of these to bid against each other for the purchase of livestock, the farmer felt protected by the relatively high prices paid for his livestock. The interest of the freezing firms, however, was best served by being able to buy cheaply at home and to sell dear in Britain. The River Plate firms were better situated to achieve this end than their Australasian counterparts.

As the trade increased part of the secret of commercial success in Britain lay in controlling the arrival of frozen meat supplies so as to avoid the disasters of a glutted market. This need was particularly apparent given the inadequate cold storage capacity in Britain in the 1880s and early 1890s. The three River Plate companies, in a powerful oligopolistic position as purchasers of Argentine cattle, were better able to co-ordinate the arrivals of supplies in Britain than the numerous small scale Australasian businesses. Ultimately, of course, the situation came to rebound upon the Australian and New Zealand farmers. If, as was the case with a lot of the early export of mutton from Queensland, the meat was forwarded to London at the growers' risk, farmers were rapidly made aware of the consequences of a bad market when their cheques from London were insufficient to cover their freezing and freight charges and their own costs of production.

Attempts on the part of those engaged in the Australasian trade to regulate shipments to maintain prices in London were never a success. So many different individuals and groups with widely divergent interests and views shared in the trade that it was always impossible to obtain any agreement over the management and the avoidance of crises. The first conference of producers was held as early as October 1887 to consider 'combined action amongst consignees of New Zealand mutton to support prices'. At that meeting representatives of seven firms together with three individuals considered a scheme to regulate supplies, limit prices and concentrate sales, and rejected it. Two further conferences were held before the end of the century, in 1893 and 1898, both of which failed to achieve any agreement. (27)

Considering the whole structure of the Australasian frozen meat trade it is difficult to see that there was ever any possibility of regulating this trade in the manner of the River Plate. Continuous supplies of sheep and cattle were forthcoming to the South American frigorificos but not to either the Australian or New Zealand meat freezing plants. In Australia the practice of sending surplus sheep for export when wool prices were low introduced one element of discontinuity into the trade. Another was caused by the uncertainties of climate and the ravages of drought which had disastrous effects upon flock numbers in the areas affected, thus reducing or completely eliminating any surplus available for export. Australian farmers tended to have their main animal surplus available for export at seasonal intervals; after lambing, the four months from December to March, was the period when the works, killing and freezing, were busiest, and they were comparatively slack for the rest of the year. Some even closed down for part of it. Although New Zealand was not usually bothered by drought, the mutton and lamb trade from that colony was also seasonal, though the killing season lasted longer than the Australian. It opened around the start of December in the North Island and about a month later in the South Island and continued until June or July. (28) This shortness of the killing season in Australasia was a further reason why the number of meatworks was large in relation to the total output. To some extent Australasia was able to supplement its exports of mutton by sending frozen beef as well, climate permitting, but New Zealand with its heavier concentration on sheep never developed this trade to any extent.

These differences in the conditions governing the structure of the Australasian and South American frozen meat industries before 1900 were reflected in the way the meat plants themselves were operated. There appears to have been considerably less surplus capacity in the South American meat companies than among the Australasian firms. It is difficult to arrive at a precise statement of overall capacity in this industry as the enlargement of existing freezing works or the addition of new ones was continually undertaken before 1914. Even in South America, which had the same number of firms between 1886 and 1902, modifications to the layout of existing plants meant that capacity was not constant. However, the figures in Table 10.1 indicate a marked difference between the Australian and New Zealand frozen meat industries and the River Plate. In 1899 the three River Plate works utilized 66 per cent of the freezing capacity whereas the forty-three Australasian works between them operated at less than 23 per cent of their rated capacity.

The general view among those engaged in the frozen meat trade was that the South American industry was organized and operated in a much more efficient manner than that of either Australia or New Zealand. Argentina possessed one advantage over Australasia in that it was much nearer the final market. To compensate for this, storage capacity in Australia and New Zealand was greater than in South America. But despite this ability to hold over greater quantities at home in anticipation of a good market, arrivals of Australasian meat in Britain tended to be very irregular in comparison with South American frozen imports. This is explained in part by the numerous points of shipment for meat from Australasia in

TABLE 10.1 Number of works freezing meat for export in Argentina, Australia and New Zealand, in 1899, each country's total capacity, and the percentage utilized by imports of frozen meat from those countries into the United Kingdom in 1899

	(a)	(b)	(c)	(d)	(e)
	No. of freezing works	Total daily capacity	Total annual capacity	Imports of frozen meat into United Kingdom	Imports into United Kingdom as a proportion of annual capacity
		(56 lb carcases)	(56 lb carcases)	(56 lb carcases)	(%)
Argentina	3	13,000	3,900,000 (97,500 tons)	2,583,160 (64,579 tons)	66
Australia	17	34,300	10,290,000 (257,250 tons)	2,269,880 (56,747 tons)	22
New Zealand	25	46,700	14,010,000 (350,250 tons)	3,220,280 (80,507 tons)	23

Columns (a) and (b). W. Weddel and Company, 'Review of the Frozen Meat Trade', 1899, p.15.

Column (c) is an estimate based on (b). It assumes a year of 300 working days to allow for rest days and time spent on plant maintenance.

Column (d) includes frozen mutton, lamb and beef.

Column (e). For Argentina and New Zealand, exports to the United Kingdom accounted for all their exports of frozen meat. Australia in 1899 had additional markets as she was provisioning the British Army in South Africa and the US Army in the Phillipines with frozen beef and mutton. No statement of the quantities involved is available, however. In addition the United Kingdom received frozen rabbit, mostly from Australia. If these were taken into account they would raise Australia's percentage of capacity utilized above that of New Zealand.

comparison with South America. In 1899 New Zealand mutton was
shipped from twelve ports, six on each island. The largest shipments from Lyttelton in the South Island accounted for under 30 per
cent of the year's total. Shipments of Australian frozen meat were
made from four States; New South Wales, Victoria, Queensland and
South Australia. This pattern of shipping from numerous points made
it impossible to ensure regular and continuous arrivals in the
United Kingdom. It also involved extra delay and cost for this
journey as a vessel had to call and load at several places before
it could set out for the final destination.

    There were considerable variations in the pattern of shipping
and the arrangements for ocean freight between the South American
and Australasian industries. In 1899 there were 113 vessels
engaged in the Australian and New Zealand trade together, and thirty
in the River Plate trade. As imports from Australia and New
Zealand in that year were approximately only twice the quantity of
those from the River Plate (137,254 tons and 64,579 tons respectively), it might at first sight appear that the balance of efficiency
was strongly in favour of the South American trade with a fleet of
refrigerated ships less than a third of the size of the Australian
trade's. The position is slightly complicated, though, by
differences in the carrying capacities of ships operating along the
various routes, and the number of voyages it was possible to make in
a year. Although the ships operating between Australia and New
Zealand and the United Kingdom had the largest carrying capacity
(93,100 56 lb carcases) and those in the South American trade the
smallest (36,200), there was some compensation in the greater number
of voyages which could be made between the River Plate and United
Kingdom in each year. But even when these things are taken into
account, the South American fleet of frozen meat ships in 1899 (not
an untypical year) was still more fully employed than the carriers
of Australasian frozen meat. In that year almost 60 per cent of the
available tonnage between Australasia and the United Kingdom was
unfilled, while over 80 per cent of the available freight between
the River Plate and the United Kingdom was filled (see Table 10.2).
As with the utilization of freezing capacity on shore, the most
serious under-employment occurred in the Australian trade where
approximately 70 per cent of shipping space was unfilled. The
problem of surplus capacity was not so severe for shipping space as
it was for on-shore freezing plant. In all cases the performance of
the shipping companies in this respect was better than the record of
the freezing firms. The shipping companies were independent of the
freezing plants, and exporters in Argentina or Australasia merely
engaged shipping space some time ahead of when it was required. As
the River Plate plants had the clearest idea of what the level of
their trade would be in, say, three months shipping capacity could
be more closely matched to actual requirements by the companies
engaged in this trade. Some surplus capacity was always inevitable
as monthly shipments (even from South America) were subject to
variation. The 81 per cent utilization of shipping capacity in the
Argentine trade was probably the maximum it was possible to achieve
under normal trading conditions. Shipping companies fitted out
their ships with refrigeration plant and cold chambers on the basis
of past demand and predictions of the future growth of the industry.

TABLE 10.2 Number of vessels carrying frozen meat from Argentina and Australia to the United Kingdom in 1899, their carrying capacity and the percentage of that capacity utilized by imports of frozen meat from those countries into the United Kingdom in 1899

Country of origin for journey to the United Kingdom	(a) Vessels	(b) Carrying capacity each voyage		(c) Estimated maximum annual importing capacity	(d) Annual voyages per vessel	(e) Imports into United Kingdom as a proportion of annual shipping capacity
		(b1) Total	(b2) Average per vessel			
	(No.)	(56 lb carcases)	(56 lb carcases)	(56 lb carcases)	(No.)	(%)
Argentina	30	1,086,500	36,200	3,200,000	2.95	81
Australia	76	2,942,800	38,700	7,300,000	2.48	29(f)
Australia & New Zealand	7	652,000	93,100	1,300,000	1.99	41
New Zealand	30	2,034,500	67,800	4,500,000	2.21	61(f)

Columns (a), (b) and (c). W. Weddel and Company, 'Review of the Frozen Meat Trade', 1899, p.15.

$$\text{Column (d)} = \frac{\text{Column (c)}}{\text{Column (b1)}}$$

Column (e). Imports into the United Kingdom are taken from Table 10.1, column (d). Shipping capacity is taken from column (c) of the present table.

(f) In estimating these values the tonnage operating from both Australia and New Zealand has been distributed between each country in the same proportion as the imports of meat from each country in 1899 (taken from column (d) of Table 10.1) i.e. 59% of 1.3 million (767,000) 56 lb carcases to New Zealand and 41% of 1.3 million (533,000) 56 lb carcases to Australia.

The figures in this Table and Table 10.1 (columns (e) in both cases) accord well with the statement in W. Weddel, 'Review of the Frozen Meat Trade', p.16, viz. 'The River Plate Freezing Companies work up to within 75 per cent, while New Zealand Freezing Companies only attain about 40 per cent, and Australian to 25 per cent of their capabilities, as these are estimated by the owners of the various Works and by shipowners.'

Predictions were never entirely reliable but they were made by W. Weddel and Company, a firm engaged in the Australian and New Zealand trade, in their annually published 'Review of the Frozen Meat Trade' which began in 1887, the year the firm started. This publication provided a good idea of the meat firms' potential capacity to freeze meat, and official trade statistics of various governments revealed the actual size of annual flows. Therefore it was easy for the shipping companies to keep their capacity below that of the freezing plants (see Tables 10.1 and 10.2, columns (c)).

3   MARKETING METHODS IN THE UNITED KINGDOM

Differences in United Kingdom marketing arrangements between South American and Australasian meat corresponded to differences in the organization of these industries in their countries of origin. The three firms on the River Plate, in keeping with their operations in Argentina, had far more efficient and streamlined marketing machines in the United Kingdom than their numerous competitors. Partly they were able to take advantage of economies of scale: the volume of meat handled by any one of the Argentine firms was far greater than the quantity exported by any single Australasian company. Also the continuity of supplies from South America made it profitable for these firms to erect a comprehensive distribution network. The irregular arrivals from Australia and New Zealand made it much harder to establish a regular marketing system.

The success of the three Argentine firms in regulating the arrivals of meat in Britain can be seen in Figure 10.2. In 1900 there was a maximum variation around the mean of +30 per cent and -35 per cent in monthly arrivals of frozen mutton in Britain from the Argentine. For arrivals of the same type of meat from Australia and New Zealand, with a larger number of exporting concerns and consequently less overall control over the flow of supplies, the amplitude of fluctuations was twice as large. Australian imports of frozen mutton varied between +99 per cent and -68 per cent and those from New Zealand between +73 per cent and -79 per cent around their monthly means for 1900.

Although the irregular arrivals of Australasian mutton constitu-ted a considerable marketing difficulty, this argument did not always apply in the case of lamb. Prior to around 1900 the British demand for this meat had a strongly seasonal character, following the seasonal availability of home-grown lamb. It is therefore doubtful if importers had aimed at maintaining the level of their supplies throughout the year that they would have obtained any great benefit. In the frozen lamb trade the main secret of success was to bring the meat onto the market at the right time to obtain the maximum of that season's prices. The season was short, lasting the three months from April to June with the highest prices in June, so that importers had to spread the bulk of their arrivals over these months to obtain the best all-round results. After June the demand for lamb usually fell sharply, along with the demand for all other meats during the hot summer months of July to September. In their attempts to match arrivals of frozen lamb to periods of greatest demand, importers could make serious mistakes. This

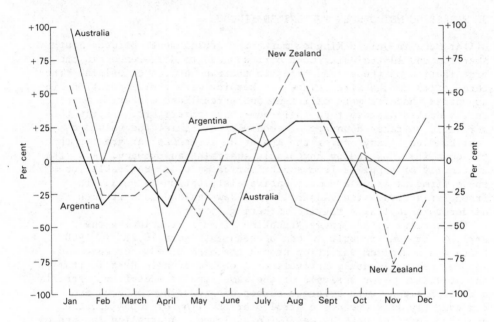

FIGURE 10.2 Monthly fluctuations in United Kingdom imports of
frozen mutton, 1900

Source: W. Weddel and Company, 'Review of the Frozen Meat Trade',
1900, p.5.

happened in 1899 when large quantities of New Zealand lamb arrived
in London during February and March before the proper season had
opened. The finish of the season was equally unsatisfactory as the
heaviest supplies came to hand in July, after the proper season was
over. But events like these did have the effect of changing and
extending the lamb season when repeated in following years.
Weddel's 'Review' explained the changes in the following terms: (29)
    Frozen lamb, from being a strictly 'season' trade, is slowly but
    surely becoming an all-the-year-round business; but in the 'off'
    months the demand is still very limited, and only small shipments
    can be disposed of satisfactorily. When a large number of
    shippers simultaneously endeavour to 'catch' the early or the
    late trade, it is more than likely to prove worthless to all, as
    happened in 1899.

In 1900, which was a better regulated and more successful season, from the Australasian exporters' point of view, it was observed: (30)

Each succeeding season tends to establish the lamb trade on more and more of an all-the-year-round basis, and during 1900 there was not a single day throughout the year in which some frozen lambs were not sold on the Smithfield market.

There was no competition in the frozen lamb trade between the Australasian and South American firms, as imports of this item from the River Plate were practically insignificant. Frozen meat, especially in the early years, had to face a considerable degree of indifference on the part of the consumer. To overcome this, the product needed to be tenaciously marketed over a period of time. Once consumer allegiance to the product had been won in a particular area, it needed to be retained by a dependable flow of supplies in the future. Failure to do so meant the benefits of consumer education were lost by the supplier as demand was transferred to more easily obtainable substitutes among other types of imported meat or the cheaper sorts of what was available from local production. This was a problem that was felt most acutely by the importers of Australian beef, lamb and mutton - the most unpredictable of all arrivals. In one month in 1899 Australian cargoes of mutton amounted to 9,000 carcases, in another, 224,000 carcases. (31) In 1902 arrivals of Australian frozen beef were so spasmodic that there was no real trade in that description of meat. The general character of shipments in that year also bore unmistakable evidence of the trying experience through which Queensland cattle had passed in recent years of drought, so little of the product was of prime quality. By the end of the year Australian beef had completely lost its position in provincial markets and in most districts had been supplanted by Argentine frozen beef. The same thing happened in that year to Australian mutton. In the country and in London the ground gained among retailers by the steady arrivals between 1896 and 1901 was lost almost completely as it proved impossible to keep a connection together with an average import of only 15,000 carcases a month after 66,000 in 1901. (32)

The South American firms took a very close interest in matters of detail when arranging for the sale and distribution of their meat in Britain. They preferred to manage their own network of agents and cold stores in this country. By contrast the Australasian firms were content to leave the mechanics of meat distribution very largely in the hands of British wholesalers. Although they did take a greater part in marketing in this country after the importation of frozen meat had become established, their participation in bringing their product before the consumer was always less than that of the River Plate companies. The South American firms were prepared to become involved in their marketing on a national scale. Taking advantage of the pre-existing network of James Nelson and Sons, Nelson's River Plate Fresh Meat Company sent frozen meat vessels to Liverpool in 1886 and the Sansinena Company followed suit. Both these companies established their own private cold stores in that port to assist the distribution of their product in the north of England. The Australasian firms did not adopt similar tactics until 1892; throughout the 1880s they preferred to ship their meat

only to London. Early shipments of New Zealand mutton, sent on
account of the growers, were often consigned to various finance and
investment companies or wool houses based in London and doing business with the colony. (33) Presumably the farmers, ignorant of the
wholesale meat trade in Britain, used them because they were their
only commercial contacts in this country. These organizations were,
if anything, even more ignorant of meat selling than the New
Zealand farmers, nor had they any inclination to diversify their
interests in that direction. Therefore they placed the documents
and all matters concerned with the meat into the hands of regular
meat brokers and commission agents in London and, after a few
consignments, the farmers' companies in New Zealand came to deal
with these men directly. When the Australasian firms came to take a
closer interest in selling in Britain there was often a considerable
duplication of effort and personnel and what was described as a
'needless multiplication of selling agents'. (34) Given the smaller
scale of these firms, in terms of the consignments sent, it probably
meant that they had a greater proportion of their resources concentrated in their marketing operations than did the South American
firms. Also the small scale of the Australian and New Zealand firms
made their marketing operations less efficient, and the resources
embodied in them were employed less effectively than the larger
firms of the River Plate.

The early concentration of the Australasian firms on London and
the diversification of the River Plate companies into the markets of
the north via Liverpool suited, and was partly determined by, the
differences in the products of the two continents. The lighter
carcases of mutton from South America were in stronger demand outside London, especially in the manufacturing towns of northern
England. (35) There appears to be no really satisfactory explanation for this regional variation in consumer taste, but it applied
to other meat besides mutton. (36) It was also a thing of long
standing and in the 1840s and 1850s the animals that did best in the
London market were well fed, but not over-fed so that the carcase
contained vast quantities of fat. (37) Again, in the 1860s and
1870s lightweight continental sheep found their way to Manchester,
the west Midlands and Wales. (38)

In the early 1880s carcases of Argentine mutton were described as
having almost lamb-like proportions. In 1884 the average weight of
River Plate sheep was 48 lb, almost 15 lb lighter than the
Australian. Its average price was 3d. to 4d. per lb, at the same
time the average price of New Zealand mutton was between 4½d. and
5d. per lb. (39) There was no improvement in the weight of
Argentine sheep in the 1880s - in 1889 the average weight of
carcases sent to Britain was 45 lb, (40) while the weight of
domestic sheep was around 70 lb each on average. (41) Liverpool was
the principal destination for these lightweight South American
carcases. In 1886 the Argentine firms landed 103,454 carcases
there and 331,245 in London. But thereafter London dropped to
second position a long way behind Liverpool which became the first
port for the reception of South American mutton. In 1892
Liverpool's share of the trade was 1,263,915 carcases while London
with only 109,808 had less than 8 per cent of the total. (41) At
the same time, however, the bulk of the Australasian arrivals was

centred on London.

The move by Australian and New Zealand firms towards making direct shipments to Liverpool, instead of relying completely on distribution via London, was connected with trade difficulties and the first serious fall of London prices in the 1890s. But even in the 1880s, after the high profits made by the initial pioneering shipments, there were rumours and reports of difficulties among the trade, though they appear to have been most serious among the Australian companies. (43) In an article in the 'Quarterly Review' of 1887, W.E. Bear reported: 'With respect to Australia, some of the large companies engaged in the frozen meat trade have failed.' South American firms also experienced difficulties, and, according to the same article: 'At the recent meeting of the River Plate Fresh Meat Company, a loss of £37,000 on ten months' trading was declared.' In part, the early problems of the trade rested with the extreme variation in the quality of different consignments. Prices for the best quality frozen mutton were high, but often they do not give an accurate indication of average prices. (44) There was considerable overlapping in the price bands for frozen mutton from the three countries that supplied it. One of the lists issued by the New Zealand Loan and Mercantile Agency in 1887 showed prices ranging from $3\frac{1}{2}$d. per lb upwards for Australian mutton, $3\frac{1}{2}$d. to $4\frac{1}{4}$d. for South American, and all prices between 3d. to 5d. per lb for New Zealand. Exporters' expenses, that is slaughtering, freezing, freight, storage and commission in Britain, were variously put at between 3d. and $3\frac{1}{2}$d. per lb. Also a considerable proportion of the cargoes were described as 'irregular', that is their quality was poor and so the price was low. Bear doubted whether a fraction over 4d. per lb had been received, on an average, for all the mutton sent from New Zealand in 1886. As $1\frac{1}{4}$d. per lb was represented as the bare minimum a New Zealand farmer needed to make over his expenses before exporting became a paying proposition, clearly a considerable proportion of this meat made a loss for the producer. At the same time most New Zealand mutton received favourable reports about its quality in the British press. Also, it was alleged that retail prices for this meat did not adequately reflect the level of whole-sale prices. Bear expressed the case in the following terms:

the middleman in this country gets a great deal more than the producer out of the frozen mutton, as, indeed, he does on the meat supply generally. A great deal has been written lately about exorbitant butchers' profits, and no one who knows anything about wholesale or retail prices can doubt that they are enormous. This is doubly injurious to producers; for, in the first place, they do not obtain a fair share of what consumers pay, and secondly, the extreme prices charged by the butchers reduce the demand for meat and thus tend to keep down the prices. But there are other middlemen besides the butchers, and British and foreign meat alike often passes through several dealers' hands before it gets to the consumer.

Bear was generally an accurate and informed commentator on economic affairs, but the weakness of this particular argument lies in his inability to produce comparative figures to demonstrate that the margin between wholesale and retail meat prices gave 'enormous' profits to the middleman. This is not surprising as very little is

known about retail prices in general for the nineteenth century;
most series relate to wholesale prices. For example, M.G. Mulhall's
'History of Prices Since 1850' (London, 1885), which surveys the
movement of prices (together with resources) during the so-called
mid-Victorian boom, contains no instance of retail prices; they are
all wholesale. In the absence of hard facts the popular orthodoxy
supported the assertion, based on varying degrees of information
and judgment, that the middleman made a large profit. (45) This
assertion was strong in the case of food distribution and was
applied with particular vigour to the butchers and other middlemen
in the meat trade.

The only attempt to test these allegations and to arrive at some
sort of figure for retail butchers' profit margins was made by James
Long. (46) In addition, a pamphlet published by the Co-operative
Union in 1890 intended as a guide for societies contemplating the
establishment of their own butchering departments presents some
hypothetical costings. (47) The results of their figures are
presented in notes 46 and 47 to this chapter. They show profits of
15 per cent, 19 per cent and 21 per cent between the cost and
selling prices to the butcher of home-grown mutton, cattle and pigs
respectively. However this makes no allowance for overheads in the
form of labour, rent, fuel, interest and depreciation, etc. Also
these percentages do not allow for the full costs of distribution
because they take no account of the mark-up in prices between the
farmer and the meat wholesaler or cattle dealer.

In a sense, however, the refinements of elaborate costings and
precise calculations of profits did not affect the issue so far as
it concerned the farmers and others engaged in the colonial mutton
and lamb trade with Britain. It is unlikely that they needed to
give a lot of consideration to the part played by the wholesalers
in equalizing supplies of meat to the varying regional levels of
demand, both for different amounts and types of meat. The colonial
importers were probably more strongly influenced by the differences
in the ex-farm and wholesale prices of frozen meat and the amount
ultimately paid for their frozen joints by the British public. Also
they most likely listened to allegations, usually by popular newspapers, that frozen mutton was sold by unscrupulous butchers as
home-grown, at the higher prices of home-grown meat, yet the frozen
meat importers were themselves aware that the wholesale price of
even the best New Zealand frozen mutton and lamb was about one third
below the comparable home-grown article. The opportunity to make
this deception probably only existed with the best frozen mutton.
One later example was given in a series of articles in 'The Parish
Councillor' (48) of 1896 by its editor, Thomas Farrow, who visited
the Old Welsh Mutton House in the Strand where, he alleged, the
butcher covered a leg of frozen New Zealand mutton with flour 'to
give it a more "Welsh like" appearance' and charged him 10½d. per lb
for it - 'thus obtaining a fraudulent profit of from 3d to 4d per
pound'. Here, the object of the exercise was not to protest about
underpayment of the New Zealand producer but against the British
farmer being subjected to unfair competition from the imported
article. This particular offending limb was immediately borne, no
doubt in triumph, to the House of Lords where it was shown to the
Select Committee taking evidence on the Agricultural Produce (Marks)

Bill (49) as tangible evidence of the need for the compulsory marking of foreign meat.

Reports and stories such as these, whether or not ill-founded or
exaggerated, encouraged New Zealand and Australian farmers and meat
shippers to follow the example of their River Plate competitors and
take a closer interest in all the stages of marketing their meat in
Britain. This interest was a persistent feature of this section of
the frozen meat trade, and was expressed in a number of ways. One
proposal was for the colonies to establish in London their own
private cold stores, presumably to exercise closer control over the
distribution of their meat. As this plan came at a time when the
United Kingdom had more than sufficient cold storage capacity, it is
difficult to see how there could have been any benefit in the idea.
Also past attempts by the City of London and other powerful local
bodies to move markets even a few hundred yards did not make it
advisable for colonial governments to sink capital in such enterprises. (50) Another scheme, which was examined in 1903, was for
the New Zealand government to open retail shops to sell frozen meat.
This plan was also abandoned after investigation by a committee
appointed by the New Zealand government, on the grounds that the
distribution network was already sufficiently developed and the
scheme offered no prospect for any great improvement over that
already existing. (51)

The extent of involvement outside London for the South American
firms always remained much larger than for the companies importing
colonial meat. Figure 10.3, based on information given in the
advertisements appearing in the 'Meat Trades Journal' for 1904,
illustrates this point. The two firms dealing only in South
American meat had, between them, branches in fifteen towns. The two
firms handling both South American and colonial meat had a much
smaller geographical coverage with branches in a total of only seven
towns. Finally, the two firms who handled nothing but colonial meat
had branches in only three towns between the pair of them.

4 DECENTRALIZED DISTRIBUTION

Associated with this development was the move away from reliance on
London alone as the port of discharge for cargoes of frozen meat
from the colonies. This move was first made in 1892 when 55,250
carcases of Australian mutton and lamb and 34,228 carcases of New
Zealand mutton and lamb were landed at Liverpool. This attempt at
geographical diversification was not an immediate success, however.
The Australian experiment was not repeated during the next two
years, and although New Zealand persevered with the experiment in
1893 and 1894 it was abandoned thereafter and the next cargo of New
Zealand meat consigned to the outports was 17,503 carcases landed at
Cardiff in 1903. Australia sent small amounts to Liverpool and
Manchester in 1895, and though she continued to ship to one or other
of these places (and to Cardiff in 1902) the amounts were insignificant before 1905, compared with the quantities unloaded at London.

The advantages of shipment to the outports, such as greater
proximity to the point of consumption and the elimination of a
longer rail journey for the frozen meat from London to the north and

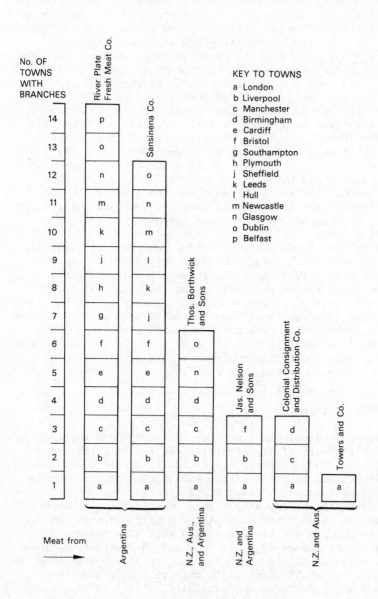

FIGURE 10.3 Branches of six firms in the frozen meat trade, 1904

Source: 'Meat Trades Journal', 1904 passim.

west, were in fact not as great as shippers had at first expected.
Throughout the 1890s London was predominantly the distribution
centre for all meat and the facilities at the outports were
decidedly inferior in all respects. There was a general improvement
in provincial cold storage, for instance, after 1890, but where
this was carried out by firms in the South American trade, it was
obviously not available for use by colonial shippers. There were
two other more serious disabilities facing traders attempting to
send Australasian meat to the outports. In the first place the
arrangements made by the shipping firms ensured that London was
served by faster services than the outports. This effectively
ensured that a cargo of meat for, say, Liverpool or Cardiff
dispatched from New Zealand took three months to complete the voyage
whereas a consignment for London took only two. This was an
important consideration for the New Zealand lamb trade. A January
shipment from New Zealand to Liverpool or Cardiff was not available
for buyers' use any earlier than a February shipment from the same
source via London, or than a March shipment from the River Plate.
Usually the market value of a February shipment of lamb was at
least $\frac{1}{8}$d. per lb under the value of January shipments, and therefore
as by the mid-1890s cost of railage from London to either Cardiff or
Liverpool was not more than $\frac{1}{8}$d. per lb, and the risks of rail
transit were quite nominal, there was not much inducement for
Cardiff or Liverpool buyers to make purchases from Australia or New
Zealand for direct shipment to their markets. Further, by purchasing for delivery in London, provincial buyers had the choice of
taking advantage of a strong market there on arrival or of sending
the goods on by rail to their final destination. The second dis-
couragement to the direct trade with the outports was the right
assumed by ship owners, in the conditions of the bill of lading, to
rail goods from any other port at which a vessel might call, to
either Cardiff or Liverpool, instead of sending the vessel on to
discharge direct into the cold stores at these ports. (52) This
practice at times was more convenient and cheaper for ship owners.
If they could empty and re-load a vessel at one port both time and
money was saved over the more cumbersome piecemeal discharging at
several places. But provincial buyers of colonial meat did not like
to receive their goods via London if they had arranged with ship
owners that they should be unloaded elsewhere, and the practice led
to a certain amount of friction between the parties involved. (53)

The slow service to the west coast ports persisted for a number
of years. In 1908 the Colonial Consignment and Distribution Company
commented that colonial shippers still lacked a service to west
coast ports (54) as speedy as that to London. (55) This was a
distinct disadvantage to the trade and to some extent outweighed the
attractions of these ports as receiving centres. Foremost among
these were lower dock labour costs and in certain cases superior
wharfside arrangements for unloading ships, compared with London.
At the Port of London most ships had to discharge their cargoes into
lighters which took them to the wharfs where they were again unloaded and transferred to the cold stores. But in many of the
provincial docks, where the installations were newer, like Avonmouth
and Manchester, steamers could berth directly alongside the wharfs
and unload by crane straight into trucks that ran a short distance

into the cold stores. This was the easiest and most convenient
method of discharging frozen meat; it involved the minimum of handling and consequently there was less chance of damage to the carcases on their way from ship to store, than at London. (56)   Hull
offered similar convenient methods of discharging frozen cargoes.
In addition it was argued that provincial markets could be supplied
at lower cost via their local port than from London. For example
in 1911 the rate to Bradford on 1 ton of frozen meat, including
receiving from ship, conveyance to cold store, sorting, rent for 28
days, weighing at time of delivery to and from store to railway
companies and conveyance to destination, from London was about 70s.
9d., while from Hull it was only 41s. - a difference of around 30s.
per ton in favour of Hull.

The crucial factor which limited the extent of the direct trade
to the outports was not the length of the voyage or the time of
arrival for vessels, but the size of their markets. The warning
constantly repeated to shippers intending to exploit the provincial
markets for themselves was that smaller markets were easier to
over-supply. However, the move to these places was encouraged in
the 1890s by the decline in prices obtained in London. This was
associated with an increase in total meat imports into the United
Kingdom. In 1893-4 imported meat, of all kinds, accounted for 32.4
per cent of the estimated United Kingdom supply, but by 1900-1 this
had risen to 45.4 per cent. Between the same dates the amount of
meat imported rose from 12.5 million cwt to 20.9 million while the
home-produced supply remained virtually the same at 26.0 million and
25.2 million cwt respectively. (57)

The importing firms were encouraged to undertake experiments in
direct shipments to the outports by the belief that higher prices
were obtainable in the provinces than in London for the same
qualities of frozen meat. This claim is impossible to test as the
only price series for frozen meat apply to the metropolitan market.
If there was any differential, experience proved that it was easily
lost by the sudden arrival of a large consignment of colonial meat.
In 1906 an important distributor of colonial frozen meat, the
Colonial Consignment and Distribution Company, observed: (58)

   The belief that better results will be achieved for all classes
   of frozen meat by increasing the centres of distribution still
   appears to be largely held in the colonies. Development in this
   direction may, and probably will enable larger supplies to be
   more readily dealt with when they come forward, but scarcely
   sufficient attention is given to the fact that in a small country
   like Great Britain, such centres tend to become to a large extent
   competitive. The experience of the past year has shown that the
   limits of consumption are easily reached in the outports'
   markets, and that the prices realized have shown no advantage
   over the London market. In fact the balance has frequently been
   the other way.

However, this does not mean that there was no advantage in sending
certain classes of frozen meat directly to the outports. For
instance, in 1907 Australian lambs and considerable numbers of
lightweight New Zealand lambs (both of which came in the lower
quality ranges) found a satisfactory market in the provinces at
prices frequently very close to those paid at Smithfield for prime

brands. (59) At times, however, the experiments to test a new market by direct shipments proved self-defeating. In July 1903 some 4,000 Canterbury sheep and 13,400 lambs were landed at Cardiff. But these were not consumed locally and were sold to a River Plate firm which promptly dispatched them to depots in the north of England and the Midlands for consumption there. (60)

Although the proportion of frozen meat directly shipped to the outports grew between 1892 and 1914, this provides no guide to the quantity entering non-metropolitan consumption as substantial amounts were also railed to these markets after being discharged from vessels at the Port of London. By 1904 a large proportion of the forward sales of colonial meat - and these accounted for a large section of the trade - were made to wholesale buyers in the provinces, who in turn acted as distributors in their immediate neighbourhood. The most important channel for the distribution of colonial meat was the small country buyer. His requirements as to weight and quality of carcase were supplied by the large importing and wholesale firms. A large amount of this business was carried out through London with consignments discharged at the Port of London, sorted in London and then railed to their ultimate destination. The Colonial Consignment and Distribution Company had branches in Manchester and Birmingham but its head office was in London. An analysis of a typical day's output of this company alone showed that it dispatched meat to over 700 towns and villages in the United Kingdom in 1903. (61)

The movement by the importers of all frozen (and chilled) meats into the provincial markets after 1890 diminished the relative importance of London as a distributing centre. This relative, but not absolute, decline is shown in Table 10.3 for the frozen mutton and lamb trade. These changes were also reflected in the way the meat trade in London itself was conducted. At about the turn of the century there was some check to the total supplies of meat, both home-produced and imported, passing through Smithfield, as shown in Table 10.4.

TABLE 10.3 United Kingdom imports of frozen mutton and lamb (carcases)

Year	Total UK imports	No. received by London	% received by London
1891	3,358,823	2,389,129	71
1901	7,094,782	4,770,801	67
1910	12,981,044	8,572,788	66

Source: J.T. Critchell and J. Raymond, 'A History of the Frozen Meat Trade', London, 1912, p.211.

TABLE 10.4 Meat (tons) passing through the London Central Markets, 1893-1912

Year	Total supplies	Year	Total supplies
1893	318,162	1903	415,909
1894	342,329	1904	415,970
1895	348,138	1905	415,296
1896	380,543	1906	421,297
1897	393,307	1907	417,057
1898	400,112	1908	409,732
1899	405,916	1909	420,060
1900	410,378	1910	419,550
1901	415,510	1911	433,723
1902	405,013	1912	430,283

Source: 'Report of Departmental Committee on Combinations in the Meat Trade', P.P., 1909, XV, Appendix XII, p.302. W. Weddel and Company, 'Review of the Frozen Meat Trade', 1908-12.

It seems that the North American firms dealing in chilled meat took the initiative in 'decentralizing' the meat trade and reducing the extent of their reliance on Smithfield, but the other companies handling South American and Australasian meat were quick to follow their example. Part of the explanation has already been given - that there were increased landings of frozen (and chilled) meat at the outports. But also meat landed at London was being sent straight to the rail depots and forwarded elsewhere without ever passing through the halls of Smithfield. The system grew up of delivering frozen meat 'ex-store'; such meat instead of, as formerly, being brought to Smithfield was being sold there by what amounted to sample, and the bulk was dispatched from the cold store. This practice aroused a strong reaction from the Corporation of the City of London which owned and ran Smithfield. With the character- istic zeal it always displayed whenever its financial interests were threatened, the Corporation claimed the right to collect tolls on meat sold at Smithfield although delivered from store without going on to the market. This proposal would have required a change in the by-laws governing the market's constitution. It was naturally opposed strongly by the Frozen Meat Trade Association and the Agents General for the colonies and other interested parties. Such changes required the sanction of the President of the Board of Trade and the opposition were able to have a public enquiry arranged to consider the objections to them. However, the Corporation, presumably having little confidence in the outcome of a public presentation of their case, had the enquiry permanently postponed. Instead the Corporation compromised and entered into agreements with its tenants holding market stalls whereby some account was taken of sales of meat not physically passing through the market. The episode was described as 'a protest on the part of the Corporation of London against the decentralization of the chilled and frozen meat trade from the Central Markets'. (62)

5   THE FORWARD TRADE

A new development in the organization of the frozen meat trade began
in the 1890s. (63) This was the forward buying and selling of meat,
pioneered by the New Zealand freezing firms. Probably the first
transaction of this nature was the sale in 1888 of 2,000 Dunedin
sheep to Messrs W. and R. Fletcher Ltd by Messrs A.S. Paterson and
Company, of Dunedin, through their London agents, Messrs W. Weddel
and Company. Prior to then, wholesale buyers in Britain had always
bought frozen meat as and when it appeared at Smithfield, in what
were called 'spot' purchases. The forward trade involved a contract
between buyer and seller. The buyer agreed to take a certain amount
of meat at a fixed price in a specified month in the future and
agreed to pay the cost, insurance and freight of the consignment.
For his part, the seller was obliged to deliver the agreed amount
(and quality) of meat on the date in question. This system was also
called the c.i.f. trade. It did have a certain speculative element
to it as price fluctuations affected the level of profits involved.
In the early 1890s the English firm of Nelson Bros Ltd had annual
contracts with farmers in New Zealand to ensure a regular supply
and freight arrangements. However when they lost £102,000 on the
trade in one year because of falling prices, the firm had to ask the
sheep farmers of Hawkes Bay to reduce the contract price. The
provision of annual contracts was not a success in a trade subject
to such wide price fluctuations and the practice was accordingly
discontinued. (64) Some forward sales were made as much as six
months in the future but it was more usual to sell month by month.
In 1909, when frozen lamb fell 50 per cent in price on the rates of
the previous year, forward buyers lost money heavily. However, the
extent of speculative buying was small in proportion to the total
size of the trade.

The successful operation of the c.i.f. trade depended on modifications in the structure of demand as well as adaptations in the
supply side of the industry. In the 1890s the first large chains of
multiple butchers' shops were assembled in London and the provinces.
These organizations provided a regular outlet for meat of a predictable quality and weight and they found that they could partly cover
their requirements for many months if they contracted to buy in
advance on a cost, freight and insurance basis. At the same time
the introduction of the grading process in New Zealand made it
possible for buyers to know in advance the precise quality they were
purchasing. The system was one of mutual convenience for the seller
and buyer. To some extent being able to purchase in advance of
their requirements protected the large retailers from the effect of
sudden and untoward changes in prices. The system also enabled the
farmers to find a market for their animals by selling outright to
the freezing companies, free of any worry about future prices. The
grading of carcases was in fact the foundation of the c.i.f. trade.
This was according to weight and type of animal, that is sheep,
wethers or maiden ewes. The first firm selling forward to grade for
weight was the New Zealand Refrigerating Company at Dunedin. In the
first instance the British demand was for relatively heavy mutton,
but as the trade developed it was found that the requirements at
Smithfield were for lighter weights of carcases. In 1887 the most

favoured weight was for a 64 lb carcase but by 1910 it was from 48
to 52 lb. The smaller the carcases the smaller the joints they were
cut into. The tendency for the smaller joint to become more popular
was a matter of consumer preference. It was argued that the English
working people wanted more variety on their table and that the
English housewife was less bothered to prepare dishes from cold
mutton. However, the preference for small joints was a general
phenomenon affecting all kinds of meat.

In the years after 1890 the system of grading became more complex and the grades more numerous and precise. In 1890 the New
Zealand Refrigerating Company had five separate grades. By 1910
there were nine accepted Canterbury grades for sheep and lamb in
general use at Smithfield.

The system of grading was most developed in the New Zealand
trade, and these grades gave a firm and reliable guide to quality.
In Australia the grading of meat was never so thoroughly developed.
Without reliable grading the forward trade was also handicapped, and
although a higher proportion of trade from Australia was conducted
on a c.i.f. basis than from New Zealand, the lower prices of the
Australian meat were partly to cover this faulty grading. In New
Zealand there was a fair degree of uniformity in systems of grading
between the two islands and also between different firms, although
there was never complete uniformity. The various firms in that
colony also branded their own products and in many cases these brand
marks were also a guide to qualities. By 1912 there were twenty
different brands in use, representing that number of companies in
the New Zealand frozen mutton and lamb trade. Much of the
Australian grading was vestigial compared with that in use for New
Zealand. The two most common were 'f.a.q.' and 'g.a.q.' which stood
for 'fair average quality' and 'good average quality' respectively.
These descriptions were far more ambiguous than the New Zealand
quality grades of 'prime quality' and 'second quality'. In the
Argentine each company graded its own meat in its own way. The
first forward sales of River Plate mutton, lamb and beef were not
until 1903. (65) This delay is presumably associated with the much
tighter control these firms had over their marketing and distributing system. In all countries beef was graded as well as mutton and
lamb. As the carcases were heavier the weight grades for beef had
wider intervals than for mutton and lamb. In the case of mutton and
lamb the usual interval between weight grades was between 5 and 8
lb, for beef the 20 lb interval was common.

The forward trade had other problems in addition to those over
grading Australian meat. Irregular, and therefore unpredictable,
arrivals were one source of contention between parties. In 1899
serious difficulties arose in the New Zealand trade over the late
shipment of orders. Shipping arrangements out of the ports of New
Zealand were at best poor and at worst utterly disorganized. Delays
were frequent as numerous ships waited to load relatively small
consignments. It was estimated that the saving of only one day in
loading and one day in discharging would mean an economy for all the
vessels engaged in the Australasian trade (making 141 voyages in
1899) of between £10,000 and £15,000 per annum or around £500 per
voyage. Such delay would be crucial for buyers in Britain as the
monthly variation of prices might result in their losing the price

they had expected to make when they negotiated the contract. When
this happened buyers were reluctant to pay the full price they had
originally agreed in the forward contract, although the freezing
companies protested the delay and late arrival were no fault of
theirs and advised the buyer to seek his redress with the shipping
company. The freezing companies and the shippers might also enter-
tain the suspicion that the buyer was making his claim merely
because the market had gone against him, and spot values in London
did not justify his estimation of trade three months earlier. Under
conditions of this nature the forward trade with the southern ports
of New Zealand was almost unworkable in 1899. A further difficulty
arose over claims for damaged cargoes. This complaint was most
common against the Australian mutton and beef cargoes. Disputes
arose here as to the precise nature of the fault, whether it was
because the meat was inferior in the first place or whether it had
deteriorated through faulty transit conditions. This complaint
persisted beyond the early years of the trade and when it was
alleged that shippers had enough experience to avoid these losses.
Again in 1899 it was reported that the Saturday trade at Smithfield
was notorious for getting rid of damaged and inferior Australian
sheep, and that this market day was shunned by the holders of better
class frozen meat. (66)

   Given the numerous possible, and in the event actual, causes for
dispute over forward sales, attempts were made to fix a standard
form of c.i.f. contract for frozen meat. It was standard practice
by 1900 in most other produce businesses where forward sales were
made, but it proved an unattainable ambition of the frozen meat
trade. At various times specimen forms of contract were put forward
by the various bodies which represented the frozen meat trade before
1914. For instance, one was introduced in 1903 by the Frozen Meat
Trade Association but was not adopted owing to the conflicting
opinions among businessmen as to its merits. In the absence of a
generally recognized form of agreement each buyer remained practically a law unto himself regarding many of the details of contracts.
(67)

6   DEVELOPMENTS IN THE ARGENTINE MEAT INDUSTRY AFTER 1900

Changes in the structure of the Argentine meat export business took
place after 1900. For the purposes of analysis two stages of change
can be identified. The first, between 1902 and 1905, was the entry
of new firms into the trade. These newcomers were British and
Argentine firms. The second phase of development began in 1907 with
the entry of North American firms already engaged in the international meat trade into the South American section. This was accom-
plished by taking a controlling interest in some of the firms
already established in Argentina between 1902 and 1905. (68)

   The first two of the new firms who entered the industry in 1902
were La Société Anonyme de Viandes Congelées La Blanca (La Blanca)
with a capital of £300,000 and the La Plata Cold Storage Company
with a capital of £400,000. La Blanca was an Argentine concern,
financed by leading cattle ranchers or estancieros. The La Plata
Cold Storage Company was more international in its origins. It was

originally formed after there had been difficulties in obtaining
frozen beef for the South African market. In 1902 Australia had
temporarily abandoned that trade because of drought, and it had been
impossible to persuade existing River Plate companies to switch
supplies to any great extent from their established markets. Therefore, a group of mainly British businessmen, based in Cape Town,
built a freezing works at La Plata, some 25 miles below Buenos
Aires. However, by the time the works were ready to export beef,
the Boer War had finished and the South African demand for imported
supplies declined as the economy returned to a peace-time basis. La
Plata therefore turned its attention to the British market.
Although the company was multi-national in its origins and was
registered in Cape Town, the bulk of its capital was British owned
so it can be fairly regarded as a British company. (69) Another
native firm was formed in 1903, the Frigorifico Argentino with a
capital of £250,000, which began operations in June 1905. Finally,
another British enterprise, the Smithfield and Argentine Meat
Company, was also founded in 1903 with a capital of £200,000 and its
freezing establishment at Zarate was started in February 1905. (70)
Thus, by 1905 there were seven firms freezing and exporting meat
from the River Plate. The three established prior to 1902 were the
two British firms, the River Plate Fresh Meat Company Ltd (1882) and
James Nelson and Sons Ltd (1886) who carried on their South American
trade under the name of the Las Palmas Produce Company. The one
long standing Argentine firm was the Sansinena Company who had been
exporters of frozen meat since 1884.
   The entry of the four new firms in 1902 was a response to
increased profits and new market opportunities. After the comparative stagnation for a decade following the Baring crisis of 1890,
both investment and immigration into Argentina were at a high level
before the First World War. Exports were encouraged by the favourable and improving terms of trade. Changes also occurred in the
demand for, and composition of Argentina's exports of frozen meat.
Up to around 1900 the great staple of meat exports had been frozen
mutton; during 1890-8 an annual average of 38,500 tons of mutton and
lamb and 2,800 tons of beef were exported. After 1900 beef exports
grew fastest so that by 1905-9 an annual average of 167,300,000 tons
of frozen and chilled beef were exported as well as 72,200 tons of
mutton and lamb. (71) The growth of beef exports was the result of
two factors. First, in May 1900 the British government forbade the
imports of live animals from Argentina and Uruguay on account of
foot-and-mouth disease in those countries. The regulations were
relaxed briefly between 3 February and 12 May 1903 but reimposed
permanently thereafter when it was apparent that the disease was
endemic in South America. Although these imports were not large,
they had increased steadily since they started in 1889 and had
averaged 70,756 head per annum between 1895 and 1899. (72) After
the ban of 1900 and 1903 the only way to market these animals
abroad was to send them as beef, either chilled or frozen. In
addition there was in Britain a strong demand for imported fresh
beef. In the 1890s imports of mutton and beef were more or less the
same; between 1890 and 1899 the United Kingdom imported an average
of 2,474,584 tons of fresh mutton and 2,453,174 tons of fresh beef
per annum. But between 1900 and 1904 an annual average of 3,634,416

tons of mutton and 4,170,780 tons of beef were imported. A continuing high level of real wages and an easily available supply meant that the British consumer was able to demand and to obtain an increased quantity of 'imported beef. At the same time the Argentine producer increased his share of this supply by new investment in the industry as a whole.

The buoyant level of demand for Argentine meat was reflected in the profits of the companies involved, especially in 1902. This year was in fact a special case; supplies of meat from Australia were reduced by drought and also shipments from the USA to Britain were down in that year. At the same time there was an increased demand from South Africa to supply the troops there. This shortage had a dramatic effect in raising the level of wholesale prices and firms supplying the British market from South America reaped huge windfall profits. In 1903 James Nelson and Sons Ltd declared a trading surplus of £426,000 on the previous year's business - the annual turn-over was around £2 million. In that year they undertook fresh investments of £21,000 in Britain and £160,000 on their works at Las Palmas, they transferred £200,000 to their reserves and declared a dividend of 50 per cent for the ordinary shareholders. The two other businesses in the River Plate also declared profits on a similar scale. The immediate effect of this news was to induce competition. For some time there had been interests wanting to enter the trade but they had previously found it impossible to raise the necessary capital; however after 1902 they no longer had any difficulty in raising what they wanted. The possibility of increased competition was not neglected by established firms. In April 1905 the chairman of James Nelson and Sons observed 'that their large earnings of 1902 had enabled them to enlarge and practically reconstruct their plant at Las Palmas' - and at the same time to augment their working capital and 'so we are in these important respects well equipped for the sharp struggle in which it is quite possible we may before long be engaged'. (73) For instance, the estancieros' frigorifico, La Blanca, was promoted by agriculturists, inspired by the spectacle of the existing firms making huge profits, determined that they should take a hand in it themselves.

Although the increased competition was apparent by 1905, the British share of Argentina's meat freezing capacity did not decline greatly before the entry of North American firms after 1907. It is true that prior to 1900 the two British firms controlled more than two-thirds of Argentina's frozen meat exports, as the Sansinena Company's prime interest was the home market, but the investment of British capital after 1902 was on a sufficient scale to retain control of nearly two-thirds of the country's freezing capacity. Also the new Argentine firms tended to concentrate on the domestic market so British firms continued their domination of the export business. (74)

The second stage of structural changes in the River Plate industry began in September 1907 when the North American firm, Swift and Company, purchased the (predominantly) English firm, La Plata Cold Storage Company. The reason for this move lay in changes in the beef supply of the USA. It was an insurance by the North American firm against the time when the USA would have no surplus of meat available for export. (75) In 1909 a second group of Americans

entered the trade when a company representing and controlled by the
three meat packing firms, Swift, Armour and Morris, bought the
Argentine estancieros' plant at La Blanca. This sale marked the end
of attempts by agriculturists to participate in the trade and henceforth the meat industry of the River Plate resumed the rigid division of functions between farmers and freezing firms. The entry of
the US firms into the industry was probably facilitated by the
failure of profits to live up to the high expectations of 1902-3.
The River Plate Fresh Meat Company, after declaring dividends of 14
and 25 per cent in Britain in 1902 and 1903 respectively, declared
only 10 per cent in 1905 and 1906 and no dividends in 1904, 1907 and
1908. (76) The other new British company, the Smithfield and
Argentine Meat Company Ltd, formed in 1903, did not pay its first
dividend - a modest 10 per cent - on its ordinary shares until 1908.
(77)

Associated with the US companies, though by no means initiated by
them, was the growth of exports of chilled beef from the River
Plate. Prior to 1900 all beef exports from the River Plate had
consisted of frozen meat; the softer, more palatable and higher
priced chilled beef had only been available from North America. The
improvement of refrigeration techniques after 1900 enabled the more
perishable chilled meat to be exported, principally to Britain,
where the US firms had already established an elaborate network to
distribute this product. Therefore after 1900 it is impossible to
make the same rigid distinction between chilled and frozen meat
regarding either country of origin or entrepreneurial personnel that
applied in the nineteenth century. For the first time a country
exported both products and there were firms that also handled both
frozen and chilled meat. (78)

This development also had repercussions for the pastoralists of
Argentina. The companies, led by the US firms, required top quality
beef for chilling and encouraged the ranchers to produce it.
Another major category was added to the cattle bred for slaughter.
(a) The top grade were the 'chillers', specially fattened on alfalfa
pastures. (b) Next were the 'freezers', sometimes specially fed and
sometimes not, but which remained an important class of animal.
(c) Beef for local consumption was called bife de chorizo and was of
a lower quality, frequently from cows instead of steers which made
up most of the first two grades. (d) The lowest quality of all were
the thin, largely unimproved cattle, that were boiled down into
Leibig's meat extract or turned into corned beef. (79)

The North American firms' geographical diversification into this
section of the fresh meat trade was a signal for the first blast of
fierce competition felt by both the British and Argentine companies.
The 1909 Departmental Committee on Combinations in the Meat Trade,
which was formed as a response to the fear that US firms were
controlling Britain's meat supplies, reported on the evidence available to it during the months it sat that such control was unlikely.
There is, however, a strong indication that they could, at least for
a limited time, exercise a powerful influence in controlling meat
supplies from a limited area - in this case Argentina.

In 1906 and up to September 1907 the four British firms controlled 74 and 63 per cent respectively of exports of River Plate
beef to Britain. (80) But the US firms rapidly enlarged the size of

their plant soon after their purchases in 1907 and 1909 and entered
into aggressive competition with existing British and Argentine
firms to gain more of the trade for themselves. Between January
1909 and November 1911·US firms increased their share of the South
American beef trade with Britain from 35 to over 44 per cent; most
of this at the expense of the British firms (see Table 10.5).

TABLE 10.5 South American beef exports to Britain, 1909 - June
1914, according to national origin of the companies involved

Companies	Unrestricted competition			Price agreement	Unrestricted competition
	1909	1910	Jan. - Nov. 1911	Dec. 1911 - March 1913	April 1913 - June 1914
	%	%	%	%	%
British (3)	37.0	33.9	30.2	32.5	24.4
Argentine (2)	27.7	24.9	25.1	24.9	17.6
USA (2)	35.3	41.2	44.7	42.6	58.0
	100.0	100.0	100.0	100.0	100.0

Source: 'Inter-Departmental Committee on Meat Supplies', P.P.,
1919, XV, p.9.

The methods employed by the US companies to achieve this end were
to purchase large numbers of cattle to force up prices in South
America, and shipping large quantities of beef to London thus push-
ing down the prices at Smithfield. In 1910 higher prices were
actually being realized for frozen Australian beef than for
Argentine chilled as a result of the artificially low prices being
accepted by the US firms (81) for their undoubtedly superior
product. In November 1911 a conference of all South American beef
companies was called to limit beef supplies and regulate prices
between the various firms engaged in the trade. In the arrangement
that followed this meeting, usually referred to as the pool, the
British and Argentine firms had to accept a permanent reduction in
their share of the trade though they did recover a limited part of
the ground they had lost in 1911.

This agreement lasted for fiteeen months until March 1913.
Morris and Company then complained that their share of the trade was
not being maintained and used this as an excuse for a further price
war. In the opinion of the British companies the occasion of the
dispute had been deliberately engineered by the US firms in order to
obtain a still larger share of business. If this was the case these
efforts were crowned with success. During this second price war
butchers in England were able to buy good South American chilled
beef for as little as 2½d. per lb wholesale, whereas its quoted
price for 1913 was 4¼d. per lb. It seems unlikely that the full
extent of this fall in wholesale prices was passed on to the
customer. Instead butchers were able to enjoy widened profit
margins for beef, and the US firms were held in high esteem by the

British retailer for this unexpected windfall. (82) The multi-
national structure of the US firms was a great assistance to them
in these tactics. They had a bigger trade, which included the
enormous domestic market of the USA, than their largest rivals in
South America, who were solely dependent on Argentine beef supplies.
Also their greater capital reserves and cash in hand provided a
cushion against the losses they certainly made on the trade from
the River Plate to Britain. In fifteen months of unrestricted
competition, until the outbreak of the First World War, the British
firms were forced to accept a more serious reduction in their
portion of the trade from 32.5 per cent to under 25 per cent. (83)

There is also no doubt that some of the much noted efficiency of
the 1890s was lost after 1900. After the first price war of January
1909 to November 1911 there was unused freezing and chilling capacity in every plant. The three long established concerns, the
River Plate Fresh Meat Company, James Nelson and Sons and Sansinena,
were operating at under 60 per cent of their rated capacity, though
the US firms dictated for themselves a rather better bargain. (84)

The operations of the US firms in underselling their competitors
between 1909 and 1911 highlights a general feature of the imported
meat trade in Britain which became well known and remarked on in the
decade prior to the First World War. Although wholesale prices
fluctuated monthly, weekly, daily and even hourly, according to
salesmen at Smithfield, particular years often emerged in retrospect
as years of high or low prices. The standard of judgment employed
in these cases was no doubt often very arbitrary, amounting to
little more than a comparison with prices at the same time the year
before and whether those obtained currently were in advance of or
less than expected among traders. Nevertheless, particular years
did emerge as years of high or low prices. The influences that
operated to produce these impressions were manifold. Special
circumstances affecting the quantities forthcoming from the several
sources of foreign supplies, like drought in Australia or disease
among livestock in South America, was one. Then war or even the
rumour of impending conflict made up another extraneous factor. The
level and prices of domestic supplies of meat as well as the level
of home demand - determined by weather, the level of wages, and the
extent of unemployment - were some of the indigenous price determi-
nants. The precise weight to be attributed to each is not important, but traders noticed that the years of high and low prices did
not affect all sections of the meat business alike. The important
difference to emerge was between wholesalers and retailers. During
years of high prices the maximum benefits were reaped by those on
the wholesale side of distribution, and in years of low prices these
benefits were transferred to retail traders. The business of a
retailer is to buy his meat as cheaply as possible whereas a wholesaler always sells for the highest price possible. During a slump
in prices the wholesalers found their profit margins squeezed,
whereas retailers were able to increase the volume of their sales
without any appreciable increase in their fixed costs. Also
institutional 'stickiness' of retail prices ensured that they never
fell to the same extent as wholesale prices. Conversely, however,
during times of high wholesale prices the retailer's fixed costs
were still the same and the volume of sales was most likely reduced,

or else consumers switched to lower priced cuts of meat.

The British firm of James Nelson and Sons Ltd was in a position to insulate itself from these fluctuations to some extent as, in addition to importing Argentine meat, it also had about 1,000 retail shops in 1902 which it increased to between 1,200 and 1,300 by 1911. (85) This firm discovered that it was rarely possible to make much profit simultaneously in both the wholesale and retail trade; in 1902 when their wholesale trade was making enormous profits the retail side of the business was barely able to hold its own. (86) Another firm engaged in the South American trade but without the insurance of a retail division was the River Plate Fresh Meat Company. A comparison of the profit record of this enterprise, and Eastmans Ltd which since 1900 was engaged solely in retailing chilled and frozen meat, shows that between 1905 and 1907 the profits of the two concerns moved in opposite directions. In 1906, when the price of beef on the English wholesale market was low, Eastmans (retailers) made a profit of over £86,000 while the River Plate Company (wholesalers) made a loss of almost £20,000. In 1907, when the wholesale price of beef rose, the River Plate Company turned their loss into a profit of £24,000 while there was a £10,000 drop in Eastmans' profits (see Table 10.6). (87)

TABLE 10.6   Comparison of net profits between Eastmans Ltd and the River Plate Fresh Meat Company, 1905-7

	Net profits		
	1905	1906	1907
	£	£	£
Eastmans	85,527	86,588	76,585
River Plate Company	29,658	-19,799	24,392

To some extent James Nelson and Sons also cushioned themselves against the high prices of stock in Argentina and the low wholesale prices in England after 1909 by supplementing their own imports with wholesale purchases at Smithfield, when these could be made on advantageous terms. In this way the company lowered the average cost of meat supplied to their large system of retail outlets. This required the company to extend their working capital and have on hand large sums of ready cash. It was done in two ways. First, there had been a steady policy of building up a reserve from surplus profits after dividend distributions, fresh investments, etc., in the years before the US firms entered the River Plate. Thus by 1905 they were reported to have accumulated a reserve of £300,000. In addition to this the managers were in the habit of raising debenture capital. For instance at the end of 1908 this item stood at £105,000. In a business where opportunism in buying was at a premium the demand for ready cash was highly elastic. In 1909 the chairman reported, 'our accounts show that even last year, if we had had at our command £150,000 more of available cash, we could have added a considerable sum to our gross profits, which would have left a good margin after paying interest on the additional capital'.

Therefore, the amount of the debenture stock was steadily increased
from £105,000 in 1908 to £167,884 by 1913. In 1913 the total share
capital of the firm stood at £500,000 of which £300,000 was ordinary
shares and the remaining £200,000 7 per cent preference shares. The
issue of debenture stock was not the only method of obtaining working capital but at 6 per cent it was certainly the cheapest. James
Nelson's oldest rivals, the River Plate Fresh Meat Company, adopted
the more expensive method of financing their current operations with
bills of exchange. (88)

   In 1911 the diversified structure of James Nelson and Sons Ltd
was not a sufficient insurance against loss during the special
circumstances of that year. At this time the first price war waged
by the North American firms was at its height. Although wholesale
prices in Britain were high at the start of the season, delays to
the company's shipping prevented them obtaining any benefit. When
these problems had been resolved and consignments arrived in
England there was a general severe fall in prices and shipments
could only be realized at a heavy loss. It seems that these losses
were so severe that the usual policy of purchasing in Britain did
not succeed in wiping them out. Also the value of meat on the
wholesale market was further prejudiced by large quantities of
British meat prematurely marketed owing to a lack of pasture for
growing animals as a consequence of the protracted drought of 1911.
In addition the long hot summer of 1911 hindered the retail trade as
did the dock and railway strikes both during and after their
continuance. Therefore, James Nelson and Sons, who had been
steadily increasing their retail shops, found themselves more
vulnerable than when the scale of their business had been smaller.
The end result of these factors was to transform a profit of £73,000
of the previous year into a loss of £37,000 in 1911 and to force the
company to draw on a special reserve fund established in 1905 to pay
any dividends. (89)

   The increased competition, not only from the US firms, made the
future much less certain for all companies. At the end of every
annual report the chairman of James Nelson and Sons Ltd always
declined to enter into any predictions about the future year's
trade. He had better reason for such coyness than the usual businessman's reluctance to arouse the appetites of shareholders with
hints of rich dividends which twelve months hence might well remain
unsatisfied. The uncertain nature of the trade in South American
meat in Britain was reflected in the sharply fluctuating value of
the shares belonging to the various companies. The 'Economist'
warned its readers that the £1 shares of the River Plate Fresh Meat
Company, currently valued at 14s. in March 1908, moved up and down
so rapidly that they were very hard to value and should certainly
not be touched by any but the most speculative investors. Five
years earlier James Nelson and Sons had denied that their board of
directors - largely members of the family - had anything to do with
the ups and down of their shares on the Stock Exchange. (90)

   Informal meetings between the North American beef companies in
Britain to fix the price of their own meat in provincial markets and
to arrange the daily supplies each company put on the market were an
attempt to stabilize the situation, and they continued for some time
after 1909. There is evidence that these meetings persisted until

TABLE 10.7 Imports of frozen beef into the United Kingdom, 1883-
1913

Year	Australia cwt	New Zealand cwt	South America(a) cwt	Total cwt
1883	1,522			1,522
1884	2,754		500	3,254
1885	7,778	8,844	930	17,552
1886	10,195	10,962	6,736	27,893
1887	18	8,398	270	8,686
1888	864	40,490	3,678	45,032
1889	24,865	75,131	8,665	108,661
1890	21,426	88,495	8,933	118,854
1891	41,615	107,433	14,485	163,533
1892	56,568	62,065	8,309	126,942
1893	210,983	14,686	35,383	261,052
1894	301,896	2,617	5,279	309,792
1895	485,851	16,317	23,384	526,552
1896	494,975	28,803	50,095	573,873
1897	560,829	73,426	84,673	718,928
1898	531,651	92,756	108,288	732,695
1899	609,216	134,427	150,368	894,011
1900	413,991	310,667	412,262	1,136,920
1901	243,348	228,126	771,929	1,243,403
1902	65,860	237,257	923,748	1,226,865
1903	77,656	159,830	1,152,211	1,389,697
1904	76,345	175,012	1,675,271	1,926,628
1905	19,025	145,338	2,640,731	2,805,094
1906	34,457	236,587	2,811,493	3,082,537
1907	126,030	391,299	2,756,965	3,274,294
1908	112,583	347,872	3,685,697	4,146,152
1909	409,397	454,368	2,509,467	3,373,232
1910	878,469	532,830	2,330,391	3,741,690
1911	708,388	256,466	2,423,363	3,388,217
1912	892,334	261,733	2,934,000	4,088,067
1913	1,347,464	244,168	2,353,231	3,944,863

Source: 'Annual Statement of Trade', P.P.
(a) South American frozen beef was principally from Argentina with
minor amounts from Uruguay from 1905 onwards. The figures for
1900-8 include a certain amount of chilled beef which was first sent
in small quantities from Argentina in 1900 and was not separately
enumerated before 1909. J.T. Critchell and J. Raymond, 'A History
of the Frozen Meat Trade', London, 1912, pp.423-4, have an
unofficial series of figures giving chilled beef exports from
Argentina between 1900 and 1908. They are, however, estimates and
are not totally reliable.

TABLE 10.8 Imports of frozen mutton and lamb into the United Kingdom, 1882-1913

Year	Australia(a) cwt	New Zealand cwt	South America(b) cwt	Total cwt
1882	31,469	5,814	-	37,283
1883	31,747	71,942	3,571	107,260
1884	63,511	240,613	40,230	344,354
1885	53,574	284,013	112,223	449,810
1886	37,711	346,565	207,820	492,096
1887	42,445	395,638	277,709	715,792
1888	44,489	498,628	345,392	888,509
1889	42,100	568,499	395,303	1,005,902
1890	109,826	787,322	440,985	1,338,133
1891	167,331	896,126	447,325	1,510,782
1892	211,726	765,668	481,469	1,458,863
1893	287,158	900,300	525,143	1,712,601
1894	468,430	971,072	592,505	2,032,007
1895	499,920	1,171,048	726,577	2,397,545
1896	774,020	1,079,109	801,733	2,654,862
1897	706,752	1,302,333	1,007,268	3,016,353
1898	619,489	1,314,619	1,106,201	3,040,309
1899	525,733	1,475,719	1,141,208	3,142,660
1900	446,049	1,487,197	1,114,795	3,048,041
1901	518,639	1,488,217	1,271,654	3,278,510
1902	279,134	1,635,037	1,352,501	3,266,672
1903	181,269	2,035,434	1,485,770	3,702,473
1904	163,014	1,626,893	1,522,397	3,212,304
1905	505,413	1,524,981	1,462,537	3,492,931
1906	616,870	1,748,188	1,433,097	3,798,155
1907	858,226	2,005,078	1,402,302	4,265,606
1908	636,034	1,737,606	1,556,746	3,930,386
1909	943,753	1,987,023	1,646,264	4,577,040
1910	1,525,399	2,104,173	1,631,185	5,260,757
1911	1,291,696	1,981,467	1,939,705	5,212,868
1912	977,668	2,165,433	1,715,528	4,858,629
1913	1,665,859	2,200,525	1,347,873	5,214,257

Source: 'Annual Statement of Trade', P.P.

(a) Small experimental consignments arrived in 1880 and 1881: 400 and 17,275 carcases respectively. Frozen meat was not enumerated separately until 1882: prior to that date it was included with 'Meat, unenumerated, salted or fresh'. The figures for Australian mutton in 1880 and 1881 are found in Critchell and Raymond, op.cit., p.422.

(b) South American mutton and lamb was principally from Argentina. Minor amounts are included from the (British) Falkland Islands between 1886-7 and 1890-7 and Chile and Uruguay from 1905 onwards.

at least 1912. Their frequency, however, diminished before that
date. This was not because the US companies were ceasing to act in
concert, but because the use of the telephone, together with the
agreement that companies' representatives had the right to inspect
each other's works, made even unminuted meetings unnecessary. (91)

It was a continued matter of debate as to how successful these
companies were in their combined action. Their opponents always
argued that they were strong enough, when acting together, to
influence beef prices, at least in the short run. The companies'
reply was that any attempt to regulate imports to drive up prices
would encourage the expansion of home supplies, after even a few
days. The US firms claimed that their joint action was necessary
merely to prevent losses as they were handling large amounts of a
highly perishable commodity. The question arises whether their
actions were ever harmful to the interests of the British consumer.
It is hard to see how the low prices and easy availability of
Argentine beef between 1909 and 1911 could have prejudiced working-
class living standards: indeed, the reverse was the case. But this
initial period of unrestricted competition, when the pool shared out
quotas for shipments between themselves, did present a potential
threat, not only to consumer prices but to retail profits. However,
there seems to be no evidence that beef prices moved markedly out of
line in 1912 - the year the pool was operated. Average wholesale
prices of Argentine beef in 1911, 1912 and 1913 were $3\frac{1}{2}$d., $4\frac{1}{8}$d. and
$4\frac{1}{4}$d. respectively. (92)

Their allegedly precarious market position did not prevent one of
their number, Morris and Company, from becoming large buyers of
British and Irish cattle in the years just before the war. The
result of this diversification of interests was that by 1913 US meat
companies operating in South America contributed 20 per cent of the
total beef supply of the United Kingdom or about 50 per cent of the
total beef imported; at Smithfield, which was still the centre of
the trade, they controlled over 45 per cent of the total beef supply
and 57 per cent of the imported supply. (93) The British wholesale
trade viewed this situation with alarm, mainly on the grounds of
fears that in the future a similar control might be extended to
other branches of the meat trade, though the large retail firms
apparently preferred the increased guarantee of stable prices which
they supposed it implied. (94) In the event the fears and hopes of
both sides of the trade may not have been justified as there is no
guarantee that market share is the same as market power.

CONCLUDING REMARKS

The steady growth in the size and extent of the meat trade in the seventy years or so after 1840 was the result of a number of complementary factors. First, a general rise in real incomes, particularly from 1850, meant a substantial increase in the effective demand for all livestock products. From a level of around 80 lb per head in the 1840s, the per capita consumption of meat rose to a peak of 132 lb in the quinquennium 1900-4, and only declined very slightly thereafter up to 1914. The increase in consumption was also accompanied by a rise in the numbers employed in the industry. In 1911 there were almost three times as many butchers in the United Kingdom as there had been in 1841. Much of this increased consumption and employment was only made possible through the agency of foreign trade. In 1840 practically the whole demand for meat in this country was satisfied from domestic sources of supply, but by 1914 over 40 per cent of all meat supplies were imported. But the extension of this trade was a gradual process. For all practical purposes, foreign sources of meat and livestock were unexploited prior to the Free Trade budget of 1842. After that date both meat and livestock imports were freed from a considerable portion of the duties they had carried and thereafter the trade grew.

In addition to this liberalized tariff policy, the imported trade was made possible by technical developments that also had a profound effect on the domestic meat and livestock supplies. Up to 1820 most fatstock were driven to market by road. This meant an inevitable loss of weight and condition before these animals appeared as meat in the butchers' shops, especially if the town where they were consumed was some distance from the region where they were fattened. But the development of steamships in the 1820s and the railways from the 1830s allowed animals to go straight from the centres of production to the places of consumption without delay or waste. This change allowed greater scope for regions that were some distance from the centres of population to specialize more effectively in meat production. This argument applied just as well to the north east of Scotland as it did to central and south eastern Europe and, at a later date, to North and South America and finally to Australia and New Zealand. In the case of the extra-European sources of supply, these could not be properly exploited until the development of mechanical refrigeration techniques which solved the problem of preserving meat during a journey of some thousands of miles.

But although the long-term effects of these developments were undoubtedly beneficial because they allowed a growing population to enjoy an increasing supply of animal protein, some of them did highlight and even exacerbate short-term difficulties. For instance, in the 1840s and 1850s the increased flow of livestock traffic to the large cities of the United Kingdom, and here the best example was London, revealed serious flaws in the urban meat distribution system. Thus many town meat and livestock markets were not geared to cope efficiently with the large volume of supplies that the growth of population required and the development of transport made possible. This was not just a matter of handling larger numbers of livestock because the railways in particular allowed the animals to be slaughtered near to the place of production and the carcases only to be sent to the place of consumption. Again this put a premium on swift and efficient distribution once the meat arrived at its ultimate destination.

The importation of livestock from 1842 also caused its own problems. These took the form of the animal diseases that were allowed into the country along with imports of livestock. For a time these were regarded almost in the way of a necessary nuisance and it was not until the outbreak of cattle plague in 1865 that the government was prepared to consider any serious measures of control. The 1869 Contagious Diseases (Animals) Act was the first of a series of legislation designed to restrict the entry into the country of animals suffering from diseases and to control their movement, once they were in, to prevent them from infecting the domestic herd. But although dealers found these controls inconvenient they did not have the effect of halting the European livestock trade. In the case of imports of animals from North America the erection of cold stores at the ports was one method by which traders adapted their business operations to suit the new conditions that were applied to this trade after 1878.

Parallel with the development of these measures of a veterinary nature, to control disease among livestock, there was also a mounting concern about the more strictly public health aspects of the meat trade in as much as these had a bearing on the health of the human population. The unsatisfactory state of town meat markets and the more or less general sale of meat from diseased cattle and other livestock for human food in the 1840s and 1850s were both aspects of this question. At first controls in this direction were inadequate, but the general appointment of local Medical Officers of Health from 1875 onwards and the operation of the Public Health Acts of the nineteenth century also restricted the evils here. Thus both veterinary and medical measures meant more official intervention in the affairs of the meat trade. It was often unwelcome. In the 1890s there was considerable controversy over the danger to humans from tuberculosis in cattle and this was a matter that caused great anxiety in the meat trade, principally because butchers felt they were in danger of being called upon to stand the financial loss if animals they had bought in good faith were declared to be unfit for food by the public health inspectors. Butchers also resisted the attempts by municipal authorities, again on the grounds of public health, to close down small private slaughterhouses in the towns and to replace them with public abattoirs.

After 1892 animal disease legislation virtually ended imports of European livestock. But it is doubtful whether these would have continued in any case as increasing population and rising living standards diminished the livestock surplus those countries had for export. Imports of beef and cattle from North America reached their peak around 1900 but increasing population pressure also eliminated exports from there by 1914. However, bacon and hams still continued to come from North America and bacon was imported from Denmark, which largely adapted its agriculture to supply the British market. After 1900 Britain had to rely on those countries of the southern hemisphere, with small populations, to supply its imports of fresh meat. Although imports of frozen meat began properly in 1882 they became important in the 1890s. In this decade a substantial number of cold stores were erected in London and the provinces and the firms engaged in this trade perfected a national distribution network. Although frozen meat came from Australasia and South America the industry was organized in quite a different manner in each continent. In the former there was a multiplicity of firms while in the latter the trade was in the hands of a few British and Argentine companies before 1907. In that year the US firms entered the South American trade, as the export surplus from their own country seemed likely to disappear. This move was followed by a period of cut-throat competition as the US firms embarked on a successful attempt to capture a large part of the South American trade. These changes in the international meat trade provoked some anxiety in Britain as to whether there was a danger of a few firms gaining effective control of the whole meat trade. However this did not happen, for although large firms, which were unknown in 1840, took a share of the trade in 1914, there was still room for effective competition, both within the imported meat trade and between the imported and domestic trade, where the small scale individual retailer remained the norm.

NOTES

1 IMPORTANCE OF THE MEAT TRADE, 1840-1914

1 Statistics were collected for Scotland between 1854 and 1857 but this was discontinued because of complaints over the cost involved. For these early returns see P.P., 1854-5, XLVII; P.P., 1856, LIX; P.P., 1857, XV; and P.P., 1857-8, LVI. The Irish returns were collected by the police, following the disastrous famine in 1845-6. The early history of the statistics for Great Britain is described by J.T. Coppock in two articles in The Statistical Assessment of British Agriculture, 'Agricultural History Review', vol. IV, 1956.
2 J.R. McCulloch, 'A Statistical Account of the British Empire, ... etc.', London, 1837, 2nd ed. 1839. The 3rd and 4th eds, published in 1847 and 1854 respectively, are called 'A Descriptive and Statistical ... etc.'.
3 W.G. Mulhall, 'The Dictionary of Statistics', London, 1884; 2nd ed. 1886, 3rd ed. 1892, 4th ed. 1899.
4 On the basis of these returns (P.P., 1912-13, X) the Ministry of Agriculture made official estimates of the production of beef, veal, mutton, lamb and pigmeat in the United Kingdom. This series was extended to cover the period from 1900 to 1924, giving figures for each year. They were published in the 'First Report of the Royal Commission on Food Prices', P.P., 1924-5, XIII, Annex IV, p.162.
5 P.G. Craigie, On the Production and Consumption of Meat in the United Kingdom, 'British Association for the Advancement of Science, Report', 1884, pp.841-7.
6 R.F. Crawford, Notes on the Food Supply of the United Kingdom, Belgium, France and Germany, 'Journal of the Royal Statistical Society', vol. LXII, 1899, pp.597-629. The Food Supply of the United Kingdom, 'Journal of the Royal Agricultural Society of England', 2nd series, vol. XI, 1900, pp.19-34.
7 R.H. Rew, The Food Production of British Farms, 'Journal of the Royal Agricultural Society of England', vol. 64 (of entire series), 1903, pp.110-22. Report on the Production and Consumption of Meat and Milk in the United Kingdom, 'Journal of the Royal Statistical Society', vol. LXVII, 1904, pp.368-427.

8 R.H. Hooker, The Meat Supply of the United Kingdom, 'Journal of the Royal Statistical Society', vol. LXXII, part 2, 1909, pp. 304-76.

9 R.H. Rew, Memorandum on Some Estimates made by Various Authorities on the Production of Meat and Milk, 'Journal of the Royal Statistical Society', vol. LXV, 1902, pp.666-79.

10 R. Herbert, Statistics of Live Stock and Dead Meat for Consumption in the Metropolis, 'Journal of the Royal Agricultural Society of England', vol. XX, 1859, pp.475-6, 480.

11 R. Herbert, Statistics of Live Stock in the United Kingdom, 1853-1863, 'Journal of the Statistical Society', 1864, pp.520-5. This article is not as comprehensive as it sounds, and in fact is largely concerned with the changing numbers sent to London from different parts of the United Kingdom.

12 Notably, P.G. Craigie, Twenty Years' Changes in our Foreign Meat Supplies, 'Journal of the Royal Agricultural Society of England', 2nd series, vol. XXIII, 1887, pp.465-500, and J. Long, The Sources of our Meat Supply, 'Co-operative Wholesale Societies' Annual', 1891, pp.380-444.

13 The following list is not comprehensive but it covers the period from 1842 to 1908. 'Return Relating to the Past and Present supply of Live Stock and Dead Meat to the Country and the Metropolis', P.P., 1867-8, LV. 'Report of the Select Committee on Cattle Plague and the Importation of Livestock', P.P., 1877, IX. 'Select Committee on the Agricultural Produce (Marks) Bill', P.P., 1897, VIII. 'Report of Departmental Committee on Combinations in the Meat Trade', P.P., 1909, XV. In addition, the 'Statistical Abstract for the United Kingdom' which first appeared in 1854 (P.P., 1854, XXXIX) and annually thereafter contains a digest of imports, among them food, from 1840 onwards.

14 On this subject see Lord Ernle, 'English Farming Past and Present', London (6th ed.), 1961, pp.377-92. C.S. Orwin and E.H. Whetham, 'History of British Agriculture, 1846-1914', London, 1964, pp.240-386.

15 This is E.M. Ojala, 'Agricultural and Economic Progress', London, 1952, which has a statistical appendix (pp.191-217) that presents estimates of the gross and net output and income from agriculture in the United Kingdom. These are in the form of annual averages for groups of years from 1867 to 1939. The choice of these groups was prompted by special consideration. In the absence of any series for farm prices (i.e. paid to farmers for their products) before 1906 he used the annual prices in the Sauerbeck index of wholesale prices. The assumption here is that farm prices fluctuated in the same proportion as did wholesale prices. While this may not be true for individual years it was considered acceptable for groups of years. The groups chosen were those used by Colin Clark in 'National Income and Outlay', London, 1937, p.246, who chose the periods to commence three years after each main peak in the trade cycle. (Ojala, op.cit., pp.191-2.) This means these groups of years are of irregular length.)

16 Ojala, op.cit., pp.208 and 209.

17 T.W. Fletcher, The Great Depression of English Agriculture,

1873-1896, 'Economic History Review', 2nd series, vol. XIII, 1961, pp.417-32. Reprinted in W.E. Minchinton, ed., 'Essays in Agrarian History', vol. II, London, 1968. See pp.417-18 for Fletcher's review of the imperfections of the Sauerbeck price index and the appendix, p.432, for his new estimates.

18 Ojala, op.cit., p.208.

19 K.A.H. Murray, 'Factors Affecting the Prices of Livestock in Great Britain', London, 1931, pp.78-9, appendix II, table I.

20 Ibid., appendix I, table I.

21 This included a substantial store traffic from Ireland.

22 In 1911 this group comprised 116,722 bakery workers, 121,503 selling from bakers' shops, and 37,221 confectioners (makers and dealers).

23 See pp.41-9 of this book. In addition, part of the meat supply of towns went there on the hoof and was purchased by butchers who did their own slaughtering.

24 They added: 20 per cent to the original cost of meat, vegetables, butter and cheese, milk and eggs, fruit; 24 per cent to fish; 30 per cent to wheat (which became bread). Report of the Committee ... on the Present Appropriation of Wages ..., 'British Association for the Advancement of Science, Report', 1881, pp.276-9.

25 Ibid., p.279.

26 See pp.25-7 of this book.

2 CHANGES IN THE DOMESTIC LIVESTOCK TRADE, 1840-64

1 Descriptions of the Scottish cattle trade with England are found in the work of the famous cattle breeder and dealer, William McCombie of Tillyfour, Aberdeenshire, 'Cattle and Cattle Breeders', Edinburgh, 1867. The Welsh trade is described in C. Skeel, The Cattle Trade Between Wales and England from the Fifteenth to the Nineteenth Centuries, 'Transactions of the Royal Historical Society', 4th series, vol. IX, 1926, pp.135-58. Although all markets and fairs were noted as either chiefly fatstock or predominantly for the sale of lean animals, specimens of both could be found at any of these gatherings.

2 A.R.B. Haldane, 'The Drove Roads of Scotland', London, 1952, chapter 12.

3 G. Menzies, Report on the Transit of Stock, 'Transactions of the Highland and Agricultural Society of Scotland', 4th series, vol. II, 1868-9, p.463.

4 See Table 2.2.

5 On the progress of improvement see M. Gray, Scottish Emigration: the Social Impact of Agrarian Chance in the Rural Lowlands 1775-1875, 'Perspectives in American History', vol. VII, 1973, pp. 95-174. In this comprehensive survey of Scottish farming the author states: 'Scottish agiculture which had seemed so unshakeably backward in 1750 or even 1770 had by 1830 the reputation of outstanding efficiency .... The crescendo of change came between 1780 and 1830 ...' (p.112).

6 This was the large livestock market about 15 miles north of Newcastle from which the north east of England was supplied.

7 J.H. Smith, The Cattle Trade in Aberdeenshire in the Nineteenth
   Century, 'Agricultural History Review', vol. III, 1955, p.116.
8 Anon., On the Preparation of Live-Stock and Meat in Reference to
   their Exportation by Steam Vessels, 'Quarterly Journal of
   Agriculture', vol. VIII, June 1837 - March 1838, pp.246-7. The
   question of transport problems is neglected by J. Blackman in
   her article, The Cattle Trade and Agrarian Change on the Eve of
   the Railway Age, 'Agricultural History Review', vol. XXIII,
   1975, section vi, which deals with Scotland in the early nineteenth century. She gives the impression that there were no
   difficulties in the way of marketing fatstock caused by
   deficiencies in the transport system at this time.
9 A.R.B. Haldane says that 'already a small demand existed for
   transport of cattle from Aberdeen to Leith and London by sailing
   boat at a cost of £1 10s a head' ('The Drove Roads of Scotland',
   p.218). He is not specific as to the date but it seems that
   this was around 1820.
10 On the Preparation of Livestock and Meat in Reference to their
   Exportation by Steam Vessels, 'Quarterly Journal of Agriculture', vol. VIII, June 1837 - March 1838, p.248.
11 A. Wynter, The London Commissariat, 'Quarterly Review', vol.
   XCV, no. CXC, 1854, p.287.
12 A.R.B. Haldane, 'The Drove Roads of Scotland', pp.49-54, 206-7.
13 See p.18 of this book.
14 W. Youatt, 'Cattle: their Breeds, Management and Diseases',
   London, 1834, pp.257-8.
15 See p.18 of this book.
16 E.L. Jones and E.J.T. Collins, Sectoral Advance in English
   Agriculture, 1850-80, 'Agricultural History Review', vol. XV,
   1967. E.L. Jones, 'The Development of English Agriculture,
   1815-1873', London, 1968, pp.19-22.
17 J.M. Wilson, 'The Rural Cyclopedia', Edinburgh, 1849, vol. III,
   pp.393-4.
18 H. Tremenheere, Agricultural and Educational Statistics of
   Several Parishes in the County of Middlesex, 'Journal of the
   Statistical Society', vol. VI, 1843, p.122.
19 W.M. Acworth, 'The Railways and the Traders', London, 1891,
   p.94.
20 See J.H. Smith, The Cattle Trade of Aberdeenshire in the Nineteenth Century, 'Agricultural History Review', vol. III, 1955,
   pp.114-18; G. Channon, The Aberdeenshire Beef Trade with London:
   a Study in Steamship and Railway Competition, 1850-69,
   'Transport History', vol. 2, 1969, pp.1-24; C.S. Orwin and E.H.
   Whetham, 'History of British Agriculture, 1846-1914', London,
   1964, pp.98-9. Smith's figures for the numbers of cattle
   carried from Aberdeen after 1850 (p.115) seem to have been
   replaced by Channon's more modest totals (p.5).
21 J.H. Smith, The Cattle Trade of Aberdeenshire in the Nineteenth
   Century, 'Agricultural History Review', vol. III, 1955, p.114.
22 C.H. Lee, Some Aspects of the Coastal Shipping Trade: the
   Aberdeen Steam Navigation Company, 1835-80, 'Journal of
   Transport History', new series vol. III, no. 2, 1975, p.99.
23 Ibid., p.101.
24 G. Channon, The Aberdeenshire Beef Trade with London: a Study in

Steamship and Railway Competition, 1850-69, 'Transport History', vol. 2, 1969, p.5. Also there are no figures for 1866-9.

25   See ibid., appendix, table III.

26   G. Dodd, 'The Food of London', London, 1856, pp.265-6.

27   These differences were first noted in an important article that appeared anonymously in the 'Quarterly Journal of Agriculture', vol. VIII, June 1837 - March 1838, pp.241-81, On the Preparation of Live-Stock and Meat in Reference to their Exportation by Steam Vessels. This article was borrowed from by various compilers of dictionaries of farming practice from the 1840s to the 1860s. See, for instance, J.M. Wilson, 'The Rural Cyclopedia', vol. III, pp.393-8. Henry Stephens, 'Book of the Farm', Edinburgh, 1844, vol. II, pp.97-9, 167-71; 2nd ed., 1851, vol. II, pp.690-700. J.C. Morton, 'A Cyclopedia of Agriculture', Glasgow, 1869, vol. II, pp.402-7. Morton's account appears to have been modernized with additional material added by the writer of the article, William Ewart, cattle salesman, Newcastle-on-Tyne. Also some of the prices quoted by Ewart appear to have been revised and represent those being charged by retail butchers sometime in the 1850s. Although wholesale prices underwent some very sharp fluctuations between these two periods they appear to have been about the same in the late 1830s, mid-1840s and mid-1850s. (See Figures 2.1 and 2.2.) There is nothing to indicate that the relationship between wholesale and retail prices of meat underwent any radical change in this generation. This is considered a justification for regarding the retail prices given by the author of the original article in 1837-8 as being representative of retail meat prices in 1839-42, 1845-6 and 1854-7.

28   J.C. Morton, 'A Cyclopedia of Agriculture', vol. II, pp.402-7. Article by William Ewart, cattle salesman, Newcastle-on-Tyne.

29   A saddle comprises the entire hind quarter of a sheep - i.e. the leg and the loin. A haunch comprises the leg and part of the loin so as not to include the ribs and belly portion.

30   London prices, 'Quarterly Journal of Agriculture', vol. VIII, 1837-8, p.272. Newcastle prices, J.C. Morton, 'A Cyclopedia of Agriculture', vol. II, p.406.

31   The prices shown in Figures 2.1 and 2.2 are average wholesale beef and mutton prices in London, Newcastle, Edinburgh and Glasgow between January 1828 and December 1864, and for Liverpool from January 1844 to December 1864. All apply to the better qualities of both meats, and the graphs are unweighted annual averages of the highest and lowest prices recorded monthly. They are taken from the 'Quarterly Journal of Agriculture', May 1828 - March 1843. In July 1843 the magazine was renamed the 'Journal of Agriculture'.

32   These prices were for fat cattle, per hundredweight live weight. They are published in the 'Agricultural Returns' for Great Britain.

33   J.C. Morton, 'A Cyclopedia of Agriculture', vol. II, pp.360-5. William McCombie, the Aberdeenshire cattle breeder, records it was not 'the custom of the trade to get all our askings'. ('Cattle and Cattle Breeders', Edinburgh, 1867, p.80.)

34   See p.150 of this book.

35 Some of the famous sales continued a tradition laid down by
    Robert Bakewell in the eighteenth century and Lord Leicester at
    Holkham during the Napoleonic Wars and are mentioned by C.S.
    Orwin and E.H. Whetham, 'History of British Agriculture, 1846-
    1914', London, 1964, pp.27-8.
36 J.C. Morton, 'A Cyclopedia of Agriculture', vol. II, pp.360,
    417. 'Royal Commission on Market Rights and Tolls', P.P., 1888,
    LIII, vol. II, Q 6734.
37 J.C. Morton, 'A Cyclopedia of Agriculture', vol. II, p.265.

3   CHANGES IN TOWN MARKETS, 1840-64

1   J.R. McCulloch, 'Dictionary of Commerce', London, 1832, p.244.
2   P. Deane and W.A. Cole, 'British Economic Growth, 1688-1959',
    Cambridge, 2nd ed., 1967, pp.69-70.
3   John Gwynn, 'London and Westminster Improved', London, 1766,
    pp.18-20, 123.
4   Quoted in Joseph Fletcher, Statistical Account of the Markets of
    London, 'Journal of the Statistical Society', vol. X, 1847,
    p.357.
5   For descriptions of Smithfield at its worst see (for the 1830s)
    W. Youatt, 'Cattle: their Breeds, Management and Diseases',
    London, 1834, pp.259-60; (for the 1850s) A. Wynter, The London
    Commissariat, 'Quarterly Review', vol. XCV, no. CXC, 1854, pp.
    282-4. There is also a description of Smithfield and its
    cruelties in 'Oliver Twist'. Numbers of cattle displayed at the
    Christmas market are printed in the 'Journal of the Royal
    Agricultural Society', 2nd series, vol. XII, 1876, p.XIV.
6   J. Fletcher, Statistical Account of the Markets of London,
    'Journal of the Statistical Society', vol. X, 1847, p.360.
7   A. Wynter, The London Commissariat, 'Quarterly Review', vol.
    XCV, no. CXC, 1854, p.288.
8   Ibid.
9   J.S. Gamgee, 'Cattle Plague and Diseased Meat in their Relations
    with the Public Health ... A Letter to ... Sir G. Grey', London,
    1857, p.39. This was the first of two open letters addressed to
    the Home Secretary and revealing the scandalous conditions under
    which meat and livestock were sold, both in London and the
    country at large. The second letter was published as 'The
    Cattle Plague and Diseased Meat ... A Second Letter to Sir G.
    Grey, ...', London, 1857. Hereafter these publications are
    referred to as 'Cattle Plague and Diseased Meat', I and II
    respectively.
10 'Cattle Plague and Diseased Meat', II, pp.5-6.
11 'Cattle Plague and Diseased Meat', II, pp.11-13.
12 J. Fletcher, Statistical Account of the Markets of London,
    'Journal of the Statistical Society', vol. X, 1847, p.357.
13 Anon., Metropolitan Cattle Market, 'Journal of Agriculture',
    vol. XVIII, July 1852, pp.376, 378.
14 'Report of the Commissioners appointed by the Treasury to make
    Inquiries Relating to Smithfield Market ...', P.P., 1850, XXXI,
    Qs 793-5.
15 'Report of the Committee appointed by the Treasury to inquire

into the appropriation of the site of Smithfield, and the
establishment of a new metropolitan meat market', P.P., 1856,
XXXVII, p.xi.

16   'Return relating to the past and present supply of live and dead
meat to this Country, and the Metropolis', P.P., 1867-8, LV,
p.10.

17   A. Wynter, The London Commissariat, 'Quarterly Review', vol.
XCV, no. CXC, 1854, p.289.

18   From 1828 the following parliamentary enquiries were held
regarding Smithfield: 'First Report from the Select Committee
appointed to inquire into the state of Smithfield Market, and
the slaughtering of Cattle in the Metropolis; and to whom
several Petitions respecting the removal of Smithfield Market
were referred', P.P., 1828, VIII. 'Second Report from the
Select Committee on the same subject in a subsequent Session',
P.P., 1849, XIX. 'Report of the Commissioners appointed by the
Treasury to make Inquiries relating to Smithfield Market, and
the Markets in the City of London, for the Sale of Meat', P.P.,
1850, XXX. 'Report from the Select Committee on the Smithfield
Market Removal Bill', P.P., 1851, X. 'Report of the Committee
appointed by the Treasury to inquire into the appropriation of
the site of Smithfield, and the establishment of a new metropolitan meat market', P.P., 1856, XXVII.

19   George Dodd, 'The Food of London', London, 1856, pp.250-1.

20   W.A. Robson, 'The Government and Misgovernment of London',
London, 1939, p.45.

21   6 and 7 William IV, c 68.

22   'Quarterly Journal of Agriculture', vol. VII, May 1836, p.105.

23   J. Fletcher, Statistical Account of the Markets of London,
'Journal of the Statistical Society', vol. X, 1847, pp.355, 359.

24   31 Geo. II, c 40.

25   'Report from the Select Committee on Smithfield Market', P.P.,
1847, XIX, Qs 2101-14.

26   Ibid., Qs 5147-54.

27   Ibid., Qs 5085, 5089, 5200.

28   Ibid., Qs 5086.

29   Ibid., Qs 5096, 5116, 5121-3.

30   Ibid., Qs 5193, 5195-6.

31   G. Dodd, 'The Food of London', p.266.

32   J. Fletcher, Statistical Account of the Markets of London,
'Journal of the Statistical Society', vol. X, 1847, p.355.

33   On this subject see W.A. Robson, 'The Government and Misgovernment of London', London, 1939, especially part I, chapters I-
VIII, and part II, chapter X. Also, Sir Lawrence Comme, 'London
in the Reign of Queen Victoria', London, 1898.

34   Robson, op.cit., p.11.

35   See 'Minutes of Evidence taken before Select Committee on
Smithfield Market Removal Bill', B.P.P., 1851, X.

36   Ibid., Wolverhampton, Shrewsbury, Qs 569, 590, 597; Bristol,
Qs 323-6, 382-3, 386; Liverpool, Qs 218-19, 221-5, 434-9, 462;
Birmingham, Qs 551, 558, 561.

37   'Evidence Taken Before the Commissioners appointed to enquire
into the State of the Corporation of London', B.P.P., 1854,
XXVI, Q 4235.

38   'Smithfield Market Removal Act', (14 and 15 Vict., c 16).
39   A. Wynter, The London Commissariat, 'Quarterly Review', vol.
     XCV, no. CXC, 1854, p.287.
40   G.R. Hawke, 'Railways and Economic Growth in England and Wales
     1840-1870', London, 1970, pp.151-2.
41   Statistics of Live Stock and Dead Meat for Consumption in the
     Metropolis, 'Journal of the Royal Agricultural Society of
     England', 1859, vol. XX, p.479.
42   'Journal of the Royal Agricultural Society of England', 1859,
     vol. XX, p.479.
43   J.D. Chambers and G.E. Mingay mention that 1859-60 saw a very
     severe winter and a late spring with a shortage of fodder and a
     glut of lean stock ('The Agricultural Revolution, 1750-1880',
     London, 1966, p.179). Hawke suggests that this might have led
     to low figures for agricultural freight carried by rail in 1859
     (op.cit., p.137).
44   A. Wynter, The London Commissariat, 'Quarterly Review', vol.
     XCV, no. CXC, 1854, p.286.
45   P.G. Craigie, Twenty Years' Changes in Our Foreign Meat
     Supplies, 'Journal of the Royal Agricultural Society of
     England', 2nd series, vol. XXII, 1887, p.472.
46   The statistics of livestock passing through Smithfield and, to
     a lesser extent, Islington are not precise measures of the
     numbers actually sold. There is an element of double-counting
     as markets were held twice weekly and some animals were exhibi-
     ted more than once before a sale was made. There is also a
     disconcerting variation in the annual numbers recorded in
     different statistical sources. No satisfactory explanation of
     these variations can be offered. Therefore all these figures
     must be regarded as approximations only.
47   Number of stock in Smithfield from 1841 to 1851, 'Journal of
     Agriculture', vol. XVIII, January 1853, p.572.
48   'Return relating to the past and present supply of live and
     dead meat to this Country and the Metropolis', P.P., 1867-8, LV,
     p.32.
49   'First Report of the Commissioners appointed to inquire into the
     Origin and Nature, etc., of the Cattle Plague' (hereafter 'First
     Report Cattle Plague Commissioners'), P.P., 1866, XXII, Qs 4200.
     4235.
50   'First Report Cattle Plague Commissioners', P.P., 1866, XXII,
     Qs 4227, 4235-9.
51   Ibid., Qs 3017-18.
52   W.G. Rimmer, Leeds Leather Industry in the Nineteenth Century,
     'Thoresby Society Publications', vol. XLVI, 1961, pp.124-5. (I
     am indebted to Mr C.H. Lee for this reference.)
53   R. Herbert, The Supply of Meat to Large Towns, 'Journal of the
     Royal Agricultural Society of England', 2nd series, vol. II,
     1866.
54   'First Report Cattle Plague Commissioners', P.P., 1866, XXII,
     Qs 4048, 4079.
55   'Report of the Committee on the Transit of Animals by Sea and
     Land', P.P., 1870, LXI, Qs 267, 271-4, 114-6.
56   B. Poole, 'The Economy of the Railways', London, 1856, p.5.
57   G. Channon, The Aberdeenshire Beef Trade with London: a Study in

Steamship and Railway Competition, 1850-69, 'Transport History', vol. 2, 1969, p.15.

58 R. Herbert, The Supply of Meat to Large Towns, 'Journal of the Royal Agricultural Society of England', 2nd series, vol. II, 1866, p.441.

59 G. Channon, op.cit., pp.15-16. This is also mentioned in G.R. Hawke, op.cit., p.149. He finds 'Orwin and Whetham argue that railways made it possible for butchers to take advantage of divergent price trends for different cuts of meat in different markets'. But he goes on to observe that the 1866 Select Committee on Trade in Animals concluded that offal would not bear the cost of rail transport. The relevant passage in Orwin and Whetham would seem to be on p.99 of C.S. Orwin and E.H. Whetham, 'History of British Agriculture, 1846-1914', London, 1964, where they say: 'And it became possible to avoid altogether the cost of transporting live animals by developing the trade in dead meat, with the further advantage that the different parts of the same carcase could be marketed in different areas in accordance with local prices.' In this passage, however, Orwin and Whetham may not be thinking about offal but have in mind the cheaper meat cuts, such as flank, neck and skirt, as opposed to the heart, liver and kidneys which would be defined as 'offal'. It was not the case that offal never went by rail, although this may have been so about the time the 1866 Committee heard evidence. Traders were reluctant to send offal, preferring whenever possible to sell it locally, but sometimes local prices gave them no alternative as with one Norfolk dealer, cited on p.105 of this book, who sent offal to London after 1866.

60 'Report of the committee appointed by the Treasury to inquire into the appropriation of the site of Smithfield and the establishment of a new metropolitan meat market', P.P., 1856, XXXVII, pp.ix, xii-xiv. This committee made no intelligent recommendations for a new meat market, for example, 'we think it probable that the great and increasing pressure upon the existing market will, at no distant period, lead to a proposal acceptable to the trade and beneficial to the public while any attempt to force the business to a locality unsuitable for the purpose, would only have the effect of dispersing it through other channels' (p.xv).

4 TRADE IN DISEASED MEAT, 1840-64

1 S.A. Hall, John Gamgee and the Edinburgh New Veterinary College, 'Veterinary Record', 16 October 1965, p.1,237.

2 John Gamgee, The Relations of Veterinary to Social Science, 'Edinburgh Veterinary Review', vol. III, no. IX, January 1861, p.9.

3 J. Gamgee, 'Diseased Meat Sold in Edinburgh, and Meat Inspection in connection with Public Health. A Letter to the ... Lord Provost of Edinburgh', hereafter cited as 'Diseased Meat Sold in Edinburgh', Edinburgh, 1857.

4 J.S. Gamgee, 'Cattle Plague and Diseased Meat', I and II.

Because London was so important it has already been treated as a special case in the preceding chapter. For further information about these two pamphlets see chapter 3, note 9.

5 I am very grateful to Mr Sherwin A. Hall for bringing this important publication to my notice.

6 J.S. Gamgee, 'Cattle Plague and Diseased Meat', II, p.26.

7 Used in the traditional non-precise sense as the science of all pathogenic micro-organisms.

8 R.H. Major, 'A History of Medicine', Oxford, 1954, vol. II, pp.827-9, 837-8. E.H. Ackerknecht, 'A Short History of Medicine', New York, 1955, pp.162-4.

9 Ibid., pp.197-9.

10 State of the Public Health in the Last Quarter of the Year 1846, reprinted in 'Journal of the Statistical Society', vol. X, March 1847, p.88.

11 J. Fletcher, Statistical Account of the Markets of London, 'Journal of the Statistical Society', vol. X, November 1847, p.360.

12 J. Gamgee, 'Aberdeen Herald', 20 June 1857, and J.S. Gamgee, 'Cattle Plague and Diseased Meat', I, pp.35-6. Also 'Aberdeen Herald', 20 June 1857.

13 'Aberdeen Herald, 27 June 1857.

14 W. McCombie, 'Cattle and Cattle Breeders', Edinburgh, 1867, pp. 119-21. McCombie also refers to the farms rented by the Williamsons, whom he describes as 'the great Aberdeen butchers' fifty years before (pp.56-9).

15 Ibid., p.199.

16 'First Report Cattle Plague Commissioners', P.P., 1866, XXII, Qs 2976-8.

17 James Higgins, Inspector of Meat, Leeds: On Diseased Meat, 'Edinburgh Veterinary Review', vol. V, no. XLIII, November 1863, pp.670-1.

18 'First Report Cattle Plague Commissioners', P.P., 1866, XXII, Q 3061.

19 J. Gamgee, 'Diseased Meat Sold in Edinburgh', Edinburgh, 1857, p.22. (Originally published as correspondence to the 'Scotsman', 28 February 1857 and the 'Glasgow Herald', 27 March 1857.)

20 Ibid., pp.15-17, 22.

21 John Gamgee, Statistics of Loss amongst Live Stock in the United Kingdom: being the Opening Address at the International Congress of Veterinary Surgeons, held in Hamburg, 'Edinburgh Veterinary Review', vol. V, no. XL, August 1863, pp.476-81.

22 J. Gamgee, Diseases Amongst Domestic Animals in Kincardineshire, 'Transactions of the Highland and Agricultural Society', vol. XXII, 1857, p.37.

23 J. Gamgee, On the Importance of Legislation for the Prevention of Disease Amongst our Domestic Animals, 'Edinburgh Veterinary Review', vol. V, no. XLIV, December 1863, p.726.

24 'Edinburgh Veterinary Review', vol. V, no. XL, August 1863, p.479.

25 W.T. Lorimer, On Insurance Societies for Farm Stock, 'Journal of Agriculture', vol. XV, January 1845, pp.336-7.

26 J. Gamgee, 'Diseased Meat Sold in Edinburgh', 1857, pp.4-5.

27   'Edinburgh Veterinary Review', vol. IV, no. XXXII, December
     1862, p.815 (from the 'Scottish Farmer', 19 November 1862).
28   J. Gamgee, The System of Inspection in Relation to the Traffic
     in Diseased Animals and their Produce, 'Edinburgh Veterinary
     Review', vol. V, no. XLIII, November 1863, p.669.
29   W. Youatt, 'Cattle; their Breeds, Management and Diseases',
     London, 1834, pp.260-5, 412.
30   Cattle Disease Prevention, 'Journal of Agriculture', vol. XXV,
     July 1865 - April 1866, p.121-2.
31   D. Taylor, London's Milk Supply, 1850-1900: a Reinterpretation,
     'Agricultural History', vol. XLV, 1971, pp.34-6.
32   'First Report of Cattle Plague Commissioners', P.P., 1866,
     XXII, appendix A, pp.172-3.
33   'Return from the Town Clerks of England, of the means adopted
     for the prevention of the sale of diseased and unsound meat for
     human food; amount of such meat seized in 1861 and 1862', P.P.,
     1863, XLVIII, p.27. 'Edinburgh Veterinary Review', vol. V, no.
     XLIII, November 1863, pp.672-3. 'First Report Cattle Plague
     Commissioners', P.P., 1866, XXII, Qs 3007, 3061, 3080.
34   James Higgins, On Diseased Meat, 'Edinburgh Veterinary Review',
     vol. V, no. XLIII, November 1863, p.673.
35   That is, they were tuberculous.
36   'Report from the Select Committee on the Adulteration of Food,
     Drinks and Drugs', P.P., 1856, VIII, Qs 2151-200.
37   E. Holland, Diseases of Live-Stock in their Relation to the
     Public Supplies of Meat and Milk, 'Edinburgh Veterinary Review',
     vol. V, no. XLI, September 1863, pp.540-1.
38   'Return from the Town Clerks of England ...', P.P., 1863,
     XLVIII, p.49.
39   E. Holland, On Disease in Cattle, 'Edinburgh Veterinary Review',
     vol. V, no. XLIII, November 1863, p.657.
40   'Aberdeen Herald', 20 June 1857.
41   'Aberdeen Herald', 11 July 1857. Leading article, p.5; report
     of the trial, p.6.
42   E. Holland, Diseases of Live-Stock in their Relation to the
     Public Supplies of Meat and Milk, 'Edinburgh Veterinary Review',
     vol. V, no. XLI, September 1863, p.540.
43   Ministry of Agriculture Fisheries and Food, 'Animal Health,
     1865-1965', London, 1965, pp.9-10, 14-16.
44   J. Gamgee, On the Importance of Legislation for the Prevention
     of Disease amongst our Domestic Animals, 'Edinburgh Veterinary
     Review', vol. V, no. XLIV, December 1863, p.723.
45   On Cattle Disease Prevention, 'Journal of Agriculture', vol. 25,
     July 1865 - April 1866, p.119.
46   J. Gamgee, Disease in Town Dairies and its Prevention,
     'Edinburgh Veterinary Review', vol. V, no. XLIV, December 1863,
     pp.757-8.
47   E. Holland, On Disease in Cattle, 'Edinburgh Veterinary Review',
     vol. V, no. XLIII, November 1863, pp.658-9.
48   'Return from the Town Clerks of England ...', P.P., 1863,
     XLVIII, p.6.
49   W. Youatt, Cattle; their Breeds, Management and Diseases,
     London, 1834, p.256.
50   Ibid., pp.259-61, 261-3.

5 FOREIGN IMPORTS AND THE DOMESTIC SUPPLY, 1840-64

1 W.G. Mulhall, 'Fifty Years of National Progress, 1837-1887',
   London, 1887, p.83; 'The Dictionary of Statistics', 4th edition
   (revised), London, 1903, pp.286-7. J.T. Critchell and J.
   Raymond, 'A History of the Frozen Meat Trade', London, 1912,
   p.2, provides the imported meat figures. It must be emphasized
   that all these figures are very inexact and only represent
   relative orders of magnitude. Critchell and Raymond also give
   figures for domestic meat production (and hence total per
   capita consumption) that are less than Mulhall's, though they
   claim him as their source.
2 'Report on the Methods Employed in the River Plate for Curing
   Meat for European Markets', P.P., 1866, LXXI, p.1.
3 J.T. Critchell and J. Raymond, 'A History of the Frozen Meat
   Trade', p.9.
4 Andrew Wynter, 'Our Social Bees', chapter on Preserved Meats,
   London, 1865 ed.
5 G.E. Putnam, 'Supplying Britain's Meat', London, 1923, pp.65-6.
6 R.A. Clemen, 'The American Livestock and Meat Industry', New
   York, 1923 (reprinted 1966), pp.114-15.
7 'Journal of the Society of Arts', vol. XV, 17 May 1867, pp.414-
   15. (Evidence of Mr Henry Grainger, engaged in the foreign
   provision trade in London and Liverpool and President of the
   Liverpool Chamber of Commerce in 1864, before the Society's
   Food Committee, sub-committee on meat, 17 April 1867.)
8 Clemen, op.cit., pp.116-17.
9 S.G. Hanson, 'Argentine Beef and the British Market, Stanford,
   1937, pp.29-30.
10 'Report on the Methods Employed in the River Plate for Curing
   Meat for European Markets', P.P., 1866, LXXI, p.4.
11 'Journal of the Society of Arts', vol. XV, 17 May 1867, p.415.
12 G. Dodd, 'The Food of London', London, 1856, p.281.
13 B.R. Mitchell and P. Deane, 'Abstract of British Historical
   Statistics', London, 1962, p.19.
14 'Journal of Agriculture', vol. 18, October 1852, p.571.
15 'Economist', 12 January 1850, p.52; 23 February 1850, p.220.
16 'The Food of London', p.227.
17 Ministry of Agriculture, Fisheries, and Food, 'Animal Health,
   1865-1965', London, 1965, p.30.
18 R. Herbert, Statistics of Live Stock and Dead Meat for Consumption in the Metropolis, 'Journal of the Royal Agricultural
   Society of England', vol. XXV, 1864, p.244.
19 A.D. Bayne, 'A History of the Industry and Trade of Norwich and
   Norfolk', Norwich, 1858, p.66.
20 A. Wynter, The London Commissariat, 'Quarterly Review', vol.
   XCV, no. CXC, 1854, p.285.
21 R. Herbert, Statistics of Live Stock and Dead Meat for Consumption in the Metropolis, 'Journal of the Royal Agricultural
   Society of England', vol. XX, 1859, p.474.
22 R. Herbert, Statistics of Live Stock and Dead Meat for Consumption in the Metropolis, 'Journal of the Royal Agricultural
   Society of England', vol. XXII, 1861, p.132, and vol. XXIII,
   1863, p.367.

23 R. Herbert, Statistics of Live Stock and Dead Meat for Consumption in the Metropolis, 'Journal of the Royal Agricultural Society of England', vol. XX, 1859, p.475.

24 R. Herbert, Statistics of Live Stock and Dead Meat for Consumption in the Metropolis, 'Journal of the Royal Agricultural Society of England', vol. XXII, 1861, p.131.

25 'Journal of Agriculture', vol. 25, July 1865 - April 1866, p.119. p.119.

26 See M.W. Flinn, Trends in Real Wages, 1750-1850, 'Economic History Review', 2nd series, vol. XXVII, no. 3, 1974, pp.395-6. This article also has an excellent bibliography of contributions to the discussion on pp.412-13.

27 Mulhall, op.cit., p.286.

28 E.F. Williams, The Development of the Meat Trade, in D.J. Oddy and D.S. Miller (eds), 'The Making of the Modern British Diet', London, 1976, p.50.

29 J. Burnett, 'A History of the Cost of Living', London, 1969, pp.262-3.

30 Mulhall, op.cit., p.286.

31 F.M.L. Thompson, 'Victorian England: the Horse-drawn Society', London, 1968, p.20.

32 F.M.L. Thompson, Nineteenth Century Horse Sense, 'Economic History Review', 2nd series, vol. XXIX, no. 1, 1976, p.80.

33 F.M.L. Thompson, The Second Agricultural Revolution, 1815-1880, 'Economic History Review', 2nd series, vol. XXI, no. 1, p.7.

34 T.W. Fletcher, The Great Depression of English Agriculture, 1873-1896, 'Economic History Review', 2nd series, vol. XII, 1961, p.430.

35 For the movement of wages see G.H. Wood, Real Wages and the Standard of Comfort Since 1850, 'Journal of the Royal Statistical Society', vol. LXXIII, 1909.

36 From tables giving prices of sheep since 1818 printed each year in 'Transactions of the Highland and Agricultural Society'.

37 'Journal of Agriculture', vol. 25, July 1865 - April 1866, p.121.

38 E.J.T. Collins and E.L. Jones, Sectoral Advance in English Agriculture 1850-80, 'Agricultural History Review', vol. XV, 1967, p.79.

39 'Reports of the Medical Officer of Health to the Privy Council' - Fifth, P.P., 1863, XXV, appendix V, pp.320-456; Sixth, P.P., 1864, XXVIII, appendix 6, pp.330-49.

40 'Journal of the Society of Arts', vol. XV, 4 January 1867, p.100.

41 'Journal of Agriculture', vol.28, January 1863, p.739; vol. 20, October 1857, pp.144-54; vol.24, October 1863, pp. 164-80.

42 J.C. Drummond and A. Wilbraham, 'The Englishman's Food', London, 1939, pp.364-5.

43 J.T. Critchell and J.T. Raymond, 'A History of the Frozen Meat Trade', pp.425-30.

6 THE DOMESTIC TRADE, 1865-89

1 'The Times', 26 February 1866, p.5.
2 A.B. Erickson, The Cattle Plague in England, 1865-1867, 'Agricultural History', vol. 35, 1961, pp.100-3.
3 'Animal Health, 1865-1965', London, 1965, p.114.
4 'Board of Agriculture, Annual Report of the Veterinary Department, 1890', P.P., 1890-1, XXV, pp.58-9.
5 Ibid., pp.74-7.
6 E.H. Whetham, The Changing Cattle Enterprises of England and Wales, 1870-1910, in W. Minchinton (ed.), 'Essays in Agrarian History', Newton Abbot, 1968, vol. II, p.215.
7 Information for England and Scotland taken from 'Board of Agriculture, Annual Report of the Veterinary Department, 1890', P.P., 1890-1, XXV, pp.61-5.
8 'Board of Agriculture, Annual Report of the Veterinary Department, 1889', P.P., 1890, XXV, p.58.
9 Ibid., pp.94-5.
10 'Journal of Comparative Pathology', vol. II, 1889, p.142.
11 A convenient summary of the trial is found in ibid., pp.180-95.
12 A.J. Jackson, 'Official History of the National Federation of Meat Traders' Associations', Plymouth, 1956 (privately published), pp.315-27.
13 Ibid., p.16.
14 Sir Robert Giffen, 'Statistics', London, 1913, p.182, and the chapter on Railway Statistics, pp.181-211.
15 'First Report Cattle Plague Commissioners', P.P., 1866, XII, appendix A, p.171.
16 Ibid., Qs 3096-8.
17 Ibid., Qs 3368-71, 3378-84, 3385, 3390-3.
18 P.R. Mountfield, The Footwear Industry of the East Midlands (IV) Leicestershire to 1911, 'The East Midland Geographer', vol. 4, 1966, p.10.
19 'First Report Cattle Plague Commissioners', P.P., 1866, XII, Qs 4235-9.
20 For 1861-7, 'Transit of Animals Committee', P.P., 1870, LXI, appendix XXV, p.110. For 1869-75, 'Report of the Veterinary Department of the Privy Council for 1871 ... to 1875', P.P., 1872-6.
21 The more detailed information on this traffic after 1875 is published in the 'Reports of the Veterinary (afterwards Agricultural) Department of the Privy Council', P.P., 1877-89, and after 1889 in the 'Board of Agriculture, Annual Reports of the Veterinary Department', P.P., 1890 et seq. Also the 'Agricultural Returns', after 1883 carry tables giving some details of the Irish livestock traffic with Great Britain.
22 H.M. Jenkins, Report on the Trade in Animals, 'Journal of the Royal Agricultural Society of England', 2nd series, vol. IX, 1873, pp.204-20, for a summary of the Irish cattle trade in the early 1870s.
23 'Transit of Animals Committee', P.P., 1870, LXI, Q 617.
24 In 1888 an Edinburgh appeal court decided that the practice of dishorning cattle was not cruel. In the following year an English court decided that the operation was, resulting in the

anomalous situation where the operation was legal in Scotland and illegal in England. ('Journal of Comparative Pathology', vol. II, 1889, pp.143-5.)

25 'Board of Agriculture, Annual Report of the Veterinary Department, 1889', P.P., 1890, XXV, p.93.
26 'Transit of Animals Committee', P.P., 1870, LXI, Q 645.
27 'Board of Agriculture, Annual Report of the Veterinary Department, 1889', P.P., 1890, XXV, p.93.
28 'Transit of Animals Committee', P.P., 1870, LXI, Q 338.
29 Ibid., pp.xvii-xviii.
30 Arrangements for the Supply of Meat to the Metropolis, 'Journal of the Royal Agricultural Society of England', 2nd series, vol. II, 1866, pp.200-1.
31 Ibid., p.505.
32 R. Herbert, The Supply of Meat to Large Towns, 'Journal of the Royal Agricultural Society of England', 2nd series, vol. II, 1866, p.440.
33 'Memorial addressed to the Home Department by the Churchwardens and inhabitants of St. Sepulchre's parish regarding the Smithfield Dead Meat Market, and correspondence thereon', P.P., 1866, LIX.
34 From a report in 'The Times', reprinted in the 'Country Gentleman's Nagazine', October 1868, p.346. See also the 'Illustrated London News', 10 October 1868, p.349.
35 'Transit of Animals Committee', P.P., 1870, LXI, appendix XXII.
36 By 1895 Charles Booth reported: 'The present ... Markets ... are none too large for the trade, and the shops are now all let.' ('Life and Labour of the People of London', vol. VII, 1896, p.197.)
37 'Report of the Select Committee on Cattle Plague and Importation of Livestock', P.P., 1877, IX, Minutes of Evidence, Q 9180.
38 'Transit of Animals Committee', P.P., 1870, LXI, Qs 739, 742-5, appendices XXII and XXIV.
39 Ibid., Q 272.
40 'First Report Cattle Plague Commissioners', P.P., 1866, XXII, Qs 3036-45, 3076-7.
41 Ibid., Qs 4041-3.
42 'Report of the Select Committee on Cattle Plague and Importation of Livestock', P.P., 1877, IX, Qs 6181-92, 9032, 9166, 9561.
43 J.B. Jeffreys, 'Retail Trading in Britain, 1850-1950' (Economic and Social Studies, no. 13), Cambridge, 1954, p.181.

7 IMPORTS FROM EUROPE AND NORTH AMERICA, 1865-89

1 Ministry of Agriculture, Fisheries and Food, 'Animal Health, 1865-1965', London, 1965, pp.12-13, 391.
2 J.S. Gamgee, 'Cattle Plague and Diseased Meat, I, pp.26-7, 34-5.
3 The best accounts of the spread of the disease in 1865 and the measures to contain it are found in S.A. Hall, The Cattle Plague of 1865, 'Medical History', vol. VI, 1962, pp.45-58, and Ministry of Agriculture, Fisheries, and Food, 'Animal Health, 1865-1965', London, 1965, pp.125-34 et passim. Preventive measures were only reluctantly adopted by the (Liberal) govern-

ment after much critical delay. For a detailed study of government actions during the outbreak see A.B. Erickson, The Cattle Plague in England, 1865-1867, 'Agricultural History', vol. 35, 1961.

4 'First Report Cattle Plague Commissioners', P.P., 1866, XXII, Qs 3266-77.

5 'Report of the Committee on the Transit of Animals by Sea and Land', P.P., 1870, LXI, p.xxi.

6 P.G. Craigie, Twenty Years' Changes in our Foreign Meat Supplies, 'Journal of the Royal Agricultural Society of England', 2nd series, vol. XXIII, 1887, p.469.

7 Robert Herbert, Statistics of Livestock and Dead Meat for Consumption in the Metropolis, 'Journal of the Royal Agricultural Society of England', 2nd series, vol. III, 1867, pp.91, 93.

8 'Report of the Select Committee on Cattle Plague and Importation of Livestock', P.P., 1877, IX, Q 2213.

9 'Report of the Select Committee on Cattle Plague and Importation of Livestock', P.P., 1877, IX, Qs 5223-7.

10 W.D. Zimmerman, Live Cattle Export Trade Between United States and Great Britain, 1868-1885, 'Agricultural History', no. 36, 1962.

11 S. Plimsoll, 'Cattle Ships', London, 1890; I.M. Greg and S.H. Towers, 'Cattle Ships and our Meat Supply', London, 1894 (The Humanitarian League's Publications, no. 15).

12 'Report of the Departmental Committee of the Board of Trade and the Board of Agriculture on the Transatlantic Cattle Trade', P.P., 1890-1, LXXVIII, p.278.

13 'Report of the Select Committee on Cattle Plague and the Importation of Livestock', P.P., 1877, IX, Qs 4467-71, 4456-61.

14 Ibid., Qs 4467-71, 4456-61.

15 F. Vacher, 'The Accommodation for Discharging, Lairing, Slaughtering and Storing at the Foreign Animals Wharfs, Birkenhead', Birkenhead, 1882, pp.3-5.

16 'Report of the Departmental Committee appointed to enquire into Combinations in the Meat Trade', P.P., 1909, XV, appendix XII, p.388.

17 'Report of the Select Committee on Cattle Plague and Importation of Livestock', P.P., 1877, IX, Minutes of Evidence, Qs 7367-71, 8602.

18 'Report of the Select Committee on Cattle Plague and Importation of Livestock', P.P., 1877, IX, Minutes of Evidence, Qs 3270, 5013-14.

19 'Report of the Committee on the Transit of Animals by Sea and Land, Minutes of Evidence', P.P., 1870, LXI, Qs 801, 809, 810, appendices, pp.93, 115.

20 'Second Report of Cattle Plague Commissioners', P.P., 1866, XXII, p.ix.

21 Cattle from Schleswig Holstein were not subject to the same controls because the authorities there were able to exclude imports of livestock from areas in Europe where animal diseases were endemic. After 1877 all German cattle imports came from Schleswig Holstein.

22 M. Tracy, 'Agriculture in Western Europe', London, 1964, p.111.

23 'Select Committee on Cattle Plague and Importation of Livestock', P.P., 1877, IX, Qs 8548-53.
24 'Journal of the Society of Arts', vol. 15, no. 757, 24 May 1867,
   p.430
25 'Report of the Committee on the Transit of Animals by Sea and
   Land, Minutes of Evidence', P.P., 1870, LXI, Qs 5-10, 36, 91.
26 P.G. Craigie, Twenty Years' Changes in our Foreign Meat
   Supplies, 'Journal of the Royal Agricultural Society of
   England', 2nd series, vol. XXIII, 1887, p.477.
27 'Select Committee on Cattle Plague and Importation of Livestock', P.P., 1877, IX, appendix no. 4, pp.514 et seq.
28 'Meat Trades' Journal', no. 74, 28 September 1889, p.6.
29 'Meat Trades' Journal', no. 95, 22 February 1890, p.12.
30 'Meat Trades' Journal', no. 74, 28 September 1889, p.6.
31 P.G. Craigie, Twenty Years' Changes in our Foreign Meat
   Supplies, 'Journal of the Royal Agricultural Society of
   England', 2nd series, vol. XXIII, 1887, p.469.
32 'Annual Statement of Trade', P.P. The meat and livestock import
   figures from 1870 are gathered together in a convenient series
   of tables in appendix I of the 'Departmental Committee on
   Combinations in the Meat Trade', P.P., 1909, XV.
33 P.G. Craigie, Twenty Years' Changes in our Foreign Meat
   Supplies, 'Journal of the Royal Agricultural Society of
   England', 2nd series, vol. XXIII, 1887, p.473.
34 Because of its geographical and commercial complexity the frozen
   meat trade is dealt with as a whole from 1882 to 1914 in a
   separate chapter. In this section references to frozen meat are
   confined to comparisons with the chilled beef trade before 1890
   with particular reference to technical differences and their
   implications for marketing and distribution.
35 Moreover, this process is not commercially applicable to whole
   carcases of beef and mutton
36 J.T. Critchell and J. Raymond, 'A History of the Frozen Meat
   Trade', London, 1912, pp.26 and 190.
37 J. MacDonald, 'Food from the Far West', London, 1878, pp.4-5.
38 'Report from H.M. consular officers in Europe, North Africa, the
   United States, Brazil and the River Plate, respecting the Cattle
   Trade', P.P., 1877, LXXXIV, pp.459 and 460.
39 MacDonald, op.cit., pp.294-6.
40 Ibid., pp.252-3.
41 'Report from the Select Committee on Cattle Plague and
   Importation of Livestock', P.P., 1877, IX, p.viii.
42 'Select Committee on Cattle Plague and Importation of Livestock', P.P., 1877, IX. Index of Evidence, American Dead Meat:
   V, 1 and 2. Adverse witnesses, Qs 1619, 2865-8, 3146, 3814,
   5130, 5786, 6480, 7488-90, 7771, 9224. Favourable witnesses,
   Qs 2613, 3060-3, 4198, 4432, 4687, 6105-6, 6774, 8542-4, 8928,
   9486.
43 Ibid., Qs 5414-19, 9025-6.
44 Ibid., Qs 4237-8, 4386, 6237-45.
45 Ibid., Qs 1876-80, 1975.
46 Ibid., Qs 1882-5.
47 Ibid., Qs 2810-11, 6047-9, 7020.
48 Ibid., Qs 2873-4.

49 'Meat and Provision Trades' Review', 5 January 1878, p.9.
50 'Royal Commission on Market Rights and Tolls', vol. II, P.P.,
     1888, LIII, Qs 2932-4.
51 G.E. Putnam, 'Supplying Britain's Meat', London, 1923, pp.69-70.

8 THE DOMESTIC MEAT TRADE, 1890-1914

1 Tables showing the outbreaks of disease before 1914 are found in
    'Board of Agriculture and Fisheries, Annual Report of Proceed-
    ings under the Diseases of Animals Act, etc.... for 1913', P.P.,
    1914, XI. For accounts of the progress of official action
    against these diseases see Ministry of Agriculture, Fisheries
    ·and Food, Animal Health, 1865-1965, London, 1965, passim.
2 See above p.62 for the evidence of R.J. Richardson to the
    Select Committee on the Adulteration of Food in 1856. Presum-
    ably carcases were condemned on the grounds that they appeared
    unfit or unpleasant to eat. It is important to bear in mind
    that local action in the field of public health often preceded
    what would today be regarded as conclusive scientific proof.
    See also pp.89-90 of this book, for the procedure between 1864
    and 1889.
3 The following three Royal Commissions reported on the disease:
    (a) 'Royal Commission appointed to inquire into the effect of
    Food derived from Tuberculous Animals on Human Health', P.P.,
    1895, XXXV; (b) 'Royal Commission appointed to inquire into the
    Meat and Milk of Tuberculous Animals', P.P., 1898, XLIX; (c)
    'Royal Commission appointed to inquire into the Relations of
    Human and Animal Tuberculosis. First Interim Report', P.P.,
    1904, XXXIX; 'Second Interim Report', P.P., 1907, XXXVIII;
    'Third Interim Report', P.P., 1905, XLIX; 'Final Report', P.P.,
    1911, XLII.
4 Ministry of Agriculture, Fisheries and Food, 'Animal Health,
    1865-1965', London, 1965, p.215.
5 See, for example, the 'Report of the Royal Commission appointed
    to inquire into the effect of Food derived from Tuberculous
    Animals on Human Health', P.P., 1895, XXXV.
6 'Report of the Royal Commission appointed to inquire into the
    Administrative Procedure for Controlling the Danger to Man
    through the use of Meat and Milk of Tuberculous Animals', P.P.,
    1898, XLIX, p.8.
7 'Board of Agriculture and Fisheries, Annual Report of Proceed-
    ings under the Diseases of Animals Acts, etc.... for 1909',
    P.P., 1910, VII, pp.37-41.
8 'Board of Agriculture, Annual Report of the Director of the
    Veterinary Department for the year 1891', P.P., 1892, XXVI, p.8.
9 'Board of Agriculture, Annual Report of the Director of the
    Veterinary Department for the year 1892', P.P., 1893-4, XXIII,
    p.14.
10 'Board of Agriculture and Fisheries, Annual Report of Proceed-
    ings under the Diseases of Animals Acts, etc.... for 1912',
    P.P., 1913, XV, pp.5-13.
11 See pp.64, 67-8 of this book.
12 'Board of Agriculture, Annual Report of Proceedings under the

Diseases of Animals Acts, etc.... for 1894', P.P., 1895, XC, p.69.

13   In 1894 there were 5,682 confirmed outbreaks in seventy-three counties. The number of outbreaks dropped irregularly to a low point of 817, involving fifty-eight counties, in 1905. Thereafter there was a general rise in the disease so that by 1912 there were 2,920 confirmed outbreaks in sixty-six counties in Great Britain. 'Board of Agriculture and Fisheries, Annual Report of Proceedings under the Diseases of Animals Acts ... for 1913', P.P., 1914, XI, p.78.

14   'Board of Agriculture and Fisheries, Annual Report of Proceedings under the Diseases of Animals Acts, etc.... for 1902', P.P., 1903, XVII, pp.23-4; '... for 1906', P.P., 1907, XVII, p.28.

15   'Board of Agriculture, Annual Reports of the Proceedings under the Diseases of Animals Acts, etc.... for 1900', P.P., 1901, XVII, p.31.

16   'Board of Agriculture and Fisheries, Annual Reports of the Proceedings under the Diseases of Animals Acts, etc.... for 1913', P.P., 1914, XI, p.18.

17   'Board of Agriculture, Annual Report of Proceedings under the Diseases of Animals Acts, etc.... for 1900', P.P., 1901, XVII, pp.34-5.

18   'Board of Agriculture and Fisheries, Annual Report of Proceedings under the Diseases of Animals Acts, etc.... for 1903', P.P., 1904, XX, pp.36-7; '... for 1904', P.P., 1905, XX, pp.30-1; '... for 1910', P.P., 1911, XIII, p.49.

19   'Royal Commission on Market Rights and Tolls, Final Report', P.P., 1890-1, XXXVII, p.120.

20   In some markets the traders were against the collection of reliable price statistics as they feared it would harm their interests. For example, an assistant commissioner who collected evidence in 1888 reported from Chippenham, Wiltshire: 'The prices of cattle in this market are returned to the newspapers with some accuracy, and it appears that dealers (who buy to sell again) object very much to the system of publishing prices.' 'Royal Commission on Market Rights and Tolls, Assistant Commissioners' Reports', P.P., 1888, LIV, p.360.

21   Smithfield stones of 8 lb.

22   R.H. Rew, 'An Agricultural Faggot', London, 1913, p.151.

23   'Journal of the Board of Agriculture', March 1903, p.553.

24   'Agricultural Returns', 1912, p.262.

25   Rew, op.cit., p.149. W. Richards, 'Agricultural Distress', London, 1893, p.19.

26   It would not have been possible to shift the increased cost forward to the consumer because the retail prices of home-produced beef and mutton were linked to the retail price of the nearest imported substitutes, in this case North American chilled and port-killed beef and New Zealand lamb and mutton.

27   'Royal Commission on Market Rights and Tolls', P.P., 1888, LIII, Q 6602.

28   C.S. Orwin and E.H. Whetham, 'History of British Agriculture, 1846-1914', London, 1964, p.360.

29   A.G.L. Rogers, 'The Business Side of Agriculture', London, 1904,

pp.103-4. These small sales should not be confused with large annual fatstock sales held by substantial farmers. In the case of the latter hundreds of animals could be sold off one farm, and regular customers would attend from as far as 50 miles. For accounts of two such sales in Shropshire in the 1890s see R. Perren, 'The Effects of Agricultural Depression on the English Estates of the Dukes of Sutherland', unpublished Ph.D. thesis, University of Nottingham, 1967, pp.329-32.

30 'Inter-Departmental Committee on Meat Supplies', P.P., 1919, XXV, p.19.

31 This dispute over the rates charged for foreign and domestic produce was a symptom of an increasingly critical attitude shown towards the railway companies by British business and government in the late nineteenth century. The subject is extensively analysed by P.J. Cain in Railway Combination and Government, 1900-1914, 'Economic History Review', 2nd series, vol. XXV, 1972, pp.623-41.

32 The following account of the Southampton Case is based on that in E.A. Pratt, 'Railways and their Rates', London, 1905, pp. 111-16.

33 The meat trade between Aberdeen and London during 1904 is discussed in Pratt, op.cit., pp.150-3.

34 This information about the meat sent from Liverpool is found in ibid., p.136.

35 Ibid., p.150.

36 Ibid., pp.140-1.

37 A.J. Jackson, 'Official History of the National Federation of Meat Traders' Associations', Plymouth, 1956 (privately published), p.54.

38 Ibid., pp.60-1.

39 Ibid.

40 Some agricultural societies were disposed to make common cause with the butchers in appealing for compensation from public funds. Others argued that the butcher should have to bear personal risks just as the farmer had to when he bought cattle. However, it was generally agreed that in any conflict over this matter the farmers would be at a disadvantage because they were less efficiently organized than the meat traders. (Report of 'The Times'' view over the warranty question in 'Meat Trades Journal', vol. XXVIII, no. 323, 17 September 1908, p.323.)

41 Jackson, op.cit., p.65.

42 In 1903 the National Federation had secured special rates for its members with an insurance company. Jackson, op.cit., p.49.

43 See pp.27-9 of this book.

44 Thomas Parker, Fat Cattle and the Question of Warranty, 'Journal of the Newcastle Farmers' Club', 1909, pp.46, 77, 83.

45 Ibid., pp.76, 82, 83.

46 Conference between agriculturists and meat traders, held in the Whitehall Rooms, Westminster, 2 December 1908; typescript report in the Library of the London School of Economics and Political Science (R.F., 2284) (hereafter cited as 'Conference Between Agriculturists and Meat Traders', 1908), pp.19, 35.

47 Jackson, op.cit., pp.329, 330.

48 See pp.104-5 of this book.

49 'Meat Trades' Journal', vol. VII, no. 349, 3 January 1895, pp. 594-5; vol. XXIV, no. 967, 8 November 1906, p.475.

50 'Conference Between Agriculturists and Meat Traders', 1908, p.24.

51 'Departmental Committee on Combinations in the Meat Trade', P.P., 1909, XV, appendix XII, p.355.

52 For example, see 'Meat Trades' Journal', vol. VII, no. 349, 3 January 1895, pp.596, 598; and, vol. VIII, no. 401, 2 January 1896, p.713. Part of this decline also reflected changes in taste. In the 1850s beef was the traditional Christmas meat: by the 1890s increasing supplies of home and foreign poultry and game, at prices practically all could afford, induced many large retailers to reduce rather than increase beef and mutton purchases at the festive season.

53 'Royal Commission on Unification of London', P.P., 1894, XVIII, appendix III, pp.82-3.

54 J.C. Clutterbuck, The Farming of Middlesex, 'Journal of the Royal Agricultural Society of England', 2nd series, vol. I, 1869, p.26.

55 'Departmental Committee on Combinations in the Meat Trade', P.P., 1909, XV, Q 3584.

56 See pp.38-9 of this book.

57 'Meat Trades' Journal', vol. VIII, no. 403, 16 January 1896, p.720.

58 James Long, The Sources of our Meat Supply, 'Co-operative Wholesale Societies' Annual', 1891, p.442. J. Hendrick, The Growth of International Trade in Manures and Foods, 'Transactions of the Highland and Agricultural Society of Scotland', 5th series, vol. XXIX, 1917, p.33. Similar figures, from different sources, are given in J.B. Jefferys, 'Retail Trading in Britain, 1850-1950', Cambridge, 1954 (Economic and Social Studies, no. 13), pp.182-3.

59 Jackson, op.cit., pp.70-1.

60 Ibid., pp.56-7, 60, 67.

61 Jefferys, op.cit., p.183.

9 IMPORTS FROM EUROPE AND NORTH AMERICA, 1890-1914

1 John Clay, Cattle and Sheep Raising in the United States, 'Journal of the Board of Agriculture', vol. VII, no. 2, September 1900, p.226 (extracted from the 'Year Book of the U.S. Department of Agriculture', 1899).

2 W. Douglas, 'Douglas's Encyclopedia', 2nd ed., London, 1907, p.192. (Information taken from Bulletin no. 78, 1902, of the University of Illinois Agricultural Experiment Station.)

3 A. Bogue, The Progress of the Cattle Industry in Ontario during the Eighteen Eighties, 'Agricultural History', no. 21, 1947, p.165; Sir Francis Floud, 'The Ministry of Agriculture and Fisheries', London, 1927, chapter IV.

4 'Board of Agriculture, Annual Report of the Director of the Director of the Veterinary Department for 1892', P.P., 1893-4, XXIII, p.16.

5 I.M. Greg and S.H. Towers, 'Cattle Ships and our Meat Supply',

London, 1894 (The Humanitarian League's Publications, no. 15), p.5.

6 This included the cost of freight, insurance and all other charges, which were somewhere between £4 and £5 per animal.

7 'Report on the U.S. Cattle Raising Industry in 1896 and the Export of Cattle and Beef to Great Britain', P.P., 1897, LXXXVIII, p.1014.

8 'Agricultural Gazette', new series, XXXVII, 13 February 1893, p.167.

9 'Report on the Cattle Industry of the United States, June 1896 to June 1898', P.P., 1899, XCVII, pp.783-4.

10 'Agricultural Gazette', new series, XXVII, 13 February 1893, p.167.

11 'Departmental Committee on Combinations in the Meat Trade', P.P., 1909, XV, passim.

12 'Cold Storage and Ice Trades Review', vol. VI, no. 69, 1903, p.414.

13 'Newport and Market Drayton Advertiser', 9 August 1879; letter in 'The Times', 16 September 1879 (reprinted in the 'Agricultural Gazette', X, 13 October 1879, p.337).

14 A.H.H. Matthews, 'Fifty Years of Agricultural Politics', London, 1915, pp.303-6.

15 'Select Committee (House of Lords) on Marking of Foreign Meat', P.P., 1893-4, XII, Qs 350, 356.

16 'Report of Select Committee on the Agricultural Produce Marks Bill', P.P., 1897, VIII, Q 192.

17 'Meat Trades' Journal', no. 110, 7 June 1890, p.5.

18 D. Pigeon, Cold Storage, 'Journal of the Royal Agricultural Society of England', 3rd series, vol. VII, 1896, p.615.

19 'Departmental Committee on Combinations in the Meat Trade', P.P., 1909, XV, appendices IX and XI.

20 G.E. Putnam, 'Supplying Britain's Meat', London, 1923, p.71.

21 R.H. Hooker, The Meat Supply of the United Kingdom, 'Journal of the Royal Statistical Society', vol. LXXII, 1909, pp.350-2.

22 'Departmental Committee on Combinations in the Meat Trade', P.P., 1909, XV, pp.18-19.

23 'Meat Trades' Journal', vol. XXI, no. 1146, 14 April 1910, pp.429-30.

24 As these firms were now the chief buyers in the Chicago stock yard they also held a considerable proportion of the surplus cattle and dressed beef available for export.

25 'Departmental Committee on Combinations in the Meat Trade', P.P., 1909, XV, Q 574.

26 Ibid., Qs 1484-9.

27 'Meat Trades' Journal', vol. VII, no. 350, 10 January 1895, pp.610-11.

28 See p.198 of this book.

29 'Departmental Committee on Combinations in the Meat Trade', P.P., 1909, XV, Qs 6854-5, 6858, 6860, 6863-6, 6870.

30 E.A. Pratt, 'Railways and their Rates', 1905, p.135.

31 Ibid., pp.137-8.

32 See A.D. Chandler, Jr, 'Strategy and Structure: Chapters in the History of the Industrial Enterprise', Cambridge, Massachusetts, 1962, pp.25-6.

33 'Memoranda, Statistical Tables and Charts prepared in the Board of Trade with reference to various matters bearing on British and Foreign Trade and Industrial Conditions', P.P., 1903, LXII, p.358.

34 See p.208 of this book.

35 There was a substitution of dead meat for live imports, but even with this change the total quantity of meat imports virtually stagnated. In 1900-1 the total imported meat supply was 20,936 tons, in 1911-12 it was 21,203 tons. As the population grew at a faster rate between these two dates the per capita consumption of imported meat in the United Kingdom fell from 56.8 lb to 52.3 lb respectively. ('Agricultural Returns', 1912, p.279.)

36 'Meat Trades' Journal', 1904, passim.

37 'Report of the Royal Commission on Supply of Food ... in Time of War', P.P., 1905, LXXIX, Qs 2973-8, 3564-71, 4221; P.P., 1905, LX, p.204.

38 'Select Committee on Agricultural Produce (Marks) Bill', P.P., 1897, VIII, Q 2342.

39 W.H. Simmonds, 'The Practical Grocer', 1906, vol. III, p.109.

40 See pp.71-2 of this book.

41 'Departmental Committee on Combinations in the Meat Trade', P.P., 1909, XV, Qs 6240-3, and appendix I (b), p.245.

42 'Departmental Committee on Combinations in the Meat Trade', P.P., 1909, XV, Qs 1195, 2188, 1420, 4743, 3219. At this time 45 per cent of all meat supplies were imported in one form or another. The question of regional differences in the proportion of home-produced to imported supplies of meat consumed is also discussed in my article The North American Beef and Cattle Trade with Great Britain, 1870-1914, 'Economic History Review', 2nd series, vol. XXIV, 1971, pp.439-41.

43 C.P. Kindleberger, 'Economic Growth in France and Britain, 1851-1950', Cambridge, Massachusetts, 1964, pp.241-2, fn. 123.

44 E.H. Whetham, The Changing Cattle Enterprises of England and Wales, 1870-1910, 'The Geographical Journal', CXXIX, 1963, pp.378-80.

45 'Departmental Committee of Board of Agriculture on Inalnd Transit of Cattle', P.P., 1898, XXXIV, Qs 5159, 5160, 5168.

46 'Departmental Committee on Combinations in the Meat Trade', P.P., 1909, XV, appendix I (a), pp.229-30.

47 'Report of Proceedings under Diseases of Animals Acts ... for 1905', P.P., 1906, XXIII, p.75.

48 Simmonds, op.cit., 1906, vol. IV, p.257.

49 W.E. Bear, The Food Supply of Manchester, 'Journal of the Royal Agricultural Society of England', 3rd series, vol. VIII, 1897, pp.496-7.

50 'Royal Commission on Supply of Food ... in Time of War', P.P., 1905, LXXIX, Qs 3615, 3659.

51 These facts are taken from R.H. Rew's lecture, Co-operation for the Sale of Farm Produce, read before the Farmers' Club, February 1896, and published in his book 'An Agricultural Faggot', pp.123-5.

52 Exact comparisons are difficult to make, but in 1914 Danish output of pork and bacon was 217,000 tons or 63.8 per cent of

total meat production. (M. Tracy, 'Agriculture in Western
Europe', p.110.) Between 1911 and 1913 United Kingdom output of
pigmeat averaged 397,000 tons per annum, but was only 26.8 per
cent of total meat output. (E.M. Ojala, 'Agricultural and
Economic Progress',
53 See p.72 of this book.
54 'Select Committee on Agricultural Produce (Marks) Bill', P.P.,
1897, VIII, Q 1544.
55 'Royal Commission on Supply of Food ... in Time of War', P.P.,
1905, LXXIX, Qs 3978, 4048-51.

10 FROZEN MEAT

1 See pp.117, 130, 132 of this book.
2 There may have been a switch from investment in freezing works
in South America and Australasia to investment in cold stores in
Britain after 1894. Between 1890 and 1894, fifteen new
freezing works were opened in the southern hemisphere; between
1895 and 1899 the figure dropped to nine. (J.T. Critchell and
J. Raymond, 'A History of the Frozen Meat Trade', London, 1912,
appendix VII.) This is the sort of reaction one would expect as
the freezing capacity in the countries supplying this meat
outran the storage capacity in the country where it was
marketed. At the same time, there is no evidence of a general
decline in fresh British investment in South America and
Australasia after 1895. In the two quinquennia 1890-4 and 1895-
9 the flow of funds from Britain to these continents averaged
the same, at £19 million per annum. (M. Simon, The Pattern of
New British Portfolio Foreign Investment, 1865-1914, in A.R.
Hall, ed., 'The Export of Capital from Britain, 1870-1914',
London, 1968, pp.29 and 40.) For the revival of domestic
investment in Britain, which the authors date from 1894, see
E.M. Sigsworth and J. Blackman, The Home Boom of the 1890s,
'Yorkshire Bulletin', vol. 17, no. 1, May 1965.
3 J.T. Critchell and J. Raymond, 'A History of the Frozen Meat
Trade', London, 1912, pp.164-6.
4 Prior to 1878 the site under Cannon Street station, which was
$1\frac{1}{4}$ acres in extent, was an unrefrigerated food store. ('The
Meat and Provision Trades Review', vol. II, no. 37, 16 March
1878, p.252. Also pp.130, 132 of this book.
5 Critchell and Raymond, op.cit., pp.167-70.
6 See pp.116-17.
7 'Cold Storage and Ice Trades Review', vol. IV, no. 69, 15
December 1903, p.413; Critchell and Raymond, op.cit., p.353.
8 'Cold Storage and Ice Trades Review', vol. IV, no. 69, 15
December 1903, p.413.
9 W. Weddel and Company, 'Review of the Frozen Meat Trade',
London, 1908; Critchell and Raymond, op.cit., p.178.
10 'Cold Storage and Ice Trades Review', vol. II, no. 2, 15 May
1899, p.18.
11 Ibid., vol. III, no. 36, 15 March 1901, p.414.
12 Ibid., vol. II, no. 22, 15 January, 1900 (supplement, p.i).
13 Reported in ibid., vol. III, no. 34, 15 January 1901, p.340;

vol. IV, no. 46, 15 January 1902, p.284; vol. VII, no. 71, 15
February 1904, p.45; vol. VIII, no. 82, 15 January 1905, p.26.

14 'Ice and Cold Storage', vol. III, no. 27, June 1900, p.186.

15 Weddel and Company, op.cit.; Critchell and Raymond, op.cit.,
appendix VI.

16 Ibid., pp.177-8.

17 'Cold Storage and Ice Trades Review', vol. XIV, no. 154, 19
January 1911, p.25.

18 H.S. Ferns, 'The Argentine Republic', Newton Abbot, 1973, p.65.

19 Critchell and Raymond, op.cit., pp.74-83.

20 'Cold Storage and Ice Trades Review', vol. II, no. 22, 15
January 1900 (supplement, p.ii).

21 Critchell and Raymond, op.cit., p.305.

22 Ibid., p.258.

23 W.E. Bear, Our Meat Supply, 'Quarterly Review', vol. 165, no.
329, July 1887, pp.54-5.

24 Critchell and Raymond, op.cit., pp.61-2, 71-2.

25 In all cases this is a comparison between the average top prices
for each country's mutton paid at Smithfield.

26 James Long, The Sources of Our Meat Supply, 'Co-operative
Wholesale Societies' Annual', Manchester, 1891, pp.422-3. Also
John H. Williams, 'Argentine International Trade Under Incon-
vertible Paper Money, 1880-1900', New York, 1971 ed., pp.214-16.

27 Critchell and Raymond, op.cit., pp.264-7.

28 Ibid., p.257; W.M. Smith, 'The Marketing of Australian and New
Zealand Primary Products', London, 1936, p.222.

29 W. Weddel and Company, 'Review of the Frozen Meat Trade', 1899,
p.8.

30 W. Weddel and Company, 'Review of the Frozen Meat Trade', 1900,
p.8.

31 W. Weddel and Company, 'Review of the Frozen Meat Trade', 1899,
p.16.

32 W. Weddel and Company, 'Review of the Frozen Meat Trade', 1902,
pp.12, 6.

33 Critchell and Raymond, op.cit., p.101.

34 W. Weddel and Company, 'Review of the Frozen Meat Trade', 1899,
p.17.

35 W. Weddel and Company, 'Review of the Frozen Meat Trade', 1902,
p.9. 'Cold Storage and Ice Trades Review', vol. XI, no. 119,
20 February 1908, p.47.

36 'Meat Trades' Journal', vol. XIX, no. 819, 7 January 1904, p.24.
It was said that the people living in and around Manchester
'have ... no appreciation for beef that is generously fed'.

37 J.M. Wilson, 'The Rural Cyclopedia', Edinburgh, 1849, vol. III,
pp.394-6. The distaste for over-fat animals was expressed by
Andrew Wynter in Oh, the Roast Beef of Old England!, 'Subtle
Brains and Lissom Fingers', London, 1863, pp.159-64.

38 'Report of the Select Committee on Cattle Plague and the Importation of Livestock', P.P., 1877, IX, Qs 7367-71, 8602.

39 Critchell and Raymond, op.cit., p.260.

40 J. Long, The Sources of Our Meat Supply, 'Co-operative Wholesale
Societies' Annual', Manchester, 1891, p.422.

41 R.H. Rew, 'Memorandum on Some Estimates made by Various
Authorities on the Production of Meat and Milk, 'Journal of the

Royal Statistical Society', vol. 65, 1902, p.675.

42 W. Weddel and Company, 'Review of the Frozen Meat Trade', 1899, p.4.

43 The material for this paragraph comes from W.E. Bear, Our Meat Supply, 'Quarterly Review', vol. 165, no. 329, July 1887, pp. 54-6.

44 Although the low prices of 1886-7 were subject to remark at the time, they were not a persistent feature, and by May 1889 prices for both Australasian and Argentine frozen mutton had risen sufficiently to remove any fears for the future of the trade. ('Meat Trades' Journal', no. 54, 11 May 1889, p.3.)

45 More refined consideration of the forces operating on retail profits was given by Mill, Marshall and Wicksell - including influences such as custom, consumer preference and consumer knowledge. For example, Marshall observed: 'the customer seldom knows when the wholesale price of a thing has fallen, and will probably expect to be supplied at his old price ...'. He also pointed out that the retailer's working expenses (fixed costs) are independent of changes in the wholesale price. Hence retail prices cannot be expected to fall by the same ratio as wholesale prices. See 'Economics of Retailing - Selected Readings', edited by R.A. Tucker and B.S. Yamey, Harmondsworth, pp.17-26 and passim.

Until the end of the eighteenth century there was a whole body of restrictions, both national and (more effectively) local, designed to control the activities of all classes of middlemen dealing with food. See R.B. Westerfield, 'Middlemen in English Business, 1660-1760, New Haven, Conneticut, 1915, pp.187-201, for the London meat traders. Of all food traders, those dealing with grain and flour - the raw materials of 'the staff of life' - were subject to closest scrutiny. E.P. Thompson, The Moral Economy of the English Crowd in the Eighteenth Century, 'Past and Present', no. 50, February 1971, examines at length the assertions of profiteering during times of scarcity made against all groups involved in the supply and distribution of grain, flour and bread, including farmers.

46 A carcase of mutton weighing 51 lb and costing 4s. 10d. per stone of 8 lb was purchased wholesale for £1 10s. 9½d. and sold retail for £1 15s. 3½d., which represented a gross profit of 14.61 per cent. (James Long, The Sources of Our Meat Supply, 'Co-operative Wholesale Societies' Annual', Manchester, 1891, pp.336-7.)

47 A live bullock weighing 602 lb and costing 7s. 9d. per stone of 14 lb was purchased wholesale for £16 13s. 4d. The beef sold retail came to £17 9s. 19d., and the offals fetched a further £2 6s. 10d., which represented a gross profit of 19.04 per cent.

A live pig weighing 126 lb and costing 6s. 9d. per stone of 14 lb was purchased wholesale for £3 0s. 9d. The pork sold came to £3 14s. 9d., including 1s. for the bread used to make sausages with part of the carcase. The gross profit on the meat only came to 21.39 per cent. (H.D. Neate, 'How to Manage a Butchering Business', 1890, issued by the Co-operative Union Limited, Manchester, p.8.)

48 The Sale of Foreign Meat as British, 'The Parish Councillor',

vol. II, nos 63, 64, 65 of 17, 24, 31 January 1896, pp.167, 183, 199.

49 Ibid., no. 64, 24 January 1896, p.183.
50 See chapter 3, passim, of this book. Also W. Weddel and Company, 'Review of the Frozen Meat Trade', 1899, p.12.
51 Commercial History and Review of 1903, 'The Economist', 20 February 1904, p.9.
52 W. Weddel and Company, 'Review of the Frozen Meat Trade', 1904, p.6.
53 Ibid.
54 I.e., Liverpool, Cardiff, Bristol, Glasgow, Manchester.
55 'Cold Storage and Ice Trades Review', vol. XII, no. 130, 21 January 1909, p.14.
56 Ibid., vol. XIV, no. 155, 16 February 1911, p.47. Also vol. XIV, no. 161, 16 November 1911, pp.296-302.
57 'Report of Departmental Committee on Combinations in the Meat Trade', P.P., 1909, XV, p.271.
58 Reported in 'Cold Storage and Ice Trades Review', vol. IX, no. 94, 15 January 1906, p.8.
59 Ibid., vol. XI, no. 119, 25 February 1908, p.47.
60 Ibid., vol. VII, no. 71, 15 February 1904, p.42.
61 Ibid., vol. VII, no. 71, 15 February 1904, p.42.
62 Critchell and Raymond, op.cit., pp.193-5.
63 Unless otherwise stated the section on the c.i.f. trade is taken from Critchell and Raymond, op.cit., pp.102-12.
64 Ibid., p.379.
65 W. Weddel and Company, 'Review of the Frozen Meat Trade', 1904, p.7.
66 W. Weddel and Company, 'Review of the Frozen Meat Trade', 1899, pp.6, 8, 12, 14.
67 W. Weddel and Company, 'Review of the Frozen Meat Trade', 1904, p.7.
68 'Report of the Departmental Committee on Combinations in the Meat Trade', P.P., 1909, XV, appendix VII, pp.292-3. P.H. Smith, 'Politics and Beef in Argentina, Patterns of Conflict and Change', New York, 1969, pp.33-4.
69 Critchell and Raymond, op.cit., pp.83-4.
70 Ferns, op.cit., pp.88-9. Taking 1950 = 100, 1900-4 = 110.6, 1905-9 = 129.7, 1910-14 = 129.8.
71 Carlos F. Diaz Alejandro, 'Essays on the Economic History of the Argentine Republic', New Haven, Connecticut, 1970, pp.150-1, n. 14.
72 Imports of Argentine cattle were as follows: 1889, 19; 1890, 653; 1891, 4,180; 1892, 3,499; 1893, 6,882; 1894, 9,538; 1895, 39,494; 1896, 65,699; 1897, 73,852; 1898, 89,369; 1899, 85,365; 1900, 38,562 and 1903, 27,807. 'Annual Statement of Trade', P.P.
73 'Economist', 2 May 1903, p.792; 22 April 1905, p.688.
74 P.H. Smith, op.cit., p.54.
75 See p.168 of this book. From 1903 to 1912 beef cattle numbers in the U.S.A. fell from 37.3 million to 27.6 million. ('Cattle and Beef Survey, a summary of production and trade in the British Empire and Foreign Countries', prepared by the Intelligence Branch of the Imperial Economic Committee, June

1934, p.270.)

76   'Economist', 7 March 1908, p.495.

77   'Economist', 7 November 1908, p.895.

78   These firms also assumed a multi-national character with operations and branches in North America, South America and also Britain. But this only applied to the North American firms. For although British and South American firms handled both chilled and frozen beef from Argentina they never extended their operations to North America.

79   P.H. Smith, op.cit., p.35.

80   'Report of Departmental Committee on Combinations in the Meat Trade', P.P., 1909, XV, appendix VIII, pp.292-3. La Plata is counted as a British firm.

81   'Cattle and Beef Survey, a summary of production and trade in the British Empire and Foreign Countries', prepared by the Intelligence Branch of the Imperial Economic Committee, June 1934, pp.296-7.

82   'Interim Report on Meat', P.P., 1920, XXIII, p.6.

83   'Inter-Departmental Committee on Meat Supplies', P.P., 1919, XXV, p.9. Also P.H. Smith, op.cit., pp.57-63, and, S.G. Hanson, 'Argentine Meat and the British Market', Stanford, California, 1938, chapter IV, passim.

84   Ibid., p.171.

85   'Economist', 2 May 1903, p.792, and 13 May 1911, p.1034. Critchell and Raymond, op.cit., put James Nelson's retail shops at about 1,500 in the United Kingdom (p.208). This figure seems rather on the high side.

86   'Economist', 22 April 1905, p.688.

87   'Economist', 7 March 1908, p.495.

88   'Economist', 22 April 1905, p.688; 8 May 1909, p.991; 24 May 1913, p.1308; 4 April 1914, p.820.

89   'Economist', 25 May 1912, p.1219.

90   'Economist', 7 March 1908, p.495; 2 May 1903, p.792.

91   'Interim Report on Meat', P.P., 1920, XXIII, p.5.

92   'Cattle and Beef Survey, a summary of production and trade in the British Empire and Foreign Countries', prepared by the Intelligence Branch of the Imperial Economic Committee, June 1934, p.308.

93   'Inter-Departmental Committee on Meat Supplies', P.P., 1919, XXV, p.10.

94   'Interim Report on Meat', P.P., 1920, XXIII, pp.5, 7.

INDEX